The Linguistics of Sign Languages

The Linguistics of Sign Languages

An introduction

Edited by

Anne Baker
University of Amsterdam & Stellenbosch University

Beppie van den Bogaerde
HU University of Applied Sciences Utrecht

Roland Pfau
University of Amsterdam

Trude Schermer
Nederlands Gebarencentrum

John Benjamins Publishing Company
Amsterdam / Philadelphia

DOI 10.1075/Z.199

Cataloging-in-Publication Data available from Library of Congress:
LCCN 2015047984 (PRINT) / 2016004937 (E-BOOK)

ISBN 978 90 272 1230 6 (HB)
ISBN 978 90 272 1231 3 (PB)
ISBN 978 90 272 6734 4 (E-BOOK)

John Benjamins Publishing Co. · https://benjamins.com

Table of contents

Companion website
http://dx.doi.org/10.1075/z.199.website

Foreword

This book *The Linguistics of Sign Languages: An Introduction* is intended as an introductory textbook to the linguistic study of sign languages. A basic knowledge of linguistics is assumed, and the book demonstrates how this knowledge can be fruitfully applied to sign languages. Throughout the book, linguistic phenomena are illustrated by means of examples from many different sign languages from all continents in order to show that sign languages do not only differ from each other in important respects but also display interesting similarities with respect to certain grammatical features. This typological approach distinguishes the present book from other available textbooks that focus on one particular sign language.

The book is the result of a collaboration between four researchers, who have also been the editors: Anne Baker and Roland Pfau (University of Amsterdam, Department of Linguistics), Beppie van den Bogaerde (Hogeschool Utrecht [University of Applied Sciences] and University of Amsterdam, Department of Linguistics), and Trude Schermer (Dutch Sign Center). The three institutions have also supported this project. Chapters have been written by the four editors in collaboration with a number of other researchers: Heleen Bos, Marjolein Buré (Royal Kentalis, Groningen), Connie Fortgens (Royal Auris Group, Rotterdam), Sonja Jansma (Royal Kentalis, Amsterdam), Onno Crasborn (Radboud University Nijmegen), and Els van der Kooij (Radboud University Nijmegen).

We are extremely grateful to a large number of colleagues and fellow (sign language) linguists for their advice and practical help: Eveline Boers-Visker and Jan Nijen Twilhaar from the Hogeschool Utrecht; Joni Oyserman, Marijke Scheffener, and Vadim Kimmelman from the University of Amsterdam; Myriam Vermeerbergen from the Catholic University Leuven; Corline Koolhof from the Dutch Sign Center; Markus Steinbach from the University of Göttingen; Pamela Perniss from the University of Brighton; Josep Quer from the University Pompeu Fabra in Barcelona; Carlo Cecchetto from the University Milano-Bicocca; Caterina Donati from the University Paris-Diderot. Danny de Weerdt provided examples from Flemish Sign Language, Brendan Costello from Spanish Sign Language, Gladys Tang from Hong King Sign Language, and Andries van Nijkerk and Naomi Janse van Vuuren from South African Sign Language. An earlier Dutch version of this book has been used for several years with students of sign linguistics at the University of Amsterdam and in the interpreter and teacher training program of the Hogeschool Utrecht. We thank the students for their constructive criticism. In addition, we would like to express our gratitude to Deborah Chen Pichler for her extremely helpful feedback on the manuscript.

The sign drawings in *Salute* were composed by Marlies Vink from the Dutch Sign Center and by Roland Pfau. Additional drawings were made by Bart Koolen from the Dutch Sign Center. Some drawings and most of the photographs and video stills come from books or other sources. These are indicated in the respective chapters.

We assume that readers have a basic knowledge of linguistics but wish to expand their linguistic knowledge by delving into the linguistics of sign languages. General linguistic terms are therefore usually not explained but can, of course, be found in linguistic introductions (like, for example Baker & Hengeveld (2012), *Linguistics*, Oxford: Blackwell Wiley) or linguistic dictionaries (for instance, Nijen Twilhaar & van den Bogaerde (2016), *Concise lexicon for sign linguistics*, Amsterdam: John Benjamins). Important terms, some of which are specific to sign languages, are explained and are printed in boldface. While the discussion generally focuses on the linguistics of sign languages, we also often include comparisons to spoken languages in order to put sign languages into typological perspective.

The book consists of fourteen chapters that cover diverse aspects of sign linguistics. The conventions used for transcription, glossing, and abbreviations are set out in an appendix. In the first chapter, *Sign languages as natural languages*, a brief overview of the notions required to study sign languages is provided. The three following chapters look at the language user. In Chapter 2, *Psycholinguistics*, the mental processes involved in producing and perceiving a sign language are addressed. In Chapter 3, *Acquisition*, we consider how children learn a sign language as a first language and adults as a second language. In Chapter 4, *Interaction and discourse,* structural properties of conversations in a sign language are described.

In the next seven chapters, topics related to grammar and lexicon are covered. Chapter 5, *Constituents and word classes*, describes the manual and sometimes non-manual elements from which signed sentences are constructed. Chapter 6, *Syntax: simple sentences*, deals with properties of verbs and their arguments and with the rules for forming different types of sentences including declarative, interrogative, and negative sentences. Combinations of clauses, that is, subordination and coordination, are addressed in Chapter 7, *Syntax: complex sentences.* Characteristics of sign language lexica as well as properties of sign language lexemes are treated in Chapter 8, *Lexicon.* Various types of morphological processes, and how these are typically realized in sign languages, are discussed in Chapter 9, *Morphology*. Chapters 10 and 11 look at the structure of lexical signs. Chapter 10, *Phonetics*, describes the articulation of signs, and Chapter 11, *Phonology,* the basic phonological building blocks (or parameters) of signs.

The last three chapters cover sociolinguistic aspects of sign languages. Chapter 12, *Language variation and standardization*, considers the different types of variation occurring in sign languages and looks at language policies. In Chapter 13, *Language contact and change*, diachronic changes that may alter the form or function of signs are addressed, along with the influence that languages can have on one another. Finally, Chapter 14, *Bilingualism and deaf education*, considers the situation in Deaf communities with respect to education as well as educational policies.

The chapters build up information step by step, so that in principle, the chapters should be read in the order in which they appear in the book. The one exception is the final chapter on Deaf education which is less dependent on the other chapters and can thus be read out of sequence. Every chapter ends with a *Summary*, a section *Test Yourself*, a number of *Assignments*, and a section with *References and further reading*. In the summary, the main concepts are repeated per chapter, with the most important ones being printed in bold face, as in the chapters themselves. The section *Test Yourself* is intended to be used by the readers as a check on whether they have understood the text – all the answers to these questions can be found in the respective chapter. The assignments encourage further exploration of the concepts introduced in the chapter. These can be most usefully done in interaction with others. In the final section, we provide an overview of the sources we have used and suggest further reading. At the very end of the book, the reader will find an index of the main terms. The appendices detail the notation conventions and include examples of manual alphabets.

The book is supplemented by a website which provides extra information (http://dx.doi.org/10.1075/z.199.website). It contains the answers to the assignments as well as some suggestions for additional materials. Also, many of the examples which are represented in the chapters by glosses, drawings, or video stills are illustrated by means of video clips on the website.

Anne Baker, Beppie van den Bogaerde, Roland Pfau, and Trude Schermer
January 2016

Chapter 1

Sign languages as natural languages

Anne Baker

1.1   Introduction

> The sayd Thomas, for the expression of his minde, instead of words of his owne accord used these signs: first he embraced her with his arms, and took her by the handse, putt a ring upon her finger and layde his hande upon her harte, and held his handes toward heaven; and to show his continuance to dwell with her to his lyves ende he did it by closing of his eyes with his handes and digginge out of the earthe with his foote, and pulling as though he would ring a bell with divers other signs approved.
>
> Parish Register St. Martin's, Leicester, UK (1575)

Thomas Tillsye was deaf and made his marriage vows to Ursula Russell in sign as the parish register records. Descriptions like this, in which deaf people are recorded as signing, can be found in many countries, but rarely are the signs precisely described. The study of sign languages really only started in the 1950s when linguists began to become interested in the topic. They wanted to know what kind of structure these languages have and how they are used. But outside linguistics, there are still many strange ideas and prejudices about sign languages. Some people think, for example, that sign languages are a kind of pantomime. This, however, is clearly not true since sign languages, unlike pantomime, have grammar. Moreover, it is a common belief that there is just one universal sign language, but as we shall see in the following chapters, this assumption is also wrong, as there are actually many sign languages. Where there is a Deaf community, a sign language emerges. We thus find American Sign Language, British Sign Language, Chinese Sign Language, Nicaraguan Sign Language, Mali Sign Language, and so on. Sign languages were not invented by hearing people nor are they derived from spoken languages. Rather, they emerge as the result of natural interaction between deaf people. There are even speculations that sign languages were the first form of communication between humans in the pre-historic period – this is referred to as the 'gestural theory of language origin'. In that case, sign languages would have been around before spoken languages, and both deaf and hearing people would have used them.

The reader may have noticed that in the preceding paragraph, the term "Deaf" in "Deaf community" is written with a capital letter. This convention is generally used to refer to those deaf people who form a cultural and linguistic minority (see

DOI 10.1075/z.199.01bak
© 2016 John Benjamins Publishing Company

Chapter 14), in contrast to "deaf", which is used to refer to the medical condition of not being able to hear.

In this chapter, we shall discuss a few basic ideas about sign languages that are important for being able to understand the discussion of various linguistic aspects in the following chapters. The visual modality and its influence on the form of sign languages will be briefly discussed in Section 1.2. In Section 1.3, we will look at how a Deaf community comes into existence, and in Section 1.4, we investigate how a sign language can be influenced by contact with a spoken language. Sign languages seem to share certain universal principles with spoken languages (Section 1.5), but at the same time, they are quite different from spoken languages, and they can also be quite different from each other (Section 1.6). In order to be able to study sign languages, you have to be able to transcribe them. Conventions for such a transcription are set out in Section 1.7 (and are further detailed in Appendix 1). As mentioned earlier, the linguistic study of sign languages is a rather young research area which can be approached from different perspectives, as will be discussed in Section 1.8. Finally, we provide an overview of the structure and organization of this book in Section 1.9.

1.2   Language in space

Can you sign in the dark? Of course you can, but it does not make much sense since no one can see your signs. Signers have to make sure that their conversation partner can see them or possibly feel their hands. Sign languages are **visual-spatial** languages – they are articulated by using the hands, face, and other parts of the body, and all these articulators are visible. Signs are articulated on the body or in the space close to the body. This is in contrast to spoken languages, which are **oral-aural** languages. Also, sign languages are clearly different from pantomime, as pantomime makes use of all the space round the body and of the body as a whole while sign languages use a limited **signing space**, usually the space in front of the top half of the body and around the head, as depicted in (1).

(1)   The signing space

Signers seldom make signs outside this space and then only in exceptional circumstances. If someone is standing behind you, for example, and you cannot turn around, then you will sign behind your back, but obviously, this is quite cumbersome.

The signs for SWEET (2a) and CRUEL (2b) from British Sign Language are pictured below. Note that throughout this book, the names of sign languages are often abbreviated; for example, the acronym BSL is used for British Sign Language. Once an acronym has been introduced, it will be used further within a chapter (for a list of acronyms, see Appendix 1). The drawings of the signs in (2), and of most of the other signs in this book, are constructed in a certain way and adopt certain conventions. A single cross, for instance, indicates that there is contact between the hand(s) and a body part, here between the index finger and the cheek (2a) or the neck (2b). Two crosses on top of one another signal that the contact is repeated (see (4a) and (4b)). An arrow indicates a movement – in (2a) and (2b), the hand moves backwards and forwards in a small rotating movement. Sometimes, the hand changes shape and then the second handshape is depicted as well (see (13b) below). For a list of symbols used, the reader is referred to Appendix 1.

British Sign Language

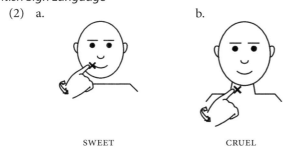

(2)   a.   b.

                SWEET   CRUEL

The signs in (2) are shown in their basic form or **citation form**, that is, in the way they are produced with no context. The meaning or **gloss** is written in small capitals to make it clear that these are signs and not spoken words (again, the reader is referred to Appendix 1 for further conventions).

The BSL signs in (2a) and (2b) are produced in two different places or **locations**, but the other formational aspects of the signs are the same. Both signs have the same **handshape**: an extended index finger. The **movement** is the same: the hand (or rather the lower arm) makes a twisting movement, and the **orientation** is also the same since the palm (when the sign starts) is facing downwards. But the sign SWEET is made at the corner of the mouth while the other sign, CRUEL, is articulated on the neck. This difference in location is contrastive and results in the two signs having a different meaning. All signs can be described in terms of these four basic form elements or **parameters**. The manual parameters – handshape, location, movement, and orientation – are always present and make up the internal structure of a sign in all sign languages.

Which parameters are the same in the pairs of signs from the Sign Language of the Netherlands (NGT) in (3) and (4), and which are different? In (3), the handshape (index and middle fingers extended), the orientation (palm is facing the body), and the location (both begin in front of the eyes) are the same. The movement is different though: in (3a), it proceeds in a straight line, while in (3b) there is a zigzag movement. In (4), the location, orientation, and movement are the same but the handshape is different. In (4a), all four fingers are extended (not the thumb), but in (4b) the thumb and index finger make contact and the other fingers are extended.

Sign Language of the Netherlands

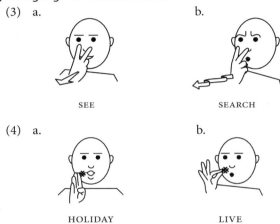

(3)   a.   b.

            SEE   SEARCH

(4)   a.   b.

         HOLIDAY   LIVE

Some signs are produced together with a mouth movement, facial expression, or body movement, as is true for the sign SEARCH (3b), where the eyebrows are lowered. These components are called **non-manual components**, because the hands are not involved. The signs in (2), for example, can be produced with a mouth movement corresponding to the articulation of the English words *sweet* or *cruel*. A mouth movement that is based on a spoken word from the surrounding spoken language is called a **mouthing**. Other mouth movements are not related to a spoken word. For instance, in BSL and NGT, the sign BE-PRESENT (5) is produced with a mouth movement *sh*, but this is not related at all to the corresponding English or Dutch word. Such mouth movements are called **mouth gesture**.

British Sign Language and Sign Language of the Netherlands

(5)

BE-PRESENT

Movements of the eyebrows, the eyes, and the nose can be important for some aspects of meaning or grammar, for example in marking a sentence as a question. This is also true for certain head and body movements.

The pictures that we presented up to now show signs out of context, in their citation form. But, of course, signs may also combine with other signs to form sentences. The combinations follow the rules of the grammar of that sign language. In German Sign Language (DGS), (6a) is a possible sentence, but (6b) is not (the fact that a sentence is ungrammatical is indicated by an asterisk '*' preceding the sentence).

German Sign Language

(6) a.   BOOK BLUE FALL.
          'The blue book falls.'
     b. *BOOK FALL BLUE.
          'The blue book falls.'

(6b) thus illustrates that there are restrictions on the possible orders of signs in DGS, just as in most signed and spoken languages. Of course, there are far more grammatical rules than just this one.

German Sign Language

(7) a.   MAN OLD BOOK BUY.
          'The old man buys a book.'
     b.   MAN BOOK OLD BUY.
          'The man buys an old book.'

The sentences in (7a) and (7b) contain the same four signs but in different orders. As a result, the two sentences have different meanings. Individual signs have a certain meaning and combined with other signs, they form a complex message. In sign languages, just as in spoken languages, we speak of **compositionality**. That is, the basic form elements combine to form signs, and signs in turn combine to form sentences.

1.3   Deaf communities

Within a **Deaf community**, a sign language is used to communicate. When deaf people interact over a longer period of time, a sign language emerges quite naturally. In the Middle Ages, it was thought that deaf people were mentally handicapped. As a result, they often only had contact with their direct family, or they were locked up in institutions. In these situations, deaf people did not have an adequate means of communication. Spoken language was difficult to access, and they were isolated from other deaf people. However, there are reports of deaf signers at the court of the English king in the seventeenth century and also at the court of the Turkish sultan in the sixteenth century.

In individual families, a form of communication can arise between the deaf child and the other (hearing) family members which involves the use of signs. These signs are usually not taken from the national sign language but are either based on common gestures or invented. This form of communication is called **homesign**. Homesign is not a fully-fledged sign language since the signs are understood by only a limited number of people, and there is usually little or no grammar. In situations in which deaf children grow up isolated from other deaf people and deaf people have little contact with one another, it is impossible for a sign language to emerge.

For Western countries, the likelihood of a child being born deaf is usually estimated to be one in a thousand (i.e. 0.1 %), and due to these relatively low numbers, some degree of organization is required for deaf children and adults to get in contact with one another. For some time now, schools for the deaf have been the main meeting place for deaf children. Many sign languages have also had their beginnings in such schools. A recent example is the development of Nicaraguan Sign Language (see Chapter 13). In Managua, the capital of Nicaragua, homesigners from all over the country came together in the 1970s at a school for the deaf, and within a couple of years, a new sign language had emerged that displays many of the features characteristic of established sign languages (see also Section 13.4.1). It is important that deaf people meet regularly for it to be possible for a sign language to emerge.

In various locations around the world, communities have been identified which are characterized by a considerable degree of genetic deafness: in some villages, deaf people constitute up to three percent of the entire population. Under such circumstances, a '**village sign language**' (or 'rural sign language') can emerge, although this is fairly rare. Examples of village sign languages are Adamorobe Sign Language in the south of Ghana and Kata Kolok in Northern Bali (Indonesia). Interestingly, in such communities, deafness is often not, or at least less, stigmatized, and commonly, a considerable number of hearing community members also know the local sign language.

Deaf children who are born deaf or become deaf during their first year are referred to as **prelingually deaf**, as the development of spoken language has not yet really got underway. A deaf child growing up in a deaf signing family learns the sign language in a natural way, just as hearing children learn a spoken language from their parents. The sign language is then the first language of the deaf child. Hearing children growing up in a deaf family also often learn the sign language and grow up bilingual.

Most deaf children though (90–95%) are born into hearing families. It is the parents' choice if they want to offer input in a sign language. They can decide to learn the sign language and use it at home with their child. They can also send their child to a school for the deaf where a sign language is used in teaching. Other parents prefer to send their child to a regular school or to provide instruction at home. Nowadays, in Western countries, many parents choose to have their child be given a cochlear implant. With the implant, the child can usually hear more and can learn more of the spoken language; however, this often means that the sign language is no longer provided. Being deaf therefore does not always mean that a person learns a sign language or that they form part of the Deaf community.

Deaf people who do learn a sign language and use it regularly make up the Deaf community in a particular country. There are national organizations such as the *Turkish Federation of the Deaf*, or the *National Association of the Deaf* in India. In Europe, there is also the *European Union of the Deaf* and, on an even wider international level, there is the *World Federation of the Deaf*.

1.4   The relationship between signed and spoken languages

Compare the sentences in (8). We can see that sentence (8a) contains more signs than sentence (8b). There are also different signs in (8a) compared to (8b). Why is that?

(8)   a.   THE WOMAN WORK-e-d AT SCHOOL.
      b.   PAST WOMAN WORK SCHOOL.
           'The woman worked at school.'

In schools for the deaf, the emphasis has long been on teaching the spoken language with little or no use of the sign language. Although sign languages often emerge in school settings in the contact between pupils, they are not always used in teaching. In many schools, the spoken language is used but every word is accompanied by a simultaneous translation in the form of a sign. This is what we see in (8a). Although the signs from a sign language are used (in this case, American Sign Language or ASL), this form of communication is not a natural sign language but is called a **sign system** or **manually coded language**. A manually coded language is a visual form of a spoken language. The grammatical rules of the spoken language are followed, in this case English. Therefore, the definite article 'the' is signed using an invented sign that does not occur in ASL. Also, the sign WORK combines with a past tense marker, a fingerspelled version of -*ed* that does not occur in ASL. The sign AT is an invented sign, too. In contrast, the ASL version of the sentence (8b) involves a time adverb at the beginning (PAST), but no definite article, tense inflection, or preposition are used.

The sentence pair in (8) thus illustrates that sign languages have their own grammatical rules whereas sign systems follow the grammar of the spoken language. In sign
systems, elements from a sign language lexicon are slotted into the grammar of the
spoken language. This is a form of relexification of the spoken language – a process
that also occurs in the formation of creole languages. When a sign system is used,
signing and speaking occurs simultaneously. In this case, mouth gestures are usually
omitted since it is simply impossible to speak and make other mouth movements at
the same time. Manually coded systems exist for many spoken languages: English
has Signed English, Mandarin has Wenfa Shouyu or Signed Mandarin, Afrikaans has
Signed Afrikaans, and so on.

A manually coded language is a visual form of a spoken language. Most manually
coded languages use the signs from the national sign language but, as we have seen in
(8a), some signs have also been invented by hearing people. Hearing people often use a
manually coded language to teach deaf children but also in general communication with
deaf people. Deaf people use such languages sometimes themselves in communication
with hearing people who do not sign well. The most important difference is that sign
languages are natural languages while manually coded languages are not. Further differences between these two communication systems are summarized in the table in (9).

(9)   The most important differences between sign languages
      and manually coded languages

Sign languages	Manually coded languages
– are natural languages;	– are not natural languages;
– are not derived from a spoken language but have their own grammar and lexicon;	– are derived from spoken languages: they take the grammar from the spoken language and insert lexical elements of the sign language in combination with some invented signs;
– are the first language of prelingually deaf people.	– visually support the spoken language. They are used in communication with hearing people who do not sign well or in teaching.

There are also forms that fall between sign languages and manually coded languages.
In fact, it can sometimes be difficult to evaluate to what extent the signing you are ob-
serving has been influenced by a spoken language. This can make it difficult to decide,
for example, whether a signed sentence is grammatical in a sign language or not. The
contact between signed and spoken languages will be discussed further in Chapter 13.

Some hearing people learn the manual form of the letters of the alphabet and think
that they have learned to sign. It is possible to represent the written form of the spoken
language in this way, but obviously, this is just a conventionalized code, a transliteration
of the written language, and not a real independent language. Deaf people use a **manual**

alphabet for **fingerspelling** if they need to communicate about a concept, object, or person for which there is not yet a sign. Take the following situation, for example: Mr. Mo from China is visiting America. He probably does not yet have a name sign, and so his name will have to be spelled. In (10a), we see how his name would be spelled in the American manual alphabet (see Appendix 2 for examples of manual alphabets).

(10) a.   American manual alphabet: the letters M and O

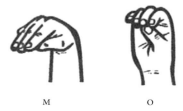

b.   British manual alphabet: the letters M and O

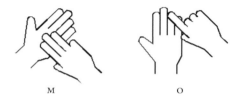

c.   Japanese manual alphabet: the hiragana character 'mo'
     and the corresponding manual form representing the syllable

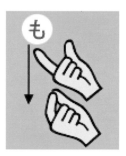

If Mr. Mo travels to Britain, his name will be spelled using the British manual alphabet. In (10b), we see the two letters of his name but these are made using two hands (see also Appendix 2). If he travels on to Japan, his name will be spelled using the Japanese manual alphabet. Interestingly, in this alphabet, his name is represented by a single form (10c). This is so because the Japanese manual alphabet is derived from the Japanese writing system where each character stands for a syllable. The character for his name from the hiragana writing system is also shown in (10c).

The spoken language is the majority language and also the language used in education. It may therefore have a considerable influence on the sign language, and this is evident in the above cases where a name, or a concept for which no sign exists, has to be spelled out. However, if such a name or concept is used frequently, the form usually changes in order to comply with the phonological rules of the sign language (see Chapter 11) or is sometimes even completely replaced by a new sign. As deaf people become more aware of their language, they can try to work against this influence and so, for example, refuse to see fingerspelled sequences as part of their language and invent new signs instead (see Section 12.7).

In (11), we see a number of conventional **gestures** that are commonly used by hearing people in different cultures and which often accompany speech. The term 'gesture' refers to such manual forms and distinguishes them from the signs of a sign language. The gesture in (11a) is used in many cultures all around the globe to express the meaning 'good', but other gestures are specific to a particular culture. The gesture depicted in (11b), for instance, means 'eat' in the Italian culture. Some gestures can have quite different meanings in different cultures: the gesture depicted in (11c) means 'mad' in Jordan but 'tasty' in the Netherlands – a considerable difference! Conventional gestures are often taken over into the national sign language and then become a real sign, that is, part of the sign language lexicon.

(11)   a.   Gesture 'good'   b.   Italian gesture 'eat'

    c.   Jordanian gesture 'mad' / Dutch gesture 'tasty'

The **index sign** is an example of a gesture that is used in all sign languages investigated to date. This manual form is most commonly made with the index finger, but it is also possible to point using the whole hand. When used in a sign language, it is often glossed as INDEX. This pointing sign can have many different grammatical functions in different sign languages, for example to refer to people and objects in conversations. INDEX can also be used to refer to locations, and these can be real locations in space or abstract locations (see Chapter 5). It is striking to observe that signers usually locate entities in the signing space, as viewed from their own perspective. For example, if a cupboard is standing to the right of a table, then the signer will locate the table in the space in front of him and then the cupboard to the right of it. But for the conversation partner – at least if he is facing the signer – the cupboard will then be to the left of the signer. In order to understand the correct spatial relationship, he therefore has to mentally rotate the spatial set-up by 180°. That is, he has to change his mental image. This cognitive task appears to be no problem for skilled signers.

1.5 Sign languages and linguistic universals

On the face of it, sign languages appear to be quite different from spoken languages. They are produced and perceived in the visual-spatial modality – in contrast to the spoken languages, which employ the oral-aural modality. In linguistics, typologically diverse languages are studied to find out which properties are common to all languages, that is, in order to identify **linguistic universals**. The intriguing question is whether sign languages share universals with spoken languages or whether they display grammatical characteristics that are specific to the visual-spatial modality – in other words: **modality-specific** universals. Let us consider an example of a universal that has been suggested for spoken languages (12a).

(12) a. All languages make use of consonants and vowels. From these small elements, all larger units are built and these in turn are combined to form sentences.

It is quite obvious that this universal is not applicable to sign languages – after all, sign languages do not make use of consonants and vowels. At first sight, (12a) may thus be a good candidate for a universal that is specific to the oral-aural modality. Remember, however, that we argued earlier in this chapter (Section 1.2) that signs are also composed of smaller building blocks: handshape, orientation, location, and movement. That is, once we substitute the part "consonants and vowels" in (12a) by "small meaningless elements", the modality-specific flavor of the universal disappears, and it can be applied to spoken and signed languages. Yet, unlike in spoken languages, the meaningless elements in sign languages are combined simultaneously. It is simply impossible to articulate a handshape without at the same time creating a location and orientation. Consonants and vowels, on the other hand, are ordered sequentially. But, as we have seen, signs are combined in sequence to form sentences just as words are combined to form sentences.

(12) b. In all languages, the users can express a negative statement, can ask a question, and can issue an order.

A second example of a universal is given in (12b). Does this universal also apply to sign languages? Of course, it does. In many sign languages, a negative statement is expressed by means of a non-manual component, namely a headshake. This movement has been adopted from a gesture that commonly signals negation in spoken languages – be it by itself or accompanying a negative sentence. In some cultures, however, the gesture for negation is a backwards movement of the head, and it is therefore not surprising that the same head movement is also found as a non-manual marker of negation in the sign languages used in these cultures (e.g. Greek Sign Language and Turkish Sign Language; see Chapter 6.8 for further discussion).

What about potential modality-specific universals then? The fact that all sign languages studied to date make use of the signing space for grammatical purposes seems to be a good candidate for a universal specific to the visual-spatial modality.

1.6   Differences between sign languages

Sign languages have only been the subject of linguistic study for a comparatively short time as we mentioned earlier. It is therefore too early to make strong claims about sign language specific universals. But more and more information is becoming available about different sign languages, providing insight into the possible variation among sign languages.

One area where we see great variation is the lexicon. Compare the signs in (13).

(13) a. *Portuguese Sign Language*   b. *German Sign Language*
          Flemish Sign Language, etc.

BABY   CAT

c.   *Swedish Sign Language*   d.   *SL of the Netherlands, British Sign Language*

CAT

HOLIDAY (NGT) /
TOILET (BSL)

The sign BABY in (13a) is transparent in meaning since the form of the sign imitates the cradling of a baby. Such **iconic signs** are attested in every sign language, and given the clear relation between form and meaning, one might expect them to be universal – this, however, is not the case. We know that a sign very similar to (13a) is used in many sign languages including, for instance, Portuguese Sign Language, Flemish Sign Language (VGT), but also Asian sign languages (e.g. Khmer Sign Language) and African sign languages. But whether this form is really universal, we do not know. In (13b) and (13c), we see two signs for CAT, one from German Sign Language (DGS) and the other from Swedish Sign Language (SSL). Both signs are clearly iconic, but still they are different: in the DGS sign, the cat's whiskers are portrayed while the SSL sign shows the stroking of the soft paws.

This indicates that iconicity in itself does not necessarily mean that the sign will have the same form in different sign languages. The sign in (13d) has two different meanings in two different sign languages: it means HOLIDAY in NGT but TOILET in BSL. This sign is not iconic, as the relationship between form and meaning is arbitrary. The vocabulary of sign languages shows more iconicity than that of spoken languages, but in general, the lexicon is to a large extent culturally determined and thus different in each language (see Chapter 8).

If an **arbitrary sign** is very similar in form and meaning to a sign from a different sign language, then it is likely that there has been some form of language contact. The form of the sign SPORT depicted in (14), for instance, is exactly the same in DGS, Italian Sign Language (LIS), and VGT.

(14)   *German, Italian and Flemish Sign Languages*

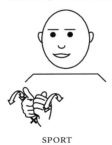

SPORT

The fact that the three sign languages use the same sign may either be due to a common historical source or to the fact that there was contact between European sports people in the past. Comparative studies have also revealed that there is considerable overlap in the lexica of Australian Sign Language (Auslan), New Zealand Sign Language (NZSL), and BSL, and in this case, we know for sure that BSL is the common historical source. Many early immigrants to Australia and New Zealand came from Great Britain and brought BSL and the system of deaf education with them.

Some signs are made with two hands and some with just one. The same sign can vary in this aspect between sign languages: the sign GLASSES, for example, is signed with the same handshape, location, and orientation in Brazilian Sign Language (Libras) and Russian Sign Language, but it is one-handed in the former and two-handed in the latter. If a sign is one-handed, then it is usually produced by the dominant hand of the signer, that is, the right hand of a right-handed signer or the left hand of a left-handed signer. The other hand is the non-dominant hand when used in two handed signs.

Besides the lexicon, sign languages may also differ in the forms they use. There are, for example, many possible handshapes in sign languages. These handshapes are often labelled according to their use in the different manual alphabets. However, since these labels may vary per country, we will avoid using them in this book. Rather, we will indicate handshapes by using a convenient handshape font (that has been developed at the University of Hong Kong). It is worth noting that not all handshapes are used in every sign language. For instance, the ⍟-handshape, which is used in ASL (the letter 'T' from the ASL manual alphabet: thumb stuck between index and middle finger) is not found in several other languages, where it may even be taboo since it resembles an obscene gesture (see Section 4.7 for more on pragmatic adequacy).

The syntactic structure of different sign languages may vary, too. For instance, the forms used for different grammatical functions as well as the order of signs within a sentence may be subject to cross-linguistic variation (see Chapter 6). In certain areas, the grammars of sign languages may display patterns that are different from those of spoken languages. Think, for instance, of the possibility to articulate two signs simultaneously by using the two hands. Clearly, a comparable phenomenon is not attested in spoken languages. As for similarities across unrelated sign languages, it has been observed that sign languages do not have a copula such as 'is' in the English 'Inge *is* clever'. Consequently, a sentence like INGE CLEVER is perfectly grammatical in BSL, DGS, LIS, and other sign languages. Still, this is not a modality-specific universal, as numerous spoken languages behave similarly in this respect, for instance, Mandarin, Turkish, and many creole languages. In subsequent chapters, we will discuss more examples of similarities and variation across sign languages.

1.7 Transcribing sign languages

In (15), we see an example of an NGT sentence. The signs are represented in the form of drawings, and the meaning of each sign and some grammatical aspects are presented in the form of English words. We will discuss this sentence in some detail to illustrate how sign languages can be represented in writing and to introduce the glossing conventions we will use in the remainder of this book.

Sign Language of the Netherlands
  (15)

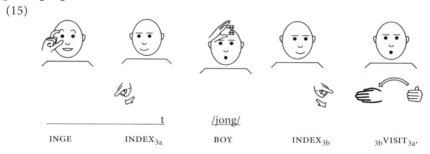

    'As for Inge, the boy is visiting her.'

The representation of the sentence in (15) is useful, but it does not represent a writing system for signs. Actually, there is no standardized way of writing down signs that would be comparable to the International Phonetic Alphabet (IPA) commonly used for spoken languages. There have been attempts to create a **sign writing** system for sign languages, for example SignWriting, but such systems are not systematically used in every country. A single sign contains a considerable amount of phonological information, such as the four parameters handshape, movement, location, and orientation, and all of these, as well as their simultaneous interaction, have to be represented by dedicated symbols. Consequently, a sign writing system may look more like the character writing system of languages like Chinese than an alphabetic writing system or IPA.

Learning such a system is also more complex. For research purposes, a few **notation systems** have been developed. Using these, all linguistic information can be registered using special symbols, but these systems are too detailed and complex for daily use. For example, systems have been created to register the exact form of individual signs, such as HamNoSys or KOMVA (see Section 10.5). Other notation systems have been developed to provide information about the morphological form of complex signs and signed sentences, such as the Berkeley Transcription System (BTS).

Let us now return to the example in (15). We see that there is an English word below each sign drawing. These words are called 'glosses'. Glosses do not provide any information about the form of the sign, just about the meaning. The gloss is, of course, taken from a spoken language, in this case English, to make the meaning transparent for the reader, but the gloss might as well be given in Dutch in a Dutch context, etc. Given that the gloss is taken from a different language than the sign language it represents, it should be considered an approximation of the meaning of the sign. Therefore, it only represents one possible translation. The sign VISIT, for instance, could also be glossed as PAY-A-VISIT-TO. In the case of concrete notions such 'cat' or 'chair', the relationship between the sign and the gloss is quite clear but in many cases, alternative glosses may exist. Also, the use of glosses in sign language dictionaries does not always do justice to the full range of meanings of signs. In this book, we will use English glosses, but the reader should keep in mind that at times, a gloss may not be the perfect translation of a sign.

As for the shape of signs, throughout this book, we will be using a special font when referring to handshapes, for example, 🖐 or ✊. As explained above, in other publications, handshapes are often labelled according to the role they play in a manual alphabet, for example 'B-hand' or 'C-hand', but this is tricky, as one and the same handshape may represent different letters in different sign languages (e.g. the ✊-hand represents the letter 'T' in NGT but the letter 'F' in DGS). Moreover, sign languages also employ elements that are not articulated with the hands, the non-manual components. Such components are usually produced simultaneously with a manual sign. In Example (15), we can see a line above the sentence-initial constituent [INGE INDEX$_{3a}$] with 't' written at the end of the line. This line signals the use of a non-manual marker that is articulated simultaneously with manual signs. The length of the line indicates which signs are accompanied by the marker (that is, the scope of the non-manual), and the abbreviation indicates the function of the component, here the marking of a topic (important information that has previously been introduced in the discourse; see Section 4.6), which involves raised eyebrows. Other non-manual components are indicated by other symbols; for example 'sucked-in cheeks', which often expresses the meaning 'small', is represented by brackets ')(' – see the illustration in (16) from Inuit Sign Language. In this case, the symbol refers to the form of the non-manual component, not to its meaning. Many of these conventions are listed in Appendix 1.

Inuit Sign Language

(16)

sucked-in cheeks expressing
the meaning 'small'

In (15), the gloss BOY is accompanied by the Dutch element /jong/, which is part of the Dutch word *jongen* 'boy'; this indicates that this mouthing has been articulated at the same time as the manual sign. Yet, this convention does not necessarily imply that the word was articulated using the voice; it only indicates that corresponding mouth movements have been produced. If voice had been used, this would have to be transcribed by means of a separate symbol, for example, '+voice'.

The gloss INDEX is accompanied by a subscript 3a to indicate that the indexical sign is pointing towards an area of the signing space located to the side of the signer (either right or left). By using this sign immediately after the signs INGE and BOY, these two (non-present) referents are localized in space, and these locations can be used later in the discourse to refer back to the referents. Similarly, in other sentences, the subscripts 1 and 2 are used to refer to the signer (first person) and to the addressee (second person). The **localization** of referents is important in the syntax of the sentence. The sign $_{3b}$VISIT$_{3a}$ is produced with a sideways movement, in this case from left to right from the perspective of the signer. The fact that the same subscripts are used in (15) is meaningful: the initial location of the verb (3b) corresponds to the location introduced for BOY, the subject of the verb, while the final location (3b) corresponds to the location introduced for INGE, the object. In the following chapters, we shall talk about the "syntactic signing space" when the signing space is used for syntactic purposes.

In Example (15), the sign drawings provide a pictorial representation of the signs; these representations are helpful but they are necessarily simplified. In the computer-based transcription system ELAN, it is possible to link the transcription of a signed utterance to a video. The screenshot in (17) shows a BSL example. The red vertical bar indicates the exact point in the recording; that is, the signer is just articulating the sign GET. Below the video, we see a detailed transcription on different tiers. These tiers can be defined by the researcher. In (17), the topmost tiers refer to the articulation of the right hand (RH), followed by an English translation and tiers for the left hand (LH). The next couple of tiers specify different types of non-manual information (e.g. head position, brow movement). Obviously, this type of multi-tiered annotation is very complex and thus very time-consuming. Because of the considerable amount of information to be encoded, and thus the increased chances of missing valuable details, it is considered good practice to make the video material available alongside the written transcription, as is possible in a system such as ELAN.

(17)   Example of an ELAN transcript from a BSL story

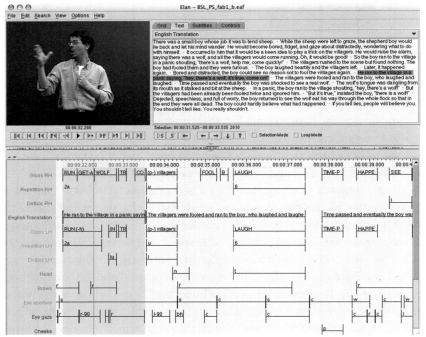

1.8   The history of sign linguistics

Until roughly 1980, sign languages were hardly mentioned in any introductory text book on linguistics. Although linguistic research had been done on sign languages, primarily on ASL at that time, since the early 1960s, this work had not had any influence on mainstream linguistics. The first published studies emphasized the similarities between sign languages and spoken languages in order to convince the scientific world that sign languages were real natural languages. By now, this situation has changed radically. In linguistics, sign languages are now generally accepted as genuine objects of research. Basically every introductory text book refers to sign languages, at least in passing, and there is considerably more interest in the differences between signed and spoken languages, that is, in the modality differences.

We are steadily gaining access to more information about the use and structure of quite diverse sign languages. The growing data pool facilitates the comparison of sign languages with each other and thus the description of differences and similarities. This has given the impetus to a young and thriving research area, **sign language typology**, and a search for possible universals, as we described in Section 1.5, is now possible. As mentioned above, most of the early linguistic studies focused on ASL, but soon after 1980, research started on various European sign languages (including BSL, NGT, and SSL), Auslan, and Libras. More recently, sign languages from Africa and Asia have been added to the research agenda, such as, for example, South African Sign Language, Ugandan Sign Language, Taiwan Sign Language, Indopakistani Sign Language, and Hong Kong Sign Language. As mentioned earlier, there are also communities with an unusually high percentage of deaf people, and there is also an increasing body of research on the sign languages used in these communities, which sometimes display typologically unusual properties. Although research on sign languages is increasing, there are still many sign languages that have not been described, or maybe not even been discovered, yet.

When research on a sign language begins, one of the first things to be done is usually the making of a dictionary. In (18), we see an entry from an older ASL dictionary.

(18)   Lemma from an ASL dictionary

drink
beverage

DRINK, n.v. DRANK, DRUNK, DRINKING.
(The natural sign). An imaginary glass
is tipped at open lips.

Such dictionaries are usually far from complete – after all, it takes years to compile a relatively complete dictionary for any language, as the centuries work on the Oxford English Dictionary illustrate. A choice is often made to start with a basic vocabulary, around one thousand signs. Older dictionaries appeared in book form but currently, more use is being made of DVDs or on-line videos. Many such dictionaries contain a description of the form of the sign, as in (18), sometimes complemented by some grammatical information. In (18), for instance, the sign is categorized as being both a noun (n) and a verb (v). In addition, some dictionaries include example sentences.

Sign dictionaries are above all **descriptive**, but by including certain signs while excluding other variants, they can have a **prescriptive** influence (see Sections 8.5 and 12.7).

Grammatical descriptions (or sketches) in book form or on DVD are available for few sign languages. These are often intended for use in teaching and are thus **pedagogical grammars**. Other grammars are more descriptive in nature and have been written from various theoretical linguistic perspectives. Since so little is known about individual sign languages, the information contained in such grammars is often seen as prescriptive.

1.9   The content of this book

In the previous sections, we have provided some initial information on sign languages which is required to be able to read this book further. We are assuming that the reader has some basic knowledge of linguistics and wishes to expand her/his linguistic knowledge by delving into the linguistics of sign languages. General linguistic terms are therefore usually not explained, and the reader is advised to consult an introductory textbook on linguistics should a term be unclear. Terms that are specific for sign linguistics will of course be explained. While the discussion generally focuses on the linguistics of sign languages, we also provide comparisons with spoken languages in order to put sign languages into typological perspective.

In Chapters 2 and 3, we focus on the language user. Chapter 2, *Psycholinguistics*, discusses the mental processes involved in sign language use. How is a sign language represented in the brain? Is the organization of memory, for example, comparable to that for spoken languages? How do signers use linguistic rules in comprehension and production? In Chapter 3, *Acquisition*, we look at how children and adults learn a sign language. Learning a sign language as a second language is discussed together with bilingualism. The language learning situation of deaf children is complex, but an important question is in how far the process of sign language acquisition is influenced by the structures of the languages involved and by the modality. The role of cochlear implants will also be addressed here. In Chapter 4, *Interaction and discourse*, we look at conversations in sign languages and how these are conducted. How do you take a turn in a visual language? Are the turn-taking rules different from those in spoken languages? How do you refer to people and things that are present or not present? What are the rules for encoding different types of speech acts?

The next five chapters deal with topics around grammar and lexicon. Chapter 5, *Constituents and word classes* describes the basic building blocks of sentences in sign languages. Are these the same as in spoken languages? Are there distinct word classes such as nouns and verbs? Are there grammatical elements that are attested in spoken languages but not in signed languages, or vice versa? Chapter 6, *Syntax: simple sentences*, discusses the rules used to form sentences from the constituents described in Chapter 5. What role do grammatical and semantic roles play in the syntax of sign languages? How are questions distinguished from declarative clauses, and how can sentences be negated? Strategies for constructing subordinate and coordinate clauses are addressed in Chapter 7, *Syntax: complex sentences*. Above, we already pointed out that some signs show a relationship between form and meaning, called iconicity. What is the role of iconicity in sign languages? How is the lexicon of a sign language organized? In Chapter 8, *Lexicon*, these questions will be subject to discussion. Chapter 9, *Morphology*, describes various types of word formation processes in sign languages. Do we find compounds in sign languages? Can verbs change their form according to who is performing the action? How is plurality expressed? Again, it will be interesting to consider whether certain morphological operations are modality-specific.

Chapters 10 and 11 provide a description of the structure of individual signs. Chapter 10, *Phonetics*, covers the actual articulation and perception of sign. Which joints are involved in the articulations of signs? How much variation can there be in the articulation of a sign for it still to be understood? We will also return to the issue of notation in this chapter. In Chapter 11, *Phonology*, the parameters of signs are discussed. How many different handshapes are there? Are some more frequent than others? Are there (possibly universal) constraints on the formation of signs? How are non-manual components integrated in signs? In addition, this chapter briefly addresses phonological structure at the sentential level, that is, prosody.

The last three chapters deal with sociolinguistic aspects of sign languages. Chapter 12, *Language variation and standardization*, covers the variation that can occur within a sign language. Which external factors may have an influence on the use of a sign language? For instance, are the signs used in a conversation in a café different from those used in a formal lecture? Are there dialects in sign languages? Is there such a thing as a standard form of a sign language? If so, how does it come into existence? In Chapter 13, *Language contact and change,* the influence that languages can have on one another will be discussed. In this context, the influence that a surrounding spoken language may have on a sign language is very important. We also ask whether sign languages change over time in the same way as spoken languages do. Finally, Chapter 14, *Bilingualism and deaf education*, describes the language situation within Deaf communities around the world. Deaf people usually grow up bilingual since they have to learn the spoken language of their environment. How does the educational system influence the sign language? What kind of educational strategies exist for deaf children?

Summary

Sign languages are fully-fledged, natural languages articulated in the **visual-spatial modality** in contrast to spoken languages, which make use of the **oral-aural modality**. Sign languages are not derived from spoken languages but have their own lexicon and grammar. Signs are produced on the body or in a three-dimensional space in front of the body, the **signing space**, which is different from pantomime, where there are no such restrictions and the whole body may be used. Signs produced in isolation, that is, outside of the context of a sentence, are said to be in their basic or **citation form**. The meaning of a sign is usually given using a **gloss** that consists of one or more words from a spoken language.

Every sign is made up of four different basic elements or **parameters**: the **handshape**, the **location**, the **movement**, and the **orientation**. Some signs are produced simultaneously with a **non-manual component**, that is, an element that is not articulated by the hands but by the mouth, face, or upper body. Words or parts of words that are articulated are called **mouthings**, while mouth movements that are not derived from words are called **mouth gestures**. All these elements are combined in signs, and signs in turn are combined to form sentences, which demonstrates that sign languages display **compositionality**, an essential property of natural languages.

People who are born deaf or who become deaf in their first year are called **prelingually deaf**. If these deaf people use a sign language on a regular basis, then they are members of the **Deaf community**. Most deaf children grow up in hearing families. When these children are isolated from other deaf people, they may develop a form of **homesign**, that is, a manual communication system that is used within a single family. A fully-fledged sign language can only develop when deaf people have regular contact with each other. In some rural communities in which there is a higher percentage of deafness, a **village sign language** may emerge.

A sign language is different from a **sign system**. In a sign system (or **manually coded language**), individual signs of a sign language are used, but the sentences follow the grammar of the surrounding spoken language. Sometimes invented signs are added. Sign systems are often used in the communication between deaf people and hearing people who do not know the sign language well. Often they are also used in the education of deaf children.

The **manual alphabet** (used for **fingerspelling**) allows a signer to convey concepts or names from the spoken language for which no signs exist. Different types of manual alphabets exist, but they are not really a part of the sign language. **Gestures** that are used by hearing people, often in combination with speech, are commonly integrated into the sign language. A prominent example is pointing which is used in all sign languages and is glossed as INDEX. Among other things, an INDEX can be used for the **localization** of referents.

Research into sign languages still has to produce more evidence so that we can determine which **linguistic universals** are **modality-specific**, that is, hold true for both signed and spoken languages, and whether there are also universals that are specific to sign languages. There is no generally accepted **sign writing** system for sign languages. In research, use is made of different **notation systems** in order to transcribe signed utterances. **Glosses**, the translation of a sign in a spoken language, provide information on the meaning of a sign but not on its form. There are clear differences between individual sign languages in their structure and lexicon despite the significant proportion of **iconic** signs. Iconic signs are not necessarily identical across sign languages. Also, many signs are **arbitrary**. Not every sign language uses the same handshapes, and the grammatical rules are also diverse. **Sign language typology** is a young research area, but there are still too few sign languages described to be able to come up with a comprehensive typological picture. Existing descriptions of sign languages are usually **descriptive**, but are sometimes used **prescriptively**. The first step in describing a sign language is usually making a dictionary or sign book. There are a number of **pedagogical grammars** being used in education.

Test yourself

1. Name three common misconceptions about sign languages and explain why they are not true.
2. What is the difference between a gesture and a sign?
3. What is homesign?
4. What is the definition of prelingually deaf?
5. Which articulators are used for non-manual components?
6. What is the difference between a mouthing and a mouth gesture? Find an example of both types of non-manual components in a sign language you know.
7. Name three characteristics of a sign system.
8. What is an INDEX?

Assignments

1. There is no universal sign language. Why is this the case? Some hearing people find this a 'wasted opportunity'. Where does this judgement come from?
2. Signs are made up of parameters. These are said to belong to the *phonology* of sign languages. Is this true?
3. Find three signs from a sign language that you know or look them up on internet. Describe as accurately as possible the manual parameters of these signs (handshape, location, movement, and orientation).
4. What are the differences between pantomime and sign languages?

5.   Find two iconic signs and two arbitrary signs from a sign language that you know. You need to know the etymology of the iconic signs. Describe the iconic aspects of the iconic signs. Are the two equally iconic? Are the two arbitrary signs equally arbitrary?
6.   Is fingerspelling part of a sign language?
7.   Why is a sign system not a real language?

References and further reading

A non-linguistic book that offers an introduction to deafness and sign languages in general is *Seeing Voices* by Oliver Sacks (1989). A recent handbook covering all aspects of sign language linguistics is Pfau, Steinbach & Woll (2012a). Introductory books on the use and structure of specific sign languages (in English) exist for BSL (Sutton-Spence & Woll 1999), Auslan (Johnston & Schembri 2007), ASL (Valli & Lucas 1992/1995), Israeli Sign Language (Meir & Sandler 2008), Irish Sign Language (Leeson & Saeed 2012a), and Kata Kolok (Marsaja 2008). Only a few descriptions of deaf communities are available in English; the Spanish deaf community, for example, is described by Vallverdú (2001). Characteristics of deaf communities in general are addressed in Woll & Ladd (2003). Various chapters in Brentari (2010) provide an overview of a selection of sign languages in different parts of the world. Nyst (2012) and De Vos & Pfau (2015) offer convenient overviews of the use and structure of village sign languages, including a discussion of cross-linguistically unusual features. The use and structure of homesign is discussed in Goldin-Meadow (2003, 2012); Nicaraguan Sign Language (and its emergence) is the topic of the study by Kegl, Senghas & Coppola (1999). Use of sign language at the Ottoman court is described by Miles (2000).

Many sign language dictionaries are available on-line, for example for ASL on www.lifeprint.com, but the glosses are often in the spoken language of the respective country. An incomplete list can be found on http://www.yourdictionary.com/languages/sign.html. Edited volumes that offer explicit comparisons of grammatical characteristics of sign languages are Baker, van den Bogaerde & Crasborn (2003) and Perniss, Pfau & Steinbach (2007); the issue of sign language typology is addressed in Zeshan (2008) and Pfau (2012). Taub (2012) provides an overview of the role of iconicity in sign languages, and Perniss, Thompson & Vigliocco (2010) offer a highly informative survey of iconicity in spoken and signed languages. An excellent overview of the history of sign language research is provided in McBurney (2012). Woll (2013) discusses how sign language research has developed over time. Challenges of sign language transcription are described in Frishberg, Hoiting & Slobin (2012).

The quote from Thomas Tillsye is taken from Sutton-Spence & Woll (1999), as is the BSL SWEET/CRUEL example. ELAN is available from the Max-Planck-Institute in Nijmegen (http://www.mpi.nl/tools/elan.html). The Inuit Sign Language example is taken from Schuit (2013). The drawing program used for some of the drawings in this book is *Salute*, a program which unfortunately is not available anymore.

Chapter 2

Psycholinguistics

Trude Schermer & Roland Pfau

2.1 Introduction

Linguists strive to uncover how exactly a language is structured, and they try to describe its structure on different levels: phonology, morphology, syntax, lexicon, and pragmatics. Psycholinguists, on the other hand, do not focus so much on the language itself, but rather on linguistic behavior. Sometimes, the area of language acquisition is included under psycholinguistics, but in this book, we will discuss this topic in a separate chapter. In the present chapter, we will address three broad issues: language in the brain (Section 2.2), language comprehension (Section 2.3), and language production (Section 2.4), and will ask questions like: where is sign language stored in the brain (Section 2.2.1), and what is the effect of modality on the way language functions in the brain (Section 2.2.2)? What actually happens when a signer suffers from a brain lesion? Do we see differences in language disorders like aphasia between hearing and deaf language users (Section 2.2.1)? In order to gain insights into language disorders, we must know how human beings understand and produce language. An interesting question is whether there are differences between spoken languages and signed languages when it comes to the identification of the linguistic signal (Section 2.3.1) and the storage and processing of signs (Section 2.3.2). Sign languages are visual languages that contain relatively many iconic elements, as we already pointed out in the previous chapter. Research into the differences and similarities between signed and spoken languages have focused on the degree in which iconicity plays a role in language comprehension, both at a lexical level (recognizing signs) and a grammatical level (the role of spatial and linguistic elements in the use of space); these issues will be addressed in Sections 2.3.3 and 2.3.4, respectively. Language users generally know exactly what they want to communicate, but occasionally, something goes wrong in the production process, and the message is not transmitted as intended. This may happen both in spoken and signed languages. In Section 2.4, we first consider the so-called tip-of-the-finger phenomenon (Section 2.4.1). Subsequently, we turn to spontaneous speech errors, slips of the hand, which provide important information about the process of language production; in this context, we take a look at grammatical (Section 2.4.2) and phonological coding (Section 2.4.3). Finally, in Section 2.4.4, we consider the articulation of signed utterances.

DOI 10.1075/z.199.02sch
© 2016 John Benjamins Publishing Company

2.2   Language and the brain

Language is a distinctive feature of human beings. It is thus not surprising that we want to know how we are able to understand and produce language. Somewhere in our brain, there must be a language system, but where is it and how does it work? By looking at language disorders as a result of brain lesions, we can learn a great deal about our language system: what exactly goes wrong when part of our brain is damaged? There are two parts in the brain: the left and right halves, also called the **left** and the **right hemisphere**. In right-handed people, the left hemisphere is usually the dominant hemisphere for language; in a small percentage of left-handed people, the right hemisphere is dominant for language. For ease, we will assume the most frequent case in the following discussion.

It was only in the nineteenth century that the first studies were carried out on hearing subjects to find out where exactly spoken language is located in the brain. In these studies, the location of damage in the brain was related to problems in language production and comprehension of the patient. Language disorders as a consequence of a brain lesion are generally called **aphasia**. Damage in the front of the brain in the left hemisphere, **Broca's area**, causes mainly problems in **language production** (see (1)). A patient with damage in Broca's area usually has difficulty speaking, is hardly able to produce grammatical sentences, but seems to understand language quite well. If the damage in the brain is more to the back of the left hemisphere, in the **area of Wernicke**, the patient has problems with **language comprehension**, and less with language production. These early studies thus showed that the left hemisphere is very important for language, but that lesions in different parts of that hemisphere of the brain have different effects.

(1)   Language areas in the left hemisphere

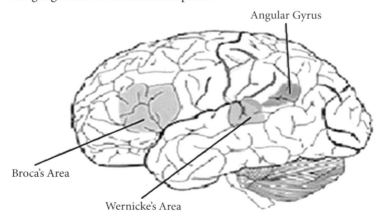

More recently, neuro-imaging techniques such as functional Magnetic Resonance Imaging (fMRI) have been used to examine brain activity on-line as people perform linguistic tasks. Various areas in the brain have been shown to be responsible for the ability to comprehend and produce language, although these are predominantly in the left hemisphere. However, these techniques have revealed that the right hemisphere also plays a role, although it is less involved in these tasks than the left hemisphere. It is in discourse skills, particularly in telling narratives, that both hemispheres seem to play a role. We have to be careful in interpreting test results though, since language production and comprehension include more than the ability to produce separate words or sentences. Nevertheless, we can still safely conclude that the left hemisphere is the hemisphere that – in most people and for most language abilities – is specialized for language.

In contrast, motor and visual processing are localized predominantly in the right hemisphere. Sign languages are visual languages with the hands as articulators, and they thus involve motor and visual abilities. Now, given that language is localized predominantly in the left hemisphere and motor and visual activities mainly in the right hemisphere, research on deaf sign language users should allow us to provide an answer to the question whether modality influences the localization of language in the brain. As we know from Section 1.8, early research on sign languages predominantly focused on the similarities between signed and spoken languages in order to prove that sign languages are equal to spoken languages. Early neurolinguistic work therefore also focused on similarities – if language is localized in the brain independent of modality, this implies that sign languages are equivalent to spoken languages. Since the 1990s, psycholinguistic and neurolinguistic research on sign languages has been receptive to also identifying patterns different from those described for spoken languages. Research on languages in another modality thus contributes in a significant way to our understanding of the processes that are involved in language and of the brain more generally. In the next two subsections, we will consider evidence from aphasia and neurolinguistic studies of signers.

2.2.1 Aphasia in deaf signers

Studies on aphasia in spoken language users have shown that the left hemisphere is predominantly responsible for language production, use, and perception. So, if there is a lesion in specific areas in the left hemisphere, a language disorder will result. In the 1980s, American researchers considered the question of a possible influence of modality on the typical consequences of aphasia. In one study, the sign language skills and visual-spatial skills of six deaf subjects were studied: they had acquired American Sign Language (ASL) at a young age and used it on a daily basis, but had later suffered a brain lesion. The patients with a lesion in the left hemisphere made mistakes in their sign language; for instance, they produced grammatical and/or phonological errors, and had problems with the system of reference (e.g. use of INDEX without specifying the referents first). The patients with a lesion in the right hemisphere, on the other hand, showed no special disorders in their use of sign language.

Research into the effects of brain lesions in deaf sign language users yields very similar results as studies on hearing people with brain lesions: the sign language use of deaf subjects is affected following left hemisphere damage. Deaf aphasics with a left hemisphere lesion in Broca's area show the same symptoms as hearing aphasics with a similar lesion: language comprehension is more or less unimpaired, whereas language production is problematic. In the fragment in (3), an ASL signer tries to describe the picture in (2), which shows a woman doing the dishes without noticing that the sink is overflowing with water. Behind her back, a boy and a girl are at the same time stealing cookies from the cupboard. Note that the examiner also used ASL, but his utterances are transcribed in English.

(2)   Aphasia test picture – the "cookie theft" scene.

American Sign Language

(3)   Examiner: What's happening here? [Pointing to the water spilling on the floor]
      Patient: WHAT? [Points, gestures, mouths "oh"]
      Examiner: What is that? [Pointing to the water again]
      Patient: f- … e- … f- … a- … l- … l. [fingerspells "fall" laboriously]
      Examiner: What is the woman doing there?

Patient:	[Fumbles and gestures, then signs] PLATE
	t- … e- … o- … w- … l. [Attempts to fingerspell "towel"]
Examiner:	What is the woman doing?
Patient:	TURN-OFF. TURN-OFF.
Examiner:	What does the girl want?
Patient:	[Mouths "cookie" but puts finger to lips as does girl in picture]
Examiner:	What does the boy want?
Patient:	c- …a- … o- … o- … k- … e. [Attempts to fingerspell "cookie"]

The transcript in (3) shows that the patient is not capable of giving a description of the picture. She hardly produces any signs and substitutes even highly frequent signs with fingerspelling. However, even fingerspelling is difficult for her and she often confuses letters. This patient was diagnosed with Broca's aphasia. It is typical for Broca aphasics to only produce isolated content words (e.g. the noun PLATE and the verb TURN-OFF in (3)) but hardly any grammatical elements such as agreement and tense affixes. The aphasic signers were also unable to use the signing space correctly, for example, in order to localize referents. For the sake of comparison, we provide an English example in (4), in which an aphasic patient describes the same picture.

English

(4) Researcher: What happened?
    Patient: Cookie jar … fall over … chair … water …
                empty … ov … ov …
    Researcher: Overflow?
    Patient: Yeah.

This hearing patient, too, only uses content words and is unable to integrate these correctly into a grammatical structure. This telegraphic speech, which is typical for Broca aphasics, is also called **agrammatical** speech.

A trauma in the area of Wernicke, on the other hand, does not severely affect language production but causes considerable problems with language comprehension. Even though patients with Wernicke's aphasia can speak or sign fluently, they sometimes make lexical and morphological mistakes. An ASL signer with Wernicke aphasia, for example, produced **lexical substitutions** like the ones in (5a). Similar examples produced by German aphasics are given in (5b) (see Section 2.4.2 for examples of substitutions in unimpaired signers).

American Sign Language (a) and German (b)

(5) a. BED   instead of   CHAIR

          DAUGHTER   instead of   SON

          FLOOR   instead of   ROOM

   b. *Kran*   instead of   *Bagger*

        'crane'   'excavator'

        Karaffe   instead of   *Glas*

        'carafe'   'glass'

        Haartelefon instead of   *Kamm*

        'hair telephone'   'comb'

The examples above make it clear that modality does not influence the area where language is localized in the brain. Nevertheless, there are certain differences between deaf and hearing patients with a brain trauma, as we shall see in Section 2.3.4.

It is important to include discourse processes in testing all aphasics, whether hearing or deaf. In many studies, only word and sentence level processes have been tested. It may appear from the studies described thus far that only the left hemisphere is responsible for language. Current research on right hemisphere lesions, however, suggests otherwise. A signer with a right hemisphere lesion was able to refer back to a referent in the same sentence, but not to a referent in a previous one. That is, she functioned without problems at the sentence level, but often got confused at the discourse level. A more accurate generalization seems to be that the left hemisphere is responsible in both modalities for more local linguistic phenomena (phonological, morphological, and syntactic structure), while the right hemisphere is important in the processing of more global processes (for instance, discourse structure).

2.2.2 The effect of modality on the brain

As mentioned above, new **brain imaging techniques** have been developed for investigating and measuring brain activity in healthy subjects. Using these techniques, such as functional Magnetic Resonance Imaging (**fMRI**), we are now able to see which brain areas are active when certain language tasks are carried out. As a result, we now know that Broca's area is not only involved in speaking, but to some extent in comprehension as well. The fMRI pictures in (6) show the brain activity (indicated by light areas) in the left hemisphere (top picture) and the right hemisphere (bottom picture). In the left hand column, we see the images of the brains of English speakers presented with sentences such as *I will send you the date and time* or *The woman handed the boy a cup*. The left hemisphere (top) shows much more activation than the right hemisphere, although the right hemisphere (bottom) is involved to some extent. The same is true for British Sign Language (BSL) signers who are presented with similar sentences in BSL, as shown in the right hand column.

(6) fMRI scan of left (top) and right (bottom) hemispheres of (a) English speakers presented with spoken English and (b) British Sign Language signers presented with BSL. Brain activity is indicated by the light areas.

a. English speakers   b. BSL signers

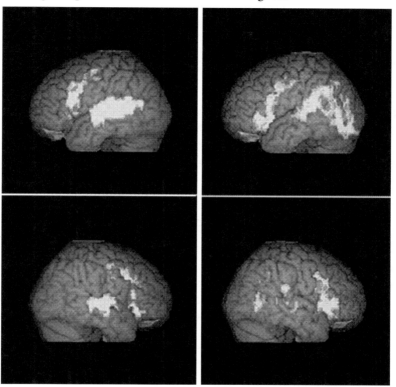

A different technique, which measures electric activity in the brain over time, is electro-encephalography (**EEG**). EEG is used to indicate how and especially how fast language users respond to features of language input. For example, do language users react to grammatical features of the language input or just to semantic features? In sentence (7b), the ASL verb CHASE is wrongly marked (indicated by '*'), as the direction of movement suggests that the girl is chasing the boy; the correct version is shown in sentence (7a).

American Sign Language

(7) a. BOY INDEX$_{3a}$ GIRL$_{3b}$ TWO-OF-THEM PLAY++.

        BOY $_{3a}$CHASE$_{3b}$. GIRL$_{3b}$, WRONG INDEX$_{3b}$ FALL$_{3b}$.

        'There was a boy and a girl and they were playing.

        The boy chased the girl, but oops, she fell.'

(7) b.   BOY INDEX$_{3a}$ GIRL$_{3b}$ TWO-OF-THEM PLAY++.
         BOY $^*_{3b}$CHASE$_{3a}$. GIRL$_{3b}$, WRONG INDEX$_{3b}$ FALL$_{3b}$.

The EEG measures the brain activity while a subject processes such (non-deviant or deviant) sentences. The output of an EEG is an Event-related Potential (ERP). ERP studies have shown that signers react to syntactic violations as in sentences like (7b) by showing specific brain activity at about 600 milliseconds after the violation was presented (known as the P600 effect). Just as in hearing people's reactions to sentences in a spoken language, this does not occur in grammatically correct sentences like (7a).

However, a sentence like (8b) that contains a semantic violation (unexpected use of the sign BED) triggers a different effect at about 400 milliseconds after exposure to the semantically awkward word (the N400 effect), whereas (8a) does not. Such evidence proves that the distinction between grammar and meaning, on the one hand, and between correct and incorrect, on the other hand, is equally valid in sign languages.

American Sign Language
(8) a.   HISTORY CLASS STUDENTS DISCUSS WORLD POLITICS, HOT DEBATE.
    b.   HISTORY CLASS STUDENTS DISCUSS WORLD **BED**, HOT DEBATE.

As we have seen, the ability of signers to use language depends on the way certain areas in the brain function, just as is the case in hearing people using a spoken language. The timing of reactions in the brains of signers also reflects the different status and the distinct processing of grammatical and semantic information as in hearing subjects. The question remains as to what (cognitive) steps signers have to take in order to interpret and produce language.

2.3   Language comprehension

Language users do not have much influence on their understanding of language. In fact, it regularly happens that people make mistakes or do not understand each other immediately. Psycholinguists are not only interested in where language is located in the brain, but also in how we understand each other: what processes take place in our brain? In what way do signers remember what has been signed to them, and how do they detect signs in the stream of movements that they see? And, again, is there a difference between signed and spoken languages? Can the difference in modality provide us with insights into the processes occurring in the brains of hearing speakers and deaf signers?

With these questions in mind, we turn to the issue of **language comprehension**. Speakers of a language can discriminate meaningful sounds without much difficulty from the flow of sounds they hear, as long as the sounds belong to the inventory of their own language. Second language learners can have problems in this respect – for example, Japanese learners of English have difficulty in distinguishing the 'l' and the 'r' since their first language, Japanese, does not distinguish these two sounds. A signer also has to learn to distinguish the parameters of a sign: after all, small differences in handshape, movement, and location can make a big difference in meaning, as we saw in Section 1.2.

2.3.1 Identifying the signal

Speech is a **continuous signal**. This is very obvious when you listen to a language that you do not know: it sounds like an incoherent jumble of sounds. Sounds are not always the same, they are **variable**. For example, the 'm' in 'moon' is different from the 'm' in 'mark', as the pronunciation of a sound may be influenced by a preceding or following sound. When non-signers look at a sign language, they also only see a jumble of movements and handshapes accompanied by all sorts of facial expressions. Signers, however, have no problems in identifying the signs that belong to their sign language and in distinguishing these from non-linguistic movements. Contrary to common belief, signers do not constantly look at the hands of their conversation partner. Rather, they generally fix their eye gaze on a point near the face of the other signer, since important grammatical information is expressed on the face (see Chapter 6 for discussion). The articulation of the parameters of a sign is variable, just like that of sounds. The Sign Language of the Netherlands (NGT) sign TRAIN can be made with two ⊘-hands (9a), but also with two ⊘-hands, as is shown in Example (9b), but such variation in thumb position does not seem to interfere with comprehension. The context will often be important in determining whether one of the options is chosen over the other; for instance, if TRAIN is preceded by a sign with extended thumb, then option (9b) may be the preferred one.

Sign Language of the Netherlands
  (9) a.   b.

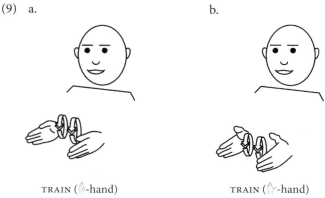

TRAIN (⊘-hand)   TRAIN (⊘-hand)

In Section 10.4, we will look at the variation in the articulation of signs in greater detail. The visual perception system is specialized in the processing of simultaneous information, far more so than the system for auditory perception. This makes simultaneous processing of different sources of visual information less complex than might be expected. This is important since sign languages regularly employ many different sources simultaneously, such as facial expression, position of the head, body posture, handshape, and position of the hands in space.

An important issue in the study of **sign perception** is the amount of information needed to identify a sign: must the whole sign be visible, or is it clear which sign is meant on the basis of the handshape and the initial location? Much research has been done on speech perception in spoken languages. According to most investigators, listeners already begin to consult their mental lexicon as soon as the first speech sounds of a word have been perceived. For example, when hearing the initial *b-*, this activates all words in the mental lexicon that begin with this sound (*bear*, *big*, *book*, *bone*, *blossom*, *break*, etc.). Once the next few sounds of the word have been perceived, for example *-los-*, the first selection is reduced and the listener can already decide that the word must be *blossom* (or perhaps a related word like *blossoming* or *blossoms*). This form of perception, that is, the use of a set of phonologically related words called a cohort, is of course dependent on the fact that words are composed of sequentially organized sounds in spoken languages.

In contrast, signs are characterized by simultaneous structure, that is, the simultaneous combination of parameters, and therefore, the **cohort model** cannot work in the same way as in spoken languages. Studies indicate that the recognition of signs proceeds in two steps: firstly, the identification of the parameters handshape, orientation, and location defines a cohort, followed by the identification of movement. Signs are also identified very rapidly: from experiments with Deaf native signers, it appears that only about 35% of a sign needs to be perceived before it can be identified, compared to 83% of a word. This difference seems to be due to the fact that important information is provided simultaneously by all parameters and that there are few signs that are identical in terms of handshape, orientation, and location.

Context is as important in sign perception as it is in speech perception. In a context in which a signer talks about illness, the recognition of the sign FLU from NGT will be easier, and it will be less likely that it will be confused with the NGT sign CHARACTER that closely resembles it in terms of the manual parameters, as can be seen in Examples (10a) and (10b).

Sign Language of the Netherlands

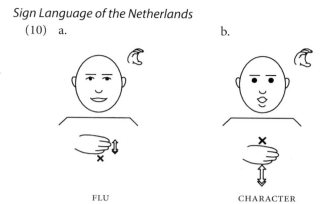

(10) a.   b.

FLU   CHARACTER

2.3.2 Storage and processing of signs

As we discussed in Section 2.2, an important reason for comparing signed languages to spoken languages is the question whether processes in the brain are different as a consequence of the difference in modality. Research on the manner in which language is temporarily stored in the brain also relates to this question. The main question is then: how does the **working memory** of signers work in comparison to that of speakers of a spoken language? There are different interpretations of the term working memory, but here we will use a definition according to which the working memory is a form of memory with both a storage and a processing function. Working memory is thus used to retain information for a short time and also to work with the stored information.

Extensive research on working memory in spoken languages has led to different theories and models. However, research on the working memory in sign language users has concentrated mainly on one model, the so-called **multiple-component model**. This model consists of various components that enable people to process input from their surroundings, mentally reflect on this information, retain recent information, and support the processing of new knowledge. We will not discuss all components of the model here.

One component of working memory that is of particular interest when comparing spoken languages to signed languages is the so-called **phonological loop**. This component is specialized in the temporary storage of phonological material like speech sounds. The information that the phonological loop can contain is limited. The information disappears within two seconds, unless it is repeated sub-vocally. This means that the words to be remembered have to be repeated by mentally articulating them without voice – think, for instance, of memorizing a telephone number while searching for a pen to write it down (this is similar to normal articulation, except that the muscles are not fully activated). By supposing the existence of a phonological loop, the problems that people have in retaining words that are phonologically very alike can be explained (like, for instance, *bed, bad, cat*), as opposed to words that are not alike (e.g. *bed, crate, door*). The crucial question is whether this phonological loop is specialized for auditory material. In other words, are signs retained in the working memory in the same way as spoken words? If the phonological loop is not just specialized for auditory material, but for linguistic material in general, then there should be comparable processes in working memory for signed and spoken languages. By studying the mistakes that deaf signers make when remembering and reproducing signs, it has been established that the mistakes are based on phonological rather than semantic features. These studies have also found that remembering signs that are phonologically very similar (as in (10)) is far more difficult for deaf sign language users than remembering signs that are phonologically very different. On the basis of such studies, researchers have concluded that the existence of a repetitive loop in the visual-spatial part of working memory, a **visuo-spatial loop**, is highly plausible.

To see whether deaf signers also repeat signs mentally without articulating them, participants in an experiment were asked to make meaningless movements (for instance, imitating playing the piano) whilst taking a memory test. It turned out that they performed worse in the memory test when they had to produce such meaningless manual movements, suggesting that signers also repeat lexemes mentally to aid short term memory, just as hearing people do. Finally, just as fewer words with many syllables can be retained in spoken languages, studies have revealed that fewer signs with a longer movement can be retained compared to signs with a shorter movement.

In sum, we see that research on working memory has yielded comparable results for sign language users and spoken language users. From this, we can conclude that the phonological loop is not specialized in auditory material, but rather in 'linguistic' material. This implies that there are no differences as a consequence of modality in the storage and processing of signs. Yet, there appears to be a difference between speakers and signers, namely a difference in the capacity of the working memory. Some studies suggest that signers can store fewer items than speakers. A possible explanation that has been offered is that the articulation of a sign takes more time than the articulation of a word. This, however, is not a consequence of the difference in modality. The amount of time it takes to articulate an item determines the number of items that a person can retain in working memory, whether it is in a spoken or signed language. This, by the way, does not lead to a difference in skills between signers and speakers, because the amount of simultaneity in sign language grammar compensates for the limitation in working memory.

2.3.3 The role of iconicity in processing signs

As we mentioned in Section 1.6, words have a form and a meaning, and the relationship between these two is generally **arbitrary**; for instance, the sounds that make up the English word 'chair' have no bearing on the object chair. There are a few exceptions, such as the verbs for animal sounds, like *meow* for a cat or *squeak* for a mouse, or other mechanical sounds like *toot* for a car horn, and so on. In signs, however, a relation between form and meaning is attested more frequently – that is, signs are more likely to be **iconic** than words (see also Chapter 8). This results from the fact that it is simply much easier to represent visual aspects of an entity or an action with your hands than with your voice. Some people have interpreted this fact as an indication that sign languages are a form of pantomime rather than natural languages, but, of course, we know by now that this interpretation is misguided. Still, there are also many signs in which the relation between form and meaning is arbitrary. In (11) to (13), we provide examples from various sign languages to illustrate different types of form-meaning relations.

The meanings of signs like New Zealand Sign Language (NZSL) DRINK (11a) and Indopakistani Sign Language (IPSL) BABY (11b) are rather easy to guess, even for non-signers. These two iconic signs are therefore called **transparent** signs. Sometimes signs become less transparent over time. For instance, the French Sign Language (LSF) sign MOBILE-PHONE (11c) is highly transparent in 2016, but it is quite possible that it will be less transparent ten years from now if the design of mobile phones changes. In (12), examples are given of signs that are not, or no longer, transparent. The Spanish Sign Language (LSE) sign for MILK (12a) used to be transparent when cows were milked by hand, but nowadays, this traditional procedure is much less well known. The same applies to the NGT sign COFFEE (12b), which depicts the grinding of coffee. The Italian Sign Language (LIS) sign MIRROR in (12c) has actually never been highly transparent. Examples of arbitrary signs from NGT, BSL, and German Sign Language (DGS) are given in (13).

(11)   Transparent signs
        a.   b.   c.

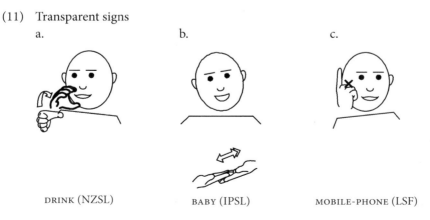

DRINK (NZSL)   BABY (IPSL)   MOBILE-PHONE (LSF)

(12)   Non-transparent iconic signs

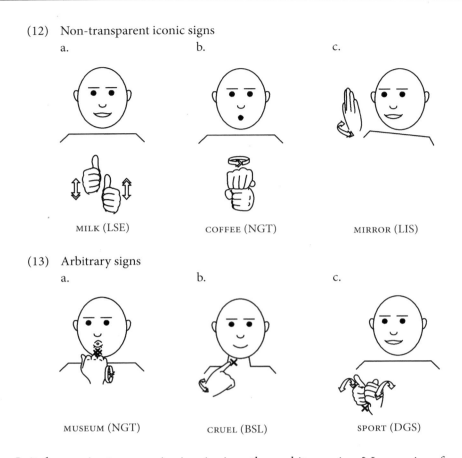

a.   b.   c.

MILK (LSE)   COFFEE (NGT)   MIRROR (LIS)

(13)   Arbitrary signs

a.   b.   c.

MUSEUM (NGT)   CRUEL (BSL)   SPORT (DGS)

Is it then easier to recognize iconic signs than arbitrary signs? In a series of experiments, hearing people who did not know sign language and deaf signers of different sign languages were shown a set of arbitrary and iconic signs. The subjects had to guess the meaning of each sign. The assumption was that if a sign was iconic, it would be easy to guess its meaning, even for people with no knowledge of a sign language. This assumption proved to be wrong. Hearing non-signers performed far worse than all signers in the recognition of both transparent and non-transparent iconic signs. Furthermore, a recent experiment revealed that iconicity helped deaf children to distinguish signs that were similar to each other in form. The children made fewer errors and took less time to identify signs that were similar and transparent than to identify signs that were similar but not transparent.

Iconic signs are also easier to learn and remember for hearing second language learners. Once they know the meaning of a sign, it is easier for them to remember its form when it is iconic. Interestingly, iconicity has little influence on the phonological and lexical acquisition of signs in young children (see Chapter 3), although it may influence other areas of language. On the basis of these studies, we can conclude that iconicity has some effect on recognition and memory in native signers but less than might be expected. In second language learning, the effect of iconicity is clearly stronger.

2.3.4 Spatial versus linguistic information

As we have already discussed, sign languages are visual-spatial languages and the right hemisphere is responsible for visual-spatial perception. It might therefore be expected that a lesion in the right hemisphere would also lead to a disorder in, for instance, the production of verbs which can be spatially modified. As we explained in Section 1.7, people and objects can be located in space, and some verbs change their movement according to where such objects or people have been located in space (as in (7) above; see Section 9.5 for further details). Research has indeed shown that deaf people with a lesion in the right hemisphere are unable to describe a room or to provide spatial information (topographic use of space). In contrast, they are still able to form grammatical sentences in which space plays a role. We should remark here that in some cases, damage in the right hemisphere does lead to a disorder in sign language comprehension, and in this respect, deaf and hearing aphasics are not quite the same. There seems to be a difference in the processing of signs that are localized an arm's length or more from the body in space (the **extrapersonal space**) as opposed to signs localized closer to the body (the **intrapersonal space**). It is argued that spatial relations in the extrapersonal space are first processed in the right hemisphere and then are transmitted to the left hemisphere to be coded linguistically. Deaf aphasics with a left hemisphere disorder do not understand spatial grammar, because they cannot decode it, but deaf aphasics with a right hemisphere disorder fail to understand some spatial syntax that involves the extrapersonal space.

2.4   Language production

By **language production**, we understand the process of formulating and articulating sentences. At the beginning of this process, there is an abstract idea that the speaker or signer wishes to convey in a message. This preverbal message must be transformed into a linguistic form. In order to do this, speakers or signers have to retrieve lexemes (words or signs) from their mental lexicon and combine these according to the rules of the language (grammatical coding). This grammatical structure must then be converted into a phonological form (phonological coding), and will ultimately be articulated.

At first glance, this seems an easy task, but in fact, many things can, and regularly do go wrong during language production. It is only when something goes wrong that it becomes clear how exactly the planning of an utterance proceeds and which types of linguistic units are relevant during the planning phase. In principle, it might be the case that sentences are planned and produced as a whole. Spontaneous speech errors, or slips of the tongue, however, show that this is not the case, since they may occur at different linguistic levels, that is, in the lexicon, in the grammar, and in the phonological component. Slips are sometimes funny and sometimes embarrassing – but they are also natural. Researchers estimate that speakers produce a slip approximately once in every thousand words, but when a person is drunk or tired, slips may, of course, occur more frequently. Given that speech errors are such a natural and common phenomenon, we may expect them to also occur in sign languages; we are then dealing with **slips of the hands**. But what do they look like? And do we find the same types of errors as in spoken languages?

Signers do indeed make errors during language production, and these slips are as intriguing and informative as slips in spoken language. Slips of the hand have so far been collected and analyzed for ASL and DGS. The ASL-corpus contains solely spontaneous slips (in total 131) which were collected using the so-called pen-and-paper method, whereby the person who observes a slip (in a conversation or on TV) writes it down – this method is, of course, a bit more cumbersome for sign language than for spoken language. The DGS corpus includes a number of spontaneous slips, but mainly consists of slips that were elicited experimentally (in total 944 slips). The informants were asked to retell picture stories under various stress conditions (e.g. speed, forced repetition of parts).

In the following, we address various aspects of sign language production. We first discuss problems in accessing a lexical item (Section 2.4.1). Then we turn to production errors at the word level (Section 2.4.2), the phonological level (Section 2.4.3), and finally at the level of articulation (Section 2.4.4).

2.4.1 The tip-of-the-fingers phenomenon

Once a signer/speaker has come up with a message s/he wants to convey, one of the first things to do is to retrieve the appropriate elements from the **mental lexicon**. At this stage, it may happen that the meaning of a word/sign is known, but that (parts of) its phonological form cannot be retrieved. When this happens in a spoken language, we speak of a 'tip-of-the-tongue' (TOT) state – a phenomenon that is probably familiar to everyone and that may be rather frustrating. In a sense, one has the word on the tip of one's tongue but still cannot articulate it. In this situation, speakers are often able to access a part of the word's phonological form, mostly its beginning and its syllable structure. For instance, when trying to retrieve the word *carnivore*, a low-frequency word, speakers would come up with *cannibal* or *carnival*.

In a study with ASL signers, researchers tried to experimentally evoke a similar state, that is, a **tip-of-the-fingers** (TOF) state. Just as in spoken languages, the TOF-state occurred mostly with proper names. Signers reported that they could access the meaning of the lexical item (they could, for instance, paraphrase its meaning), but that they were unable to retrieve its full phonological form. The parameters most likely to be recalled were handshape, orientation, and location, while recall of the movement parameter was less likely. This parallels the findings for perception reported in Section 2.3.1. Apparently, these three parameters have a similar status as the beginning of words, which are also most often recalled in a TOT-state. The patterns also confirm the idea that signs are recalled in a two-stage process. Finally, it is noteworthy that iconicity did not play a role in what could be remembered.

2.4.2 Grammatical encoding: word level

When signers start to retrieve the elements from their mental lexicon that are appropriate for the intended message, they do this on the basis of the meaning of these elements. The meaning-lexicon contains so-called **lemmas**, rather abstract elements that may be specified for word class, but that are not phonologically specified.

An error may already occur at this early stage. It sometimes happens that a signer chooses a lemma from the mental lexicon that resembles an intended sign in meaning. We call this **semantic substitution**. Semantic substitutions show that the mental sign language lexicon – just like the mental lexicon of, say, English speakers – is organized like a network: lemmas that share meaning characteristics are grouped close together. This is, for instance, true for the two signs TRAIN and LORRY, which both refer to large vehicles. While retelling a story, one of the DGS signers meant to sign LORRY but instead produced TRAIN (14a). The example illustrates another interesting phenomenon: the **self-correction** of a slip (indicated by '//'). The signer realizes that something went wrong, laughs at his mistake, and then produces the correct sign. Researchers estimate that about 50% of all slips are self-corrected, but often the speaker or signer is not even aware of the slip and the self-correction. For comparison, consider the German slip in (14b). Here, too, we witness a semantic substitution – instead of *Fenster* 'window', the speaker says *Tür* 'door'. The speaker also corrects himself, but unlike in Example (14a), the self-correction is somewhat delayed, as it does not happen immediately after the slip. Also, the utterance contains an overt comment on the slip.

German Sign Language (a) and German (b)

(14)   a.

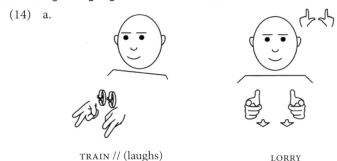

TRAIN // (laughs)   LORRY

b.   du   musst die **Tür**   dann festhalten, Quatsch,   das Fenster
     you must the door then   hold,   nonsense, the window
     'You must hold the door then, nonsense, the window.'

Once the correct lemmas have been selected, they must be integrated in a syntactic structure, that is, they must be combined into a grammatical sentence according to the rules of the language. At this point, too, errors may occur. A lemma – usually a noun or a verb – can appear in a sentence position where it does not belong; it can appear too early (**anticipation**), too late (**perseveration**), or two lemmas can be **exchanged** (this is also called **metathesis**). For instance, in (15a), we observe a perseveration of the noun BALL, followed by a self-correction ('y/n' represents a non-manual marker – eyebrows up – that marks yes/no questions in DGS; see Section 6.7.1 for further discussion).

German Sign Language (a) and English (b)
(15)   a.   DOLL, CLOWN, BALL, BEAR SMALL, EVERYTHING-THROW-INTO.
            _____y/n
            BALL // SHOE, NOTHING
            'The doll, the clown, the ball, the small bear, everything was
            thrown into [a box]. But the ball, eh, the shoe? It wasn't there.'
       b.   From which book did you copy these **books**, eh, articles?

The slip of the hand in (15a) makes clear that signs are units that are manipulated during language production. That is, the language processor deals with individual signs during grammatical encoding, not with whole sentences. Similarly, words are manipulated in spoken language production. The English slip in (15b) is very similar to (15a): a noun is perseverated, and the speaker corrects himself. Here, we only present examples involving a perseveration, but in both signed and spoken languages, anticipations and exchanges of lemmas also commonly occur.

The impact of meaning on sign production is also evident from an experiment conducted with ASL signers. In this experiment, signers were asked to provide the sign for an object shown on a picture. When they were presented with a picture of an object that was related in meaning to the object on the previous picture, their reaction time was slowed down. Obviously, the previous meaning was still slightly activated in their mental lexicon, and this interfered with naming the semantically related target object. This indicates again – as we saw for TOF-states in the previous section – that in the first instance, meaning is accessed when starting to produce a sign.

2.4.3 Phonological encoding

The result of grammatical encoding is an abstract representation of a sentence. The lemmas are already in the correct order, but the sentence elements have not yet been phonologically specified. At the next stage of production, the phonological forms of the lemmas (**lexemes**) are retrieved from the phonological lexicon. The mental lexicon thus consists of two parts: the meaning lexicon and the form lexicon, as illustrated in (16).

(16)   The mental lexicon

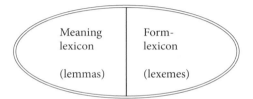

The selection of lexemes from the form lexicon is also a potential source of errors, namely **phonological substitutions**. We already know that the (manual) building blocks of signs (the phonological parameters) are handshape, orientation, location, and movement. Signs that are similar in their phonological form are in close proximity to each other in the form lexicon, and just as in the meaning lexicon, this proximity may give rise to the selection of an erroneous element. An example of a phonological substitution is given in (17a). The two DGS signs FASHION and HOTEL are phonologically very similar (but have no semantic relation). They share the phonological parameters handshape (-hand), orientation (fingers upwards, palm to the left), and location (just below the right shoulder), but are different in movement: HOTEL has a short, repeated straight movement, while FASHION has a repeated circular movement. In both signs, the thumb makes repeated contact with the body. In the slip, the signer produces FASHION instead of HOTEL. Please note that when there is no self-correction between the target utterance (on the left) and the slip (on the right), an arrow '→' indicates this. Again, we provide an English phonological substitution for the purpose of comparison in (17b).

German Sign Language (a) and English (b)

(17)   a.

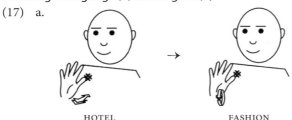

          HOTEL   FASHION

    b.   prohibition against incest → prohibition against **insects**

We know from research on spoken languages that once sentence elements have been phonologically specified, further phonological errors can occur. For instance, phonemes can appear in positions where they are not supposed to be; that is, just like lemmas (15), they can be anticipated, perseverated, or exchanged. Such slips are evidence that phonemes, too, play an important role in language production. If this were not the case, slips like (18) could never occur. (18a) is a case of a consonant exchange, while (18b) is a consonant anticipation followed by a self-correction. Interestingly, in both examples, the phonological error results in existing English words.

English
(18)   a.   with this ring I do wed → with this wing I do red
       b.   shown in the pleasant, I mean present slide

The phonological structure of signs differs clearly from the phonological structure of words. While the phonological building blocks of words – vowels and consonants – are sequentially ordered, the phonological parameters of signs can be produced simultaneously. In fact, it is simply impossible to produce the parameters handshape, orientation, and location of the sign HOTEL in (17a) sequentially. Clearly, it is an important question whether this simultaneous organization has an influence on the occurrence of phonological errors. After all, one might suspect that building blocks that are simultaneously realized are not as easily extracted from the lexeme, that is, they are not as easily manipulated individually.

Well, the speech error evidence suggests otherwise. One of the most interesting findings from research on slips of the hand is the fact that individual phonological parameters – despite their simultaneous organization – can be involved in slips. We will discuss two examples, one from DGS and one from ASL. The DGS example in (19a) is a handshape anticipation; the handshape of the second sign PARENTS ($\text{\includegraphics}$-hand) replaces the $\text{\includegraphics}$-hand of the first sign, the possessive pronoun POSS$_{3a}$ ('his/her'). The result is a possible, but non-existent sign. In both the DGS and the ASL corpus, handshape is by far the phonological parameter that is most frequently affected in a phonological slip.

German Sign Language (a) and American Sign Language (b)

(19) a.

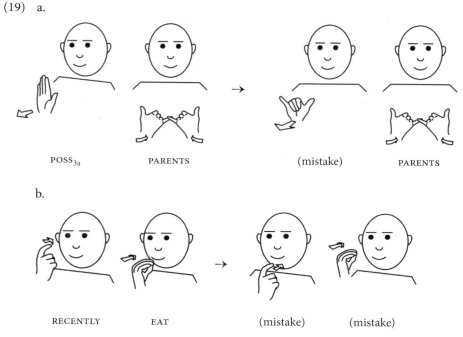

b.

The ASL Example (19b) differs from (19a) both in the type of slip and in the phonological parameter involved. What we observe here is a location exchange. The sign RECENTLY is produced next to the head, the sign EAT near the mouth. In the slip, the first sign is produced near the mouth and the second near the head. Handshape and movement, however, are retained. This slip also results in two possible, but (at least in ASL) non-existent signs.

The last type of slip of the hand we will discuss are **blends**. In blends, too, the phonological structure of signs plays an important role: two signs that appear adjacent in a sentence blend into a single sign which combines phonological parameters of both signs. In (20), the signer intends to produce the two DGS signs BICYCLE and SHOP. However, he blends them into one sign, which has the location (neutral space) and orientation (palm down) of both original signs, but takes the movement (alternating circular movement) from BICYCLE and the handshape (5-claw: ✋) from SHOP. The resulting sign is not only a possible sign, but coincidentally also an actual sign in DGS, namely the sign ANIMAL.

German Sign Language
(20)

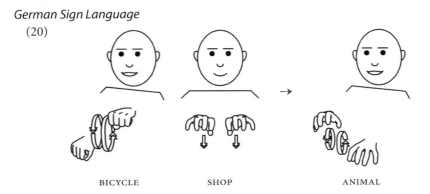

BICYCLE   SHOP   ANIMAL

2.4.4 Articulation

When an utterance has been phonologically encoded, instructions are given to the articulatory organs to produce the sentence. During this process, phonological changes can also take place and errors can occur.

During the articulation of a sentence, we can often observe **assimilation** processes; these increase with the speed of articulation. When you listen closely to a sound recording of a spoken conversation, you can often hear, for instance, that phonemes and pauses are reduced or even disappear. So, for example, "I don´t know what he said" can become "Idunnowotised". We can see similar processes at work in sign languages. In Israeli Sign Language (ISL), a signer wanted to sign SHOP INDEX₃ 'the shop over there'. SHOP is signed with two ⟩-hands that move downward in front of the body, INDEX with a ⟨-hand. During the downward movement, the dominant hand changes from a ⟩- to a ⟨-hand and already produces the INDEX while the non-dominant hand completes the downward movement of SHOP. In other words: part of the movement (of the dominant hand) of SHOP is deleted, and the pause between the two signs disappears.

A well-known problem in the articulation of a spoken language is **stuttering**. Stuttering is characterized by a repetition of sounds or syllables, which decreases the fluency of the articulation, for instance 't-t-t-t-t-train'. Stuttering seems to occur in all known spoken languages, and of course the question is whether it also occurs in sign languages. If so, what would it look like? Unfortunately, not much research has been done in this area. There are informal reports of signers only being able to form the handshape and the beginning part of the movement. The movement also seems to be spasmodic. It has also been stated that stuttering of this type is affected by stress, just as it is in spoken languages.

Summary

Psycholinguistics studies the linguistic behavior of language users. A crucial question is whether and to what degree the modality has an influence on the way in which language functions in the brain. By looking at language disorders caused by brain lesions (**aphasia**), we learn a great deal about where language is located in the **left** or **right hemisphere**. For most people, deaf and hearing, right- or left-handed, the left hemisphere is broadly specialized for language. Simplifying somewhat, a lesion in **Broca's area** results in problems in **language production**, in particular **agrammatism**, while a lesion in **Wernicke's area** leads to problems in **language comprehension**, and also to **lexical substitutions**. The right hemisphere, however, also plays a role, in particular at the discourse level. There is a difference between deaf and hearing aphasics which is due to the role of the right hemisphere in the processing of spatial relations and the differences in **extrapersonal space** and **intrapersonal space**. Research on language comprehension gives insights into the way people understand language. Various **brain imaging techniques** such as **fMRI** and **EEG** can be used to measure brain activity during spoken and signed language comprehension. Speech is a **continuous signal** and sounds are **variable**. The same is true for sign languages. Studies on **sign perception** indicate that the movement parameter in particular is decisive in the recognition of a sign. But **context** also plays a role. The **cohort model** that has been suggested for spoken word recognition is not easily applied to signs because of their partly simultaneous nature.

Research into the way language is stored in the brain has led to different theories concerning the **working memory**. Researchers have focused mainly on one model, the '**multiple-component model**'. For the comparison with sign language, the **phonological loop**, the part where phonological material is temporarily stored, is particularly interesting. Sign language users store information based on the form of signs. This has been established on the basis of research on mistakes that signers make when remembering and producing signs. A **visuo-spatial loop** has been discovered, comparable to the phonological loop. Like spoken language users, signers have difficulties with lexemes that are phonologically very similar. There appears to be a difference between hearing and deaf subjects in the capacity of working memory: signers can retain fewer items than speakers. This probably has to do with the fact that the articulation of a word takes less time than the production of a sign.

The relation between form and meaning of a word is usually arbitrary. Signs are different in this respect, as they are more likely to display a relation between form and meaning. There are **arbitrary signs** and **iconic signs**, and some of the latter are **transparent**, which implies that their meaning is immediately clear. Psycholinguistic research on the role of iconicity has shown that it can have some influence on sign processing, and that such signs are definitely easier to remember for second language learners.

Studies on the **tip-of-the-fingers** phenomenon and spontaneous speech errors have provided insights into the process of **language production**. Meaning is the first part to be accessed during production, followed by the phonological form of the signs. **Slips of the hand** reveal how sign language production proceeds and which units are relevant. First, **lemmas** are retrieved from the **mental lexicon**. At this point, **semantic substitutions** may take place. When the selected lemmas are combined in a grammatical structure, **anticipations**, **perseverations**, and **exchanges** can occur. Only in the next step, phonological forms, **lexemes**, are retrieved from the phonological lexicon. When something goes wrong in the selection of a lexeme, we observe a **phonological substitution**. Just like lemmas, phonological elements can also be anticipated, perseverated, and switched. Moreover, adjacent signs can **blend**. Ultimately, in the language production process, the articulatory organs must articulate the sentence. At this point, processes of **assimilation** can be observed. It is unclear at present, whether **stuttering** exists in the visual-spatial modality.

Test yourself

1. Which part of the brain is important for language?
2. Why is research on the difference in modality interesting?
3. Are deaf and hearing aphasics completely comparable?
4. Which processes play a role in the storage and processing of signs?
5. What is the role of iconicity in the retention of signs?
6. What do tip-of-the-fingers states reveal about sign production?
7. What evidence demonstrates differences between the topographic and grammatical use of space in deaf aphasics?
8. What are slips of the hand?
9. In what way does phonological coding take place?
10. What are assimilation processes? Think of some examples.

Assignments

1. If an aphasic deaf signer (with a left hemisphere lesion) had to describe the route to her/his house to a stranger, what types of errors might s/he make and why?

2. Look at the following fragment of an exchange between an examiner and a deaf aphasic patient. What type of aphasia is the patient suffering from? Argue your case. (Examiner's signs are given in English; dots indicate hesitation; see Appendix 1 for further notational conventions).

Examiner:	What else happened?
Patient:	CAR … DRIVE … BROTHER … DRIVE … I … s-t-a-d
	[attempts to gesture "stand up"]
Examiner:	You stood up?

Patient: YES … BROTHER … DRIVE … DUNNO.

               [attempts to gesture "wave goodbye"]

Examiner: Your brother was driving?

Patient: YES … BACK … DRIVE … BROTHER … MAN … MAMA …

               STAY… BROTHER … DRIVE …

3.   In an experiment, a set of 15 signs were taught to hearing adults, who had no previous knowledge of any sign language. This set consisted of 5 transparent iconic signs, 5 non-transparent iconic signs, and 5 arbitrary signs. After they had been presented with the signs three times (with the meaning in a spoken language provided), the adults were tested after five minutes on their comprehension and production of the signs. The test was carried out again after 1 hour and after 24 hours. For comprehension, the meaning given to the sign by the adult was noted, and for production, the realization of the parameters of the sign was noted, for example the handshape, etcetera.

   a.   Which results do you expect for the comprehension of these signs? And why?
   b.   Which results do you expect for production? And why?
   c.   Do you expect a difference in the results of the test carried out after 5 minutes, 1 hour, and 24 hours?
   d.   Signs that are similar in form to a gesticulation were excluded. What do you think motivated this decision?
   e.   Do you expect the same results in another sign language?
   f.   Try to do this experiment yourself with friends or colleagues using a sign language you know.

4.   Based on a sign language you know, construct three examples of slips of the hand and describe what kind of slips these are.

References and further reading

A general, comprehensive, and accessible introduction to psycholinguistic aspects of signing is the book by Emmorey (2002). Recent reviews on topics addressed in this chapter are by Dye (2012) on sign language processing, Hohenberger & Leuninger (2012) on sign language production, and Corina & Spotswood (2012) on neurolinguistic findings. The consequences of aphasia in deaf signers were studied by Poizner, Klima & Bellugi (1987), Poizner & Kegl (1992), Corina (1999), Hickok, Bellugi & Klima (2001), and Campbell, MacSweeney & Waters (2008). Important research on the localization of sign languages in the brain has been conducted by MacSweeney et al. (2002) and, using an ERP study, by Capek et al. (2009). A model of the working memory (in spoken language) is presented by Baddeley & Logie (1999); studies on aspects of the working memory are reviewed in Carroll (2004). Research on working memory in sign languages – with different conclusions concerning its capacity – is reported in Wilson & Emmorey (1997), Emmorey (2002),

Emmorey & Wilson (2004), Bavelier et al. (2008), and Geraci et al. (2008). Perception studies for sign languages have been reviewed by Emmorey (2007) and, for children, by Ormel et al. (2009). For the effect of language experience, see Morford et al. (2008); for insights from misperceptions, see Adam et al. (2011).

The classical study on the role of iconicity in ASL is Klima & Bellugi (1979). A cross-linguistic and cross-cultural study on sensitivity to iconicity in signers and non-signers is presented by Pizzuto & Volterra (2000). The role of iconicity in sign language processing is addressed in Baus, Carreras & Emmorey (2013). Thompson, Emmorey & Gollan (2005) describe the tip-of-the-fingers phenomenon. The first study on sign language production and slips of the hand (in ASL) is the one by Newkirk et al. (1980). Slips of the hand in DGS are analyzed by Hohenberger, Happ & Leuninger (2002) and Leuninger et al. (2004); these authors also compare error types and error units to those found in German slips of the tongue. Lexical access is investigated for Catalan SL by Baus et al. (2008). For a review of stuttering in ASL, see Whitebread (2014).

The examples of aphasic production in ASL and English are taken from Poizner, Klima & Bellugi (1987); the German examples were found in Leuninger (1989). The English slips of the tongue come from the, by now classic, study of Fromkin (1971) and from Fromkin (1988). The DGS slips are described in Glück et al. (1997), Hohenberger, Happ & Leuninger (2002), and Leuninger et al. (2004).

Chapter 3

Acquisition

Anne Baker, Beppie van den Bogaerde & Sonja Jansma

3.1 Introduction

Mark is three years of age and deaf from birth. He is playing with his mother, who is also deaf. In (1), an excerpt is given from a dialogue between Mark and his mother (see Appendix 1 for notational conventions).

Sign Language of the Netherlands

(1) a. Mother ALL TRAIN GO_{3b} EFFATHA SCHOOL
$INDEX_{3b}$ LOOK-AT CLOWN PLAY CYCLE JUGGLE.
'We all went by train to Effatha, and there we saw a clown playing and cycling and juggling with balls.'

                   `_____aff` `_____neg`

  b. Mark JUGGLE, MOMMY $INDEX_{mother}$ CANNOT.
'Yes, juggling. Mommy can't do that.'

                   `_____neg`

  c. Mother PU MOMMY CANNOT $INDEX_1$.
ALL CANNOT.
'No, mommy can't. Nobody can, actually.'

           `_____neg` `_____neg`

  d. Mark $INDEX_1$ CANNOT, NOT ALL, L J M.
'I can't, nobody, Laura, Jonas, Mark can't.'

                   `_____aff`

  e. Mother LAURA JONAS MARK, ONLY CLOWN.
$INDEX_{Mark}$ CAN $INDEX_{Mark}$ JUGGLE? CAN $INDEX_{Mark}$?
'Yes, Laura, Jonas and Mark, only the clown.
And you, can you juggle, can you?'

  f. Mark $INDEX_1$ $_2WATCH_1$ $AUX\text{-}OP_1$ JUGGLE $INDEX_1$.
'Me – watch me, I can juggle!'

  g. Mother CLEVER BOY $INDEX_{Mark}$.
'What a clever boy you are!'

  h. Mark $_2WATCH_1$ CLOWN, "nod", "nod" $INDEX_1$.
'Watch me, like a clown, yes, me.'

DOI 10.1075/z.199.03bak
© 2016 John Benjamins Publishing Company

In this conversation in Sign Language of the Netherlands (NGT), Mark and his mother are referring to a performance of a clown at school. Mark is talking about what he saw at the time. He believes he can juggle, too, and that everybody would then look at him, just as they watched the clown. Although his story is not altogether clear, his mother fills in the gaps, and she knows exactly what he is talking about.

Any three-year-old, in whatever language, is still learning the form, the structure, and the rules for language use. In a signed language, this is no different from a spoken language, provided the child is offered **input** in that language (Section 3.2). Deaf and hearing children who are raised in a deaf family usually receive sign language input. For convenience sake, when we talk about deaf children in the following, we mean children who are learning a sign language. Sign language acquisition follows the same path as spoken language acquisition, although aspects that are characteristic for a sign language are sometimes acquired a little later (Section 3.3). Some people, both deaf and hearing, learn a sign language as a second language. This acquisition process has certain typical features that are different from first language acquisition (Section 3.4). Deaf children grow up in a hearing society and are usually bilingual both in a signed and a spoken language. Since a sign languge is involved, that is, a language in a different modality, this is often called **bimodal bilingualism**. How the process of bilingualism develops is strongly dependent on the surroundings of the child (Section 3.5).

3.2   How do children learn a sign language?

Hearing parents talk to their children from birth. Often they are already talking to the child while it is still in the womb, and hearing babies can in fact hear their parents' voices. The parents immediately start talking to their hearing baby, even though they do not expect an answer for some time. Hearing parents also talk to their deaf baby, even when they know the child is deaf, because the urge to talk is so strongly embedded in their communication pattern. Deaf signing parents equally feel this urge to communicate – only they use sign language. The child cannot yet use signs but even so the parents continue to offer language. It is irrelevant whether their child is deaf or hearing, deaf parents will use their first language, sign language, with their baby. Of course, hearing children of deaf parents will also acquire the spoken language – from other relatives of from the deaf parents themselves (see Section 3.5). If hearing parents start following a sign language course as soon as the child has been diagnosed as deaf, they too will be able to begin using signs with their child from an early age.

The way in which deaf children acquire a sign language is strongly dependent on the way the language is offered at home and elsewhere, and on when such an input begins. Parents are an important source of language for their child. The child receives a large amount of input during the daily activities at home – during meals, when being changed or bathed, at play, etc. Children are also offered language outside the family home, by other relatives, friends, and neighbors. This can also happen in the context of a day-care center or preschool where input is offered by adult caregivers and peers. There can be considerable variation in the signing input from parents and from the people in the child's environment.

Many deaf children are offered only spoken language from birth, that is, they receive no sign language input (see Chapter 14). Such children will often use the gestures they observe in their surroundings and also invent signs of their own, thus creating an idiosyncratic form of communication called *homesign* (see Sections 1.3 and 3.5). Because spoken language is almost inaccessible for these deaf children, language acquisition, as a process, proceeds very slowly. They often do not come into contact with sign language until they start going to school. The age at which children go to school varies from one country to another so that some children will not start learning to sign until they are five years of age or even older. Such children are called **late learners**. The fluency level that these children reach in their sign language may be considerably lower than that of children who have been offered sign language from birth, but also lower than that of hearing people who have learned a sign language at an even later age.

When sufficient signed input is offered from the beginning, a sign language develops more or less parallel to a spoken language in hearing children (see Section 3.3). The sign language is then acquired as a first language. In the process of first language acquisition, the innate language acquisition device plays a role. This device is not specific for spoken language, but also functions for signed languages. When too little input is provided in sign language, or when signed input is offered too late, say after the age of three, the language acquisition process shows similarities to second language acquisition (see Section 3.4 and Chapter 14), and there is the chance that a native level competence in the sign language will never be reached. Independent of the input, a deaf child may of course have a language learning problem. This may be due to a problem such as ADHD or autism. It is also possible for deaf children to have a problem more specific to language just as hearing children can have Specific Language Impairment (SLI). This chapter will focus on deaf children with no such disorders.

As mentioned earlier, first contact with a sign language may not occur until the child visits a day-care center or kindergarten. The possibilities differ considerably between countries. In some countries, for example the Netherlands and Great-Britain, there are preschools where both a signed and a spoken language are offered, but in many countries, no such schools exist. The child then receives sign language input for the first time at a primary school for the deaf. There, the linguistic input is defined by the language policy of the school. Some schools for the deaf make a choice for bilingual input, that is, input in both a signed and a spoken language (see Chapter 14). Other schools opt for a sign system (see Section 1.4 and for more detail Section 13.5.1) like Signing Exact English in the US. Of course, in this case, the input is different: the lexicon of the sign language is usually used, but not the grammar. Even if a school officially does not allow sign language, the children still learn a form of sign language from each other. It is also possible that a child is in contact with members of the Deaf community, and in this way receives more and varied language input. A child of signing deaf parents encounters sign language in a natural way, through his parents, friends, and relatives. In contrast, deaf children of hearing parents are dependent on the choices their parents make regarding actively searching for contacts in the Deaf community (see Section 1.3). Television programs, theatre, and movies in sign language for deaf children or interpreted programs are also a source of language input, but there are only relatively few countries where these are available.

3.3   The path of sign language development

3.3.1 The pre-linguistic stage

In the **pre-linguistic stage** (or period), that is, from birth to approximately the first birthday, the deaf child does not yet produce signs. But still, there is a lot of communication going on – through eye contact, facial expressions, gestures, and signs, and also through speech and touch. The child also smiles for the first time. The attention of the child, deaf or hearing, is focused on the face of the adult, and the child will try to imitate facial expressions and mouth movements. In turn, the adult reacts to these imitations, and thus a kind of proto-conversation takes place in which both baby and adult take turns. Although the hands provide much information in a sign language, the focus of attention stays on the face in a sign language conversation, even in adults (see Section 10.3).

In the Netherlands and several other countries, deaf and hearing parents are encouraged to offer as many signs as possible to their deaf child, and to imitate the hand movements the child makes. This is comparable to the imitation of sound sequences by parents of hearing children and is also a form of proto-conversation. As children grow older, they focus more on the world around them and start to become interested in objects and people in their direct environment. When interacting with a hearing child, it is possible for the adult to label an object while the child is looking at it, for instance: "Look, there's the train!" This is not possible with deaf children. They have to learn how to divide their attention between the object and the sign TRAIN that refers to it. Learning the appropriate visual attention for sign language communication is a lengthy process that will only be finished around two and a half or three years of age.

When they are around seven or eight months old, deaf children begin to produce rhythmic hand movements. These hand movements are compared, by some researchers, to the vocal babbling of hearing children, that is, the rhythmic repetition of articulatory movements. These researchers claim that only children exposed to a sign language make such movements, and that **manual babbling** is the precursor to the first 'real' signs. Other researchers maintain that such movements can be observed in all children (also children not exposed to a sign language), which implies that they cannot be seen as the precursors of the first signs.

Even if these movements or babbles have no fixed meaning, they are interpreted as such by the adults. The NGT conversation in (2) between Laura and her mother, at the age of eleven months, illustrates this. We will use the convention 'year;months' from here onward to indicate the age of the children.

Sign Language of the Netherlands
(2) Mother and Laura, age 0;11;
Laura and her mother are looking at a picture book together.
a. Mother   PENGUIN.
b. Laura   "arm movement" (right arm, spread open hand, up-and-down movement, before chest)
c. Mother   YES, INDEX_{book} PENGUIN INDEX_{book} PENGUIN.
'Yes, this is a penguin.'

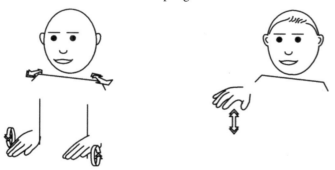

Adult form in (2a):   Child movement in (2b)
PENGUIN

The form of Laura's arm movement in (2b) is not yet recognizable as the sign for PEN-GUIN, but is being interpreted as such by her mother.

Later in this pre-linguistic stage, the children will begin to initiate communication, and will show that they understand a great deal. The mother could ask, for instance, CLOCK WHERE? (*Where is the clock?*), and immediately the child will look at the clock. Language comprehension in this period clearly is more advanced than language production. At this stage, children cannot yet produce the sign CLOCK, but they understand their mother's utterance. This process is comparable to the spoken language acquisition of hearing children.

Around the age of nine months, the children start to point at objects and people. Initially, these pointing gestures are undistinguishable from the pointing gestures made by hearing children. They have not yet acquired the grammatical function of INDEX (see Sections 1.4 and 1.7).

In the pre-linguistic period, deaf adults make sure that they sign and/or speak to their deaf child when the child is actually looking at them. They can also explicitly gain the child's attention by tapping the child, by waving their hand in the visual field of the child, or by signing on the child. Often signs are moved into the visual field of the child. The two-handed ASL sign RABBIT, for example, which normally is signed with both hands on either side of the head, can be articulated in the visual field of the child, for instance, close to a picture of a rabbit in a book, or on the head of the child. The ways in which visual attention is sought, that is the **attention strategies** used by deaf parents, are visually oriented from the beginning. The children themselves still have to learn the correct looking behavior; they sometimes look up too late or look away too soon, so that they miss (part of) the adult's utterances. Adults, in turn, articulate their signs more slowly and often repeat their sentences in the communication with young deaf children, thus making it easier for the child to actually see their signs.

3.3.2 The one- and two-word stages

In the early linguistic period, between one and two-and-a-half years, children begin producing their first **referential signs** as well as pointing gestures – that is, assuming that the deaf child receives enough language input, as discussed above. Referential signs have a fixed form and refer to an established referent. In the **one-word stage**, the number of referential signs quickly (sometimes in one big jump) increases, although there are large individual differences between children. At this stage, problems in language acquisition may become apparent. We do not yet know very much about language disorders in deaf children, or in hearing children who acquire a sign language as a first language, but the few available case studies suggest that those problems that do occur are more or less the same as in spoken languages. Children with Down's syndrome, for instance, have a delayed and sometimes deviant sign language acquisition.

At this stage, it is common for children to use a form with a much broader meaning than adults (**overextension**); this happens in sign languages, too. For example, they may use the sign CAT for all small animals, or the sign GRANDPA for all older men.

In their **phonological development**, children at this stage are still making mistakes in the form of the signs – in the handshape, the movement, or the location of the sign. In (3), we see an example of an error in handshape. A girl produces different forms of the target sign DADDY in American Sign Language (ASL). In (3a), the correct sign is shown, which consists of a 👋-hand twice making contact with the forehead; in (3b), (3c), and (3d), the location and movement are correct but the handshape is incorrect.

American Sign Language (correct form and child forms)

(3) a.   b.   c.   d.

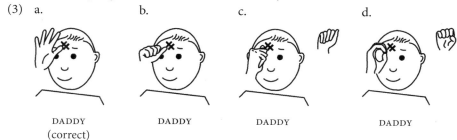

| DADDY | DADDY | DADDY | DADDY |
| (correct) | | | |

Although children at this age are physically able to produce the handshapes of their own sign language in terms of motor development (just like hearing children can produce all sounds of their own language), they do not always produce them correctly in signs (that is, linguistically). The handshapes in (4) are acquired first.

(4)   Frequent handshapes

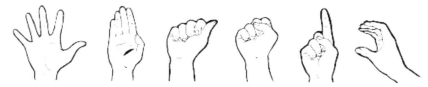

These handshapes are easy to articulate and occur in many sign languages. They are called **unmarked handshapes** (see Section 11.2). A handshape with only the thumb and pinky extended (5), for instance, is motorically more difficult than the handshapes in (4). As has been observed for various sign languages, children often replace a difficult (marked) handshape by an unmarked handshape; this is referred to as a **substitution**.

(5)

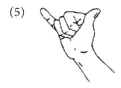

In the adult form of the NGT sign AMERICA (6a), the two hands make a circular movement in front of the body. In (6b), Mark is producing the sign for America, but he makes a movement with his whole body, unlike the circular movement of the hands and arms in the adult sign. The articulation of the movement has been displaced from the hands to the whole body. During motor development, children first gain control over the trunk, then the shoulders, the elbows, the hands, and lastly the articulators furthest away from the trunk, that is, the fingers. Mark makes the movement for AMER-ICA with his trunk, instead of his hands.

Sign Language of the Netherlands

(6)   a.   b.

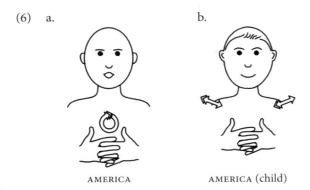

AMERICA   AMERICA (child)

The articulation of a sign by a body part or a joint closer to the trunk is called **proxi-malization** (see also Section 10.2). This is comparable to the development of motor control of the speech organs; for example, consonants produced in the front of the mouth are easier than consonants in the back, and full closure is easier than partial closure. Hearing English-speaking children thus often say *tom* instead of *come* because it is easier to produce a front plosive [t] than a back plosive [k] – this phenomenon is called **phonological simplification**.

In the **two-word stage**, usually around 1;8, children also begin to combine two signs, initially often combining an INDEX with a referential sign, and later also two referential signs. The pointing gesture, INDEX, slowly acquires linguistic meaning and begins to function as a demonstrative pronoun or a personal pronoun. Still, the linguistic status of pointing in combination with a referential sign is often unclear. Early in language acquisition, hearing children not exposed to a sign language also frequently combine a referential word with a pointing gesture. In this case, the pointing gesture is analyzed as a gesticulation and not as a linguistic element. However, when a deaf child produces the same form, it is often impossible to determine whether it should be analyzed as a gestural or a linguistic element. A pointing gesture clearly has a linguistic status as INDEX when the child uses it to localize a non-present referent or when it starts to acquire other grammatical functions (see Section 1.4 and Section 5.5.1).

Deaf children, just like hearing children, label things and express semantic relations such as attributes, for example BICYCLE RED 'the bicycle is red', or ownership, as in MUMMY PENCIL 'that's mummy's pencil'. Hearing children produce similar utterances in this period like *bicycle red* or *mummy pencil*. Just like hearing children, deaf children talk only about the **here-and-now**, that is, they communicate only about present objects or persons. The topics of conversation are also similar: who is doing something, what is being done, often related to eating, drinking, toys, actions, etc. The lexicon rapidly grows around these topics. It is, however, striking that deaf children learn signs for 'deaf' and 'hearing' quite early, whereas hearing children learn these terms much later. Combinations of signs slowly expand from two to more elements, but the utterances of the children in this phase are still simple. We hardly see inflected verbs, for example (see Chapter 9), but the sign order is usually correct. The phonological form of signs is also often not yet fully accurate.

As we described in the previous section for the pre-linguistic period, signing adults usually make sure that the child can see the signs offered. From this period on, the child learns to actively pay visual attention to communication. Example (7) shows how Mark is looking at his mother while she is signing the NGT sign AIRPLANE.

Sign Language of the Netherlands
(7)   Mark (2;6) looks at his mother signing

Initially, children sometimes start to sign without checking for visual attention, but around the age of two, they become aware that their conversation partner needs to be able to see their signing. They now begin to check whether the other person is looking at them *before* they start to sign themselves. Children also start looking spontaneously at their conversation partner in order to see if perhaps signs are being offered, and they react better to movements (by looking up), both in their visual field and the periphery.

3.3.3 The differentiation stage

In the **differentiation stage** (2;6–5;0), sentences increase in length. The children's language becomes more complex, and the acquisition of grammatical structures really starts. In this period, the children begin to use non-manual elements, like facial expressions, the head, and their body for grammatical purposes. In the NGT conversation between Mark and his mother (see (1) at the beginning of this chapter), Mark nods his head to express confirmation and shakes his head for negation. These aspects are acquired quickly and quite early on in this phase. The correct use of facial expressions for yes/no questions and wh-questions also begins to emerge (see Section 6.7.1). This may seem late, but these are complex markers that have to be produced simultaneously with manual signs. Deaf mothers do not start using non-manual markers in a grammatical manner in their input until children are between 2;0 and 2;6, so it is not surprising that acquisition of these aspects starts rather late. Moreover, these grammatical aspects marked on the face are rather complicated for children to learn because the face is also used to display emotion. The child has to learn to distinguish these two functions and then encode them correctly.

Syntactic relations are expressed in the signing space (see Section 1.3). The area that is used for this is thus often called the syntactic signing space (see Section 6.4). In the syntactic signing space, the relation between the verb and its subject and object are indicated. In the differentiation phase, children learn how to use agreeing verbs, as we can see in the example produced by Mark in conversation with his mother at three years of age (Example (1f), repeated here for the sake of convenience).

Sign Language of the Netherlands
    (1)   f.   Mark   INDEX$_1$ $_2$WATCH$_1$ AUX-OP$_1$ JUGGLE INDEX$_1$.
                       'Me – watch me, I can juggle!'

The movement of the NGT verb WATCH begins at the location of the second person, marked with a subscript '2' (in the example, the 2 refers to his mother) and ends at the first person, Mark, marked with subscript '1'. In this way, Mark makes clear that his mother should watch him. This particular instantiation of agreement is correct here, but correct realization of agreement is not always the case (see Section 9.5.2 for discussion of agreement). In agreeing verbs, we may find **overgeneralization**, that is, cases in which a particular grammatical rule is used where it should not be used. In the example, we can see that Mark combines the verb WATCH with the auxiliary AUX-OP (see also Chapter 9). AUX-OP can be marked for both a subject and an object (agreement), but it is not usually used with verbs that can show agreement, like WATCH. In this respect, Mark's utterance in (1f) is thus unusual. Also, in Mark's sentence AUX-OP agrees with the object only (as indicated by subscript '1'), where it should agree with both subject and object: $_2$AUX-OP$_1$.

Moreover, all sign languages studied to date also have verbs that cannot be marked for agreement in this way (see Section 9.5.2), and these are sometimes inflected incorrectly, as in the ASL example in (8a). Here the child inflects the verb LIKE by moving the hand towards the locus associated with the object. The adult target form (8b), however, does not allow such a directional movement.

American Sign Language

(8)   a.   b.

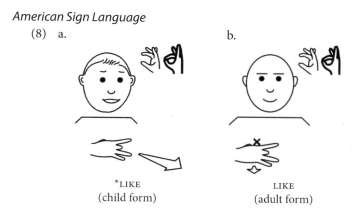

*LIKE	LIKE
(child form)	(adult form)

Children have to learn how to express these grammatical relations correctly, and during this process, we see developmental errors such as those just described. They also make mistakes in not specifying what the subject of the sentence is, or by forgetting to produce the object.

Taken together, aspects that are specific for sign languages (see the following chapters) are acquired at this stage, like the use of non-manual markers as a grammatical part of a sentence (see Chapters 6 and 7), or the use of the signing space in front of the body, as well as the use of classifiers in spatial verbs (see Section 9.6.2). Pointing gestures now acquire clear grammatical status. When a noun is signed for the first time in a conversation (e.g. MAN), this sign is localized in the syntactic space (see Section 1.5). Usually this is done by means of an INDEX. When, at a later point in the conversation, the child points again to this location, it is clear that she refers to that noun (MAN) and that this pointing gesture now functions as a personal or demonstrative pronoun. This abstract use of space now starts to be acquired by the children. Of course, they often make mistakes. Sometimes they place more than one referent in one location (*stacking*), which makes it unclear to whom they are referring or what they mean exactly. This can be compared to the use of personal pronouns by children acquiring a spoken language, for instance, when they are talking about two men, and keep on using 'he' without specifying which 'he' they are referring to.

The lexicon has been continually expanding in the previous phase and this continues in this phase. In hearing children acquiring a spoken language, a lexical spurt has often been observed around three years. This is not so clear in the few studies of lexical development in signing children; vocabulary expansion seems rather to continue steadily.

In this phase, children also talk far more about events that do not take place in the *here-and-now*, as in Mark's story about the clown he saw at school a week earlier. This has consequences for the way children use language. For example, they have to estimate what their conversation partner knows about the topic of the conversation, and what s/he doesn't know. They also have to refer to people, objects, and events that are not in the here-and-now in a grammatically correct way. In other words, besides grammatical skills, we see a development in pragmatic skills in this period (see Chapter 4). When children tell a story, the narrative is often still vague and unstructured, and is mostly about personal and quite recent events. The actions of different people at different times in the story are not yet correctly linked with one another; the child often tells parts of the story as if they were separate. In all these aspects, development is similar to that seen in the acquisition of a spoken language.

3.3.4 Reaching the adult level

Between five and nine years of age, the finer details of the language are acquired. Basic knowledge of both grammar and the lexicon is now in place. The lexicon increases continuously, of course, also in adults. Grammatical aspects, like more complex forms of verbs, additional non-manual grammatical markers, or complex sentences with subordinate clauses are also acquired. In this phase, fingerspelling (see Section 1.4) is learned, usually as a result of being at school where fingerspelling also supports beginning literacy. In many European sign languages, the mouth plays a larger role than, for instance, in ASL, which uses more fingerspelling. This difference, of course, influences the acquisition of these various elements in a specific sign language.

An important development can be seen in narrative skills. As the children grow older, they start using more grammatical elements correctly in order to increase the cohesion of their stories (see Chapter 4). The focus here is on learning how to introduce new elements in a story and to refer back to these elements in an appropriate way. This is mainly achieved by using referential signs, through the use of INDEX, and classifiers (see Chapters 5 and 9). Just as in spoken languages, the acquisition of pragmatic skills – for example, the correct structure of a narrative – takes a long time, and continues even past the age of nine.

3.4   Second language acquisition

Age of acquisition is an important factor in learning a sign language as a second language, just as with spoken languages. Generally, children are better in acquiring native skills in a foreign language than adults. This observation has contributed to the discussion about learners having a so-called **sensitive period** for language learning. The late learners, as discussed in Section 3.2, certainly have problems in reaching a near native-like level in a sign language, but it is not clear if this is strictly due to there being a sensitive period.

Aspects that second language learners of a sign language find difficult are phonology, non-manual aspects, and the grammatical use of space. These are aspects that are clearly specific for signed languages and do not occur in spoken languages. The phonological inventory of a sign language, for instance, is completely different from that of any spoken language. The variation that always exists in any language, like the use of synonyms, regional variation, or a particular register (see Chapter 4.7), is often especially difficult to learn in a sign language.

The first language of a learner also plays a role in the acquisition or learning of a second language. For instance, where the word order in a sign language is different from that in the surrounding spoken language, the second language learners are likely to make errors in this grammatical domain. On the other hand, we can also view this type of **interference** as a type of **interlanguage**, a phase that a learner goes through before the correct form of a language has been acquired. By interlanguage, we mean here a language variety with characteristics of two language systems: the interlanguage functions as a transition between these two systems. All learners of a second language have to deactivate their first language in order to avoid interference. When learners of a sign language have a spoken language as their first language, the spoken language has to be deactivated. Because it is physically possible to produce a sign while *simultaneously* producing a word (see Sections 1.2 and 1.4), as in bimodal bilingualism, a mixture of signs and words can be the result (see Section 13.5).

What is also important in learning a new language is the degree to which it can be used and practiced, in this case through contact with native signers. There is no 'deaf country' that one could visit to practice the language, and contact with native signers is often sporadic. There are few opportunities to have access to natural sign language input, except through direct contact with deaf people. Moreover, in many countries, there are no television programs in the national sign language (but see the BBC in the United Kingdom with *See Hear!*). In only a few countries is a sign language interpreter provided to interpret spoken language television programs. Also, there is hardly any written literature translated into sign languages on DVD, for example, and cultural forms like poetry, theatre, and film are still relatively scarce. The chances of seeing or using a sign language outside the deaf community are therefore small, even though modern technology like internet nowadays provides an increasing number of examples of signed cultural expressions, such as poetry.

The ultimate level of skill reached in a sign language is thus determined by a complex of features closely related to the motivation to learn the language, the aptitude for language learning, the age of learning the language, and the opportunities to actually use the language. This ultimate level and the speed and rate of acquisition may thus vary considerably. However, the order of acquisition is almost the same for all learners, and is similar to the first language acquisition process, although there are also a few modality-specific challenges. As mentioned earlier, most hearing learners will have problems in acquiring the correct facial expressions and the use of the signing space, but also the verbal system. In the domain of phonology, it has been shown that second language learners – just like children acquiring a sign language – are less likely to correctly produce marked handshapes. Also, it has been found that second language learners generally articulate iconic signs less accurately than arbitrary signs, probably because the direct form-meaning mapping prevents learners from focusing on the exact phonological structure of the sign.

3.5   Bilingual development

Before the introduction and application of cochlear implants in Western countries in the 1990s, deaf children and deaf adults were almost always bimodal bilinguals (see Chapter 14). Bilingualism is functionally defined here: people are bilingual when they use two languages on a daily basis. For deaf people, these two languages are a sign language and a spoken language (or only its written form). It could be the case that even more languages are used, for instance, when a family originates from a different country than where they are resident and the home language is not the national language. In a number of countries, sign language has been considered since the 1980s to be the native language of deaf children and the spoken/written language the second language. Actually, deaf children who learn to sign do not really have a choice about their bilingualism. In order to be able to function in the hearing society, they must learn the spoken language, or at least its written form. In many Western countries, a large proportion of deaf children nowadays receive a cochlear implant. This may allow them to acquire spoken language to a much better degree than deaf children without such a device. If the parents, or the child, then choose not to sign, then such deaf children are not in contact with the deaf community and consequently, with sign language. These children often grow up monolingual in the spoken language (see Section 3.5.3).

Bilingualism can be achieved in different ways. We speak of **simultaneous bilingualism** when both languages are offered during the early phases of language acquisition (before the age of three). This can also be the case for deaf children. However, the one person – one language strategy, that is, a situation in which one language is used by one of the parents and the other language by the other parent, is less likely since the spoken language is usually offered in the form of a signed system. It is also possible that at home, a different language is used than outside the home, for instance in kindergarten. This may be the case with deaf children who have a cochlear implant: at home, the spoken language is used, while at school, a signed language, or sign-supported speech can be offered. When a child first acquires a sign language, and later, after the third year, a spoken language, this is called **sequential bilingualism** (see Chapter 14).

The parents' choice to offer a sign language is dependent on having a diagnosis of deafness of their child. If deafness is discovered relatively late, that is, after the child is two years of age, the child will already have a delay in language acquisition. This is a frequent occurrence in many parts of the world. The age at which diagnosis is possible depends on the availability of hearing tests. Nowadays, it is possible to test hearing status immediately after birth using Otoacoustic Emission, which measures the evoked response to a sound. The sooner parents know that their child is deaf, the earlier they can make choices: yes or no to using a sign language, yes or no to bilingualism, yes or no to special education (see Chapter 14), etc. The choice of parents seems strongly influenced by the social facilities and the language policies in their country. Is family counseling offered? Is there financial support for the parents? Is language policy in favor of or against sign language? It still happens regularly that a school for the deaf is asked to accept a child aged three or four who has no language to speak of (minimal language skills). These children must begin from scratch with language development, that is, learn to pay attention to the face, learn to make eye contact, and discover that communication is fun, intimate, informative, and useful.

In Section 3.2, we discussed that there is a huge variation in the population of children who learn a sign language. In the discussion on development of bimodal bilingualism in a signed and a spoken language, we can distinguish four groups of children. We shall briefly discuss each group.

3.5.1 Deaf children of deaf parents

In deaf children of deaf parents, first language acquisition follows the normal acquisition path – but of course only if a sign language is in the input – and is subject to the same input conditions as are relevant for a spoken language. As sign languages have been suppressed in many countries for a long time, not all deaf adults use a sign language in their daily lives, not even in communication with their children. In those families where a sign language is the home language, the children can acquire this language as their first language.

Many deaf parents offer their young babies both a spoken language and a sign language, at least until they know whether their child is hearing or deaf. But even after they discover that their child is deaf, many still offer the spoken language. However, the intelligibility of the spoken language input varies greatly, and it remains a fact that a deaf child only has visual access to a spoken language. There is a considerable amount of exposure to the spoken language through the environment of the child, for instance from a hearing baby sitter, caretakers in kindergarten, the media, etc. These children are raised in a situation of simultaneous bimodal bilingualism, even though there might be a delay in the acquisition of the spoken language.

3.5.2 Hearing children of deaf parents

The hearing children of deaf signing parents are also exposed to sign input. Both the signed and spoken languages are fully accessible to these children and they are thus in the ideal situation for bilingual bimodal development. In principle, the signed and the spoken language can be offered in parallel. Research has shown that deaf parents indeed offer both languages to their hearing child, but usually in a blended form in which the grammar of the sign language is followed (see Section 13.5.1), not a sign system which follows the grammar of the spoken language (see Section 1.4). The spoken language of course also is widely used in the child's surroundings: hearing relatives, neighbors, caretakers in kindergarten, and the media all provide input in the spoken language. We can speak of simultaneous bilingualism in these children, too.

3.5.3 Deaf children of hearing parents

The majority of deaf children have hearing parents: 90–95%. These children initially receive spoken language input, at least during the period before the parents discover that their child is deaf. This language input of course makes little impact on the deaf child, because it is offered in a modality that is hardly accessible, or even inaccessible, to the child. The degree of residual hearing determines the accessibility of the spoken language.

If hearing parents are unfamiliar with sign language, or choose not to use it, they sometimes create an individual form of communication using invented gestures, that is, a homesign system, as already discussed in Section 1.3. Homesign is a rather simple form of communication where a deaf person uses his own system of gestures with a small group of people, usually family members. These gestures are often based on the gestures used in a particular culture, but they may also be invented. The homesigns are usually highly iconic (see Chapters 1 and 8), since the conversation partners are dependent on iconicity in order to establish the meaning. Further characteristics of homesign are the absence of complex grammar and a restricted set of handshapes.

If parents do choose to learn sign language, they have to follow sign language classes. In the course of time, as the parents improve their signing skills, the sign language input to their children will increase and become richer. Hearing siblings of deaf children also often learn to sign well. In some countries, the child can attend a special kindergarten for deaf children and then a deaf school. There, too, the second language, that is, the spoken language, will be offered (see Chapter 14). It is therefore possible for deaf children of hearing parents to also become bimodal bilingual at an early age provided that they receive a form of schooling where the two languages are offered.

3.5.4 Children with a cochlear implant (CI)

Since the beginning of the 1990s, deaf children in some countries can receive a **cochlear implant** (CI), provided they meet the selection criteria. A cochlear implant (9) is an electronic prosthesis that spans the outer, middle and inner ear. It is inserted into the cochlea during a surgical operation. The implant changes sound into electronic pulses that stimulate the auditory nerve. With a CI, general sounds and speech can be heard, but they sound quite different from the sounds people with normal hearing hear.

(9)   Cochlear implant (CI)

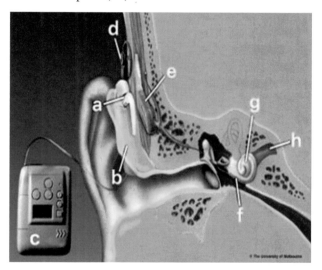

- a.   Sounds and speech are picked up by the microphone.
- b.   The information from the microphone is sent to the speech processor.
- c.   The speech processor analyzes the information and converts it into an electrical code.
- d.   The coded signal travels via a cable to the transmitting coil in the headset. Radio waves from the transmitter coil carry the coded signal through the skin to the implant inside.
- e.   The implant package decodes the signal. The signal contains information that determines how much electrical current will be sent to the different electrodes.
- f.   The appropriate amount of electrical current passes down the lead wires to the chosen electrodes.

g.   The position of the stimulating electrodes within the cochlea will determine the frequency or pitch of the sounds. The amount of electrical current will determine the loudness of the sounds.

h.   Once the nerve endings in the cochlea are stimulated, the message is sent up to the brain along the hearing nerve. The brain interprets the stimulation as a meaningful sound.

A cochlear implant gives many deaf children better access to spoken language than a regular hearing aid. Because they can perceive the spoken language better, they develop considerably better receptive and productive skills in a spoken language. The group of children with a CI is very diverse. Some children are raised and educated monolingually; in most cases, this will be in a spoken language and by hearing parents. We also find children who have considerable signing skills at the time of implantation. Some deaf signing parents may also choose to have their child implanted. These children, with sign language input and better access to the spoken language, can become fluent in both languages.

An increasing group of children receive a CI at a very young age, before their first birthday. This makes the spoken language wholly or partly accessible to them in the very early phases of language acquisition. For all these children, it depends on their parents' choice whether or not they will be mono- or bilingual. Some parents decide after implantation to raise and educate their child only in a spoken language, and in fact, this is often the advice of the hospital CI teams. These children can be integrated in regular education for hearing children, or they can go to a deaf school providing monolingual education or education for hard-of-hearing children, where the spoken language is the instruction and target language. Other parents still decide to raise and educate their child bilingually. The language policy of the school of their choice will determine in what form bilingualism is offered (see Chapter 14). Children with a CI can become bilingual, depending on the choice of their parents.

Even with a CI, acquiring a spoken language remains quite a challenge for many deaf children. A large number of children with a CI achieve a better level of spoken language than deaf children with conventional hearing aids. Research indicates that the earlier a child receives a CI, the better the chances of good results in the spoken language. Most children with a CI have some delay compared to hearing children, but it is not yet known whether they can catch up in the course of time. Possibly, the delay will increase. It is certainly not the case that all children profit in the same way from their CI. There are still children who, even several years after implantation, have no or very limited spoken language skills.

Summary

Children learning a sign language are, as all children, dependent on adequate language **input**. The language input of signing deaf parents is natural, but hearing parents of deaf children must make a huge effort to learn the sign language and offer it to their child. The environment is also an important source of language input for deaf children, for instance kindergarten or daycare centers. Some deaf people are exposed only to spoken language and learn it with considerable difficulty. They come into contact with sign language only at a later age; such **late learners** usually reach a relatively low level in sign language. The stages that children go through in the sign language acquisition process are comparable to those in spoken language acquisition.

In the **pre-linguistic period** (0–1 year), children produce **manual babbling** and begin to develop **attention strategies** by looking at their conversation partner. Parents adapt their language input to the child's level by repeating signs and by signing slower. In the early linguistic phase (1;0–2;6), children produce **referential signs**. In the **one-word stage** and the subsequent two-word stage, this category increases rapidly and **overextension** occurs. In the child's **phonological development**, handshapes that are difficult to produce motorically are replaced by easier forms, that is, **unmarked handshapes**. The same is true for movements. Such replacements are called **substitutions**. Another type of **phonological simplification** is **proximalization** whereby a sign is articulated by a joint that is closer to the trunk. In the **two-word stage**, children combine signs, but they still mainly sign about the **here-and-now**. In the **differentiation stage** (2;6–5;0), general communication skills have been acquired and the children are beginning to learn specific grammatical aspects such as non-manual elements, localization in the signing space, and verb agreement; **overgeneralization** can occur. After the age of five, the lexicon is still expanding, complex structures are acquired as well as many pragmatic skills.

Some hearing people learn a sign language as a second language later in life. The level they can acquire is dependent on factors such as age, motivation, and language aptitude. Age plays an important role, and this is linked to the discussion of there being a **sensitive period** for language acquisition. Specific aspects of grammar like verb inflection and non-manual aspects remain difficult. Sometimes **interference** of the grammar of the spoken language occurs; this mixed form can be considered an **interlanguage**.

Most deaf people use a signed and a spoken language. This is called **bimodal bilingualism**. Children either acquire both languages at the same time (**simultaneous bilingualism**), or one after the other (**sequential bilingualism**). This is highly influenced by the age of diagnosis of deafness and the parents' choice for, or against, sign language. Some children are diagnosed with deafness late. There are four different groups of children who can be bilingual in a signed and a spoken language: deaf children of deaf parents, hearing children of deaf parents, deaf children of hearing parents, and children with a **cochlear implant** (CI). These groups can differ greatly in their fluency in both languages.

Test yourself

1. Which are the most important features of the early linguistic stage?
2. What are the most important differences in the conditions under which a deaf child of deaf parents acquires language compared to a deaf child of hearing parents?
3. Please explain why a deaf child must develop attention for communication.
4. What is a CI? Describe the influence of a CI on the language acquisition situation of a deaf child.
5. What does interlanguage mean in the context of a signed and a spoken language?
6. What is meant by the term late learner in the context of a sign language and what is the influence on the ultimate language level?
7. What is proximalization?
8. At which stage does a deaf child of deaf parents with sign language input learn to conjugate verb signs?
9. Mention three features of sign language input of parents to their children.
10. What is the difference between simultaneous bilingualism and sequential bilingualism in the context of deaf children?
11. What influence does the moment of diagnosis of deafness have on the language acquisition situation?

Assignments

1. Imagine that hearing parents of a deaf child immediately start taking sign language lessons and using signs in the communication with their deaf infant. But quite quickly the deaf child is implanted with a CI and the parents increasingly use Sign Supported English with their child. What will be the first language of this deaf child?
2. A 2–3 year old boy acquiring Finnish Sign Language uses the 🖐-hand:
    -   instead of the ✋-hand in MOTHER, BOY;
    -   instead of the 👆-hand in BROKEN;
    -   instead of the 👆-hand in BINOCULARS.

    What do you call this process in phonological acquisition?
3. The South African Sign Language (SASL) verb KNOW is produced with a bent 👆-hand, palm facing downwards, on the side of the head with a repeated movement. The SASL verb REMEMBER is produced with a 👆-hand, palm facing sideways, on the side of the head with a repeated movement. You can predict that children will learn to correctly produce the verb KNOW before the verb REMEMBER. What is the basis for this prediction?

SASL ᴋɴᴏᴡ   SASL ʀᴇᴍᴇᴍʙᴇʀ

4. How would you describe the language acquisition situation of a hearing child in a deaf family who is offered both a sign language and a spoken language? What makes this situation different from the sign language acquisition of a deaf child of deaf parents, and the spoken language acquisition of a hearing child of hearing parents?

5. Decide whether the following sentences are typical for (i) the early linguistic stage, (ii) the differentiation stage, or (iii) a later stage:

    a. sentence with an inflected verb;
    b. sentence with a non-manual negation;
    c. sentence with INDEX and a referential sign;
    d. sentence with a complex set of verbs and non-manual elements.

6. Which aspects of the conversation in NGT at the beginning of this chapter are characteristic for the differentiation stage?

References and further reading

How language acquisition generally takes place has been described in many texts, for example Clark (2009). Amongst the first general studies on sign language acquisition are the ones by Newport & Meier (1985) and Bonvillian & Folven (1993), both on ASL; a recent comprehensive survey is provided by Chen Pichler (2012). Petitto & Marentette (1991) first described sign babbling. The acquisition of phonological aspects has been described, for instance, for ASL by Bonvillian & Siedlecki (2000) and Conlin et al. (2000), for BSL by Morgan, Barrett-Jones & Stoneham (2007), and for Libras by Karnopp (2002). Boyes Braem (1990) and Meier (2000) studied the influence of motor development on phonological development.

As for the acquisition of morphological and syntactic aspects, Schick (1990) investigates the acquisition of classifiers, Meier (2002) provides an overview of the acquisition of verb agreement, and Chen Pichler (2008) reports on the acquisition of word order. Lillo-Martin & Chen

Pichler (2006) review the acquisition of syntactic aspects, and Reilly (2006) does the same for non-manual markers. The use of first (referential) signs is addressed by Folven & Bonvillian (1991), while lexical development is sketched in Anderson (2006). The acquisition of pragmatic skills has been studied by, for instance, Morgan (2006) and Baker & Van den Bogaerde (2006). Richmond-Welty & Siple (1999) and Van den Bogaerde (2000) looked at the role of visual attention in sign language interaction.

Methodological aspects of language acquisition research in deaf children are discussed in Baker, van den Bogaerde & Woll (2005) and more recently by Lieberman & Mayberry (2015). Spencer & Marschark (2006) and Schick, Marschark & Spencer (2006) include reviews on various aspects of acquisition from a more educational point of view. Marschark, Tang & Knoors (2014) focus on the role of bilingualism.

Developmental language disorders have not been addressed in this chapter. Actually, the study of such disorders in sign language is in its infancy, but for information on symptoms (e.g. of SLI, autism) and assessment, the interested reader is referred to the overview by Woll (2012a) and various chapters in Quinto-Pozos (2014).

Late learners and the effects of age of acquisition were first studied by Mayberry (1993) with many subsequent studies (e.g. Boudreault & Mayberry 2006). There are only few studies that investigate the acquisition of sign language as a second language; for phonological aspects, see Rosen (2004), Chen Pichler (2011), and Ortega (2013). Recent reviews of learning a sign language as a second language can be found in Woll (2012b) and Chen Pichler & Koulidobrova (2015). Bimodal bilingualism in adults has been studied by Emmorey et al. (2008) and Bishop & Hicks (2009). Studies in children have been carried out by Baker & Van den Bogaerde (2014) and Chen Pichler, Lee & Lillo-Martin (2014). How to study bimodal bilingualism is discussed in de Quadros et al. (2015). A recent overview of the influence of communication mode on language development in deaf children with a cochlear implant is offered by Walker & Tomblin (2014).

The example of a child-mother conversation in NGT is taken from the Amsterdam longitudinal database (Van den Bogaerde 2000). The CI picture comes from www.bionicear.org/mhg/cichowcochlearimplantswork.html, which also provides more explanation about the device. The example from Finnish Sign Language was taken from Takkinnen (1994); the SASL examples come from the National Institute of the Deaf dictionary (2001).

Chapter 4

Interaction and discourse

Anne Baker & Beppie van den Bogaerde

4.1   Introduction

Having a conversation is the most natural thing in the world, but if you do not comply with the conversational rules, you are often misunderstood. In a signed conversation, it is also necessary to adhere to certain (implicit) conversational rules to ensure that your conversation partner can follow you. Both linguistic and non-linguistic information is important in understanding an utterance.

In this chapter, we will discuss these rules – many are comparable to those used in spoken languages, while others are clearly different. In Section 4.2, the principles are discussed that signers use in order to understand each other well. Subsequently, in Section 4.3, we will look at how turn-taking takes place in a signed conversation. Coherence is an important aspect of any conversation and is the focus of Section 4.4. Utterances can be motivated by many different kinds of intentions, and different intentions result in different speech acts. How this is achieved in sign languages is the topic of Section 4.5. In Section 4.6, we will address a number of aspects that can have an influence on how linguistic information is organized in a discourse, namely definiteness, information structure, and role shift. Ideally, the style of an utterance fits the context in which it is uttered as well as the conversation partner, that is, it is pragmatically adequate. Still, it is, of course, also possible to be rude or impolite in a sign language, just as it is in a spoken language. The issue of pragmatic adequacy is addressed in Section 4.7. Many of the examples in this chapter are taken from Sign Language of the Netherlands (NGT), but most, if not all, of the principles we discuss can certainly be generalized to other sign languages.

4.2   Cooperating in conversations

Let us start by having a look at the fragment of a conversation between four female Deaf friends in British Sign Language (BSL), given in (1). Tanya (TA), Trish (TR), Nancy (NA), and Frances (F) are talking about teachers from their former high school. For the reader's convenience, we first provide the translation, followed by the transcript, which

DOI 10.1075/z.199.04bak
© 2016 John Benjamins Publishing Company

is given in a sort of score notation, such that overlapping utterances of the participants also overlap in the score (note that some of the conventions in (1) are slightly different from those listed in Appendix 1; e.g. YOU instead of INDEX₂).

British Sign Language

(1)   Conversation between four women

Translation:

Tanya: That's interesting. Maths. You see.
Nancy: You see! It's strange. He was clever but crap. It makes you wonder why…
Trish: Me too. I had an art teacher who was similar. Yes, similar, with his odd
             clothes. That's artists for you. Odd and wear odd clothing.
Frances: Odd like you then, Trish.
Tanya: Yes, that's why you're odd.
Frances: You went to art school, didn't you Trish?
Trish: Yes, I did art but I left.
Frances: <comments not clearly visible>
Trish: Not really, but he was deaf. Hey, that's the point, he was deaf. Only the
             hearing teachers were odd.
Tanya: Yes, you're right, that's true. I had an art teacher=
Trish: = with a horrible mohican cut
Tanya: Yes, he had a mohican cut and a handle-bar moustache. He had long hair
             and wore white clothes […]. I dunno. There's something different about
             art teachers. It must be because of their love of art. They are very strange.

```
TA │ INTERESTING   MATHS            YOU-SEE
TR │ WELL NOW       INTERESTING---------------
N  │                YOU-SEE IT'S-STRANGE HE CLEVER BUT CRAP
F  │

TA │
TR │      HEY       HEY-----------      ME-TOO        ART TEACHER      SIMILAR
N  │ MAKE YOU       WONDER WHY
F  │      HOW-MANY------ WHAT

TA │
TR │ SIMILAR-----   YES-BUT SIMILAR--------      OH-YES SIMILAR ODD CLOTHES
N  │ HAVE (XXX)   CLOTHES  ART     THEIRS      MEANS      THAT
F  │

TA │            YES-RIGHT I AGREE   YOU              HOW YOU?
TR │ ART        ODD-----------------  CLOTHING
N  │                                      ODD                    "laughs"----
F  │                                              SAME YOU        ODD
```

```
TA │ THAT'S-WHY ODD
TR │              ME-----------     GET-OUT-OF-IT--------        ME ART------
N  │ -------->
F  │              YOU BEFORE YOU    ART            SCHOOL     YOU---- MEAN

TA │                        UGH                    TRUE------------
TR │     "shakes head"   NOT-REALLY BUT DEAF       HEY! DEAF ONLY
N  │     "shakes head"
F  │ (xxx)

TA │              YOU'RE-RIGHT    TRUE        THAT'S-IT   ME      TEACHER ART
TR │ HEARING      ONLY            HEARING     ODD         THAT'S-IT HORRIBLE
N  │              "nods firmly"
F  │

TA │              TEACHER MOHICAN HANDLE-BAR-MOUSTACHE LONG-HAIR WHITE
TR │ MOHICAN
N  │
F  │

TA │ CLOTHES [...] I-DUNNO DIFFERENT THEIR WAY LINKED ART LOVE STRANGE.
TR │
N  │
F  │
```

The transcript shows how all four signers contribute to the conversation. Their turns are not very long. As far as we can tell, they do not lie and do not provide wrong information on purpose. Also, they give relevant answers to questions. In other words, they comply with the **cooperative principle** that applies to all conversations. Within that principle they adhere to the rules, or **maxims**, of **quantity**, **quality**, and **relevance**. In order to adhere to these maxims, the signer needs to provide enough information, tell the truth, and communicate what is important for the conversation partner to know.

But now consider Example (2). In this short conversation, Marie's answer does not seem to match Jack's question. He is asking whether she will be coming along to a party, but in her answer, she does not even mention the party. At first sight, it seems as if her answer is irrelevant.

Sign Language of the Netherlands

(2) Jack: TONIGHT PARTY, INDEX$_2$ COME-ALONG?
             'Are you coming along to this party tonight?'
     Marie: TOMORROW EXAM.
             'I have an exam tomorrow.'

But a closer look tells us that this is not the case. Of course, Marie means to imply that she must study for her exam, which will prevent her from going to the party. Although she does not directly answer Jack's question, he will have no trouble interpreting her answer as a 'no'. He derives a **conversational implicature** from Marie's utterance. So, what is going on in Example (3)?

Sign Language of the Netherlands

(3) Jack: TOMORROW WILLIAM INDEX₁ PERFORM. ROMEO.
'Tomorrow William and I have a performance. Romeo.'

                                                     wh
    _____
Marie: ROMEO PERFORM WHO?
'Who will play Romeo?'

Why does Marie have to ask this question? Well, Jack has not made clear who will take the part of Romeo. Of course, he should have done this by repeating either the name sign WILLIAM or the first person pronoun INDEX₁ in the second clause. Given that he did not provide enough information to make his utterance interpretable, Jack failed to comply with the maxim of quantity.

Example (4) contains a reference to people present in the physical surroundings. Consequently, the use of INDEX_girl is deictic here. This use complies with the maxim of quantity if, but only if, the conversation partner can also see the person referred to. The references to the first and second person – that is, the signer and the addressee – are clear, but the girl referred to has to be visible to the addressee.

Sign Language of the Netherlands

                                                     y/n
                                      _____
(4) Jack: INDEX_girl COFFEE DRINK, INDEX₂ TOO?
'She's going to have a coffee, you too?'
Marie: GREAT. INDEX₁ THIRSTY.
'Great. I'm thirsty.'

Just as in spoken languages, it is necessary to comply with the maxims of the cooperative principle to ensure a fluent conversation in any sign language.

4.3   Turn-taking

The transcript of the BSL conversation in (1) shows how often the four friends are signing simultaneously. Sometimes as many as three participants sign at the same time. At first, this may appear rather chaotic, but the participants do not seem to experience their conversation like that. Cultures, and thus languages, differ in how commonly speakers or signers can speak or sign at the same time. In Scandinavian countries, for instance, only little **overlap** is allowed in conversations, while in Britain, more overlap is acceptable, and in Spain even more. In informal situations, overlap is more often allowed than in formal situations (see Section 12.4).

In the conversation in (1), the roles of the participants are quite complex; they construct the conversation together. Overlaps consist of minimal comments like TRUE or nodding, or a repetition of one's own sign (e.g. SIMILAR) or a sign made by somebody else (e.g. ODD), but completing someone else's utterance also occurs. For instance, Nancy asks why the math teacher was odd, and at the same time Trish adds that she also had had an odd art teacher in the past. Later Frances asks Trish whether she didn't go to art school, and Trish almost simultaneously replies that she did but that she dropped out. All these overlaps are tightly connected to the topic of the conversation. This can only be successful if all participants adhere to the cooperative principle.

Despite there being overlaps, signers, just like speakers, take turns in conversations. For effective **turn-taking**, it is necessary to have the attention of your conversation partner. Sometimes signers explicitly ask for attention before taking a turn to ensure that the partner will see their contribution. Across sign languages, it is common to tap the other person on the arm or shoulder, but nowhere else, and this should always be done gently (5a); conventions may differ per culture, of course. In (5b), the signer is waving her hand to attract the attention of the person seated. An alternative strategy is to articulate the manual signs in the visual field of the other person, but not too close, since that is often felt to be impolite.

Sign Language of the Netherlands

    (5)   a.   Attention strategy: tapping   b.   Attention strategy: waving

Other ways of attracting attention are to bang on the table, or stamp on the floor, at least if the floor or table can transmit vibrations – a concrete floor does not work. Turning the light on and off is yet another possibility. These are all very explicit ways to attract attention, but usually signers are more implicit. They will more often wait for a signal from the conversation partner that they are willing to hand over their turn. A signer can indicate this in various ways – by dropping the hands, by changing the speed of signing, by tilting the head and making eye contact. Signals that are used to take a turn are called **turn regulators**.

In many studies of spoken languages, it has been found that the speaker usually looks away from the listener at the beginning of an utterance (or just before) and looks back to the listener towards the end of the utterance. The listener looks at the speaker far more than the other way around. Interestingly, in conversations between Philippine deaf adults in Philippine Sign Language, a similar pattern has been observed: the signer looks away at the beginning of a turn, and eye contact is re-established to mark the end of the turn. The conversation partner is looking at the signer more or less continuously, since, of course, s/he has to be able to see the signing. Nevertheless, there are moments when the two conversation partners do not look at each other in a signed conversation. In mixed conversations, that is, conversations between hearing and deaf people where an interpreter is also present, the participants often forget to check whether the deaf participants are actually looking at the interpreter at the beginning of a turn. This easily causes communication problems.

As for the role of eye gaze in turn-taking, it is also important how many people are participating in the conversation. It is logical, for instance, that a dialogue is totally different from a classroom interaction in this respect. Obviously, individual eye gaze in a dialogue works differently than group eye gaze. When a teacher signs a question in class, then it is clear who should give an answer on the basis of the direction of the teacher's eye gaze. If the teacher is not looking at anyone in particular, but rather continuously and rhythmically looks around at all the students, this means that no-one in particular is addressed, and thus all pupils are given the chance to answer.

We know little about differences between sign languages in turn-taking. A British deaf woman once said that she hardly managed to get a turn in conversation with deaf Americans – the turn-taking pattern was too fast for her. A Swedish deaf woman reported the same experience in the Netherlands. These are just personal anecdotes but they suggest that there may well be differences between sign languages when it comes to turn-taking patterns. However, more research is needed to verify this hypothesis.

4.4   Coherence

In the conversation between the four friends in (1), we can see that all contribute to the general topic "teachers in school". There is a minor exception when they talk about Trish's previous art training, but even this fits in with the general topic of art teachers. According to the maxim of relevance, all utterances together should form a coherent whole. **Coherence**, an essential element of both signed and spoken communication, requires a relation between the parts of the linguistic content of a text, and this in turn must be related to the non-linguistic context.

In order to achieve coherence, utterances also need to be related to each other. In sign languages, the verbal means that are used to connect utterances are quite different from those used in spoken languages. Have a look at the short NGT conversation in (6).

Sign Language of the Netherlands

(6) a. NEW NEIGHBORS HAVE INDEX$_1$. YESTERDAY SEE.
       'I have new neighbors. I saw them yesterday.'

     b. MAN INDEX$_{3a}$ WOMAN INDEX$_{3b}$ UNIVERSITY AMSTERDAM WORK.
       'The man and the woman work at the University of Amsterdam.'

     c. INDEX$_{3a}$ PHILOSOPHY TEACH INDEX$_{3b}$ BIOLOGY.
       'He teaches philosophy and she biology.'

Sentence (6c) refers back to the man and woman in sentence (6b). This is established by means of an INDEX. The use of a linguistic form like INDEX to link sentences is called **cohesion**. In (6c), two different locations in the signing space are used to indicate two persons who are not present in the discourse context; these locations are labeled '3a' and '3b' (see Section 1.2). These abstract locations are used to make clear who is being talked about. The locations have already been established in the previous sentence (6b). In this way, it is possible to refer, without repeating the nouns MAN and WOMAN. The use of **abstract locations** for establishing reference is comparable to the use of anaphoric pronouns in spoken languages. It is a way to create cohesion in a text (see Section 6.9 about pronominalization).

In the second sentence of (6a), it is striking that there is no explicit sign that refers to the subject of the sentence, the signer herself. In many sign languages, an INDEX can be left out if the context makes clear who is performing the action. In this case, the subject is clear as it has been mentioned in the previous sentence. Similarly, in (6c), the verb TEACH is not repeated, because the context makes clear what the action is. Such forms of **ellipsis** are often used in sign languages and also contribute to the creation of cohesion. In addition, sentences can be linked to each other by using certain syntactic constructions like temporal or causal clauses. Such embedding also constitutes a form of cohesion and will be subject to further discussion in Chapter 7.

4.5 Speech acts

When we look at pragmatic aspects that determine the form and meaning in the use of language, we can distinguish two levels: the linguistic form of an utterance on the one hand and the communicative intent on the other. As was discussed in Section 4.2, in Example (2), Marie's answer not only provides the explicit information that she has an exam the following day, but also includes implicit information: having to study will prevent her from coming to the party. This communicative intent is called a **speech act**. This linguistic term is also applied to sign languages even though the term "speech" is used. The literal form of an utterance, the **locution**, taken together with the communicative intent, called the **illocution**, determines the meaning of the utterance.

Just like spoken languages, sign languages distinguish **direct** from **indirect speech acts**. Marie's reply in (2) exemplifies an indirect speech act, as the locution and illocution are different. Alternatively, this illocution could have been formulated as in (7). In this case, the locution and illocution are the same, and we are thus dealing with a direct speech act.

Sign Language of the Netherlands

(7) Marie: CAN-NOT, TOMORROW EXAMS INDEX$_1$, STUDY MUST.
            'I cannot [come], tomorrow I have exams, and I have to study.'

Another example of a direct speech act is given in (8).

Sign Language of the Netherlands

(8) Jack: PROMISE, TOMORROW BOOK BRING INDEX$_1$.
            'I promise that I will bring the book tomorrow.'

The illocutive meaning of this speech act is immediately clear and explicit, because the verb PROMISE is used (the promise that is being made). Verbs of this type, which indicate explicitly the illocution of the utterance (e.g. *inform, promise, warn, ask* in English), are called **performative verbs**.

Most utterances do not, however, contain a performative verb and are thus indirect, as is true for the example in (9). The conversation partner will probably interpret this sentence as a promise, even though this is not explicit.

Sign Language of the Netherlands

(9) Jack: TOMORROW BOOK BRING INDEX$_1$.
            'Tomorrow, I will bring the book.'

The form of the sentence can help the addressee to interpret the illocution of the utterance. Across sign languages, the type of sentence – for example, declarative, interrogative, or imperative – is mainly indicated by specific non-manual markers such as facial expressions (see Sections 1.2 and 6.7). In general, indirect requests in spoken languages are expressed in the form of a yes/no question, as in *Can you pass me the salt?* Obviously, this is not a real yes/no question, as a reply like *Yes*, without further action, would be considered inappropriate or awkward. Rather, the question involves a request. A first descriptive study on the form of indirect speech acts in NGT has revealed that similar strategies are applied in this sign language.

In NGT and several other sign languages, real yes/no questions are accompanied by the following facial expression and head movement: (i) eyebrows up and (ii) head tilted forward (see Section 6.7) – and these non-manual markers indeed accompany the yes/no question in (10a). However, in an indirect request, like the one in (10b), the chin is often lowered instead of the forward head tilt, and we therefore gloss the combination of non-manual markers as 'ir' (indirect request) in this example. Moreover, a 'general request sign' (glossed as REQUEST) is often used in NGT in such contexts. This sign seems to explicitly distinguish yes/no questions that are used as indirect requests from real yes/no questions.

Sign Language of the Netherlands

$$\overline{\qquad\qquad\qquad\text{y/n}\qquad\qquad}$$

(10) a. INDEX$_2$ SCHOOL GO INDEX$_2$?
          'Are you going to school?'

$$\overline{\qquad\qquad\qquad\qquad\qquad\qquad\qquad\text{ir}}$$

  b. IX$_2$ REQUEST CAN IX$_1$ CHILDREN IX$_2$ FOOTBALL TAKE?
      'Can you please take my children to football?'

How form and meaning relate to each other has to be described specifically for every language, spoken or signed, since besides language-specific linguistic features, cultural and social aspects also play a crucial role in how speech acts have to be expressed and interpreted.

4.6   Structuring the discourse

Language is used to exchange information between people, and a conversation is thus a continuous flow of information. The information that is exchanged, however, can be old (known) or new to the respective addressee, and it is positioned and marked within an utterance in such a way that the exchange is systematically structured. In order to emphasize information in an utterance, intonation is often used in spoken languages but grammatical means can be used as well. Exactly the same is true for sign languages, where non-manual marking often fulfils the function of intonation (see Section 11.10). In the following, we address three phenomena that are crucial in structuring signed discourse: the use of articles and pronouns, information structure, and role shift.

4.6.1 The use of articles and pronouns

To distinguish new from old information in English, for example, the choice of the definite article (*the*) versus the indefinite article (*a/an*) is important. An article (definite or indefinite) has, amongst other things, the function of signaling whether the noun it accompanies is already known to the listener or not. The couple that is introduced in

(11a) is unknown, and therefore an indefinite article is used. In the subsequent sentence (11b), however, the couple – and thus implicitly the man and the woman – has already been mentioned; it is old information, and consequently, definite articles must be used. The alternative sentence in (11c) is not really ungrammatical, but would be considered pragmatically awkward in this context.

English
   (11)   a.   I saw *a* couple sitting on a bench.
          b.   *The* woman was obviously angry with *the* man.
          c.   *A woman was obviously angry with *a* man.

At present, very little is known about (in)definite articles in sign languages. For American Sign Language (ASL), it has been suggested that an INDEX preceding a noun can function as a definite article, but in other sign languages, an INDEX that combines with a noun does not necessarily contribute definiteness. In the NGT example in (12a), for instance, the noun phrase MAN GERMAN is accompanied by an INDEX, which follows the noun phrase and associates the referent with an abstract location in the signing space. Yet, the noun phrase is interpreted as indefinite, as it constitutes new information at this point.

Sign Language of the Netherlands
   (12)   a.   MAN GERMAN INDEX$_{3a}$ UNIVERSITY WORK.
               'A German man works at the university.'
          b.   INDEX$_{3a}$ WANT COLLEAGUE INDEX$_{3b}$ LONDON $_{3a}$VISIT$_{3b}$.
               'He wants to visit a colleague in London.'

Still, in the subsequent discourse, the use of an INDEX targeting the same location will be interpreted as old information, as already discussed in Section 1.4 and in Examples (6a–c) above. Crucially, further reference to this same location implies reference to a referent already mentioned. Thus, in (12b), INDEX$_{3a}$ refers to the German man, a known referent (that is, old information) at this point. Note, however, that another new referent is introduced in (12b), the colleague, which is also localized by means of an INDEX.

In cases like (12b), INDEX$_{3a}$ functions as a pronoun, and by definition personal pronouns signal old information. There are various forms of **anaphoric reference** that occur in different sign languages. For instance, signers can direct their eye gaze to a certain location, or can lean their body towards that location. These forms can also be used for **deictic reference**, that is, in contexts in which the referent is present (see further Section 6.9).

4.6.2 Information structure

The information status of a constituent (old vs. new) and the role it plays in structuring the discourse in general, and sentences in particular, is referred to as '**information structure**'. Important terms that are used are **focus** for new information and **topic** for old information. In many spoken languages, the constituent in focus gets a more prominent place in the sentence, and is often placed in sentence-final position. The topic on the other hand is usually placed at the beginning of the sentence. In sign languages, too, focus and topic are important notions, and they are commonly marked by dedicated grammatical strategies, be they non-manual, manual, or both. Sign languages may differ in the extent to which they use these different types of markers: it has been found, for instance, that NGT uses more non-manuals to mark focus than Russian Sign Language (RSL) does.

Let us briefly consider topics first. Across sign languages, topics are marked by word order, with the topicalized element occurring in sentence-initial position, and by a non-manual marker. Both characteristics are illustrated by the Finnish Sign Language example in (13a), in which the topic constituent is marked non-manually by raised eyebrows ('re'). We must assume that the night club is old/shared information, that is, it has either been previously mentioned or it is present (visible) in the discourse context. In the RSL example in (13b), the subject is topicalized, and it is accompanied by raised eyebrows and a backward head tilt ('bht'). Note that following the topic, an INDEX refers back to the topic. Again, the referent CAT has been introduced in the previous discourse. Topics will be further discussed in Section 6.6.

Finnish Sign Language (a) and Russian Sign Language (b)

$$\overline{\qquad\qquad\qquad\text{re}\qquad\qquad}$$

(13) a. NIGHT CLUB INDEX$_{3a}$, INDEX$_1$ WORK DOORMAN
'That night club, I work (there) as a doorman.'

$$\overline{\qquad\text{re+bht}\qquad}$$

b. INDEX$_{3a}$ CAT, INDEX$_{3a}$ THINK
'The cat, it thinks.'

Focus can also be marked in different ways. Answers to wh-questions are always in focus, as they always constitute new information; this type of focus is called information focus. In (14a) from ASL, we see an answer to the question *What kind of fruit does John like?* In this case, the noun BANANA is the new information, and is thus in focus, and it precedes the subject JOHN – that is, as in (13), information structure has an impact on the word order. Interestingly, BANANA is in turn preceded by the constituent FRUIT, which is a topic, as fruit was mentioned in the question and thus is old information.

American Sign Language

$$\overline{\quad\text{t}\quad}\ \overline{\quad\text{focus}\quad}$$

(14) a. FRUIT / BANANA / JOHN LIKE MORE
'As for fruit, John likes bananas best.'

$$\overline{\qquad\qquad\qquad\text{re}\qquad\qquad}$$

b. ME DISLIKE WHAT, LEE POSS TIE
'What I dislike is Lee's tie.'

Another way to syntactically mark focus is the so-called 'wh-cleft' construction, as illustrated in (14b). The focused constituent in this ASL example is [LEE POSS TIE] 'Lee's tie'; it could thus be a reply to the question *What do you dislike?*. Note that the first part of the sentence contains the wh-sign WHAT, and that it is accompanied by raised eyebrows (see also Section 7.3.2).

In NGT, as in some other sign languages, an eyebrow raise, which we already mentioned in the context of topics, can also accompany the element in focus. In addition, so-called **body leans** can be used, that is, small or exaggerated backward, forward or sideways movement(s) of the torso, the shoulders or the head, in relation to the body posture during the rest of the utterance. In ASL and in NGT, a forward body lean has been observed as a strategy to emphasize the new information in answer to a question. The NGT example in (15) is the answer to the wh-question *Who has taken the paper?*. We can see that the new information is accompanied by a forward body lean ('forward-bl').

Sign Language of the Netherlands

<u>   forward-bl</u>

(15)   BABYSITTER CL_{person} $INDEX_{3a}$, SELF $INDEX_{3a}$.
         'The babysitter (took the paper).'

Body leans are also used to mark another type of focus, namely contrastive focus, in several sign languages. In (16) from RSL, a contrast is established between the man and his action and the woman and her action. This is marked by two body leans in different directions, as is illustrated in the images below the example.

Russian Sign Language

                   <u>   bl-left   </u>   <u>   bl-right   </u>

(16)   MAN WAS [CL:SIT CL:HORSE.RIDE]. WOMAN [BIKE CL:RIDE.BIKE].
       'The man rides a horse. The woman rides a bike.'

In the NGT example in (17), contrast between two aspects is also marked by body leans to the left and to the right. This contrast, however, involves a correction of what has been said. Signer A utters an assumption. Signer B then corrects this assumption. He repeats the element FRIEND from A's utterance but negates it by a non-manual marker ('neg'). Also, he localizes this element to his left. The new, correct element (BROTHER) is then localized on the right (and accompanied by a forward head tilt). The localization on opposite sides of the signing space in combination with the corresponding body leans creates a clear contrast between the two elements.

Sign Language of the Netherlands

(17) A Context:

'I thought your friend was learning ASL.'

bl-left		bl-right	
neg		forward head tilt	

B   NO FRIEND INDEX$_{3a(left)}$, BROTHER INDEX$_{3b(right)}$, SELF INDEX$_{3b}$.

'No, not my friend, my brother [is learning ASL].'

Moreover, body leans can also accompany positive and negative answers. In general, a forward body lean accompanies a positive answer while a backward body lean is observed in a negative one. Again, use of the body leans implies contrast. In the short dialogues in (18) from NGT, we see how B in both cases contradicts what A has said, but in (18a), he does so by means of a positive reply with a forward body lean, and in (18b) with a negative reply and a backward body lean. We represent the utterances here in English, with the actual body leans made by the NGT signer in italics.

Sign Language of the Netherlands

(18) a. Positive answer   body-lean

A: I don't believe your brother is learning ASL.

B: Yes, my brother is learning ASL.   *forward*

b. Negative answer

A: Your neighbor has sold his car.

B: No, he did not sell his car.   *backward*

However, depending on the leaning behavior of the conversation partner (A), the mapping between utterance and body lean can also be the other way around, as is shown in (19).

Sign Language of the Netherlands

(19) A: So – your brother learned ASL.   *backward*

 ˙ B: No, my brother did not learn ASL.   *forward*

The direction of movement of the signer can therefore not be solely explained by the opposition forward = positive, and backward = negative. It rather appears that the leaning behavior of the signer providing such a contrast is closely related to the behavior of the signer posing the question: the direction of the lean – be it forward or backward – is the opposite of the previous leaning behavior of the conversation partner. Obviously, pragmatic aspects are required to explain the realization of body leans in NGT.

4.6.3 Role shift

Many sign languages have a specific form to convey information and to give form to the discourse, namely **role shift**, also known as *role taking*, *perspective shift*, or *constructed action*. Within a role shift, the signer can take on the role of a protagonist in a story. By changing the body posture (often only subtly), called **body shift**, and often also the facial expression, the signer can express words or thoughts from the point of view of a protagonist in the story. In spoken languages, this is usually achieved by means of direct quotes, as shown in the English example in (20), where Marie reports an utterance of her brother. In the NGT example (21), the signer employs a role shift: starting with the sign TOO, which marks the beginning of the quote, she turns her upper body slightly towards location 3a and (optionally) takes on the facial expression of the brother (glossed as 'fac.expr.' – possibly a sulky expression in this case) (see Section 7.2.2 for further discussion of role shift).

English
(20)   Marie: My little brother said: "Me too, I want to get on the swing."

Sign Language of the Netherlands

<u>bl-3a+fac.expr. brother</u>
(21)   Marie: BROTHER INDEX₃ₐ SAY TOO SWING WANT.

But role shift is used for more than only the expression of direct quotes. Within a role shift, a signer can also represent an action from the **perspective** of the person she is talking about – therefore the alternative term 'constructed action'. Look at the video stills in (22). When retelling the story of a cartoon involving Sylvester and Tweety in Jordanian Sign Language (LIU), the signer shifts her body to indicate how the cat and the bird are looking at each other through binoculars. In (22a), she takes the perspective of the cat, and in (22b) the perspective of the bird.

Jordanian Sign Language
(22)   a.   b.

In the same story, the signer also renders that Tweety was chased by taking on the role of Tweety. Through facial expression (looking backward, frightened) and modified signing (FLY-VERY-FAST), she tells the event as the bird experienced it, that is, she becomes the bird herself. Of course, comparable strategies – facial expressions, body movements, and change of intonation – are also commonly applied by skilled storytellers in spoken languages when reporting the adventures or utterances of a character.

4.7 Pragmatic adequacy

In sign languages, it is possible to sign **informally** or **formally**, just as in spoken languages. The **pragmatic adequacy** of the language used is not only determined by the choice of lexical signs, but also by characteristics of the signing: the speed of signing, the size of the signs, and the (intensity of) expression. In NGT, for instance, formality and politeness can be conveyed by articulating an INDEX with a -hand, palm up, instead of using the index finger. In the context of a meeting with people who do not know one another, the INDEX could thus take on this form, as illustrated in (23).

Sign Language of the Netherlands

$$\overline{\qquad\qquad\qquad\text{y/n}\qquad}$$

(23)   COFFEE WANT INDEX$_2$? (with -instead of a -hand)
'Would you like some coffee?'

Signing style is, amongst other things, determined by the context, by those present in the discourse situation, and by the topic of conversation, and it should fit the social situation of that context. Consequently, the NGT sign PISS-OFF (24a) will not often be encountered in, say, a conversation between a teacher and a pupil; rather, in such a context, a polite alternative will be used to express disagreement, such as the sign AGREE combined with a negative headshake (24b) (the mouthing 'sop' in (24a) is a heavily reduced form of the corresponding Dutch expression).

Sign Language of the Netherlands

		/sop/			neg
(24)	a.	PISS-OFF	b.		AGREE
		'Oh, piss off man!'			'I don't agree with you/that.'

Specific terminology or **register** can be used by different groups. Terms like PHONOLOGY, SYNTAX, or PRAGMATICS, for instance, belong to the register of linguistics.

For second language learners of a sign language (or a spoken language, for that matter), it is often more difficult to estimate *how* something should be appropriately said in a given context, than to actually formulate the message. It is very difficult for second language learners to judge the social context accurately in another culture.

Consequently, even though they may know a sign for a certain concept, they will often be in doubt as to whether it is the right sign in that specific situation. So, if you only know the sign PISS-OFF to indicate that you do not agree with someone, you will probably be considered very rude by the Dutch Deaf community!

4.7.1 Whispering and shouting

Recent research has provided us with some information about whispering and shouting in sign languages, that is, the use of signs in circumstances in which the signer wishes to make his message less obtrusive (whispering) or more obvious (shouting). In the latter case, the signer will articulate signs with larger movements and with more pronounced facial expression. The signing space as a whole (see Section 1.2) will also often be larger and higher. In contrast, when whispering, the signing space will be smaller and lower than usual, and the head and shoulders are continuously tilted forward. The head is thus brought closer to the signing space. Actually, the posture resembles somebody sitting or standing close to the addressee and whispering as in a spoken language. Not only is the head brought closer to the hands, but the hands are also shielded from the gaze of others by a turn of the upper body. Often two-handed signs (see Section 11.7) are made with one hand, and most signs are articulated lower and nearer to the body. Another characteristic of whispering is that the movement amplitude of signs is reduced as a result of **distalization**, that is, the use of joints that are more distal to the torso (e.g. the wrist and the finger joints) than the joints that would normally be used (e.g. elbow or shoulder joint) (see Section 10.2).

4.7.2 Influence of the hearing status of the conversation partner

As we indicated earlier, the conversation partner may also have an influence on the signing style. It matters, for example, whether the addressee is known to the signer, has the same status, or is a woman or a man. While the same factors play a role in spoken conversations, in sign conversations, the **hearing status** also plays an important role. For a long time, in many communities, signing was only used among the Deaf themselves (see Section 1.3). As soon as a hearing person approached, signing stopped. The low status of sign languages has long had an influence on the language use of the deaf in the presence of hearing people (see Chapter 13 for further discussion). Fortunately, this situation has changed. Nowadays, Deaf people in many countries take pride in their language and use it in the presence of hearing people. However, the presence of hearing people, or rather their fluency in signing, may still influence the language use. If the hearing person is not very fluent in signing, the form of signing will likely change, for instance by speaking simultaneously or by signing more slowly and more simply. A sign system may also be used (see Section 1.4). In Chapter 12, we will further discuss this issue.

Summary

Conversations in all languages are conducted following the **cooperative principle**. This means that the **maxims of quantity** (not too much or too little information), **of quality** (as much correct information as possible), and **of relevance** (information that is relevant to the theme of the conversation) are respected. Sometimes information is given implicitly; this is called a **conversational implicature**. Signers and speakers take turns in contributing to the conversation. In many languages, simultaneous speaking or signing, that is **overlap**, is tolerated, when the information contributes to the development of the conversation. Still, cultures, and thus languages, differ in this respect. **Turn-taking** is managed by using diverse signals or **turn regulators**. For sign languages, the following regulators have been described: lowering of the hands, change in speed of signing, change of head position (head tilt), and eye contact. **Coherence** in a signed conversation is ensured by making all contributions relevant to the topic of conversation, just like in spoken languages. The linguistic means used to indicate coherence or **cohesion** between the contributions, however, are different in sign languages. Sign languages make use of INDEX to refer to **abstract locations** where persons or objects have been previously localized. **Reference** is an important means for creating cohesion. **Ellipsis** is also used as well as complex sentences.

An utterance is a **speech act**, in which the literal form, the **locution**, is combined with the communicative intent, the **illocution**. **Performative verbs** explicitly express the illocutive meaning. There are **direct** and **indirect** speech acts that can vary in their form across languages. The structure of a discourse or story is determined, amongst other things, by **information structure**, that is, by whether information that is provided is old (**topic**) or new (**focus**). The use of **anaphoric** and **deictic reference** is important here. Among the means to indicate focus are **wh-clefts** and the direction of movement in **body leans**. Another linguistic strategy to structure information is **role shift** which allows the signer to present information from a particular **perspective**, also using **body shift**. The discourse situation and the people participating in the conversation determine the **pragmatic adequacy** of the utterances, which thus often differ in **formal** and **informal** contexts. **Registers** for specific groups or situations are also found in sign languages. Choosing the right style is particularly challenging for second (spoken and signed) language learners. It may, for instance, be difficult to know when it is appropriate to whisper (whereby **distalization** can occur). The **hearing status** of the conversation partner(s) also has an influence on sign language use.

Test yourself

1. Name three maxims that are part of the cooperative principle.
2. What is meant by conversational implicature? Provide an example.
3. How do signers regulate turns?
4. What is the difference between coherence and cohesion?
5. Name three linguistic means used in sign languages to create cohesion.

6.   What is the function of abstract locations for reference?
7.   What is meant by locution and illocution?
8.   Give an example of anaphoric and deictic reference.
9.   In what way can a signer place a part of the sentence in focus in a more prominent position?
10. Body leans have different functions. Name two.
11. What determines the choice of a signer for a particular register?
12. What is distalization?

Assignments

1.   Construct some short conversations in a sign language that you know that violate the maxims of quantity, quality, and relevance. Present these conversations to others, if possible, in your group and have them work out which maxims are violated.

2.   Which information is implicit and which explicit in the following NGT example? If there is implicit information, please provide the technical terms for it.

Jan: INDEX$_{man}$ CAR EXPENSIVE ALWAYS BUY.
        'He always buys expensive cars.'
Marie: FAST DRIVE WANT.
        'He wants to drive fast.'
Jan: NEVER JOIN INDEX$_1$.
        'I will never join him.'

3.   Formulate three suggestions for people working with sign language interpreters about how they should manage turn-taking.

4.   Formulate the locution and the illocution of the following NGT speech act.

_____ y/n
INDEX$_2$ WINDOW CLOSE CAN INDEX$_2$?
'Can you close the window?'

References and further reading

There are to date no handbooks on language use in sign languages, but there are many articles and chapters in books – see for an overview Baker & van den Bogaerde (2012), where most aspects addressed in this chapter are covered in somewhat more detail. The maxims of the cooperative principle are from Grice (1975), who formulated them on the basis of research on spoken languages. Speech acts have been described for NGT by Nonhebel (2002) and for ASL by Campbell (2001). Reviews of the realization of information structure in sign languages are provided by Wilbur (2012) and Kimmelman & Pfau (in press). Kimmelman (2014) offers a detailed comparison of the realization of information structure in RSL and NGT, and Sandler & Lillo-Martin (2006) discuss the realization of focus, topic, and role shift in ASL. Properties of role shift in LIU are described by Hendriks (2008). For a comprehensive overview of research on role shift, see also Lillo-Martin (2012).

Coates & Sutton-Spence (2001) did research on turn-taking, in particular gender differences, in BSL; the conversation at the beginning of this chapter is taken from their study. Baker (1977) discusses turn-taking strategies in ASL, and Mather (1987) and Dively (1998) address specifically the role of eye gaze direction in turn-taking. Martinez (1995) describes characteristics of turn-taking in Philippine Sign Language, Baker & van den Bogaerde (2006) investigate the phenomenon for NGT, and Groeber & Pochon-Berger (2014) for Swiss German Sign Language. Mather (1994) analyzed class interaction in ASL. Wilbur & Patschke (1998) studied the functions of body leans in ASL, and Van der Kooij, Crasborn & Emmerik (2006) did the same for NGT. Characteristics of whispering and shouting in sign have been described for NGT by Crasborn (2001), and for ASL by Mindess (2006). Van Herreweghe (2002) investigated the influence of hearing participants in conversations in Flemish Sign Language (VGT).

In the section on information structure, the FinSL example is taken from Jantunen (2007), the RSL examples from Kimmelman (2014), the ASL examples from Lillo-Martin & de Quadros (2008) and Wilbur (1996), and the NGT examples from Van der Kooij, Crasborn & Emmerik (2006). The video stills that illustrate role shift in LIU were found in Hendriks (2008).

Chapter 5

Constituents and word classes

Anne Baker & Roland Pfau

5.1 Introduction

The newspaper heading 'Man catches child with gun' is ambiguous. Who had the gun? The man or the child? Both interpretations are possible. The interpretation crucially depends on how we divide the sentence into units. In both cases, the sentence consists of four parts: the subject *man*, the object *child*, the verb *catches*, and the modifier *with gun*. Such sentence units we call **constituents**. Constituents are made up of words, and they may combine with each other in various ways. And here lies the crucial difference between the two interpretations: in one case, the modifier combines with the object (*child with gun*), thus further specifying the noun, while in the other case, it combines with the verb (*catches with gun*), thus specifying the action expressed by the verb.

In this chapter, we will discuss constituents that occur in sign languages (Section 5.2) and how these can be identified. In spoken languages, a constituent consists of a head and (optionally) modifiers. Is this also true for signed languages? The answer can be found in Section 5.3. In Sections 5.4 and 5.5, differences between signs with a lexical content and signs with a grammatical function are addressed.

5.2 Constituents

In Example (1a), we present a sentence from Italian Sign Language (LIS).

Italian Sign Language
(1) a. MAN YOUNG CAR EXPENSIVE BUY.
         'The young man buys an expensive car.'
     b. [[MAN YOUNG] [[CAR EXPENSIVE] [BUY]]].

The sentence in (1a) consists of different types of signs: MAN and CAR are nouns, YOUNG and EXPENSIVE are adjectives, and BUY is a verb. These signs belong together and together form a sentence, but they have different relations with each other. The brackets in (1b) indicate how the sentence is split up into constituents, that is, which elements belong together. It is intuitively clear that YOUNG does not go with CAR, although it might if we only consider the linear order of signs, and that EXPENSIVE does not modify

DOI 10.1075/z.199.05bak
© 2016 John Benjamins Publishing Company

MAN. The brackets in (1b) also show that the constituents [CAR EXPENSIVE] and [BUY] together form one larger constituent.

To test which elements belong together, we can carry out the so-called replacement test. If two (or more) signs can be replaced by one other sign, then it is evident that we are dealing with a constituent. For instance, instead of [MAN YOUNG], we could produce the pointing sign INDEX$_{man}$. Similarly, MOTOR could very well replace CAR EXPENSIVE. The constituent that consists of the two parts [CAR EXPENSIVE] and [BUY] might be replaced by a verb that does not require an object, like SWIM. Such a replacement test works in signed languages in exactly the same way as in spoken languages.

The example in (2a) shows that the order of sentence elements can vary. Note that in this sentence, the direct object is in sentence-initial position, that is, it is separated from the verb.

Italian Sign Language
> (2)   a.   [CAR EXPENSIVE] [MAN YOUNG] [BUY].
>   b.   *EXPENSIVE MAN YOUNG CAR BUY.

The example in (2b) makes clear, however, that signs cannot be combined randomly. Signs that are part of a nominal constituent, for instance, usually cannot be separated. Therefore, sentence (2b), in which EXPENSIVE is separated from CAR, is ungrammatical. Still, constituents are commonly displaced as a whole in the sentence, as in (2a), where we are dealing with a phenomenon called 'topicalization'. Most sign languages studied to date have a fairly flexible constituent order; yet, as far as we know, in all of them the order of elements within a sentence is subject to certain restrictions. We will discuss this issue further in Chapter 6. Constituents can also be whole clauses. When talking about constituents that are not clauses, we will use here the term **phrase**, and the nature of phrases will be the focus of this chapter. Constituents that are clauses will be discussed in detail in Chapter 7.

From analyses of spoken languages, we know that in most of them, four different word classes have to be distinguished: nouns, like *child*, verbs like *catch*, adjectives like *beautiful*, and adverbs like *often*. We assume here that the same word classes also exist in sign languages; this will be the topic of Section 5.4. Individual constituents can be subdivided in relation to these word classes. Please note: it is important to take the signed sentence as a starting point, and not the translation into a spoken language. MAN and CAR are **nouns**, because they refer to entities; BUY is a **verb**, because it describes an event; and YOUNG and EXPENSIVE are **adjectives**, as they describe properties. As was shown in (1), signs may combine to form more complex constituents, that is, phrases. Nouns and adjectives, for instance, may combine in **noun phrases**, such as [MAN YOUNG] and [CAR EXPENSIVE]. Verbs, on the other hand, commonly combine with noun phrases to form **verb phrases**, as is true for [CAR EXPENSIVE BUY], where the noun phrase [CAR EXPENSIVE] constitutes the direct object of the verb. Note that in principle, adjectives may also combine with other elements within adjectival phrases (e.g. *very expensive*). In the above example, however, the adjectives are not combined in this way and thus constitute **adjectival phrases** by themselves. In Section 5.3, we will come back to this issue.

We have not yet addressed the fourth word class, the **adverbs**. When a phrase with a modifying function is primarily used to specify properties of a verb, it is known as an **adverbial phrase**. In the German Sign Language (DGS) example in (3), for instance, the adverbial phrase OFTEN attributes a property to the verb TRAVEL, namely repeated occurrence of the event.

German Sign Language
> (3)   POSS$_1$ BROTHER OFTEN TRAVEL.
>   'My brother often travels.'

Finally, phrases can also have a **relational function**. Examples of this type of phrase, here **adpositional phrases**, from different sign languages are given in (4) and (5). The Russian Sign Language (RSL) example in (4) involves an adposition with a comitative meaning ('with'), while in the NGT example in (5), we observe a temporal adposition (this example will be discussed in more detail in Section 5.5.2).

Russian Sign Language
> (4)   CINEMA INDEX$_3$, INDEX$_1$ GO$_3$ [FRIEND WITH]
>   'I go to the movies with a friend.'

Sign Language of the Netherlands
> (5)   right: [MEETING   BEFORE], WE-TWO TEA DRINK
>   left: MEETING INDEX$_{3b}$ -------
>   'Before the meeting, we drink tea.'

We must point out, however, that adpositional phrases are uncommon in sign languages since adpositions themselves – in particular those that specify a spatial relation (e.g. *in, on, next to*) – are not frequently used, as will further be discussed in Section 5.5.2.

The examples in (1) to (4) involve phrases in which signs occur one after the other, in other words, phrases that are sequentially organized. Interestingly, in (6a) and (6b), we witness a different type of organization – in these examples, an adjectival or adverbial meaning is expressed simultaneously with the **manual** nominal or verbal sign it modifies. In (6a), the fact that the ball is small is given form by two means. First, the manual sign BALL is signed with only one hand and a smaller handshape; second, a **non-manual modifier** is added, that is, sucked-in cheeks. When signers want to indicate that the ball is being rolled slowly, the verb ROLL (6b) can be modified by slowing down the movement – again this modification is imposed simultaneously on the base sign, yet it is a manual, not a non-manual modification.

Sign Language of the Netherlands

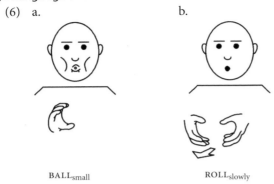

(6)   a.   b.

BALL_{small}   ROLL_{slowly}

Such simultaneous modifications that function as adjectives (6a) or adverbs (6b) appear to occur in most if not all sign languages studied to date. Because these markers are part of either the noun (BALL_{small}) or the verb (ROLL_{slowly}), they are not considered separate phrases. A possible spoken language parallel is the German diminutive suffix *-chen* (e.g. *Hemd* 'shirt' and *Hemdchen* 'small shirt'), or in English *-ie* (e.g. *dog–doggie*). These suffixes are not considered separate phrases either; rather, they are bound morphemes. Crucially, however, they are realized sequentially, not simultaneously.

The noun phrases that we have discussed so far refer to concrete entities, to persons or objects. Nouns, however, can also have an abstract meaning that is related to an event or a condition, like the nouns *dream* or *fear*. In English and many other languages, such nouns often carry a morphological marker that determines the word class; in the nouns *refusal* and *irritation*, for instance, the suffixes *-al* and *-ion* change verbs into nouns. Such morphological processes seem to be rare in sign languages. Usually the linguistic **context** in which a given sign appears determines its word class. In (7a), the linguistic context suggests that WORK must be interpreted as a verb.

American Sign Language

(7)   a.   INDEX₁ TEND WORK EIGHT HOUR.
           'I usually work eight hours.'
      b.   TODAY WORK BORING.
           'The work today is boring.'

In contrast, in (7b) WORK is used as a noun. The adjectival predicate BORING refers to this noun. From the linguistic context, it is thus clear that WORK cannot be a verb. Comparable phenomena are observed in many spoken languages. Consider, for instance, the English and Samoan examples in (8) and (9), in which the same phonological form (in bold) refers to a noun in the (a)-examples but to a verb in the (b)-examples.

English

    (8) a.   I had a bad **dream** last night.

          b.   I often **dream** of horses.

Samoan

    (9) a.   Ua   malosi le   **la**.
               ASP strong the sun
               'The sun is strong.'

          b.   Ua **la** le   aso.
               ASP sun the day
               'It is a sunny day.' (literally: 'The day sun-s.')

In English, this phenomenon is attested only for a relatively small number of cases (e.g. *dream, paint, love*), and it is often difficult to determine whether the verb- or the noun-meaning is the more basic one. In contrast, in Samoan, this phenomenon appears to be more the rule than the exception. In all cases, both the grammatical and the semantic context are very important in determining the word class. In (9a), the element *la* 'sun' is combined with an article and thus functions as a noun (note that the same is true for *dream* in (8a)). In (9b), the same element appears with an aspectual marker (ASP), which – given that only verbs can combine with aspectual markers – indicates that in this sentence, *la* functions as a verb.

5.3   The structure of phrases

Let us take another look at the LIS sentence we presented in (1).

Italian Sign Language

    (1) a.   MAN YOUNG CAR EXPENSIVE BUY.
               'The young man buys an expensive car.'

          b.   [[MAN YOUNG] [[CAR EXPENSIVE] [BUY]]].

In (1b), we see that a phrase can be part of another phrase: the noun phrase [CAR EXPENSIVE] is embedded within the complex verb phrase [[CAR EXPENSIVE] [BUY]]. The structure of phrases in sign languages can be represented in exactly the same way as has been suggested for spoken languages. One way is to use square brackets with subscript labels (10a); another way is to use tree structures (10b).

Italian Sign Language

    (10) a.   [[[MAN]$_N$ [[YOUNG]$_{Adj}$]$_{AdjP}$]$_{NP}$
                      [[[CAR]$_N$ [[EXPENSIVE]$_{Adj}$]$_{AdjP}$]$_{NP}$ [BUY]$_V$]$_{VP}$]$_S$
               'The young man buys an expensive car.'

(10) b.

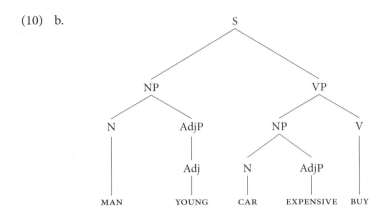

Note that in this book, the following abbreviations for types of constituents and phrases are used.

N	–	noun	NP	–	noun phrase
V	–	verb	VP	–	verb phrase
Adj	–	adjective	AdjP	–	adjectival phrase
Adv	–	adverb	AdvP	–	adverbial phrase
Adp	–	adposition	AdpP	–	adpositional phrase
S	–	sentence			

No matter which of the two strategies is used, the structures can be interpreted in the following way: the signs YOUNG and EXPENSIVE are adjectives and form their own adjectival phrases. Together with the nouns MAN and CAR, respectively, they form noun phrases. The noun phrase [CAR EXPENSIVE] in turn combines with the verb BUY to form a verb phrase. Finally, the noun phrase and the verb phrase together form a sentence.

The order of constituents is clear in sentences where constituents are sequentially ordered, like in (10). In this example, every manual sign is part of a phrase and these are sequentially ordered. But we already know from Chapter 1 and from the discussion of the examples in (6) that sign languages allow for an alternative strategy of organizing sentence elements: simultaneous structures. When attempting to analyze an NGT sentence like (11), we realize that the organization of phrases is less clear.

Sign Language of the Netherlands

(11)   BOY BALL_{small} ROLL_{slowly}.
       'The boy slowly rolls a small ball.'

The noun BALL in this example is accompanied by a non-manual modifier, as was illustrated in (6a), which contributes the meaning 'small'. This simultaneous adjective has the form of sucked-in cheeks and squinted eyes. Similarly, the verb in (11) is modified by a simultaneous marker that functions as an adverb. In this case, however, the adverbial meaning 'slowly' is not expressed non-manually; rather, the movement of the verb ROLL is changed in that it is articulated more slowly. Crucially, such simultaneous modifiers, no matter whether they involve a manual or a non-manual change, cannot occur independently – it is, for instance, impossible to sign BALL and subsequently suck in the cheeks. These modifiers must therefore fuse, as it were, with the manual signs which they modify. The resulting structure is obviously not sequential. Therefore, as stated above, sometimes a choice is made not to represent such simultaneous markers as separate phrases. Alternatively, it could be argued that a non-manual adjective, for example, occupies the same position in the tree structure as the manual adjectives in (10b). Given that the non-manual cannot be articulated by itself, it will have to fuse with the adjacent manual sign. We cannot further elaborate on this question here, but our brief discussion should make clear that the **simultaneity** of sign languages is a challenge for the presentation of signed clauses in a mainly linear structure.

Within different phrases, different types of signs function as **head** of the phrase. Within a noun phrase, for instance, the head is always a noun or a pronoun. Above we have seen that a noun phrase may consist of a noun and an adjective. Alternatively, an NP can contain a noun and an INDEX, as in (4), where INDEX$_3$ fulfils a localizing function, or only an INDEX with a pronominal function, as is true for INDEX$_1$ in (7a).

Under certain conditions, the head of a constituent can be omitted. In the NGT example (12), the noun FLOWER can be omitted in the second sentence. In other words: the head of the nominal constituent in the second sentence is empty.

Sign Language of the Netherlands
(12)   FLOWER++ INDEX$_{\text{arc-3a}}$ BEAUTIFUL. INDEX$_1$ BLUE WANT.
       'The flowers over there are beautiful. I want the blue (ones).'

In such sentences, the referent modified by the adjective BLUE is clear from the previous context. Similar constructions are also attested in some spoken languages, such as Spanish (13) and German. English is somewhat different in that it requires the replacement of the omitted noun by means of the pronoun *one* (14).

Spanish
(13)   Estas flor-es   son   bonita-s. Prefiero   las azul-es.
       these flower-PL   are.PL nice-PL. prefer.1SG the blue-PL
       'The flowers are nice. I prefer the blue (ones).'

English
(14)   These flowers are nice. I would like to have the blue ones.

5.4   Lexical signs

In the previous section, we argued that in signed languages, just as in spoken languages, four word classes may occur: nouns, verbs, adjectives, and adverbs. These can be distinguished on the basis of their meaning and function in the sentence. Nouns refer to concrete or abstract entities which may be countable (*apple, idea*) or non-countable (*rice, health*). Verbs describe activities (*to write*), processes (*to melt*), or states (*to live*; note that states in English often involve the copula verb *to be*, as in e.g. *to be clever*). Finally, adjectives and adverbs specify properties or qualities of nouns and verbs, respectively. Signs that belong to one of these four groups have lexical content, and thus are called **lexical signs** or sometimes **content signs** (see Chapter 8).

In spoken languages, these word classes can sometimes be distinguished on the basis of their form. We therefore have to ask whether this is also the case in sign languages. In Section 5.4.1, we will discuss the differences between nouns and verbs before turning to possible distinctions between adjectives and adverbs in Section 5.4.2.

5.4.1 Nouns and verbs

In Examples (15a) and (15b) from American Sign Language (ASL), we see two pairs involving a verb and a corresponding noun. In both pairs, the signs are semantically related, but different in their phonological form. Take a moment to compare the two signs in each pair. It is obvious that the movement in the verbal signs differs from that of the nominal signs. The ASL verbs SIT and FLY have a single longer (and more relaxed) movement, whereas the corresponding nouns CHAIR and PLANE are articulated with a short, more tense, and repeated movement.

American Sign Language
 (15)   a.

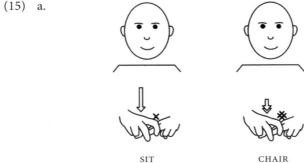

   SIT   CHAIR

   b.

   FLY   AIRPLANE

A comparable systematic difference between nouns and verbs has also been reported for Austrian Sign Language (ÖGS), Australian Sign Language (Auslan), and Russian Sign Language. It has to be pointed out, however, that this systematicity is only attested in cases where the noun and the verb are semantically related in the sense that the noun refers to a concrete object and the verb to an action performed with this object. Comparable phonological differences, however, have not been found in all sign languages. In NGT, for instance, a comparable **systematic relation** between nouns and verbs cannot be established. The manual part of the signs for SIT and CHAIR, which are both signed with a ꝗ-handshape, thus looks identical in some signers. Others perform CHAIR with a turn of the wrist which is not found in SIT. The two-handed noun BICYCLE is usually signed with a single alternating circular movement while the related verb CYCLE has multiple repetitions – exactly the opposite of the ASL pattern described above. In a dictionary, these identical forms are indicated in the gloss with a slash between them, e.g. CHAIR/SIT. Thus, a difference in movement is certainly not systematic for noun-verb pairs in NGT. This fact may be related to the frequent use of mouthings in NGT. By means of an accompanying mouthing, two manually identical signs can be distinguished (see Sections 1.2 and 11.6). Moreover, an accompanying INDEX may also indicate that a given sign is a noun.

It therefore appears that the form of a sign can sometimes reflect its word class, at least in some sign languages. Note that the gloss for a given sign may at times be misguiding. The BSL sign in (16), for instance, is often glossed as PRESENT, and this can create the impression that it is an adjective (as in *the present king*). Closer inspection, however, reveals that this sign is realized differently in different contexts and thus rather resembles a verb. For instance, it can be marked for agreement and aspect (see Section 9.5). This property makes it likely that we are actually dealing with a verb and as such, the sign should rather be glossed as BE-PRESENT.

British Sign Language
(16)

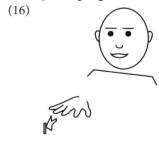

BE-PRESENT

The Flemish Sign Language (VGT) examples in (17a) and (17b) involve two verbs that differ in handshape; still, the same gloss is used for both forms: LIE-ON. In both cases, the handshape is related to the subject of the sentence, that is, to the entity that is being located. In (17a), the ꝗ-hand in the verb LIE-ON reflects form features of BOOK, whereas in (17b), for the same meaning, a ꝗ-hand is used that is motivated by form characteristics of the sign APPLE. These specific verbs make use of **classifier-handshapes** (see Section 9.6.2 for further discussion of classifiers).

Flemish Sign Language

(17) a.   b.

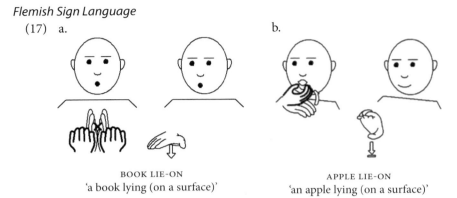

BOOK LIE-ON   APPLE LIE-ON
'a book lying (on a surface)'   'an apple lying (on a surface)'

In sum, we see that at least some sign languages make a systematic formal distinction between some nouns and verbs, but we do not know yet whether similar strategies are attested in the majority of sign languages. The discussion also revealed that even in sign languages in which we do not find systematic form differences, the syntactic context and/or the use of mouthings may disambiguate between verbal and nominal uses of manually identical signs.

5.4.2 Adjectives and adverbs

In English, adverbs are often distinguished from adjectives by attaching the suffix -*ly* – compare *quick* with *quickly*. Similarly, French adverbs are usually marked by the suffix -*ment* – compare *rapide* 'quick' with *rapidement* 'quickly'. It seems that sign languages do not systematically distinguish adjectives from adverbs, and in that respect they are comparable to many spoken languages such as, for example, German or Chinese. Usually, the context will make clear what type of phrase we are dealing with. Let us compare the NGT sentences in (18). The form of NICE modifying WOMAN (18a) is identical in form to the adverb NICE modifying TEACH (18b).

Sign Language of the Netherlands

(18) a.   [WOMAN NICE INDEX$_{3a}$] SCHOOL INDEX$_{3b}$ TEACH.
            'That nice woman teaches in the school.'
      b.   WOMAN INDEX$_{3a}$ SCHOOL INDEX$_{3b}$ [NICE TEACH].
            'That woman teaches nicely at school.'
      c.   WOMAN INDEX$_{3a}$ [SCHOOL NICE INDEX$_{3b}$] TEACH.
            'That woman teaches in a nice school.'

The adjective NICE in (18a) is positioned between the noun WOMAN and the INDEX and is therefore clearly part of the noun phrase. As such, it cannot modify the verb, which means that it cannot be interpreted as an adverb. The interpretation of the sign as an adjective is thus clear. In contrast, in (18b), the (phonologically identical) adverb NICE appears next to the verb. It is separated from the noun SCHOOL by means of an INDEX and can thus not modify the noun. Often the rhythm of signing also indicates which constituent a sign belongs to. In (18b), there would probably be a short pause between INDEX$_{3b}$ and NICE. In (18c), the adjective NICE is adjacent to SCHOOL but precedes the INDEX. This clarifies the interpretation of NICE as an adjective modifying SCHOOL.

Note that there are also signs that can only function as adverbs, most importantly, temporal adverbs like OFTEN. Similarly, there are certain adjectives which are highly unlikely to modify verbal meanings, for instance, color terms like BLUE.

As we have already discussed, certain adjectives and adverbs can also have a **non-manual form**. In the BSL examples (19a) and (19b), we observe that the non-manual form which conveys the meaning of 'small' is the same in both cases although it adds adjectival meaning in (19a) but adverbial meaning in (19b). The non-manual component is similar, but the manual sign that it accompanies is a noun in (19a) and a verb in (19b). As before, the linguistic context will disambiguate the function of the non-manual element in these cases.

British Sign Language
   (19)   a.   b.

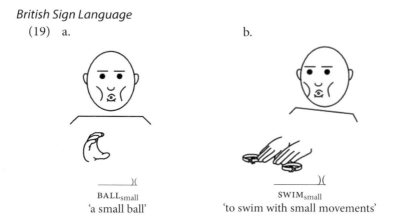

BALL$_{small}$ SWIM$_{small}$
'a small ball'   'to swim with small movements'

While the range of non-manual adjectives appears to be very small (possibly limited to the meanings 'small' and 'big'), the set of non-manual adverbs is more extensive. It appears that non-manual adverbs generally involve movements and configurations of the lower face (mouth, lips, cheeks). Actually, there are non-manual markers that can

only be used as adverbs. For ASL, a number of non-manual adverbs have been identified. One of these markers, where the lips are pursed in a relaxed manner, is glossed as
'mm'. When this marker is articulated simultaneously with a verb (e.g. WALK), it adds
the meaning of 'in a relaxed way' to the action.

In the LIS example in (20), we see an adjective that modifies MIRROR. The movement of this sign is in the form of a contour and by this reflects the form of the object:
this particular mirror is square. These **contour signs** or **size-and-shape specifiers** are
a special and fairly common type of adjective in sign languages. They generally modify
nouns and are thus easily identified as adjectives.

Italian Sign Language
(20)

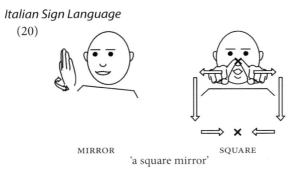

MIRROR   SQUARE

'a square mirror'

Summarizing: in the sign languages studied so far, adjectives and adverbs do not seem
to differ systematically in form. Therefore, in most cases, the context must reveal which
word class the sign belongs to. Nevertheless, there are also manual and non-manual
elements that can only function as an adjective or an adverb.

5.5   Function signs

Besides content words, many spoken languages have at their disposal quite a large
inventory of function words, including adpositions (pre- and postpositions), articles,
conjunctions, and particles. In (21), we provide an English sentence with the function words (or functional elements) marked in boldface. We see that it contains the
definite article *the*, the indefinite article *a*, the conjunction *that*, the preposition *in*,
and the copula *is* (we neglect bound functional elements like the agreement marker *-s*
attached to the verb *say*). Compare the English sentence with its French Sign Language
(LSF) translation in (22). Interestingly, the latter example only contains content signs,
namely nouns and verbs.

(21)   **The** doctor says **that a** bed **in the** hospital **is** broken.

French Sign Language
  (22) Doctor say bed hospital break.

Note that this property of LSF cannot be related to a structural difference between individual sign languages. It rather appears that sign languages in general have very few
signs with a purely grammatical function. Of course, there are also spoken languages
that make only little use of function words, like Malay (23).

Malay
  (23) harimau makan babi
        tiger   eat   pig
        'The tiger eats a pig.'

Actually, this sentence can have various meanings, not just the one we offer in the
translation, e.g. 'tigers eat pigs' or 'a tiger eats the pig'. While in English (21) and many
other languages, grammatical functions like definiteness or plurality are usually expressed by means of function words, in Malay, such functions and the accompanying
interpretive differences have to be provided by the context.

    However, the fact that the LSF example (22), just like the Malay example (23), does
not contain functional elements is not meant to imply that sign languages have no
functional signs at all. In the following subsections, we will discuss a couple of **function
signs** that are attested across different sign languages.

5.5.1 The pointing sign INDEX

In spoken languages, a (definite or indefinite) article may encode, amongst other
things, that a noun is considered to be familiar or unfamiliar to the conversation partner. In Section 4.6.1, we already pointed out that in sign languages, this difference can
be conveyed by means of a pointing sign INDEX in combination with a noun. Besides
that, however, an INDEX can also fulfil various other grammatical functions. For instance, it is possible to localize non-present referents in the signing space by means
of an INDEX, as is shown in Example (24a) from Israeli Sign Language (ISL), in which
Adam is associated with location 3a and Elaine with location 3b. Later in the discourse,
these locations can be used to refer back to these referents, again with an INDEX. In this
case, the INDEX has the function of a **personal pronoun**. In (24b), for example, INDEX$_{3a}$
targets the location of ADAM and must therefore be interpreted as 'he'. Sign languages
have other strategies to refer. The signer can look at a certain location or can tilt his
body towards that location. A combination of INDEX with such non-manual markers
is also commonly attested. Of course, a signer can also use an INDEX to refer to present
referents, for example using an INDEX$_1$ to himself (24c). Personal pronouns are further
discussed in Section 6.9.

Israeli Sign Language

(24)   a.   ADAM INDEX$_{3a}$ ELAINE INDEX$_{3b}$ TOGETHER-GO MOVIES.
'Adam and Elaine went to the movies together.'

b.   INDEX$_{3a}$ BUY TICKET.
'He bought the tickets.'

c.   NEXT-YEAR INDEX$_1$ STUDY UNIVERSITY.
'Next year, I am going to study at the university.'

When referring to a present referent, an INDEX can also function as a **demonstrative pronoun,** as in Example (25) from Spanish Sign Language (LSE). It may at times be difficult to distinguish a personal pronoun from a demonstrative pronoun, but often the movement of an INDEX which functions as a demonstrative pronoun is somewhat more tense and repeated. Finally, an INDEX can also be used to indicate a location, that is, it may function as a locative adverb. In this use, the movement and orientation of INDEX may distinguish between a location that is nearby (proximal: *here*) and a location that is further away (distal: *(over) there*). In the former case, the movement is short and the finger orientation downwards; in the latter case, we observe a longer arc-shaped movement with the finger orientation forward (25b).

Spanish Sign Language

(25)   a.   INDEX$_{person\text{-}in\text{-}the\text{-}same\text{-}room}$ DEAF.
'That (person) is deaf.'

b.   YESTERDAY INDEX$_{arch\text{-}3a}$ PARTY.
'Over there was a party yesterday.'

5.5.2   Adpositions

By means of adpositions (**prepositions** or **postpositions**) relations between persons and objects can be made clear. These relations can be of a temporal (as in *after three o'clock*), spatial (for instance, *on the table* or *to school*), or abstract nature (as in *I did it for you*). In general, sign languages appear to make little use of adpositions. As we discussed above (Section 5.2), even though some sign languages have signs that express, for example, 'with' and 'on', it is far more common to express such relations through use of the signing space. This is particularly evident for **spatial relations**. In many, if not most, sign languages spatial relations are specified by modifying the form of the verb, and not through separate signs. Example (17) illustrated this phenomenon in VGT. The movement of the verb LIE-ON specifies the relation between an object and its location (for instance, a table). In a comparable manner, locative meanings like 'in', 'under' and 'next to' can be conveyed by the form of the verb. Besides location, a verb sign can also specify a direction. In (26a), we see that the DGS verb WALK, in its base form, is articulated in front of the signer's body in neutral space. In contrast, in (26b),

WALK moves in the direction of location 3a where the locative argument SCHOOL has been located. The use of a separate sign that expresses the meaning of 'to' is superfluous.

German Sign Language

(26)   a.   WOMAN WALK.   b.   SCHOOL INDEX$_{3a}$ WOMAN WALK$_{3a}$.
            'The woman walks.'   'The woman walks to the school.'

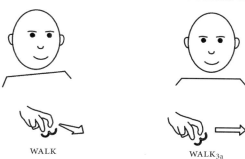

               WALK   WALK$_{3a}$

Sometimes an INDEX can fulfil an adpositional function when specifying a specific part of a locative noun phrase, as (27) demonstrates. In HKSL, the sign HILL is one-handed with the flat hand performing a convex (∩) arc movement. The INDEX in (27) points towards the topmost part of the arc, thereby expressing the meaning 'on top of'.

Hong Kong Sign Language

(27)   HILL INDEX$_{up}$ HAVE THREE
       'There were three people on top of the hill.'

Signs that specify **temporal relations**, like 'before' or 'after', seem to exist in many sign languages. But in this case, too, the signing space may be exploited to express the relation. The NGT example in (5), the relevant part of which is repeated in (28), is interesting as it involves a complex two-handed construction. The two-handed noun MEETING is localized in the signing space by means of an INDEX which is articulated by the non-dominant (left) hand; this pointing sign is then held as a sort of anchor in space while the temporal postposition BEFORE is articulated in relation to it, that is, with a movement from the location of the pointing sign towards the signer's body (thereby making use of a time line; see Section 8.7 for further discussion).

Sign Language of the Netherlands

(28)   right: MEETING   BEFORE
       left: MEETING   INDEX$_{3b}$ ---------
       'before the meeting'

Across sign languages, adpositions expressing abstract relations appear to be quite infrequent. Georgian Sign Language, however, features an interesting element that can express that an action is performed for someone else, that is, a benefactive marker. This sign, which we gloss as FOR in (29), is performed with a 🖖-handshape moving towards the location of the benefactive argument. Note that the movement is sufficient for expressing the argument; no separate pronoun ('him/her') is required.

Georgian Sign Language
   (29)   INDEX$_1$ WRITE   FOR$_{3a}$
          'I write (something) for him/her.'

In English, prepositions are sometimes used to indicate grammatical relations. In the English sentences in (30a) and (30b), we observe that the arguments of the verb *give* – 'woman', 'dog', and 'girl' – can either be marked by order or by the use of a preposition. In the first case, the indirect object *the girl* is placed before the direct object *a dog* (30a). The order of these two noun phrases can be changed, but in that case, the indirect object must be accompanied by the preposition *to* (30b). Without the preposition, this sentence is ungrammatical (30c), at least with the desired interpretation.

English
   (30)   a.   The woman gives the girl a dog.
          b.   The woman gives a dog to the girl.
          c.   *The woman gives a dog the girl.

In Example (31), we see that in NGT both orders are possible: indirect object before direct object (31a) and direct object before indirect object (31b). The use of an adposition is superfluous, because the form of the verb GIVE makes clear how the sentences must be interpreted: the verb moves in space from the location of the giver (the woman) to the location of the receiver (the girl). Just as in the English examples in (30a,b), it is possible that use of one order over the other is motivated by the discourse context; the meaning of the two sentences, however, is the same.

Sign Language of the Netherlands
   (31)   a.   WOMAN INDEX$_{3a}$ GIRL INDEX$_{3b}$ DOG $_{3a}$GIVE$_{3b}$.
          b.   WOMAN INDEX$_{3a}$ DOG GIRL INDEX$_{3b}$ $_{3a}$GIVE$_{3b}$.
               'The woman gives the girl a dog.'

Note that the examples in (31) are only meant to illustrate different word order options. Given that out of context, we cannot be certain about potential subtle differences in interpretation, we only provide one translation for the two alternative structures. The issues word order and verb modification will be subject to further discussion in Section 6.5.1 and Section 9.5.2, respectively.

5.5.3 Conjunctions

The main function of **conjunctions** is to link two clauses. The clauses involved can be two main clauses (linked by e.g. *and*, *or*), or a main clause and a subordinate clause (linked by e.g. *that*, *because*). It appears that generally, sign languages only employ few conjunctions. A conjunction comparable to English *that* (as in *I assume that she will sign the contract*), for instance, has not been identified in any sign language studied to date. Examples of conjunctions introducing subordinate clauses that have been described include the manual signs WHEN and BECAUSE in British Sign Language (BSL), and BECAUSE and IF in NGT. Moreover, the use of BUT to link two main clauses is common in NGT. In contrast, the conjunction AND is not commonly used and is usually considered as influence from spoken Dutch.

These conjunctions, or the clause they are introducing as a whole, are sometimes accompanied by specific non-manual markers like raised eyebrows or head tilt. In some contexts and in some sign languages, these non-manual elements are obligatory. The way in which complex clauses are realized in sign languages will be dealt with in more detail in Chapter 7.

5.5.4 Particles

Particles are function words that can occur by themselves and that can change the meaning of a sentence. We will focus on only two types: negative particles and modal particles. In many spoken languages, negation is expressed through independent particles, for instance, *not* in English, *no* in Italian, and *nil* and several other particles in Irish. Typological research on a number of sign languages from all around the world has shown that all sign languages have a manual **negation particle**. Some sign languages, like Jordanian Sign Language (LIU), even have several negators that convey different meanings. The LIU sentence in (32a) is negated by means of the most common particle, the neutral negation particle NEG. NEG is articulated with a ⬧-hand that makes a repeated to-and-fro movement in front of the body. When the signer wants to emphasize the negative meaning, he can use the sign NEG:EMPH (32b). This sign also has a ⬧-hand, but is performed with a single, strong sideward movement. Note that this sign is repeated in (32b) to add even more emphasis to the utterance. In addition, LIU has the sign NEG-EXIST. This sign is articulated with a ⬧-hand in front of the mouth (fingertips oriented towards the mouth), and the fingers bend repeatedly. The main function of NEG-EXIST is to deny the existence of objects (e.g. *There is no bread*), but in some contexts, it can also be used as a general clause negator (32c).

Jordanian Sign Language

(32)   a.   FATHER MOTHER DEAF INDEX$_1$ NEG, SPEAK.
            'My father and mother are not deaf, they speak.'

(32) b. NEG:EMPH SMOKE NEG:EMPH.
          'No, I certainly don't smoke.'
      c. YESTERDAY EVENING PARTY COME NEG-EXIST.
          'Yesterday evening I did not go to the party.'

It is important to note that in all sign languages that have been studied so far, manual particles are not the only means for expressing negation; non-manual markers, for instance a headshake, are also commonly used. In many sign languages, the manual element even appears to be optional. LIU is remarkable in this respect, since in this sign language, the manual signs are obligatory while the non-manual marker (which has been neglected in (32)) is optional. In Section 6.8, we will further discuss the characteristics of negation.

Modal particles also change the meaning of a sentence, but the changes they impose can be fairly subtle and are sometimes difficult to paraphrase. The use of a modal particle is illustrated by the German sentence pair in (33). The sentence in (33a) is a neutral statement of a fact. By virtue of the modal particle *doch*, the sentence in (33b) gets a clearly different meaning. The particle adds information about the speaker's attitude; it signals that the speaker is annoyed and/or surprised. In addition, it adds emphasis to what is expressed. Some spoken languages make frequent use of modal particles (e.g. German and Dutch) while in others such particles do not exist (e.g. English). In the English translation of (33b), the same meaning could be expressed by putting stress on the second syllable of *explained*.

German
(33) a. Das habe ich ihm schon erklärt.
          that have I   him already explained
          'I already explained that to him.'
      b. Das habe ich ihm **doch**   schon   erklärt.
          that have I   him MOD-PART already explained
          'I already *explained* that to him.'

Research into DGS has shown that in this sign language, comparable changes in meaning are not realized by means of manual particles, but rather by non-manual modifications. An example of such a modification is given in (34). Example (34a) contains the neutral question word WHERE which is accompanied by the usual non-manual question marking (eyebrows down). The manual part of the utterance in (34b) is exactly the same, but the non-manual marking is different. Through a combination of shrugging ('shr'), frowning ('fr'), and an energetic ('el') and somewhat desperate look ('dl'), the signer makes clear his attitude. The same attitude, annoyance combined with impatience, can be expressed in German with the modal particle *nur* and in English by a phrase like *on earth*, as in the translation of (34b).

German Sign Language

(34) a. $\overline{\qquad\qquad\text{wh}}$
POSS₂ PEN PUT-DOWN WHERE?
'Where did you put your pen?'

b. $\overline{\qquad\qquad\qquad\text{shr, fr, el, dl}}$
POSS₂ PEN PUT-DOWN WHERE?
'Where on earth did you put your pen?'

In sum, the discussion makes clear that certain changes in meaning which are commonly realized in spoken languages by means of dedicated particles, are often realized in signed languages by non-manual markers. Even though manual particles also occur in sign languages, they are often optional, and the desired changes in meaning are more frequently expressed by facial expressions and/or head movements.

5.5.5 Auxiliaries

Auxiliaries also have mainly a grammatical function in spoken languages. Their most important function is to mark tense, aspect, and/or modality (which is why they are commonly called TAM-markers), but they may also serve to connect two phrases, as in the case of the **copula**. Most sign languages do not have a copula, as has already been pointed out in Chapter 1. In the Indopakistani Sign Language example in (35), the nominal constituent GIRL INDEX₃ₐ is followed by the adjective SMART. The sentence thus contains no verb, in contrast to the English translation, where the copula *be* is mandatory (see Section 6.2 for further discussion). In this respect, sign languages are not exceptional. In fact, there are many spoken languages that have no copula, for instance, Turkish, Russian, and Chinese (36).

Indopakistani Sign Language

(35) GIRL INDEX₃ₐ SMART.
'That girl is smart.'

Mandarin Chinese

(36) Mǎlì   hěn   cōngming.
Molly very intelligent
'Molly is very intelligent.'

Across spoken languages, auxiliaries are mostly used to mark **tense** and **aspect**. In English, for instance, an event can be put in the past tense by means of the auxiliary *have* (compare *She writes a letter* with *She has written a letter*) or in the future tense by means of the auxiliary *will* (*She will write a letter*). Just like some spoken languages, many sign languages do not have such auxiliaries and use temporal adverbs like YESTERDAY and TOMORROW instead (see Section 9.5.1). ASL, too, uses temporal adverbs, but also has a few signs that have been analyzed as auxiliaries. There are, for instance, auxiliaries for future (37a) and past (37b) tense. The signs FUTURE and FINISH not only differ in form from the related temporal adverbs, they also appear in a different position in the sentence. Temporal adverbs are either in sentence-initial or -final position, whereas the auxiliaries always appear between the subject and the verb (just like other auxiliaries; see Example (41)). Furthermore, ASL has the fingerspelled marker 'e-x'. This marker can be combined with nouns (for example, e-x^PRESIDENT), but can also function as an auxiliary when talking about habits from the past (37c).

American Sign Language
(37) a. JOHN FUTURE BUY HOUSE.
'John is going to buy a house.'
b. JOHN PAST LIVE CHICAGO.
'John lived in Chicago.'
c. JOHN e-X LIKE CHOCOLATE.
'John used to like chocolate.'

Some sign languages, for instance, BSL and NGT, have separate signs that indicate that an action is finished. These signs, which are glossed as READY in (38) and (39), are analyzed by many sign linguists as a sort of aspectual auxiliary. In Section 9.5.1, we will further discuss these markers.

British Sign Language
(38) EAT READY INDEX$_{3a}$.
'He has eaten.'

Sign Language of the Netherlands
(39) WOMAN INDEX$_{3a}$ CAR FIX READY.
'The woman has fixed the car.'

Modal verbs are also considered as auxiliaries because they generally combine with a lexical verb. A **modal auxiliary** may express that an action is possible (for instance, *I can swim*) or necessary (for instance, *I must swim*), amongst other things. Sign languages also have modal auxiliaries like CAN, MAY, and MUST. In the VGT example in (40), the modal auxiliary MUST follows the lexical verb LEARN. In contrast, in ASL, the most common position for modal auxiliaries is the position between the subject and the lexical verb (41) – the same position where the temporal auxiliaries appear (37).

Flemish Sign Language
(40) INDEX$_2$ SWIM LEARN MUST INDEX$_2$.
'You must learn how to swim.'

American Sign Language
(41) JOHN CAN BUY HOUSE.
'John can buy a house.'

Interestingly, next to basic affirmative forms of modal auxiliaries, some sign languages also have special negative forms. In the DGS sentence in (42), for example, negation is integrated in the sign MAY by means of a change in movement. In DGS, this fusion of modal and negation is obligatory for the modal verbs MAY, CAN, and MUST. Unlike lexical verbs, these modal auxiliaries cannot be combined with the negative particle NOT.

German Sign Language

$$\overline{\qquad\qquad\text{neg}}$$

(42)   GARDEN INDEX$_{3a}$ CHILD++ PLAY MAY-NOT.
   'The children may not play in the garden.'

Last, we would like to point out that some sign languages have another special type of auxiliary. Unlike the auxiliaries described above, these auxiliaries do not function as TAM-markers, but are only used to mark subject and object agreement. Such agreement-markers have been found in, for example, Catalan Sign Language, DGS, Greek Sign Language, NGT, and Taiwan Sign Language. In Section 9.5.2, we will describe the characteristics of these auxiliaries in more detail.

Summary

Just as in spoken languages, sentences in signed languages are composed of different types of phrases: **noun phrases**, **verb phrases**, **adjectival phrases**, **adverbial phrases**, and **adpositional phrases**, although the last type appears to be fairly rare. The first four are related to the four main word classes. However, in sign languages, the grammatical and semantic **context** is often necessary to determine the word class of a sign. Just as in spoken languages, sign language utterances are hierarchically organized. The hierarchical structure can be represented by means of a bracketed structure or in a tree diagram. However, this type of representation is mainly linear and therefore somewhat problematic for sign language utterances which are often characterized by **simultaneity**. **Non-manual modifiers** clearly add meaning but it is not immediately clear how they can be represented in a sequentially organized phrase structure. Just as in spoken languages, phrases in sign languages always consist of a **head** that determines the type of the phrase. Under certain conditions, the head can be omitted.

Most signs are **lexical signs**: verbs, nouns, adjectives, or adverbs. The distinction between the different word classes is sometimes problematic, however, because the word class of a sign is only rarely marked, for instance by means of affixes. Here, too, the linguistic context plays an important role. For some sign languages, however, **systematic relations** have been identified between semantically related nouns and verbs. Some verbs can combine with **classifier handshapes**. Certain adjectival and adverbial meanings can be realized **manually** or **non-manually**. Furthermore, **contour signs** can also function as adjectives.

In general, sign languages have been found to employ only few **function signs**. The pointing gesture INDEX can have different grammatical functions: it can serve as a definite article, as a **personal pronoun**, and as a **demonstrative pronoun**. **Spatial relations** that are often expressed in spoken languages by **prepositions** or **postpositions** are usually expressed by spatial means in sign languages. **Temporal relations** can be encoded by means of adpositions, but here too, the use of space often plays an important role. **Conjunctions** that connect two sentences are also rather rare in sign language, but a few do exist. By means of particles, the meaning of a sentence can be changed. Sign languages differ from each other with respect to the use of **negation particles**. All sign languages appear to have such particles, but in many sign languages, their use is optional, because negation can also be realized non-manually. In some spoken languages, the meaning of a sentence can be modified by means of **modal particles**. Again, such changes are mainly expressed non-manually in sign languages. **Auxiliaries** always occur in combination with a lexical verb; their main function is to mark **tense**, **aspect**, and **modality**. While tense is mainly indicated by adverbs in sign languages, some sign languages also use specific temporal auxiliaries. Also, some aspectual auxiliaries have been described. Many sign languages regularly use **modal auxiliaries** to express the possibility or necessity of an event. A **copula** is a special type of auxiliary that is used to connect a subject and a predicate; most sign languages do not use a copula.

Test yourself

1. How can you determine the number of constituents in a signed sentence, and how can you determine the type of constituent?
2. What is a contour sign?
3. How can we distinguish adverbs from adjectives in sign languages?
4. What is the difference between a lexical sign and a function sign?
5. How often do function signs occur in sign languages? Please provide three examples of a function sign and the sign language it belongs to.

Assignments

1. Please divide the following NGT sentences into constituents. Use for every sentence the bracket model of Example (10a) and also draw a tree diagram as in Example (10b).
   a.   BOY INDEX$_{3a}$ FAST CYCLE.
        'The boy was cycling fast.'
   b.   PROFESSOR ENGLISH STUDENTS INDEX$_{3a}$ TEACH.
        'The English professor is teaching the students.'
   c.   BOOK EXACT RIGHT BE-PRESENT.
        'Exactly the right books are present.'

2.   Why are the following NGT sentences, as presented, ambiguous in structure? Provide a para-phrase of each meaning.

   a.   NOW PROFESSOR ENGLISH TEACH.

   b.   GIRL BEAUTIFUL PAINT.

3.   Do constituents have psychological reality in the comprehension and production of a sign language? Please use information from Chapter 2 in your answer.

References and further reading

There are only a few studies that focus on different types of constituents in sign languages. Constituents and their internal structure are usually discussed in the context of (often fairly formal) descriptions of phrase structure; for instance, Petronio (1993) and Neidle et al. (2000) for ASL, de Quadros (1999) for Libras, and Brunelli (2011) for LIS and NGT. A general discussion of word classes is provided in Meir (2012), and Schwager & Zeshan (2008) suggest criteria for the distinction of different word classes in sign languages. Differences between nouns and verbs have been described for various sign languages, see Supalla & Newport (1978) for ASL, Johnston (2001b) for Auslan, Hunger (2006) for ÖGS, and Kimmelman (2009) for RSL. Zwitserlood (2003) presents an overview of different types of contour signs in NGT. Non-manual adverbs were analyzed for the first time for ASL in Liddell (1980). An overview of different uses of pointing signs is provided by Pfau (2011). The use of INDEX as a definite article is discussed (for ASL) in Zimmer & Patschke (1990) and MacLaughlin (1997). Ahlgren (1990) addresses the use of deictic pronouns in Swedish Sign Language, and McBurney (2002) provides a comprehensive comparison of personal pronouns in spoken and signed languages. Characteristics of sign language pronouns are also conveniently summarized in Cormier (2012) and Meier & Lillo-Martin (2013). Waters & Sutton-Spence (2005) describe a number of BSL conjunctions. The typological study by Zeshan (2004a) offers a cross-linguistic description of the use of negation particles in different sign languages. Modal verbs (including negative modals) have been studied in different sign languages: see Ferreira Brito (1990) for Libras, Wilcox & Wilcox (1995) and Shaffer (2002) for ASL, and Pfau & Quer (2007) for DGS and LSC.

   The noun-verb pairs from ASL are taken from Supalla & Newport (1978), the other ASL examples are from Neidle et al. (2000). The ISL sentences are from Meir & Sandler (2008), the LIU examples from Hendriks (2008), and the BSL example from Sutton-Spence & Woll (1999). The DGS examples were found in the articles by Herrmann (2007) and Pfau & Quer (2007). The Georgian Sign Language example is taken from Makharoblidze (2015). Finally, the spoken language examples are taken from the following sources: the Samoan sentences from Mosel & Hovdhaugen (1992), the Malay example from Prentice (1987), and the Chinese example from Li & Thompson (1987).

Chapter 6

Syntax: simple sentences

Roland Pfau & Heleen Bos

6.1   Introduction

In the previous chapter, we distinguished four types of constituents in sign languages, similar to those occurring in most spoken languages: nominal, verbal, adjectival, and adverbial constituents. This classification was established on the basis of semantic and syntactic criteria. By combining these constituents according to language-specific rules sentences are created. In this chapter, we will address various properties of simple sentences in sign languages (which have to be distinguished from complex sentences, which are the topic of Chapter 7). These properties can be illustrated on the basis of two sentences from Sign Language of the Netherlands (NGT) in (1).

Sign Language of the Netherlands

<pre>
                             _____t   _____neg
(1) a.   INDEX₁ SISTER INDEX₃ₐ, TOMORROW INDEX₃ₐ WORK.
          'My sister, she won't be working tomorrow.'

                                          _____wh
     b.   INDEX₂ BICYCLE BUY WHERE?
          'Where did you buy the bicycle?'
</pre>

Example (1a) consists of four constituents: the verbal constituent WORK, the nominal constituents INDEX₁ SISTER INDEX₃ₐ 'my sister' and INDEX₃ₐ, and the adverbial constituent TOMORROW. These four constituents fulfil different functions in the sentence, namely the functions of predicate, arguments, and adjunct, respectively. In Section 6.2, the different functions of constituents will be discussed in detail. The valency of predicates will be the topic of Section 6.3.

In addition, nominal constituents in a sentence can have different semantic and grammatical roles; these are considered in Section 6.4. Furthermore, the way constituents are combined in sign languages is not arbitrary; rather, their combination is subject to language-specific rules – similar to what has been found for most spoken languages. For instance, in Example (1a), the verb is in final position, while in the wh-question in (1b), the same position is occupied by the question word. In Section 6.5, we will focus on sign order patterns described for sign languages, and in Section 6.6, we turn to a process that influences the sign order at the sentence level, namely topicalization, as

DOI 10.1075/z.199.06pfa
© 2016 John Benjamins Publishing Company

is also illustrated in sentence (1a), where the topicalized constituent is marked by 't'. The examples in (1) already make clear that sign order may be influenced by sentence type. Different sentence types – declarative, interrogative, and imperative sentences – and the way in which they are realized will be discussed in Section 6.7. All types of sentences can negated; in (1a), for instance, a headshake (glossed as 'neg') accompanies a part of the sentence, thereby negating it. How negation is expressed in various sign languages will be explored in Section 6.8. The constituent INDEX$_{3a}$ in (1a) exemplifies pronominalization, a phenomenon that we will turn to in the final section of this chapter, Section 6.9; in this context, we will also address the fact that pronouns may be omitted under certain conditions.

6.2   Function of constituents

Just like in spoken languages, constituents in sign languages can have one of three functions in a sentence: that of predicate, argument, or adjunct. A **predicate** usually either expresses a state or an event, possibly establishing a relation with another constituent in the sentence, or it specifies a property of a constituent. In the German Sign Language (DGS) examples in (2), the predicates are printed in bold (POSS indicates a possessive pronoun, which in DGS is signed with a ⍭-hand).

German Sign Language

(2) a. TOMORROW SCHOOL POSS$_1$ DAUGHTER CAKE **BAKE**.
         'Tomorrow my daughter will bake a cake at school.'
     b. POSS$_2$ FATHER **SWIM**.
         'Your father is swimming.'
     c. VEGETABLE **HEALTHY**.
         'Vegetables are healthy.'
     d. POSS$_1$ BROTHER **DOCTOR**.
         'My brother is a doctor.'

In Example (2a), the predicate BAKE specifies an event and expresses a relation between the constituents POSS$_1$ DAUGHTER 'my daughter' and CAKE. The predicate SWIM in (2b) also refers to an event but does not express a relation between constituents. In (2c), the predicate HEALTHY provides information about VEGETABLES, while in (2d), the sign DOCTOR further specifies the subject INDEX$_1$ BROTHER 'my brother'. Clearly, these two predicates do not refer to an event, but rather to a property.

As in most spoken languages, the predicate in signed languages is often a verbal constituent, like BAKE in (2a) and SWIM in (2b). The examples in (2c) and (2d), however, illustrate that other types of constituents can also function as predicates: in sentence (2c), we find an **adjectival predicate** (HEALTHY) and in sentence (2d) a **nominal**

predicate (DOCTOR). The sign languages studied to date appear not to make use of a copula like English *are/is* (see the translations of (2c) and (2d)). From a typological point of view, this is not particularly remarkable, as many spoken languages, such as for instance Turkish and Chinese, also do not have copula.

The second function of a constituent in a sentence is that of **argument**. This function is exemplified by the constituents INDEX$_2$ FATHER 'your father' in (2b) and VEGETABLE in (2c). These two constituents are required in order to form a grammatical sentence. In (2a), there are two obligatory arguments: INDEX$_1$ DAUGHTER and CAKE; if either of the two is omitted, the resulting sentence is ungrammatical – just like the corresponding English sentences *My daughter bakes* and *Bakes a cake* (see Section 6.3 for further discussion).

In contrast, the constituent SCHOOL in (2a) can be omitted, as it is not required by the predicate. That is, the noun SCHOOL functions as an **adjunct** – more precisely, a locative adjunct – in (2a), and adjuncts are always optional. The difference between arguments and adjuncts is closely related to the valency of predicates. This concept is explained in the next section.

6.3   Valency

The term valency refers to the number of arguments that a predicate requires in order to form a grammatical sentence. Just as in spoken languages, predicates in signed languages differ in their valency: there are one-place, two-place, and three-place predicates. The predicate DANCE in the Russian Sign Language (RSL) example in (3a), for instance, requires only a single argument, and it is therefore a one-place predicate or an **intransitive verb**. Omission of this argument results in an ungrammatical sentence (3b). An example of a **transitive** (two-place) predicate has already been given in (2a) (BAKE). In (4a), we provide another example, this time from RSL. Given that the verb BUILD is transitive, both (4b) and (4c) are ungrammatical, as one of the required arguments is missing.

Russian Sign Language
(3) a.   DIRECTOR DANCE.
            'The director is dancing.'
      b.   *DANCE.

Russian Sign Language
(4) a.   POSS$_1$ NEIGHBOUR BUILD SHED.
            'My neighbour is building a shed.'
      b.   *BUILD SHED.
      c.   *INDEX$_1$ NEIGHBOUR BUILD.

Finally, the verb SEND in (5a) is **ditransitive** (three-place) and thus requires three arguments. Again, we provide ungrammatical versions of the example in (5b–d), in order to show that all three arguments are indeed obligatory – a least when the examples are signed without a context. In contrast, the valency of a predicate does not determine the presence or absence of adjuncts; in all examples, an adjunct could optionally be added (e.g. the temporal adjunct SATURDAY).

Russian Sign Language

(5) a. BOY PARENTS PRESENT SEND.
         'The boy is sending his parents a present.'

     b. *PARENTS PRESENT SEND.

     c. *BOY PRESENT SEND.

     d. *BOY PARENTS SEND.

It is important to note, however, that not all arguments of a predicate need to be expressed all of the time. For instance, when it is clear from the context who is the recipient of the present, then that argument (the indirect object) need not be explicitly mentioned, and consequently, a sentence like (5c) may become well-formed, as shown in (6) (see Section 6.9 for further discussion).

Russian Sign Language

(6) Context: Is the boy visiting his parents for their anniversary?
     NO, INDEX₃ PRESENT SEND.
     'No, he will send [them] a present.'

As in spoken languages, predicates that express weather conditions behave differently: they are zero-place predicates. Hence, verbs like SNOW and RAIN in Flemish Sign Language (VGT) require no arguments at all and even do not allow specified arguments (7). In many spoken languages, such weather predicates are accompanied by so-called **pseudo-arguments** (also called expletive pronouns), that is, arguments that are semantically empty. The English element *it* (as in *It rains*) is of this type – clearly, this element does not contribute any meaning; yet it functions as the subject of the sentence, which would be ungrammatical without the pronoun *it*. In sign languages, however, such pseudo-arguments are not used.

Flemish Sign Language

(7) a. YESTERDAY SNOW.
         'Yesterday it snowed.'

     b. TOMORROW PERHAPS RAIN.
         'Tomorrow perhaps it will rain.'

Interestingly, under specific circumstances, the valency of a predicate can be reduced. This is attested in some languages in the case of **reciprocal constructions**. A reciprocal situation is a situation in which multiple participants are at the same time subject and object of an action. In English, such situations are expressed by means of the recipro- cal pronoun *each other*, as for example in *The children are greeting each other*. English *greet* is a transitive verb, and in this case, the pronoun *each other* functions as a direct object, thus satisfying the valency of the verb. In other languages, however, reciprocity is not expressed by a separate pronoun, but rather by a verbal affix. Just like its English counterpart, the Turkish verb *selâmlamak* 'to greet' is transitive and requires a direct object, as shown in (8a). In (8b), however, the verb appears without a direct object but with the suffix -š, which encodes the reciprocal meaning. By using this suffix, the valency of the verb is reduced.

Turkish
(8) a. Çocuk-lar öğretmen-i selâmla-dı-lar.
child-PL   teacher-ACC greet-PST-3PL
'The children greeted the teacher.'
   b. Çocuk-lar selâmla-š-tı-lar.
child-PL   greet-REC-PST-3PL
'The children greeted each other.'

Just like Turkish, DGS does not make use of an independent reciprocal pronoun, and reciprocal situations are sometimes expressed by means of a modification of the verb. Example (9a) illustrates that the agreeing verb GIVE moves from position 3a, associated with the subject, to position 3b, which is associated with the object. That is, the hand moves from right to left (see Section 9.5.2 for an extensive discussion of agreement in sign languages).

German Sign Language
(9) a.

MAN   INDEX$_{3a}$ WOMAN   INDEX$_{3b}$ FLOWER $_{3a}$GIVE$_{3b}$.

'The man gives the woman a flower.'

(9) b.

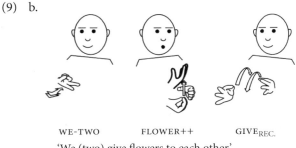

WE-TWO   FLOWER++   GIVE_{REC.}
'We (two) give flowers to each other.'

However, when two persons give flowers to each other, the form of the verb changes. As can be seen in (9b), the second (non-dominant) hand is added, and moves simultaneously with the dominant hand, but in the opposite direction. As in the Turkish example (8b), we witness valency reduction in this case: the ditransitive verb GIVE changes its form in the reciprocal construction and occurs with only two arguments, the subject WE-TWO and the direct object FLOWER++ 'flowers'.

Finally, it is noteworthy that even in English, occasionally one and the same verb may be used in intransitive and transitive constructions; that is, it may be subject to a valency alternation. Consider, for instance, the sentence pair *Peter breaks the stick* and *The stick breaks*, where *break* is a two-place predicate in the first sentence, but a one-place predicate in the second one. Yet, this difference in valency is not marked in any way on the verb. For sign languages, comparable phenomena have been described. However, it appears that across sign languages, the difference in valency can be signalled by a handshape change, as is illustrated in the American Sign Language (ASL) examples in (10).

American Sign Language

(10) a. PETER BREAK STICK.   → two ⌒-hands
          'Peter breaks the stick.'
      b. STICK BREAK.   → two ⌒-hands
          'The stick breaks.'

In both cases, BREAK is a two-handed sign involving a change in orientation, but in the transitive example in (10a), it is signed with two ⌒-hands and in the intransitive example in (10b) with two two ⌒-hands. The use of such meaningful handshapes will be further discussed in Section 9.6.2.

6.4   Semantic and grammatical roles

Just as in spoken languages, the participants or entities that are referred to by the arguments can be assigned certain **semantic roles**, such as, for example, Agent, Patient, Instrument, Source, and Goal. Semantic roles specify how a participant/entity is involved in the event or state expressed by the predicate. For instance, a participant can be the person that performs an action or the one who is the goal of the action. Furthermore, an entity can also be an instrument with which the action is performed, etcetera. Given that semantic roles are general semantic concepts, it is not surprising that semantic roles are modality-independent.

A number of these roles are illustrated in the NGT examples in (11). In Examples (11a) and (11b), the same constituent [INDEX$_1$ BROTHER INDEX$_{3a}$] occurs, but it is assigned different semantic roles: in (11a), it is the Agent of the action, while in (11b), it has the role of Patient. Two other semantic roles are exemplified in (11c) and (11d). In (11c), [BOOK] is an Instrument, while [STATION INDEX$_{3b}$] in (11d) functions as Goal.

Sign Language of the Netherlands

(11) a.   TOMORROW [INDEX$_1$ BROTHER INDEX$_{3a}$]$_{Agent}$ MOVE.
            'My brother is moving tomorrow.'
      b.   SUNDAY [INDEX$_1$]$_{Agent}$ [INDEX$_1$ BROTHER INDEX$_{3a}$]$_{Patient}$ MEET.
            'On Sunday, I will meet my brother.'
      c.   [SPIDER INDEX$_{3b}$]$_{Patient}$, [INDEX$_1$]$_{Agent}$ [BOOK]$_{Instrument}$ SMASH$_{3b}$.
            'I smashed the spider with a book.'
      d.   NOW [INDEX$_1$]$_{Agent}$ [STATION INDEX$_{3b}$]$_{Goal}$ $_1$GO$_{3b}$.
            'I am going to the station now.'

The constituent [INDEX$_1$ BROTHER INDEX$_{3a}$] does not only differ in its semantic role in (11a) and (11b), but also in its **grammatical role**: in (11a), it is the subject of the sentence, in (11b) the direct object. Note that in all four examples, the subject is an Agent. However, there is no one-to-one relation between semantic and grammatical roles. A subject, for instance, may well be a Patient (as in *The butter melts*). In many spoken languages, different grammatical roles are marked by means of case; subjects, for instance, are commonly assigned nominative case. This is not true for the sign languages that have been studied so far, where the difference in grammatical role is not expressed by a different form. Note that in English and numerous other languages, case marking is only visible on pronouns (e.g. *He moves* vs. *I meet him*), but not on nouns (e.g. *The girl moves* vs. *I meet the girl*). In NGT and other sign languages, however, even pronouns (i.e. INDEX) do not change in form depending on whether they are the subject or object of the sentence.

A clear indication that the grammatical and semantic role of arguments plays a role in the syntax of a language is the existence of a passive construction. Typically, in a passive construction, a transitive sentence is turned into an intransitive sentence, whereby the Patient-argument becomes a subject, and the original Agent-argument becomes optional. This change is obvious in the English sentence *He was asked (by the teacher)*, in which the subject *he* is Patient while the Agent-argument *teacher* is optionally expressed in a *by*-phrase. Only little is known about passive constructions in sign languages. For ASL, it has been observed that in certain constructions, an Agent is not overtly expressed but still implicitly present, as it is understood that some Agent is involved in the action. For instance, the example in (12) features the transitive verb FIX. Yet, the only argument that is present is the Patient argument BICYCLE (which is topicalized). While this may be reminiscent of a passive ('His bicycle was fixed'), we must also note that there is no passive auxiliary or passive morphology present. Scholars have therefore described such constructions as 'defocused agent constructions' rather than as true passives – and this is also reflected in the translation. It is thus possible that sign languages – just like many spoken languages – do not have passive constructions.

American Sign Language

$$\overline{\hspace{3cm}\text{t}}$$

(12)   POSS$_{3a}$ BICYCLE, NOW FIX++.
          literally 'His bicycle: now fix.'

Still, in the grammar of sign languages, grammatical roles certainly do determine the structure of sentences in a number of aspects. For instance, they influence sign order (see next section) and the phenomenon of pronoun copy (see Section 6.9).

6.5   Sign order

For most spoken languages, a basic word order can be determined at the sentence level; criteria that play a crucial role in determining a basic order are, among others, frequency (most common order) and pragmatic neutrality. Consequently, the order in, for instance, interrogative and imperative sentences is not considered, as these sentence types are not pragmatically neutral. Most sign languages for which this aspect of grammar has been investigated also seem to have a basic order.

The basic word order in a given language is established on the basis of the order found in a declarative main clause with a predicate and two nominal constituents (subject and direct object), none of which receives special emphasis. The three most common basic orders that have been identified for spoken languages, based on huge language samples, are shown in (13).

(13)   a.   Subject – Predicate – Object   →   S V O
          b.   Subject – Object – Predicate   →   S O V
          c.   Predicate – Subject – Object   →   V S O

In Section 6.5.1, we will address how the basic order of sign languages is determined at the sentence level and which factors may play a role, and in Section 6.5.2, we will discuss the order within nominal constituents.

6.5.1 Basic order at the sentence level

When we speak of 'basic word/sign order', we really mean constituent order because nominal arguments are constituents that may consist of multiple words/signs. That is, at sentence level, we are not interested in the order of individual words/signs, but rather in the order of the three main constituents, see (13). The criteria applied for sign languages are the same as those used in research on spoken languages, that is, for establishing the basic order, one looks at pragmatically neutral declarative sentences with a predicate and two nominal arguments. Still, in the following discussion, we will make a distinction between transitive and locative sentences.

As was shown in Section 6.3, a **transitive sentence** includes a two-place predicate which usually takes an Agent and Patient argument. For ASL, RSL, Swedish Sign Language, and Brazilian Sign Language (Libras), amongst others, it has been argued that the basic order in a transitive sentence is SVO, as is illustrated for Libras in (14).

Brazilian Sign Language
(14)   a.   [INDEX$_{3a}$ JUAN]$_S$ [LOVE]$_V$ [INDEX$_{3b}$ MARIA]$_O$.
            'Juan loves Maria.'
       b.   [INDEX$_{3a}$ JUAN]$_S$ [LOVE]$_V$ [FOOTBALL]$_O$.
            'Juan loves football.'

In NGT, Indopakistani Sign Language (IPSL), and Italian Sign Language (LIS), on the other hand, the basic order in such sentences is SOV, as is illustrated by the LIS examples in (15).

Italian Sign Language
(15)   a.   [GIANNI]$_S$ [MARIA]$_O$ [LOVE]$_V$.
            'Gianni loves Maria.'
       b.   [GIANNI]$_S$ [HOUSE]$_O$ [BUY]$_V$.
            'Gianni buys a house.'

In both (14) and (15), we provide two examples in order to show that the order of constituents does not depend on whether the object is animate (a-examples) or inanimate (b-examples). Still, it should be emphasized that these basic orders appear to be more common in **reversible sentences**. Note that from a semantic point of view, it is also possible in (14a) and (15a) that the woman loves the man. Hence, the correct interpretation in such sentences depends to a large degree on the order that is used. In contrast, in **non-reversible sentences** such as (14b) and (15b), a different order may occasionally be used, as such sentences only allow for one interpretation (it is, for instance, highly unlikely that the house buys Gianni). Furthermore, it has been found that in some sign languages, the word order is different – or at least more flexible – if the verb is spatially modified or inflected for aspect. RSL, for instance, has basic SVO order, but in sentences with classifier verbs or aspectually modified verbs, the order tends to be SOV (see Chapter 9 for discussion of these morphological processes).

So far, no sign language has been described with a basic VSO order. This is noteworthy, as in spoken languages, this order is not uncommon; it is attested in approximately 7% of the world's languages, including, for instance, Irish and Tagalog, the national language of the Philippines. Nor is there a sign language with a basic order in which the object precedes the subject. This, however, is less surprising, as such orders are also extremely rare in spoken languages.

Interestingly, for most of the sign languages studied to date, a different order has been identified in **locative sentences**. Locative sentences are sentences in which the position of two entities is specified in relation to each other. When signing a locative construction, it is very common to first introduce the bigger, and less mobile, entity (the ground) – as a reference point as it were – before positioning the smaller entity (the figure) in relation to the ground. This strategy, which is also called the **figure-ground principle**, is applied in the DGS examples in (16). BRIDGE and TABLE constitute the ground, while CAR and BOOK are the figures, and the locative relation between figure and ground is specified either by a verb of motion (16a) or a locative verb (16b). The RSL example in (17) also expresses a locative relation, but it does not contain a verb. In this example, it is the figure itself that is localized vis-à-vis the ground.

German Sign Language

(16)   a $[\text{BRIDGE}]_{\text{LOC}}$ $[\text{CAR}]_S$ $[\text{DRIVE-UNDER-BRIDGE}_{3a}]_V$.
            'The car is driving under the bridge.'
       b. $[\text{TABLE}_{3a}]_{\text{LOC}}$ $[\text{BOOK}]_S$ $[\text{LIE-ON}_{3a}]_V$.
            'A book lies on the table.'

Russian Sign Language

(17) $[\text{INDEX}_{3a}\ \text{WALL}]_{\text{LOC}}$ $[\text{WATERPIPE}_{3a}]$
       'There is a water pipe on the wall.'

So far, we have only been concerned with the position of arguments in the sentence – and this is indeed usually the focus of studies on word/sign order. Still, adjuncts can also have basic positions. It has, for instance, been found that in many sign languages, including NGT, **temporal adjuncts**, such as YESTERDAY, generally appear in sentence-initial position (18a), whereas the most common position of **aspectual adjuncts**, like ALWAYS, is immediately after the subject (18b).

Sign Language of the Netherlands

(18) a. [YESTERDAY]$_{TIME}$ [INDEX$_1$]$_S$ [BICYCLE]$_O$ [BUY]$_V$.
        'Yesterday I bought a bicycle.'
      b. [INDEX$_1$]$_S$ [ALWAYS]$_{ASP}$ [KEY]$_O$ [LOSE]$_V$.
        'I'm always losing my keys.'

In most spoken languages, variations on the basic word order are possible, but languages differ from each other with respect to how flexible their word order is. Obviously, the existence of alternative orders may complicate the search for a basic order. The same is true for sign languages, where various factors have been shown to have an influence on the sign order. An example is topicalization, which we will discuss in Section 6.6. In addition, a subject may appear in sentence-final position as a result of the process of subject pronoun copy; this phenomenon will be addressed in Section 6.9.

6.5.2 Sign order within the noun phrase

Up to now, we have only been concerned with the order of constituents within a sentence, but as we have already pointed out, constituents are often composed of several signs. Within constituents, signs are not arbitrarily combined either. In this section, we will look at the order within nominal constituents (noun phrases).

Within nominal constituents, nouns can be combined with different types of **modifiers**, such as articles, adjectives, numerals, possessive pronouns, and relative clauses (relative clauses will be addressed in Section 7.4). Spoken languages display interesting variation when it comes to the position of modifiers vis-à-vis the noun. In (19), we provide examples from three spoken languages that are typologically different from each other. In many languages, including Dutch and English, modifiers like possessive pronouns and adjectives always precede the noun (19a), whereas in French, we observe a split, with the possessive pronoun preceding but most adjectives following the noun (19b). In Yimas, a language spoken in New Guinea, both possessive pronouns and adjectives always follow the noun (19c).

Dutch (a), French (b), and Yimas (c)

(19) a. mijn zwarte tand
        my   black   tooth
      b. ma dent noire
        my tooth black
      c. trŋ amanaŋ urkpwicakŋ
        tooth my   black

Comparatively little is known about the order of elements within nominal constituents in sign languages. From the available data, however, we can conclude that sign languages differ from each other in this respect, too. For LIS, it has been determined that possessive pronouns (20a), demonstrative pronouns (20b), and adjectives and numerals (20c) follow the noun. The order of adjective and numeral with respect to each other, however, is flexible, as is also shown in (20c), although the order N-Adj-Num appears to be the preferred one.

Italian Sign Language

(20)   a.   COAT POSS₁
            'my coat'
       b.   BOOK INDEX₃
            'this book'
       c.   BOOK RED THREE / BOOK THREE RED
            'three red books'

The structure of the noun phrase in DGS looks a little different. As in LIS, adjectives and demonstrative pronouns usually follow the noun (21a). Possessive pronouns and numerals, however, appear in a fixed order before the noun, with the possessive preceding the numeral (21b).

German Sign Language

(21)   a.   HOUSE BLUE INDEX₃
            'this blue house'
       b.   POSS₁ FIVE BOOK THICK
            'my five thick books'

The fact that the pointing sign **INDEX** can have various functions (see Section 5.5.1) may make the identification of the order of elements within a nominal constituent tricky at times. We have already seen that this sign can be used as a personal pronoun in many sign languages – see, for instance, the NGT examples in (18). Furthermore, within a noun phrase, an INDEX can also function as a demonstrative pronoun, as in (20b) and (21a), as a locative adverbial (e.g. *the house there*), or to associate a non-present referent with a location. For ASL, it has even been suggested that an INDEX that precedes the noun can fulfil the function of a definite article (e.g. *the house*). Moreover, it is not unusual that within a nominal constituent, two INDEX signs co-occur, one before and one after the noun, as is illustrated in the ASL example in (22), where the different functions are indicated by subscripts: the pre-nominal index is a definite article while the post-nominal one functions as a locative adverbial. However, remember from the discussion in Section 5.5.1 that it is possible that different functions go hand in hand with subtle form differences.

American Sign Language

(22)   JOHN KNOW [INDEX_art MAN INDEX_adv]_NP
       'John knows [the man over there].'

6.6   Topicalization

A grammatical operation that commonly influences the order of signs within a sentence is **topicalization**. This implies that a constituent, usually a noun phrase, is placed in sentence-initial position, which is why some instances of topicalization are also referred to as 'left dislocation'. Topicalized constituents have a specific **information status** in a conversation (see also Section 4.6.2). In particular, they always contain information that is shared by the speaker and the addressee, in other words: old information. Often this information has been introduced earlier in the conversation, but this need not always be the case. By placing shared information in sentence-initial position, the speaker indicates that this is the topic of (this stretch of) the conversation about which new information will be added in the remainder of the sentence (the comment). The fact that topicalization depends on the discourse context indicates that sentences involving topicalization are not pragmatically neutral, and therefore, the word order they display cannot be considered basic.

In both DGS examples in (23), nominal constituents have been topicalized (locative and temporal adjuncts can also be topicalized, but these cases shall not be discussed here). We present sentences in isolation, but the reader should imagine that the examples were produced in contexts in which big cities (23a) or the signer's grandmother (23b) were the topic of conversation. The glosses make clear that the topics are accompanied by a particular **non-manual marker**, which we gloss as 't' (see also Examples (1a) and (12) above). This topic marker consists of raised eyebrows and a slight forward tilt of the head. Moreover, the topics are followed by a brief pause; this is indicated in the examples by means of a comma.

German Sign Language

(23) a. $\overline{\qquad\quad\text{t}}$
CITY BIG, INDEX$_1$ NEW-YORK LOVE.
'As for big cities, I love New York.'

b. $\overline{\qquad\qquad\qquad\quad\text{t}}$
POSS$_1$ GRANDMA INDEX$_{3a}$, TOMORROW INDEX$_1$ MEET.
'I am meeting *my grandma* tomorrow.'

Although in both examples, a nominal constituent is topicalized, closer inspection reveals that the two examples do differ from each other. When examining the remainder of the sentence in (23a), that is, the elements that follow the topic, it turns out that the comment is a grammatically complete sentence, as it contains a transitive verb with both its arguments. Through the topic, a constituent of the sentence is, as it were, doubled, but the topic is superordinate in meaning: New York is a member of the set of big cities. The resulting sign order is Top, SOV. Unlike (23a), the comment in (23b) – TOMORROW INDEX$_1$ MEET – is not a complete grammatical sentence, because only one of the arguments of the transitive verb MEET is present (see Section 6.3). In other words, in this example, the direct object has been topicalized, and the resulting order is O$_{Top}$, AdvSV.

As the examples in (23) show, in sign languages, topichood of a constituent can be signalled both by syntactic position and non-manual marking (the latter, however, may be optional). The translations indicate that in English, too, topicalization has an impact on syntactic structure (word order) and/or intonation (the English constituent *my grandma* in (23b) is not placed in sentence-initial position but receives stress). In some spoken languages, topics are also morphologically marked, that is, they are accompanied by a dedicated **topic marker**. In the Korean examples in (24), this is the suffix *-un*.

Korean

(24) a.   Ssaengsseon-**un** yeone-ga   madiss-da.
           fish-TOP   salmon-NOM delicious-is
           'As for fish, salmon is delicious.'
      b.   Gu chaek-un   John-i   Mary-ege suessda.
           the book-TOP John-NOM   Mary-DAT gave
           '*The book* John gave to Mary.'

The reader will notice that the examples in (24) are actually quite similar to the DGS examples in (23). Note that in (24a), we also observe a kind of doubling, just as in (23a), with the topic *fish* being superordinate to the argument *salmon*. In (24b), the part following the topic would not constitute a grammatical sentence by itself, similar to what we described for (23b).

6.7   Sentence types

Of course, topicalization is not the only syntactic phenomenon that may influence the order of constituents. As mentioned previously, the starting point for determining the basic word/sign order of a language is the neutral declarative sentence. In other sentence types, such as interrogatives (Section 6.7.1) and imperatives (Section 6.7.2), other orders may occur.

6.7.1 Interrogatives

In many spoken languages, the word order in **yes/no questions** is different from the basic order. In English, for instance, the inflected auxiliary appears sentence-initially in yes/no questions, as in *Will he sell his car?* – in contrast to the declarative counterpart (*He will sell his car*). Often, *do*-insertion takes place, but again, the auxiliary *do* occupies the sentence-initial position (*Did he sell his car?*). In contrast, in the sign languages studied so far, yes/no questions are not usually characterized by a systematic change in sign order. Rather, the fact that we are dealing with a yes/no question is generally only indicated by a **non-manual grammatical marker** (glossed as 'y/n': mostly raised eyebrows and a forward and/or downward movement of the head/chin), as can be seen in the IPSL examples in (25). In this sign language, the non-manual marker consists of eyes wide open and a forward head tilt.

Indopakistani Sign Language
  (25) a. FATHER CAR EXIST.
            '(My) father has a car.'

                            y/n
       b. FATHER CAR EXIST?
           'Does (your/his) father have a car?'

Sign linguists have suggested that such non-manual markers fulfil a function similar to that of **question intonation** in spoken languages; they constitute, as it were, the melody of the question (see Section 11.10). There are also spoken languages in which the difference between a declarative sentence and a corresponding yes/no question is only signalled by intonation, for instance Hindi. In the examples in (26), we represent a falling (26a) and rising (26b) intonation by means of a line. Crucially, the word order is the same in both examples.

Hindi

  (26) a. Bacca bemar hai.
            child   ill   be.3SG.PRS
            'The child is ill.'

       b. Bacca bemar hai?
           child   ill   be.3SG.PRS
           'Is the child ill?'

With respect to the manual part of the utterance, the only difference between declarative sentences and yes/no questions that has been observed for a couple of sign languages is the use of manual **question particles** which usually occupy a sentence-final position (and which are often optional). This is true, for instance, for Hong Kong Sign Language (HKSL). The question particle used in (27) is fairly complex, as it involves a quickly alternating repetition of the handshapes meaning 'good' (⅃-hand) and 'bad' (ᚹ-hand).

Hong Kong Sign Language

                                    y/n
  (27) NOW TAKE-PHOTO Q-PARTICLE?
        'Shall we take photos now?'

From a typological point of view, the use of a question particle is by no means unusual. Sentence-final question particles are, for instance, also attested in some Asian and African languages, like Lele, a Chadic language spoken in Chad (28) (the question particle is glossed as 'Q').

Lele
(28) Kiya hàb kùlbá ke-y **gà?**
      Kiya find cow   his   Q
      'Did Kiya find his cow?'

Wh-questions are also marked non-manually in sign languages. In most sign languages, the relevant non-manual marker involves furrowed eyebrows (possibly in combination with other markers like head forward). Typological research on sign languages from all continents has revealed that question signs (wh-signs) most commonly appear in **sentence-final position**. As mentioned in Section 6.5.1, LIS is an SOV language; an example for this basic order is provided in (29a). For wh-questions in LIS, it has been observed that the wh-sign always appears in final position, no matter whether the subject (29b), the object (29c), or an adjunct (29d) is questioned. Importantly, the wh-sign never occupies its basic position, that is, the position where the subject/object/adjunct occurs in the corresponding declarative sentence. Note that the non-manual marker must accompany the wh-sign, but may optionally spread over the entire clause (as indicated by the broken line).

Italian Sign Language
(29) a. TOMORROW GIANNI HOUSE BUY.
          'Tomorrow Gianni will buy a house.'

                    _____ ___wh
      b. FLOWER BUY **WHO?**
          'Who buys the flowers?'

                    _____ ____wh
      c. MARIA FIND **WHAT?**
          'What has Maria found?'

                    _____ ___wh
      d. LESSON START **WHEN?**
          'When does the lesson start?'

Typologically speaking, this pattern is quite unusual. In some spoken languages, the wh-word remains in the basic position, that is, in the position in which the questioned element would appear in the declarative sentence. This pattern is illustrated for Japanese, an SOV language, in (30): the wh-word *nanio* 'what' (30b) occupies the same position as the object *hono* 'book' (30a) (note that Japanese also makes use of a sentence-final question particle). Languages of this type are referred to as 'wh-in-situ' languages.

Japanese

(30) a. Jun-ga   hon-o   katta.
          Jun-NOM   book-ACC   bought
          'Jun bought a book.'
      b. Jun-ga   **nani**-o   katta   ka?
          Jun-NOM   what-ACC   bought   Q
          'What did Jun buy?'

However, typological investigations on a wealth of spoken languages have shown that in languages in which wh-words do not appear in the basic position, they almost always occupy the sentence-initial position. In the sign languages that have been studied so far, this is clearly not the case. It therefore seems that wh-questions present us with an intriguing **modality-specific pattern**.

Another remarkable and modality-specific phenomenon is **wh-doubling**. Besides the sentence-final strategy, it is possible – and actually quite common – in many sign languages to realize the wh-sign twice in the interrogative sentence, once at the beginning and again at the end of the sentence. In the Libras example in (31), the object wh-sign WHAT is doubled in this way, and in the VGT example in (32), the adjunct wh-sign WHY.

Brazilian Sign Language

$$\overline{\hspace{6cm}}^{\text{wh}}$$
(31) **WHAT** JOHN BUY YESTERDAY **WHAT?**
      'What did Juan buy yesterday?'

Flemish Sign Language

$$\overline{\hspace{4cm}}^{\text{wh}}$$
(32) **WHY** DOG BARK **WHY?**
      'Why is the dog barking?'

Wh-doubling, however, is not possible in all sign languages. IPSL is an example of a sign language that does not allow this strategy. Sentence (33a) provides an example of an IPSL declarative sentence with basic SOV order. In the wh-question in (33b), the general question sign (glossed as G-WH) appears in sentence-final position – as expected, given the above discussion. Doubling of the wh-sign, however, leads to an ungrammatical sentence, as is illustrated in (33c).

Indopakistani Sign Language

(33) a. FATHER INDEX$_3$ BOOK SEARCH.
          '(My) father is searching for a book.'

$$\overline{\hspace{6cm}}^{\text{wh}}$$
      b. FATHER INDEX$_3$ SEARCH G-WH?
          'What is (my) father searching for?'

$$\overline{\hspace{7cm}}^{\text{wh}}$$
      c. *G-WH FATHER INDEX$_3$ SEARCH G-WH?

Typologically, wh-questions in IPSL are remarkable in two more respects. Firstly, the non-manual marker 'wh' in this sign language consists of raised eyebrows (in combination with a slight backward tilt of the head), rather than furrowed eyebrows, as is evident from the still in (34). Secondly, IPSL has a minimal **question-word paradigm**: there is only one question word, the general question sign G-WH, shown in (34), which can mean 'who', 'what', 'where', 'when', 'why', and 'how'.

Indopakistani Sign Language

(34)

General question sign G-WH

Consequently, the interpretation of this sign is highly dependent on the context, as is illustrated in the examples in (35).

Indopakistani Sign Language

                                                            _____
                                                               wh

(35) a. INDEX₃ ASK **G-WH**?

'Whom/what/when/why did she/he ask?'

                                                                  wh

     b. INDEX₂ FRIEND SLEEP **G-WH**?

'Where/when/why/how did your friend sleep?'

Some of the interrogative meanings can be disambiguated by combining G-WH with another sign in a compound-like structure. Possible combinations are: FACE G-WH 'who', PLACE G-WH 'where', and TIME G-WH 'when' – basically, this is like asking 'At what time did you arrive?' instead of "When did you arrive?". For 'what', 'how', and 'why', however, a comparable strategy is not available.

    Taken together, the preceding discussion has revealed that all types of questions in sign languages are accompanied by non-manual markers, which have been argued to function like interrogative intonation in spoken languages. In yes/no questions, the sign order generally does not change. As for wh-questions, it is remarkable that, across sign languages, wh-signs often occur in sentence-final position and that they can be doubled. Sign languages differ from each other, however, with respect to the possibility of wh-doubling, and in the size of their wh-sign inventories.

6.7.2 Imperatives

While declaratives and interrogatives have received considerable attention in the sign language literature, the third sentence type that is usually distinguished, **imperatives**, has not been investigated in much detail to date. A recent cross-linguistic study on imperatives in LIS, Catalan Sign Language (LSC), and French Sign Language (LSF) has revealed that in all three sign languages, this sentence type is accompanied by specific non-manual markers, although the exact nature of non-manual marking may differ between sign languages and also between different types of imperatives (for instance, commands vs. requests). The LIS command in (36a) is accompanied by furrowed eyebrows ('fb'), but the LSF command in (37a) by raised eyebrows ('re'). Note the lack of a subject pronoun in (36a); cross-linguistically this is indeed a common feature of imperatives, even in languages that do not allow pro-drop (see Section 6.9 for discussion). As for manual marking, all types of LIS imperatives often include an indexical sign, glossed as B-INDEX, in sentence-final position (36b); this sign is articulated with a ⍟-handshape, palm facing upwards.

Italian Sign Language

		fb

(36) a. KNEEL-DOWN!
         'Kneel down!'

                                         fb

       b. EAT B-INDEX!
           'Eat!'

In LSF, requests usually involve an additional non-manual marker, namely a head nod ('hn'), as is illustrated in (37b). Moreover, in all cases, the movement of the verb may be more tense when used in an imperative.

French Sign Language

                                          re

(37) a. INDEX₂ BITE-BAR LONG!
         'Bite the bar for a long time!'

                                   hn
                                   re

       b. PLEASE INDEX₂ BITE!
           'Please, bite it!'

6.8   Negation and affirmation

It is a characteristic of natural languages that all sentence types – declarative, interrogative, and imperative sentences – can be negated. The structure of negative sentences in different sign languages will be discussed in some detail in this section, but we will also briefly look at the realization of affirmation. Again, we will see that non-manual markers play a crucial role in this grammatical domain.

All sign languages studied to date have at their disposal an independent particle to express sentential negation, just like many spoken languages (e.g. English *not*). The position of this **manual negation particle** within the sentence can differ from sign language to sign language. For instance, in LSC, an SOV language, the particle appears in sentence-final position (38), whereas it follows the subject in ASL, an SVO language (39). Still, it is not the case that there is a one-to-one relationship between basic order and the **position of the particle** within the sentence. Swedish Sign Language, for instance, is an SVO language, just like ASL, but the negative particle usually follows the verb. In (40), we illustrate the form of the manual negation particles in LSC and ASL.

Catalan Sign Language

(38)   SANTI MEAT EAT **NOT**.
       'Santi doesn't eat meat.'

American Sign Language

    neg _ _ _ _ _ _ _ _ _ _

(39)   JOHN **NOT** BUY HOUSE.
       'John is not buying a house.'

(40)   a. 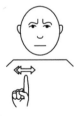   b.

           Manual negation   Manual negation
           particle in LSC   particle in ASL

A look at the examples in (38) and (39) immediately makes clear that a non-manual marker, namely a side-to-side **headshake** (glossed as 'neg'), is used in combination with the manual particle. In both LSC and ASL, the headshake can either accompany only the negative particle NOT, or it may optionally spread over the verb and the object (in the examples, optional spreading is indicated by a dotted line).

Whereas the headshake is obligatory in these two sign languages, the negative particle is optional, and in fact, it is often omitted. When this happens, the headshake is the only marker of negation, as can be seen in the examples in (41) and (42). Note that the meaning of (41) and (42a) is identical to that of (38) and (39), respectively. Furthermore, these examples illustrate that the headshake can be associated with different domains: the verb in (41), the verbal phrase in (42a), or the entire sentence in (42b). Interestingly, typological comparisons have revealed that sign languages may differ from each other with respect to the exact **timing (scope) of the headshake**. For instance, while it is possible in LSC to have headshake on only the verb in transitive sentences (41), the same has been argued to be impossible in ASL. That is, sentence (42a) with headshake on only the verb BUY would be ungrammatical; in ASL, the headshake must spread onto the object in the absence of NOT.

Catalan Sign Language

$$\overline{\text{neg}}$$

(41)   SANTI MEAT EAT.
       'Santi doesn't eat meat.'

American Sign Language

$$\overline{\hspace{3cm}\text{neg}}$$

(42) a.   JOHN BUY HOUSE.
           'John is not buying a house.'

$$\overline{\hspace{3.5cm}\text{neg}}$$

      b.   WOMAN FORGET PURSE.
           'It is not the case that the woman forgot the purse.'

Sign languages like LSC and ASL, in which sentential negation is expressed by a combination of an optional manual particle and an obligatory non-manual marker are called **non-manual dominant** sign languages, as the non-manual marker is obviously more important than the manual element. Other sign languages belonging to this group are DGS, IPSL, Libras, and NGT.

However, the non-manual dominant pattern is not attested in all sign languages. In fact, we find interesting **typological variation** in the domain of negation. In HKSL (43) and Inuit Sign Language (IUR) (44), for instance, a sentence cannot be negated by means of only a non-manual marker. Consequently, the (b)-examples are ungrammatical. Given the obligatory presence of a manual negative element, these sign languages are classified as **manual dominant**. Sign languages of this type are further characterized by the fact that the headshake is usually confined to the negative particle, that is, it cannot spread – in striking contrast to the above ASL and LSC examples. Other sign languages that pattern like HKSL and IUR in this respect are, for example, LIS, Turkish Sign Language (TİD), and Jordanian Sign Language (LIU).

Hong Kong Sign Language

neg

(43)   a.   INDEX$_{3a}$ TOMORROW FLY NOT.
          'It is not true that he is flying tomorrow.'

neg

b.   *YESTERDAY NIGHT FATHER FAX FRIEND.
          'Father didn't fax (his) friend last night.'

Inuit Sign Language

neg

(44)   a.   WOLVERINE EAT NOT.
          'I do not eat wolverine.'

neg

b.   *POLAR-BEAR SEE.
          'I didn't see a polar bear.'

Further typological variation in the domain of negation is found with regard to the form of the non-manual marker. All sign languages studied to date make use of a head-shake, but in some, an additional non-manual marker is attested: a single backward head tilt (see (45) for illustration). This is clearly an areal, culture-specific feature, as it is only attested in the Eastern Mediterranean, where a similar head movement is commonly used as a negative gesture in the hearing culture. Use of a backward head tilt in negative sentences has been described for TİD, Greek Sign Language (GSL), and Lebanese Sign Language. Just like the headshake, the backward head tilt has taken on a grammatical function in these sign languages.

Turkish Sign Language
   (45)

Non-manual negative marker
(in combination with manual particle)

In the TİD example in (46), the backward head tilt ('bht') accompanies the sentence-final negative particle, the shape of which is also illustrated in (45). As mentioned before, TİD is a manual dominant sign language. GSL also employs a backward head tilt, but still, it has been classified as a non-manual dominant sign language. This implies (i) that a sentence can be negated by a head tilt (or headshake) only (47a), and (ii) that the non-manual can spread over (part of) the sentence (47b).

Turkish Sign Language

$$\overline{\text{bht}}$$

(46)   INDEX$_1$ TURKEY BIRTH NOT.
       'I was not born in Turkey.'

Greek Sign Language

$$\overline{\text{bht}}$$

(47) a.   WORK AFTER GO, HURRY.
           'Don't be in a hurry, we will go (there) after work.'

$$\overline{\text{bht}}$$

      b.   INDEX$_1$ AGAIN GO NOT.
           'I won't go (there) again.'

So far in this section, we have only been concerned with negative sentences. However, sentences can also be positive. These two options are subsumed under the term '**polarity**' of a sentence, that is, a sentence can have positive or negative polarity. In principle, any sentence that is not negated is positive, but this is not necessarily overtly expressed – in contrast to negative polarity, which is always marked. Yet, strong positive polarity can be marked, and this is the case in affirmative sentences in which the truth of an event is emphasized. In English, for instance, the adverbial *indeed* may serve this purpose. In sign languages, **affirmation** can be expressed by means of a manual and/or a non-manual marker. The non-manual marker for affirmation ('aff') is a repeated **head nod**, which may accompany the entire sentence, as in in the LIS example in (48).

Italian Sign Language

$$\overline{\text{aff}}$$

(48)   SOMEBODY ARRIVE.
       'Someone *did* arrive.'

LIU additionally sometimes uses a manual affirmative particle, which we gloss as AFF in (49). In this case, the head nod is synchronized with the manual sign: if the sign involves a single movement, then there is also only one nod; if the sign has repeated movement, then the nod is also repeated.

Jordanian Sign Language

$$\overline{\text{aff}}$$

(49) TOMORROW PARTY GO-TO AFF INDEX$_1$.
    'I *will* go to the party tomorrow.'

The translations of the examples in (48) and (49) indicate that in English, affirmation is often expressed by intonation (emphasis on elements in italics) and/or by the auxiliary *do* – in addition to adverbials like *really* or *indeed*. In sign languages, non-manual intonation appears to be the most common way to realize strong positive polarity in the sense of affirmation.

6.9   Pronominalization and pro-drop

The last grammatical phenomenon relevant to the discussion of simple sentences that we address is **pronominalization**. We speak of pronominalization when a referent previously introduced in the discourse is referred to by a personal pronoun. This strategy is only licit when that referent is sufficiently familiar to the conversation partner, as otherwise the pronoun cannot receive an unambiguous interpretation (see Section 4.6.1). In other words, once a referent like *the brother of my girlfriend* has been introduced, this complex nominal constituent need not be repeated every time the speaker wants to refer to this referent; rather, the pronoun *he* will usually be sufficient – unless there is potential ambiguity (see (52)).

For pronominalization in sign languages, there is an additional restriction: the relevant referent must either be present or must have been localized in the signing space. Pronouns in sign languages are pointing signs that target loci in the signing space: this can be the **actual location** of a present referent (the signer himself, the addressee, or other persons or objects present in the environment) or an **arbitrary location** created for a non-present referent. We will illustrate this strategy with a fragment from an NGT conversation. In sentence (50a), the non-present referent *your cousin* is introduced and localized at location 3a by means of an INDEX. In the next sentence (50b), this referent is then pronominalized, that is, it is referred to by means of the pronoun INDEX$_{3a}$.

Sign Language of the Netherlands
(50) a. YESTERDAY INDEX$_1$ INDEX$_2$ COUSIN **INDEX$_{3a}$** SEE.
          'Yesterday I saw your cousin.'
      b. NEXT YEAR **INDEX$_{3a}$** WORLD^TRIP GO.
          'Next year, he will go on trip around the world.'

We observe here an interesting difference to pronominal reference in spoken languages. Across spoken languages, pronominalization usually involves **anaphoric reference**.

Looking at the translation of sentence (50b), we see that the pronoun *he* refers back to a previously mentioned referent that is not present in the conversational situation, in this case, the nominal constituent *your cousin* in sentence (50a). The situation is slightly different in the NGT version. Note that in the NGT sentence (50b), INDEX$_{3a}$ refers indirectly to the referent INDEX$_2$ COUSIN via the location associated with that referent; at the same time, it also refers directly to a location at which the non-present referent *your cousin* is, as it were, represented on a sort of 'mental map'. In that sense, the pronoun INDEX$_{3a}$ in (50b) is **deictic**, and not anaphoric. Indeed, on the basis of this difference, some researchers have proposed that pronominal pointing signs are more comparable to demonstrative pronouns than to personal pronouns. According to this line of reasoning, what the signer actually expresses in (50b) is 'Next year, *this one* will go on a trip'.

A modality-specific feature of pronominal reference in sign languages that is closely connected, is that **ambiguity** of pronouns is hardly ever observed. Compare the two short stories in English (51) and NGT (52), which are similar in content.

English

(51) a. Yesterday, I saw your cousin.

     b. My brother was there, too.

     c. Next year, **he** will go on trip around the world.

Sign Language of the Netherlands

(52) a. YESTERDAY INDEX$_1$ INDEX$_2$ COUSIN INDEX$_{3a}$ SEE.

       'Yesterday I saw your cousin$_i$.'

     b. INDEX$_1$ BROTHER INDEX$_{3b}$ ALSO BE-PRESENT.

       'My brother was there, too.'

     c. NEXT YEAR **INDEX$_{3a}$** WORLD^TRIP GO.

       'Next year, he$_i$ will go on trip around the world.'

In the English example, the pronoun *he* in (51c) is ambiguous: it may refer either to *your cousin* or to *my brother* because the form of the pronoun only indicates that it refers to a male referent. In other words, the pronoun encodes the features third person masculine singular, and there are two referents in the preceding context that share these features. In contrast, in the NGT example (52), use of the pronoun INDEX$_{3a}$ does not lead to ambiguity: INDEX$_{3a}$ in (52c) can only refer back to INDEX$_2$ COUSIN, because it is this referent that has been associated with location 3a while INDEX$_1$ BROTHER has been associated with location 3b (in linguistics, co-reference between a pronoun and a referent is commonly indicated by means of subscripts, and we apply this convention in the translation of (52)). In sign languages, referents are thus associated with a unique location – provided they are present or have been localized. Example (52) clearly shows that INDEX$_{3a}$, although translated as *he*, does not really mean *he*. On the one hand, the meaning of this pointing sign is more specific in this context, as it can only refer to the referent that, in this stretch of discourse, occupies location 3a. On the other hand, exactly the same pointing sign could, in another context, also refer to a female referent and thus be translated as *she*.

For almost all sign languages studied so far, the possibility to omit pronominal forms under certain circumstances has been described. This grammatical phenomenon is called **pro-drop**. Across sign languages, an important condition for pro-drop is that the argument that is omitted is indicated by the form of the verb, more specifically, by the beginning and end point of the verb's movement. It is thus possible in DGS to utter a sentence like the one in (53a), even without a context. Note that (53a) does not contain any (pro)nominal argument. However, who visits whom can be inferred from the form of the verb VISIT, which starts at the location of the addressee (location 2) and moves towards the location of the signer (location 1). The form of the verb thus indicates that the addressee is the one who pays a visit (Agent/subject) and that the signer is the one being visited (Patient/object) (this spatial modification is often referred to as 'agreement' and will be further discussed in Section 9.5.2). As a consequence, in (53a), both the subject pronoun and the object pronoun can be omitted.

German Sign Language

(53)   a.   NEXT WEEKEND $_2$VISIT$_1$ CAN.
'Next weekend, you can visit me.'

   b.   NEXT WEEKEND INDEX$_2$ INDEX$_1$ $_2$VISIT$_1$ CAN.
'Next weekend, you can visit me.'

   c.   *TWO YEARS AGO LOVE.
'Two years ago, you were in love with me.'

The alternative structure in (53b) is also grammatical, but to sign both pronouns would be considered redundant, or even pragmatically marked, in this context. Now take a look at Example (53c), which contains the verb LOVE, which cannot be spatially modified. Out of context, this sentence is ungrammatical, as the form of the verb does not specify who loves whom – consequently, the pronouns cannot be omitted. A similar relation between verb morphology and pro-drop has been established for numerous spoken languages. For instance, spoken languages in which the form of the verb unambiguously indicates person and number of the subject (such as Spanish and Turkish) usually allow pro-drop.

Still, there are contexts in which pronouns can be dropped even in the absence of a spatially modified verb. This is possible when the referent which the pronoun refers to is the topic of the conversation, that is, it is known to the addresses (see Section 4.6). Consequently, this type of pronoun drop is often referred to as '**topic-drop**' rather than pro-drop. That is, the topic of a sentence can be deleted under identity with a topic in the preceding sentence(s). We illustrate this phenomenon with the ASL example in

(54). In the first sentence, the referent DAUGHTER is introduced. This referent is at the same time subject and topic of the subsequent sentences, and given that it is the topic of conversation, repeated use of a pronoun is superfluous. Note that DAUGHTER is not localized and that none of the subsequent verbs – DECIDE, SEE, PICK-UP, FASCINATED, LOST – is modified such that it would indicate the subject (unlike VISIT in (53a)). We must therefore conclude that omission of a pronoun referring to DAUGHTER is a case of topic-drop.

American Sign Language

(54) ONE DAY, DAUGHTER NOTHING d-o, DECIDE WALK WOODS$_3$. [...]
      INDEX$_{3a}$ SEE$_{3a}$ FLOWER$_{3a}$, PICK-UP$_{3a}$.
      SEE$_{3b}$ WATERFALL$_{3b}$, [...] FASCINATED, LOST.
      'One day, the daughter had nothing to do, so (she) decided to take a walk in the woods. (She) saw there some flowers, and picked (them) up; (she) saw a waterfall; (she) was so fascinated (by it) that (she) became lost.'

Note, however, that FLOWER is localized at location 3a, and that this location appears on the verb PICK-UP. Consequently, omission of the object pronoun in this sentence is a case of pro-drop. In other words: a combination of topic-drop and pro-drop is possible. The possibility of topic-drop has also been described for spoken languages that do not allow pro-drop.

Lastly, we turn to a phenomenon whereby pronominalization may have an impact on the sign order: **subject pronoun copy**. This linguistic strategy involves the repetition of a subject argument at the end of the sentence by means of an INDEX. The subject is thus realized twice in the same sentence. Subject pronoun copy has first been described for ASL, but it is also attested in other sign languages. In (55), we illustrate the phenomenon with NGT sentences. While the subject argument in the usual sentence-initial position can be a nominal constituent (55a) or an INDEX (55b), the subject in sentence final position can only be in the form of an INDEX. Consequently, Example (55c) with the repeated subject MAN in sentence-final position is ungrammatical (see Section 7.5.3 for pronoun copy in complex sentences).

Sign Language of the Netherlands

(55) a. MAN INDEX$_{3a}$ COFFEE ORDER **INDEX$_{3a}$**.
          'The man orders coffee.'
      b. INDEX$_{3a}$ COFFEE ORDER **INDEX$_{3a}$**.
          'He orders coffee.'
      c. *MAN INDEX$_{3a}$ COFFEE ORDER **MAN**.
          'The man orders coffee.'
      d. COFFEE ORDER **INDEX$_{3a}$**.
          'He orders coffee.'

As a consequence of copying the subject argument, the sign order in (55a) and (55b) is SOVS. Occasionally, subject pronoun copy and pro-drop may co-occur within a sentence, and in this case, the resulting sign order will be OVS in NGT, as is shown in (55d). Clearly, given the criteria discussed in Section 6.5, this is not the basic word order, but rather a marked alternative order.

Summary

Signs can have different functions within a sentence; they can function as **predicate**, **argument**, or **adjunct**. When, in the absence of a copula, adjectives or nouns function as predicates, we call these **adjectival** and **nominal predicates**. Predicates differ from each other with respect to their **valency**: they can be **intransitive**, **transitive**, or **ditransitive**. In certain constructions, one may observe **valency reduction** (for instance, in **reciprocal constructions**). Furthermore, arguments can have different **semantic roles** (e.g. Agent and Patient) and **grammatical roles** (like subject and object) in a sentence.

Signs are not combined arbitrarily to form a sentence. Both at the sentence and constituent level, there are clear, language-specific ordering rules. At the sentence level, the sign order can be influenced by two factors: firstly, by whether the sentence is **reversible** or **non-reversible** from a semantic point of view; secondly, by whether the sentence is **transitive** or **locative**. In sign languages, locative sentences are usually constructed according to the **figure-ground principle**. The **information status** of a constituent can also have influence on the order. **Topics**, for instance, appear in sentence-initial position and are **marked non-manually**. Within nominal constituents, **modifying elements** can appear before or after the noun. An INDEX can perform different functions within a nominal constituent.

Non-manual markers play a crucial role in indicating different sentence types. **Yes/no questions** and **wh-questions** are marked by various positions of the eyebrows. This kind of marking has been compared to **question intonation** in spoken languages. Furthermore, some sign languages make use of manual **question particles**. Sign languages differ from each other in the size of their **question word paradigm**. In the realization of wh-questions, we also find interesting **modality-specific patterns**: wh-signs often appear in **sentence-final position**, and in some sign languages, **wh-doubling** is possible. In **imperative** sentences, facial expression and body posture play a central role. To realize **negation**, sign languages use **manual negation particles** and a headshake. In this domain, we find interesting **typological variation**. Sign languages differ from each other in the **position of the particle** within the sentence and in the exact **timing (scope) of the headshake**. Also, **manual dominant** sign languages have to be distinguished from **non-manual dominant** ones. **Affirmation** of a sentence can be signalled by a **head nod**. Negation and affirmation are subsumed under the term **polarity** of a sentence.

Pronominalization is realized in sign languages by means of pointing signs. These pointing signs either target the **actual location** of a referent or an **arbitrary location** that has been established for an absent referent. Given the fact that sign language pronouns appear to be more **deictic** than **anaphoric** in nature, **ambiguity** of pronouns is hardly ever observed. Under certain conditions, **pro-drop** is possible. In addition, **topic-drop** is attested, which is subject to different conditions. **Subject pronoun copy**, possibly in combination with pro-drop, may influence the sign order at the sentence level.

Test yourself

1. What is the valency of the following four verbs in a sign language that you know (pay attention please: (d) is a bit tricky). Please provide an example sentence in glosses for each of the four verbs.
   - a. GIVE
   - b. TEASE
   - c. CRY
   - d. HOPE
2. To what extent do wh-questions differ in sign languages from wh-questions in spoken languages? Mention two aspects.
3. The basic order in several sign languages is SOV. Why is OSV or OVS sometimes possible?
4. To what extent can sign languages differ from each other with respect to the realization of negation? Mention three aspects.
5. Provide (in glosses) three different ways to negate the following Catalan Sign Language sentence:

   TODAY INDEX$_1$ JOSEP INDEX$_3$ $_1$VISIT$_3$
   'Today, I will visit Josep.'

Assignments

1. Please identify and label the constituents in the following ASL sentence. What is special about the order in this sentence?

   _____t
   THREE BOOK POSS$_1$ SISTER BUY
   'My sister bought three books.'

2. Below you find two DGS examples, both containing two sentences. Why is the second sentence in (a) grammatical, but the second one in (b) not?
   - a. POSS$_1$ FRIEND INDEX$_{3a}$ SCHOOL WORK.

     CHILD++ INDEX$_{3b(arc)}$ $_{3a}$HELP$_{3b}$.

     'My friend works in a school. He helps the children.'
   - b. POSS$_1$ FRIEND INDEX$_{3a}$ SCHOOL WORK.

     *CHILD++ INDEX$_{3b(arc)}$ TRUST.

     'My friend works in a school. He trusts the children.'

3. What is going on in the ASL sentence below? Please describe the structure of the utterance and the function of the topics based on the description of the examples in the chapter.

    _____t _____t
    JOHN INDEX$_{3a}$, VEGETABLES, INDEX$_{3a}$ PREFER ARTICHOKE.
    'As for John, as far as vegetables are concerned, he prefers artichokes.'

4. Why is pro-drop often allowed in a sign language but not in the surrounding spoken language?

5. Create three sentences in a sign language you know in which the constituent [TABLE INDEX$_3$] 'this table' performs different functions (argument/adjunct) and (for the argument function) different grammatical roles.

References and further reading

Studies that compare sign order in different (non-related) sign languages, and also address methodological problems, are Johnston et al. (2007) and Vermeerbergen et al. (2007). Overviews of factors that may influence sign order at the sentence level are provided by Kimmelman (2012), Leeson & Saeed (2012b), and Napoli & Sutton-Spence (2014). Theoretical accounts of word order at sentence level and topicalization (for advanced students) can be found in Aarons (1996), Neidle et al. (2000), and Sandler & Lillo-Martin (2006). Janzen, O'Shea & Shaffer (2001) and Rankin (2013) discuss ASL examples that resemble passive constructions. An overview of the characteristics of different sentence types is offered in Cecchetto (2012). Zeshan (2004a,b) provides interesting typological studies on the realization of interrogative and negative constructions in different sign languages; for language-specific studies, see the articles compiled in Zeshan (2006a). Pfau (2002, 2008) compares characteristics of sign language negation to those of spoken language negation. There is an interesting (but difficult) controversy concerning the analysis of wh-questions in ASL; see Petronio & Lillo-Martin (1997), Neidle et al. (2000), and Sandler & Lillo-Martin (2006). For NGT, the realization of questions, negation, and topicalization is extensively studied in Coerts (1992). The only study investigating imperatives in sign languages is Donati et al. (in press). Sign language pronouns are the subject of a study by McBurney (2002). In this article as well as in Meier (1990), Alibašić Ciciliani & Wilbur (2006), and Cormier (2012), the particulars of sign language pronouns are discussed. Subject pronoun copy has first been described by Padden (1988). Bos (1993, 1995) describes pronominalization, pro-drop, and pronoun copy in NGT. Syntactic analyses of pro-drop in sign languages have been suggested by Lillo-Martin (1986), Bahan et al. (2000), and Zwitserlood & Van Gijn (2006).

In the section on valency, the examples that illustrate reciprocal constructions in DGS are from Pfau & Steinbach (2003), and the ASL examples are based on examples provided in Benedicto & Brentari (2004). The 'defocused agent construction' in (12) is from Rankin (2013). As for the discussion of sign order at the sentence and constituent level, we took the Libras examples from de Quadros (1999), the LIS examples from Cecchetto, Geraci & Zucchi (2006) and Brunelli (2011), the DGS examples in (21) from Happ & Vorköper (2005), the ASL example from Neidle et al. (2000), and the Yimas example from Foley (1991). The Korean topicalization examples are from Park (1997). The yes/no question from Hindi was taken from Zeshan (2004b); the HKSL example is from Tang (2006), the Lele example from Frajzyngier (2001), the LIS examples are from Branchini et al. (2013), the Libras example from de Quadros (1999), and the IPSL examples from Zeshan (2003b) and Aboh, Pfau & Zeshan (2005). The LSF and LIS imperatives are described in Donati et al. (in press). In the section on negation and affirmation, examples were extracted from the following sources: Liddell (1980) and Neidle et al. (2000) on ASL; Pfau & Quer (2007) on DGS and LSC; Tang (2006) on HKSL; Schuit (2013) on IUR; Zeshan (2006b) on TİD, Antzakas (2006) on GSL; Geraci (2005) on LIS; and Hendriks (2004) on LIU. The example that illustrates topic-drop in ASL was found in Lillo-Martin (1986).

Chapter 7

Syntax: complex sentences

Roland Pfau

7.1   Introduction

The examples presented in Chapter 6 make clear *that* the construction of simple sentences in sign languages is subject to clear rules: constituents have different functions within a sentence *and* cannot be combined at random. Also, *in order to* change the type or the polarity of a sentence, one has to follow certain rules *that* can differ per sign language. It is characteristic for simple sentences *that* they only contain one lexical predicate. This predicate is combined with obligatory arguments *and* possibly with adjuncts. In contrast, complex sentences contain two (or more) lexical predicates *that* may have different relations with each other.

Please read the sentences from the first paragraph again. What do you see? – All these sentences are complex! And yet they clearly differ from each other. Often a complex sentence involves a combination of a main clause and a subordinate (embedded) clause. As the name suggests, a subordinate clause is subordinated to a main clause. We will discuss different types of subordinate clauses in Sections 7.2–7.4. We will see that some subordinate clauses, just like nominal arguments, are obligatory (Section 7.2) while others, just like adjuncts, are optional additions (Section 7.3). Furthermore, we need to distinguish between subordinate clauses that are embedded under a verb and subordinate clauses that modify a noun (Section 7.4). Lastly, a complex sentence can also consist of two main clauses. This type of combination, which is referred to as coordination, is the subject of Section 7.5.

Can you indicate to which type of complex sentence the sentences in the first paragraph belong? The elements in italics provide some clues. If you are insecure, try again after reading this chapter.

7.2   Complement clauses and direct speech

In Section 6.3, we saw that verbs in sign languages – just like in spoken languages – can have different valencies. A transitive verb like SEE in German Sign Language (DGS) requires two arguments: a subject and an object (1a). The sentence in (1b) is ungrammatical because one argument, the direct object, is missing. In the examples presented

DOI 10.1075/z.199.07pfa
© 2016 John Benjamins Publishing Company

so far, the arguments were nouns or nominal constituents. Depending on the verb, however, an embedded clause can also function as an argument; embedded clauses of this type are called **complement clauses**. In (1c), for instance, the clause MAN INDEX$_{3a}$ BOOK STEAL (which contains a subject, object and verb) has the same function as the noun ACCIDENT in (1a), that is, it occupies the direct object slot of the transitive verb SEE.

German Sign Language
>   (1)   a.   YESTERDAY INDEX$_1$ ACCIDENT SEE.
>   'Yesterday I saw an accident.'
>   b.   *WOMAN SEE.
>   'The woman sees.'
>   c.   INDEX$_1$ SEE [MAN INDEX$_{3a}$ BOOK STEAL].
>   'I see that the man steals a book.'

In Section 7.2.1, we will further explain the syntactic characteristics of complement clauses. In Section 7.2.2, we will briefly discuss a special type of complement clause: those that function as argument of speech act verbs. We will show that such structures in sign languages are often realized in an alternative way, in particular by means of role shift.

7.2.1   Complement clauses

The combination of a main clause and an embedded clause is called **subordination**. Besides SEE (1c), many verbs in DGS and other sign languages, such as WANT, KNOW, HOPE, and DOUBT can take sentential complements. Similar to Example (1c), the sentences in (2) and (3), from Turkish Sign Language (TİD) and Sign Language of the Netherlands (NGT), respectively, would be ungrammatical if the constituents between square brackets, the complement clauses, were left out.

Turkish Sign Language
>   (2)   MELEK [CHILD GOOD SCHOOL GO] WANT.
>   'Melek wants her child to go to a good school.'

Sign Language of the Netherlands
>   (3)   ANNE INDEX$_{3a}$ KNOW [COMPUTER INDEX$_{3b}$ BROKEN].
>   'Anne knows that the computer is broken.'

In many spoken languages, main clauses and complement clauses differ from each other in their syntactic structure. Firstly, complement clauses are often introduced by a special element, a **complementizer**. In English, for instance, the complementizer *that* is commonly used. Secondly, in some languages, complement clauses differ from main clauses in their **constituent order**. German is a good example: main clauses display SVO order (e.g. *Sie weiß die Antwort* 'She knows the answer'), whereas complement clauses are usually verb-final, i.e. they display SOV order (e.g. *Ich hoffe, dass sie die Antwort weiß* 'I hope that she knows the answer'). The same phenomenon is observed in Dutch, but not in English (as the above translations illustrate).

Returning to the examples in (1c), (2), and (3), we see that neither of these features applies to these examples. In fact, the available studies suggest that sign languages in general do not employ complementizers, and that the constituent order in the complement clause does not differ from the order in the main clause. Consequently, the clauses between square brackets in the above examples would constitute well-formed independent sentences in DGS, TİD, and NGT, respectively. Still, we have to assume that these constituents are embedded clauses because otherwise, we would not be able to explain why the sentences in (1c), (2) and (3) are ungrammatical without these constituents. A comparison of the examples in (4a) and (4b) with the NGT example in (4c) reveals that a similar phenomenon is attested in English and German.

English (a), German (b), and Sign Language of the Netherlands (c)
(4) a. I hope [he will visit me tomorrow].
     b. Ich hoffe, [er kommt mich morgen   besuchen].
         I   hope he comes me   tomorrow visit
         'I hope he will come visit me tomorrow.'
     c. INDEX$_1$ HOPE [TOMORROW INDEX$_{3a}$ $_{3a}$VISIT$_1$].
         'I hope that he will visit me tomorrow.'

In all three sentences, we observe that the subordinate clauses do not contain a conjunction, and, given the word order, the sentences between square brackets could all occur by themselves. And yet, these are all complement clauses required by the verb in the main clause (the **matrix predicate**).

Besides the constituent order within the complement clause, the order of the constituents in the whole sentence is also important. Assuming that the basic order in NGT is SOV (as was mentioned in Section 6.5.1), and that the complement clause functions as direct object, we would expect the complement clause to be placed between the subject and the verb. However, this is not the case, as is evident from Examples (3) and (4c); in both cases, the complement clause appears *after* the verb. In NGT, placement of the complement clause in the expected position between subject and verb would even lead to ungrammaticality; compare the grammatical utterance with a nominal object in (5a) with the ungrammatical one containing a complement clause in (5b).

Sign Language of the Netherlands
(5) a. ANNE INDEX$_{3a}$ ANSWER KNOW.
         'Anne knows the answer.'
     b. *ANNE INDEX$_{3a}$ [COMPUTER INDEX$_{3b}$ BROKEN] KNOW.
         'Anne knows that the computer is broken.'

The displacement of a complement clause to sentence-final position is called **extraposition**. Obligatory extraposition of complement clauses has been described for several sign languages that have a basic SOV order, such as DGS and Italian Sign Language (LIS), and also for many spoken languages. Interestingly, TİD, another sign language with SOV order, appears to behave differently in this respect. Note that in (2), the complement clause appears in the expected slot between the subject and the verb. In fact, the extraposed variant has been claimed to be ungrammatical in this sign language, as is shown in (6).

Turkish Sign Language
  (6) *MELEK WANT [CHILD GOOD SCHOOL GO].
       'Melek wants her child to go to a good school.'

7.2.2 Role shift and direct speech

A special group of verbs that can take sentences as arguments in many spoken languages are **speech act verbs**, such as *say*, *claim*, and *ask*. Such constructions are referred to as **indirect speech**. In Example (7a), for instance, the embedded clause indirectly reports an utterance of the speaker's father. But utterances can also be expressed directly by means of **direct speech**, as in (7b). An important difference between the two examples is that the personal pronoun *I* refers to different referents: in (7a), it refers to the speaker, while in (7b), it refers to the father.

English
  (7) a. My father said [that I must not be late].
       b. My father said: "I must not be late."

Comparable structures have also been described for sign languages. We will illustrate this with an example from Catalan Sign Language (LSC). In (8a), an utterance by Anna is reported by means of indirect speech. In this example, INDEX$_{3a}$ within the embedded clause refers to Anna. In LSC and other sign languages it is, however, very common to present the words (or even thoughts) of another person by means of direct speech. To realize this, signers make use of a construction known as **role shift** (sometimes also referred to as *role taking* or *perspective shift*). In Section 4.6.3, we already explained that role shift can serve two ends: the expression of direct speech (constructed dialogue) and the representation of the actions of a character (constructed action); in the following, however, we will only be concerned with the former. In order to quote Anna directly, the signer in (8b) moves his body slightly towards location 3a by means of a **body shift**, and breaks eye contact with the addressee. Often a signer will also adopt the facial expression of the person whose words he is rendering. In (8b), this would most probably involve a look of exasperation.

Catalan Sign Language

(8) a. ANNA $_{3a}$SAY$_1$ [INDEX$_{3a}$ BE-FED-UP LOSE++].

 'Anna told me that she was fed up with losing so often.'

<u>   bl-3a + facial expression Anna   </u>

 b. ANNA $_{3a}$SAY$_1$ [INDEX$_1$ BE-FED-UP LOSE++].

 'Anna told me: "I am fed up with losing so often."'

Normally speaking, the personal pronoun INDEX$_1$ always refers to the signer. However, in (8b), this is not the case: in this clause, INDEX$_1$ refers to Anna. Besides the set of non-manual markers, this shift in reference is the most important feature of role shift – similar to what we described for the English example (7b).

We have discussed role shift in the section on complement clauses because, in the context of speech act verbs, complement clauses and role shift (direct speech) are two ways to express the same information. Or maybe, we should rather say: more or less the same information, as it is possible for a signer to also present the emotions of a character during a role shift. Of course, the same can be achieved in spoken languages by means of intonation changes and facial expressions. One aspect of the grammar of role shift constructions, we have to leave open at this point: whether the part that is non-manually marked in (8b) is a main clause or an embedded clause. The construction differs from the examples that we discussed in Section 7.2.1 but, just as in Examples (2), (3), and (8a), the clause between square brackets in (8b) is required; without it, (8b) would be ungrammatical.

7.3 Adverbial clauses

Unlike complement clauses, **adverbial clauses** are optional, as they are not required by the matrix predicate. In other words: the omission of an adverbial clause never leads to an ungrammatical sentence. Adverbial clauses can further specify certain circumstances and details of an event – like time, location, cause, purpose, and conditions. In the subsections to follow, we will discuss three types of adverbial clauses: adverbial clauses that specify the time of an event (Section 7.3.1), adverbial clauses that add information about the cause or purpose of an event (Section 7.3.2), and conditional clauses (Section 7.3.3).

7.3.1 Temporal clauses

Temporal information about an event is often provided by means of an adverb (*tomorrow, now*), a nominal phrase (*last week*), or a prepositional phrase (*at three o'clock*). Occasionally, however, more complex constructions are used, that is, embedded clauses that contain a subject and a verb. Take a look at the complex English sentences in (9). In all three examples, the event expressed in the main clause and the event in the embedded clause are in a temporal relation with each other. In (9a), the event in the embedded clause (between square brackets) must take place before the event in the main clause (*packing* before *leaving*). In (9b), it is exactly the other way round (*cleaning* occurs before *returning*). Finally, in (9c), the events in the main and embedded clause (*preparing* and *waiting*) take place simultaneously. A characteristic of **temporal clauses** is that, in principle, they can be replaced by one word, for instance *today* or *later*. The same is true for embedded clauses that specify a location, but these will not be discussed further here.

English
(9)   a.   We will leave [when my sister has packed her bags].
      b.   [Before his mother returned] he had cleaned the place up.
      c.   The sushi is prepared [while you wait].

To date, strategies for expressing temporal clauses in sign languages have not been researched extensively. In the following, we discuss a few examples from different sign languages, but further research is required to find out what exactly the possibilities and restrictions are in different sign languages.

To indicate that the event in the embedded clause has happened before the event in the main clause (see (9a)), Flemish Sign Language (VGT) often uses an aspectual marker that we gloss here as DONE, which occupies the final position within the embedded clause (10a). Additionally, the embedded clause is **non-manually marked** by means of raised eyebrows ('re'). Between the embedded and the main clause, there is a brief pause (and often a head nod). Optionally, the main clause may include the manual sign THEN to further clarify the temporal relation between the two events. Whereas in English (9a), the main clause and the embedded clause can be interchanged in terms of order, the same is not possible in VGT. The embedded clause must always precede the main clause, and consequently, Example (10b) is ungrammatical.

Flemish Sign Language

(10) a. $\overline{\qquad\qquad\text{re}\qquad\qquad}$
           [INDEX₂ EAT DONE], (THEN) WE-TWO SHOP.
           'When you're done eating, we (the two of us) will go shopping.'

      b. $\overline{\qquad\qquad\qquad\text{re}\qquad}$
           *WE-TWO SHOP, [INDEX₂ EAT DONE].
           'We (the two of us) will go shopping, when you're done eating.'

When the event in the embedded clause takes place *after* the event in the main clause, as in the English example in (9b), the embedded clause also appears in sentence-initial position and is marked by raised eyebrows, as the examples from DGS in (11) show. In such constructions, DGS also uses the **temporal conjunction** BEFORE. Interestingly, the examples in (11) illustrate that BEFORE can either occur at the beginning of the main clause (11a) or at the end of the embedded clause (11b) – the meaning is the same.

German Sign Language

(11)   a.   <u>   re   </u>
           [INDEX$_3$ STUDY BEGIN], BEFORE INDEX$_3$ WORLD^TRIP GO.
           'Before he begins with his studies, he will go on a world trip.'

     b.   <u>   re   </u>
           [INDEX$_3$ STUDY BEGIN BEFORE], INDEX$_3$ WORLD^TRIP GO.
           'Before he begins with his studies, he will go on a world trip.'

In fact, the non-manual marker is often the only indicator that we are dealing with a combination of a main clause and an embedded clause. Without this marker, a string of signs like the one in (11a) would be interpreted as a sequence of two main clauses: *He begins (now) with his studies. Before that he went on a world trip.*

Lastly, temporal clauses in DGS that describe an event that occurs simultaneously with the event expressed in the main clause are also accompanied by raised eyebrows. The example in (12a) describes two short (punctual) events that occur (almost) simultaneously. In contrast to this, (12b) involves two simultaneous, durative events. In this case, the sign NOW may optionally be used in the embedded clause, and the predicate in the main clause may be accompanied by head nods ('aff').

German Sign Language

(12)   a.   <u>   re   </u>
           [PERSON RING], DOG ALWAYS BE-SCARED.
           'When someone rings [the bell], the dog is always scared.'

     b.   <u>   re   </u>   <u>   aff   </u>
           [INDEX$_2$ (NOW) WAIT], PICTURE DEVELOP.
           'The pictures are developed, while you wait.'

Sometimes is it not easy to determine which of the two clauses is the main clause and which the embedded clause, especially in constructions where the two events happen simultaneously. However, as the above examples illustrate, the temporal clause always appears sentence-initially and is accompanied by a non-manual marker (raised eyebrows). In addition, from a semantic point of view, the embedded clause specifies the time of the event expressed in the main clause. Thus, in (12b), the embedded clause provides temporal information concerning the development of pictures. Of course, one might as well say/sign 'You wait while the pictures are being developed', but then the emphasis would be on the waiting event, and the embedded clause would specify what is happening during the waiting. Please note that in all of these examples, the main clause would also be grammatical without the specifying temporal clause – contrary to the examples we discussed in Section 7.2. The sentence WE-TWO SHOP in (10a), for instance, is a complete and well-formed sentence. The same is true for the examples that we will discuss in the next subsections.

7.3.2 Causal and purpose clauses

As the name suggests, **causal clauses** specify a cause that brings about the event expressed in the main clause. In order to introduce a causal clause, some sign languages make use of a dedicated causal conjunction. In NGT, for instance, the sign BECAUSE is commonly used (13); see (14a) for an illustration of this sign. The resulting structure is very similar to the structure in English and many other spoken languages.

Sign Language of the Netherlands

(13)   INDEX$_1$ ANGRY [BECAUSE INDEX$_{3a}$ ALWAYS LATE COME].
       'I am angry, because s/he always comes late.'

(14)   a.   b.

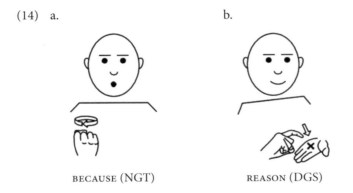

BECAUSE (NGT)   REASON (DGS)

In DGS, a comparable structure exists; however, in this sign language, the causal clause is introduced by the manual sign REASON, illustrated in (14b), which can also function as a noun (see Section 13.4.2 for further discussion). Just as in (13), the causal clause in (15a) specifies what causes the event (or rather the state: *being tired*) expressed in the main clause. In (15b), the same conjunction is used, but the interpretation is slightly different, as REASON now introduces a **purpose clause**. That is, the embedded clause specifies the goal of the action in the main clause (*work hard*; 'int' = facial expression indicating the intensity of an action). Note that the same ambiguity also characterizes the English conjunction *because*; however, in order to make the distinction clear, we use *in order to* in the English translation of (15b).

German Sign Language

(15) a. INDEX₁ TIRED [REASON NIGHT LITTLE SLEEP].
   'I am tired, because last night I got little sleep.'

   ```
               int
   ```
   b. INDEX₃ₐ WORK++ [REASON NEXT TIME EXAM SUCCESS].
   'He is working hard in order to be successful in his next exam.'

   c. NIGHT (INDEX₁) LITTLE SLEEP. (NOW) INDEX₁ TIRED.
   'Last night, I got little sleep. Now I am tired.'

It is noteworthy that causal and purpose clauses in NGT and DGS appear in sentence-final position, whereas temporal clauses always occur sentence-initially. In fact, in (15a, b), reversal of the main and embedded clause would lead to ungrammaticality. This is in contrast to many spoken languages where such a switch is allowed. Of course, the alternative construction in (15c) – without the sign REASON – is possible in DGS, but in this case, we are not dealing with subordination but rather with two main clauses (i.e. coordination; see Section 7.5). Note finally that causal/purpose clauses, unlike temporal clauses, cannot be replaced by a single word.

For many sign languages, another strategy to formulate causal clauses has been described. In the NGT sentence in (16), it seems as if the signer asks herself a question, which she then immediately answers: *Why is he sad? His cat died.* That is, the first part of (16) looks like a rhetorical question.

Sign Language of the Netherlands

```
                       re
```
(16) INDEX₃ₐ SAD WHY, INDEX₃ₐ CAT DIE.
   'He is sad because his cat died.'
   'Why he is sad, is (because) his cat died.'

However, there are crucial differences between the first part of (16) and true wh-questions (see Section 6.7.1). First, the non-manual marking is different. Whereas wh-questions are accompanied by furrowed eyebrows in NGT and most other sign languages, the eyebrows are raised in (16). Secondly, in a structure like (16), doubling of the wh-sign is impossible, while doubling is attested in true wh-questions in NGT. Based on these differences, which have first been described for American Sign Language (ASL), researchers have concluded that examples like (16) do not involve rhetorical wh-questions but should rather be analyzed as **wh-clefts** (see the alternative translation of the sentence). In Section 4.6, we already pointed out that wh-clefts (which actually may include a range of wh-signs) are commonly used to express focus.

7.3.3 Conditional clauses

Conditional clauses specify events, activities, or situations that form a condition for the events, activities, or situations expressed by the matrix predicate to take place. In other words, when the proposition in the embedded clause is not true, then the proposition in the main clause is also not true. For the English example in (17a), this implies: if it does not rain, then the garden set will also not get wet.

English

(17)   a.   If it rains, (then) our new garden furniture will get wet.
       b.   Our new garden furniture will get wet if it rains.

In most spoken languages, conditional clauses are introduced by means of a subordinating conjunction, like *if* in English or *falls* in German. Just as in many other spoken languages, the order of main clause and embedded clause is variable in English, as can be seen in (17b).

In the sign languages studied so far, conditional clauses display other characteristics. In ASL, for instance, there are **manual subordinating conjunctions** (e.g. the sign IF), but their use is optional. In fact, these manual markers are often omitted. What is more important for marking this type of embedded clause is a non-manual marker that accompanies the embedded clause (18a). For ASL, it has been established that this marker does not only involve raised eyebrows, but also a slight upward movement of the chin. Also, in striking contrast to English, ASL conditional clauses must always appear in sentence-initial position; (18b) is therefore ungrammatical.

American Sign Language

```
                  re & chin-up
       _____
```
(18)   a.   (IF) TOMORROW RAIN, REFUSE GO PICNIC.
         'If it rains tomorrow, I won't go on the picnic.'

```
                             re & chin-up
                  _____
```
      b.   *REFUSE GO PICNIC (IF) TOMORROW RAIN.
         'I won't go to the picnic, if it rains tomorrow.'

Similar patterns have been reported for other sign languages, such as DGS, NGT, and LIS. As in ASL, the conditional clause is accompanied by (at least) raised eybrows, the manual conjunction is optional, and the conditional clause always precedes the main clause.

Remember from the discussion in Section 7.3.1, that temporal clauses are also commonly marked by raised eyebrows. Consequently, in the absence of manual markers, combinations of clauses may sometimes be ambiguous, as is illustrated for ASL in (19), where the adverbial clause can receive a conditional or temporal reading. A similar ambiguity has also been described for some spoken languages, like Vai, a language spoken in Liberia, as is evident from the two possible translations of (20).

American Sign Language

<u>   re   </u>

(19) JOHN ARRIVE, CAN GO.

      'If John arrives, we can go.'

      'When John arrives, we can go.'

Vai

(20) Á   ànáèè   í-ì   à   féὲ-'à.

      he come.COND you-FUT him see-FUT

      'If he comes, you will see him.'

      'When he comes, you will see him.'

An important distinction that we have not addressed yet is the one between factual and counterfactual conditional clauses. The examples in (17)–(19) all contain a **factual conditional clause**. This means that it is possible, on the basis of our world knowledge, that the event expressed in the embedded clause will actually occur (and therefore also the event in the main clause). In other words: while we do not know for sure, it is possible that it will rain (tomorrow) and that John will arrive.

In contrast, **counterfactual conditional clauses** describe events that are hypothetical. Imagine a conditional clause like *If I were king …* – you may well fantasize about such a situation, but for most people, this will never come true. For Israeli Sign Language, it has been found that the non-manual markers accompanying factual conditional clauses are clearly different from those marking counterfactual conditionals. While the latter are predominantly marked by raised eyebrows (21a) – similar to what has been described for other sign languages –, the latter are marked additionally by a squint (21b).

Israeli Sign Language

               <u>   re   </u>

(21) a. IF INDEX$_3$ INVITE$_1$ BIRTHDAY^PARTY OF-HIM, INDEX$_1$ GO.

          'If he invites me to his birthday party, I will go.'

                     <u>   re & squint   </u>

      b. IF INDEX$_3$ STOP SMOKE, INDEX$_3$ LIVE.

          'If he had quit smoking, he would be alive.'

Taken together, this section has shown that various types of adverbial clauses in sign languages are usually non-manually marked. The most important non-manual marker appears to be raised eyebrows (in Chapter 6, we already saw that the same marker also plays an important role in yes/no questions and topicalization). As for clause order, we observed that most adverbial clauses appear sentence-initially. Causal and purpose clauses – at least in NGT and DGS – are exceptions, as they occupy a sentence-final position and are not accompanied by an obligatory non-manual marker.

7.4 Relative clauses

All types of embedded clauses discussed so far add information related to the matrix predicate, independent of the fact whether they are obligatory (complement clauses) or optional (adverbial clauses). Relative clauses are different, because they further specify nouns. Two types of relative clauses have to be distinguished: restrictive and non-restrictive (appositive) relative clauses. As the name implies, the first type restricts, as it were, the choice from a group of persons or objects. In (22a), for instance, the relative clause restricts the reference to one specific movie from a set of movies (for example, all movies that the signer and the addressee could have seen yesterday in the cinema or on TV).

English
(22) a. The movie [that we saw yesterday] was very disappointing.
      b. The Eiffel Tower, [which is located in Paris], was built in 1889.

(21b) is clearly different. Even though the relative clause adds information, this information does not result in the specification of one member from a group of objects. After all, there is only one Eiffel Tower (neglecting existing imitations in Las Vegas and Tokyo). Consequently, relative clauses of this type are called non-restrictive relative clauses. In English, the two types can be distinguished by intonation: in a sentence like (21b), there is a clear intonational break before the relative clause (represented here by the comma). In the following, we will mainly be concerned with restrictive relative clauses. Only at the end of the section, the two types will be briefly compared.

We will illustrate the structure of **restrictive relative clauses** in sign languages, as well as the attested typological variation, by means of examples from LIS and DGS. In Chapter 6, we already saw that these two sign languages share a number of syntactic properties; for instance, they are both SOV languages. It is therefore interesting to see that, despite this structural overlap, they realize relative clauses in strikingly different ways.

The noun that is modified by the relative clause (e.g. the noun *movie* in (22a)) is called the **nominal head**. In the following examples, the nominal head is printed in bold. The nominal head can have different grammatical functions in the main and relative clause. In the LIS sentence in (23a), something is said about a man who danced the day before. In this case, the nominal head MAN is subject in both the main clause (subject of *dance*) and the relative clause (subject of *bring*). In (23b), the relative clause adds information about the dog. Unlike (23a), in this example, the nominal head DOG functions as object in the main clause (object of *wash*) and in the relative clause (object of *find*). The two other possible combinations (subject of the main clause, but object of the relative clause, or object of the main clause but subject of the relative clause) are also attested, but will not be considered here.

Italian Sign Language

re

(23)   a.   [TODAY MAN$_{3a}$ PIE BRING PE$_{3a}$] YESTERDAY (IX$_{3a}$) DANCE.
'The man who brought the pie today danced yesterday.'

re

      b.   [YESTERDAY DOG$_{3a}$ FIND PE$_{3a}$] WOMAN IX$_{3b}$ (IX$_{3a}$) WASH.
'The woman washes the dog that I found yesterday.'

The relative clauses in (23) are indicated by square brackets. What is immediately clear is that in both examples, the head appears between square brackets, that is, within the relative clause. If this is the case, we speak of a **head-internal relative clause**. Two characteristics of the examples in (23) provide evidence for this analysis. Firstly, the position and interpretation of the temporal adverbs is informative. Notice that TODAY in (23a) and YESTERDAY in (23b) modify the predicates within the relative clauses (BRING and FIND). The adverbs are thus certainly part of the relative clause, and yet they precede the nominal heads (MAN and DOG). Given this order, it is clear that the nominal heads must also be inside the relative clause. Secondly, the non-manual marker provides important evidence. Relative clauses in LIS are accompanied by raised eyebrows. The glosses make clear that the non-manual marker extends over the nominal head and the adverb. In other words, both are under the **scope of the non-manual marker**, and this signals that they belong to the relative clause. Also note that LIS relative clauses include a manual marker, the sign PE, which appears in clause-final position and refers to the nominal head. This sign, which can be localized in space, is glossed as PE because it involves the oral component /pə/ (see Section 11.6 for further discussion); it is signed with a ◌-hand which performs one quick downward movement, such that the orientation of the fingertip changes from left to downward.

Crucially, the sentences between square brackets in (23) cannot occur by themselves. Of course, it is possible to sign TODAY MAN PIE BRING, but this sentence neither involves the element PE nor the non-manual marker. For that reason, the examples in (23) cannot be analyzed as combinations of two main clauses (for instance, *Today the man brought a pie. Yesterday he danced.*)

Let us now turn to DGS. The examples in (24) show that DGS is clearly different from LIS when it comes to the realization of relative clauses. First, the sentence-initial temporal adverb in (24a) modifies the matrix predicate (*dance*) and not the predicate of the relative clause (*bring*). In order to modify the predicate of the relative clause, an adverb needs to be placed after the nominal head in DGS (such as TODAY in (24a)). This is a first indication that we are dealing with a **head-external relative clause**: the nominal heads MAN (24a) and DOG (24b) are outside the relative clause. And, if the head is outside the relative clause, then an adverb preceding it can of course not be within the relative clause. Secondly – and also in contrast to LIS – the nominal head in both examples does not fall under the scope of the non-manual marker. DGS also makes use of raised eybrowas, but in addition, one often observes a body lean towards the location associated with the nominal head (indicated by 'bl-3a' in the gloss). Thirdly, relative clauses in DGS are introduced by a **relative pronoun**, glossed as RPRO in the examples. This pronoun marks the beginning of the relative clause.

German Sign Language

$$\overline{\text{re \& bl-3a}}$$

(24)   a.   YESTERDAY MAN (IX_{3a}) [RPRO-H$_{3a}$ TODAY PIE BRING] DANCE.
            'The man who brought the pie today danced yesterday.'

$$\overline{\text{re \& bl-3a}}$$

      b.   WOMAN DOG [RPRO-NH$_{3a}$ IX$_1$ YESTERDAY FIND] WASH$_{3a}$.
            'The woman washes the dog that I found yesterday.'

In fact, DGS uses two relative pronouns. When the pronoun refers to a human entity (RPRO-H), it is signed with the classifier handshape for human beings (25a); when it refers to a non-human entity or an object (RPRO-NH), then it has the form of a pointing sign (25b).

German Sign Language

(25)   a.   b.

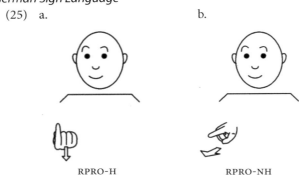

RPRO-H   RPRO-NH

Whilst the nominal head MAN in (24a) can optionally be localized in the signing space by an INDEX, this is hardly ever observed with non-human entities. If DOG in (24b) was localized, then two pointing signs would be articulated one after the other, and this would be considered redundant. It is therefore common to associate a non-human nominal head with a location by means of the relative pronoun. In this way, DOG in (24b) gets associated with location 3a, and the matrix predicate WASH is articulated at the same location.

Relative clauses are a popular subject in linguistic typology. Interestingly, the differences between LIS and DGS that we have just described reflect the most common typological patterns found for relative clauses in spoken languages: head-internal and head-external relative clauses. Compare the example from the North American language Navajo in (26a) with the LIS examples in (23). As in LIS, the sentence-initial temporal adverb *tl'eedaa'* 'last night' refers to the predicate of the relative clause; the nominal head *hastiin* 'man' is thus definitely within the relative clause. Navajo also uses an element that marks the embedded clause as a relative clause. Just like PE in LIS, this element (the suffix *-ee*) appears in final position within the relative clause.

Navajo (a) and German (b)
(26) a. [Tl'eedaa' **hastiin** yałti'-ee] ałhosh.
         last.night man spoke-REL sleep
         'The man who spoke last night is sleeping.'
     b. **Die**   **Frau**   [die   lächelt] ist meine Kolleg-in.
         the.FEM woman RPRO.FEM smiles is my   colleague-FEM
         'The woman who is smiling is my colleague.'

Spoken language structures that that are comparable to the DGS examples in (24) are easy to find. English (22a) and German (26b) feature head-external relative clauses that are introduced by a relative pronoun. In German, this pronoun agrees in gender with the nominal head (in (26b) with the feminine gender of *Frau* 'woman').

     Before concluding this section, let us briefly return to the second type of relative clauses we mentioned at the outset: non-restrictive relative clauses. This type has received considerably less attention in the sign language literature, but it seems as if it is realized in quite a different way – at least in DGS. A sentence like *In 1889, the Eiffel Tower, which is located in Paris, was built* would be signed in DGS as shown in (27). The structure of (27) clearly differs from the DGS examples in (24). First, the clause between square brackets is not introduced by a relative pronoun. Second, the non-manual markers are also different. In (27), we observe a combination of pursed lips ('pl') and a repeated head nod ('hn').

German Sign Language
                                                             <u>pl & hn</u>
(27) 1889, EIFFEL TOWER [INDEX$_2$ KNOW PARIS INDEX$_{3a}$] BUILD.
        'In 1889, the Eiffel Tower – you know, the one in Paris – was built.'

It is as yet unknown whether non-restrictive relative clauses in DGS are always realized in such a manner. In fact, it is quite likely that we are not dealing with an embedded clause in (27), but rather with a so-called **parenthetical structure**. It seems as if the signer wants to make sure that the addressee knows what he is talking about. Given these functional and formal differences, we chose to provide a translation for the sentence in (27) that does not contain a relative clause.

7.5   Coordination

So far, we have focused on different types of subordination or embedding, that is, combinations of a main clause and an embedded clause. However, complex sentences may also consist of two (or more) main clauses. In this case, we speak of **coordination** of sentences. In English, the conjunctions *and*, *or*, and *but* are commonly used to link two main clauses. It is characteristic of coordination that the sentences that are combined (the conjuncts) can also occur independently and that their order (usually) can be changed without a change in meaning.

7.5.1   Types of coordination

The two characteristics of coordination just mentioned can be illustrated by the examples in (28) from Australian Sign Language (Auslan). The two sentences, which are linked by the **manual conjunction** BUT, could well stand alone as main clauses. Moreover, changing the order of the clauses does not have an influence on the meaning (28b). This type of coordination is referred to as **adversative coordination**.

Australian Sign Language
>   (28)   a.   k-i-m LIKE CAT BUT p-a-t PREFER DOG.
>   'Kim likes cats, but Pat prefers dogs.'
>   b.   p-a-t PREFER DOG BUT k-i-m LIKE CAT.
>   'Pat prefers dogs, but Kim likes cats.'

Many sign languages appear to have a manual conjunction BUT; still, at least in some sign languages, adversative coordination may sometimes be marked by non-manual signals only, as is shown in the Hong Kong Sign Language example in (29). Both conjuncts are accompanied by head nods, but the former is marked by a slight forward body lean while the latter is marked by a backward lean.

Hong Kong Sign Language

	hn + bl forward		hn + bl backward

>   (29)   RUTH DILIGENT DO-HOMEWORK, HANNAH LAZY WATCH-TV.
>   'Ruth is diligently doing her homework (but) Hannah is lazy and watches TV.'

In (29), just as in (28), the order of conjuncts could be reversed without affecting the meaning. Sometimes, however, the predicates in sentences connected by *but*/BUT are in a clear semantic relation to each other, and in that case, the order of the two conjuncts cannot always be changed. This constraint applies to the DGS example in (30). Here the order of conjuncts implies that Roland will not learn Spanish. If the two sentences are reversed (*Roland never has time, but he would like to learn Spanish*), this implication disappears.

German Sign Language

<pre>   _____neg</pre>
(30)   ROLAND SPANISH LEARN WANT BUT IX$_{3a}$ NEVER TIME.
       'Roland would like to learn Spanish, but he never has the time.'

A second type of coordination is **conjunctive coordination** (realized in English by *and*). In order to mark this type, some sign languages may employ a manual conjunction glossed as PLUS. For at least some of them, however, the use of this sign is considered to be an influence of the surrounding spoken language (see Section 13.5). Across sign languages, it seems to be more common to mark conjunctive coordination by means of non-manual markers, in particular a body movement or **body lean**. The NGT sentence in (31) could be uttered in a context where mother and son are walking together and at a certain point are saying goodbye. While signing the first sentence, the signer's body tilts slightly towards location 3a, and while signing the second sentence towards location 3b. Of course, these two sentences can also be signed without the body lean, but then they are not coordinated. In any case, the order in which the sentences are signed does not matter. (Please note: in (31) we use the subscripts '3a/3b' and 'right/left' because on both sides of the signing space, two locations are used: to the right for MOTHER and FRIEND, to the left for MARKET and SON.)

Sign Language of the Netherlands

<pre>   _____bl-3a   _____bl-3b</pre>
(31)   MOTHER IX$_{3a}$ MARKET IX$_{left}$ GO$_{left}$, SON IX$_{3b}$ FRIEND IX$_{right}$ $_{3b}$VISIT$_{right}$.
       'The mother goes to the market (and) her son visits a friend.'

The third and final type of coordination is **disjunctive coordination** (cf. English *or*). In order to express this type of coordination, in British Sign Language (BSL), the manual sign OR can be used (32a). Once again, the order of the two clauses is not fixed. ASL has a conjunction that is glossed as COORD-L and which precedes both conjuncts, as can be seen in (32b). This sign is two-handed: the non-dominant hand has a 🤚-handshape (hence the gloss), and the dominant 👆-hand first touches the thumb (COORD-L$_1$) and then the index finger (COORD-L$_2$) of the non-dominant hand. Interestingly, this sign can be used for conjunctive and disjunctive coordination, as indicated by the two translations given for (32b). The context will have to disambiguate between the two interpretations (for instance, if the sentence is followed by DON'T-KNOW WHICH, then the meaning is disjunctive).

British Sign Language (a) and American Sign Language (b)

<pre>   _____y/n</pre>
(32)   a.   DEAF CLUB HAVE CONTINUE OR THINK DEAF CLUB DIE?
            'Do you think deaf clubs have a future or do you think deaf clubs will die?'

(32)   b.   COORD-L$_1$ [POSS$_{3a}$ PARENTS WILL BUY POSS$_{3a}$ CAR]
COORD-L$_2$ [INDEX$_{3a}$ WILL TRAVEL].
'Her parents will buy her car or she will travel.'
'Her parents will buy her car, and (then) she will travel.'

7.5.2   Ellipsis

At the beginning of our discussion on coordination, we pointed out that it is a hall-mark of coordination that the main clauses that are combined could also occur by themselves. For all of the examples discussed in the previous section, this holds true. However, we now have to qualify this generalization, as it is not always the case that two full sentences are combined in a coordinate structure. Frequently, elements that occur in both conjuncts can be left out. The omission of words (or phrases) in coordinated structures is called **ellipsis**. Consider the ASL example in (33a). The second sentence actually consists of four clauses; yet, there is only one verb, the verb BRING. Since all four clauses involve the same verb, it is redundant to repeat it four times. Therefore, the verb is deleted in the second, third, and fourth conjunct – just as in the English translation (verb ellipsis is also called 'gapping'). In (33b), we illustrate the underlying process of deletion by means of strikethrough. (33a) also shows that it is common in ASL to mark the object of the deleted verb by a head nod.

American Sign Language
(33)   a.   HAVE WONDERFUL PICNIC. INDEX$_1$ BRING SALAD,
<u>   hn   hn   hn   </u>
JOHN BEER, SANDY CHICKEN, TED HAMBURGER.
'We had a wonderful picnic. I brought the salad, John beer, Sandy chicken, and Ted hamburgers.'
b.   INDEX$_1$ BRING SALAD, JOHN ~~BRING~~ BEER, SANDY ~~BRING~~
CHICKEN, TED ~~BRING~~ HAMBURGER.

For LIS, a different type of ellipsis has been described: ellipsis of the entire verb phrase (VP-ellipsis). In this case, the elliptic clause includes the manual sign SAME, which basically functions as a place holder for the elided material, as shown in (34). Note that the tense auxiliary FUTURE may optionally be present in the second conjunct. SAME thus fulfils a function comparable to English *too*.

Italian Sign Language
(34)   GIANNI BEAN EAT FUTURE, PIERO (FUTURE) SAME.
'Gianni will eat beans, and Piero (will), too.'

Some researchers consider the **coordination of nouns** an extreme case of ellipsis. In the DGS examples in (35a), the transitive verb LIKE takes two coordinated nouns as direct objects: BREAD OLD and APPLE. It could be argued that this sentence is in fact a reduced version of 'My rabbit likes old bread and my rabbit likes apples'. As before, the material that is shared by the two conjuncts – in this case, the subject and the verb – is omitted. In (35a), the two objects are juxtaposed without any manual marker. However, in such a coordination of two nouns, the element BOTH is often added in DGS. As can be seen in (35b), this element follows the nouns, and it functions in a way similar to the English conjunction *and*.

German Sign Language

(35) a. RABBIT POSS₁ BREAD OLD APPLE LIKE.
   'My rabbit likes old bread and apples.'

   b. RABBIT POSS₁ BREAD OLD APPLE BOTH LIKE.
   'My rabbit likes old bread and apples.'

   c. RABBIT POSS₁ BREAD OLD LIKE APPLE LIKE .
   'My rabbit likes old bread and likes apples.'

Finally, it is also possible in DGS in such situations to realize the verb twice. As a consequence, in (35c), only the subject is deleted in the second conjunct. Further research is necessary to clarify whether specific non-manual markers, such as body leans, are required in elliptic constructions such as those in (35).

7.5.3 Differences between subordination and coordination

As we already mentioned above, it is not always easy in sign languages to distinguish main clauses from embedded clauses. Embedded clauses often neither contain a manual marker of subordination, such as a conjunction, nor do they show a change in word order (cf. English *I think you will like his new book*). For the same reason, it is sometimes difficult to determine whether a complex sentence involves subordination or coordination. Let us illustrate this challenge by means of the ASL examples in (36). In terms of their structure, the two examples look alike: both are combinations of two clauses and thus include two predicates (remember: ASL is an SVO language). However, there is no clear indication as to the nature of the relation between the two clauses. Given that ASL is a pro-drop language (see Section 6.9), it might well be the case that the translation of (36a) is misleading and that it should rather be 'I forced the man and he gave the boy his book'. In other words: perhaps we are dealing in (36a), just as in (36b), with coordination and not with subordination.

American Sign Language

(36) a. (INDEX₁) ₁FORCE₃ₐ MAN ₃ₐGIVE₃ᵦ BOY POSS₃ᵦ BOOK.
   'I forced the man to give the boy his book.'

   b. HOUSE EXPLODE, CAR TURN-OVER.
   'The house exploded and the car turned over.'

A number of tests have been proposed to distinguish coordinated from subordinated structures in ASL. One of these tests is the **pronoun copy test**. Remember from Section 6.9 that it is possible in ASL, as in several other sign languages, to repeat the subject at the end of the sentence in the form of an INDEX, as is shown for a non-complex ASL sentence in (37a). In (37b), we repeat the complex sentence from (36a), but this time with the subject pronoun copy INDEX$_1$ in sentence-final position; this sentence is grammatical in ASL. In contrast, in (37c), pronoun copy of INDEX$_{3a}$, the subject of the first clause, leads to ungrammaticality.

American Sign Language
  (37) a.   FATHER INDEX$_{3a}$ BUY CAR **INDEX$_{3a}$**.
             'My father buys a car.'
        b.   (INDEX$_1$) $_1$FORCE$_{3a}$ MAN [$_{3a}$GIVE$_{3b}$ BOY POSS$_{3b}$ BOOK] **INDEX$_1$**.
             'I forced the man to give the boy his book.'
        c.   *INDEX$_{3a}$ SIT$_{3a}$, [INDEX$_{3b}$ STAND$_{3b}$], **INDEX$_{3a}$**.
             'He sat here and she was standing over there.'

The difference between (37b) and (37c) suggests that the clauses between square brackets have different grammatical status: the status of embedded clause in (37b) and the status of main clause in (37c) – that is, we are dealing with subordination in the first but with coordination in the latter example. On the basis of this distinction, the following generalization has been formulated: a pronominal copy of a subject S must always occur at the end of the sentence of which S is the subject. This may sound complicated, but it is actually rather simple. Let us consider the two sentences again. The sentence (37b) contains an embedded clause, but the subject of the complex sentence is INDEX$_1$. Thus, in this case, the copy of INDEX$_1$ occurs at the end of the sentence of which INDEX$_1$ is the subject. In (37c), however, we are dealing with coordination of two main clauses. The second main clause (between square brackets) has its own subject INDEX$_{3b}$. Consequently, in this example, the copy of INDEX$_{3a}$ does not occupy the final position of the sentence of which INDEX$_{3a}$ is the subject; rather it appears at the end of the sentence of which INDEX$_{3b}$ is the subject. Thus the sentence is ungrammatical. (Note that (37b) would be grammatical if the copy of INDEX$_{3a}$ were placed directly after the first verb SIT.) In this way, the pronoun copy test can be used to distinguish between subordinated and coordinated sentences: a sentence-final pronoun copy is only possible in sentences involving subordination. While this test turned out to be a convenient tool for ASL, it unfortunately does not seem to work in the same way in all sign languages. For NGT, for instance, it has been shown that a pronoun copy referring to the subject of the main clause cannot follow an embedded clause.

Summary

Two types of complex sentences have to be distinguished: **subordination** involves a combination of a main clause and an embedded clause, whereas in **coordination**, two main clauses are combined. In spoken languages, embedded clauses are commonly marked by means of a **conjunction** and/or a change in **constituent order**. Across sign languages, however, such clues appear to be fairly rare, and it is therefore sometimes difficult to decide whether a clause is a main clause or an embedded clause. **Complement clauses** are embedded clauses that are required on the basis of the valency of the **matrix predicate**; such embedded clauses thus function as arguments, and they may be introduced by a **complementizer**. Sometimes, in an SOV language, a complement clause does not appear in the position that a nominal object would occupy, but rather follows the verb; this is called **extraposition** of the embedded clause. If the matrix predicate is a speech act verb, signers can use **indirect speech** or **direct speech**. For conveying direct speech, they will likely use **role shift**, which is flagged by specific non-manual markers (e.g. **body shift**).

In contrast to complement clauses, **adverbial clauses** are not required by the matrix predicate, i.e. they are optional. In **temporal clauses**, the events expressed in the main and the embedded clause are in a temporal relation to each other: the event in the embedded clause can occur before, after, or simultaneously with the event in the main clause. Such embedded clauses are **non-manually marked** (eyebrows up) and sometimes feature a **temporal conjunction**. **Causal clauses** that specify a cause/reason and **purpose clauses** that specify a purpose/goal are also optional additions. They are often introduced by a manual conjunction, but they can also be realized in the form of a **wh-cleft**. In the sign languages investigated to date, **conditional clauses** always appear in sentence-initial position. While the use of a **manual subordinating conjunction** is optional, non-manual marking appears to be obligatory. By means of specific non-manual markers, a sign language may even distinguish between **factual** and **counterfactual conditionals**.

Relative clauses differ from both complement clauses and adverbial clauses because they modify nouns rather than verbs. From a semantic point of view, two different types exist: **restrictive** and **non-restrictive relative clauses**. In addition, depending on the position of the **nominal head** of the construction, **head-internal** and **head-external relative clauses** have to be distinguished. The two types differ amongst other things in the **scope of the non-manual marker** and the use of a **relative pronoun**. It appears that non-restrictive relative clauses tend to be realized in a structurally different way, namely by means of a **parenthetical structure**.

Coordination, the combination of two main clauses, comes in three different types: **adversative**, **conjunctive**, and **disjunctive coordination**. In all three types, the relationship between the clauses can be expressed by **manual conjunctions** and/or by means of non-manual markers, most importantly a **body lean**. In coordinated structures, it is common to omit elements that occur in both conjuncts; this phenomenon is called **ellipsis**. A special case of coordination is the **coordination of nouns**. Sometimes it is difficult to determine whether a complex sentence involves subordination or coordination. For ASL, a couple of tests have been proposed that allow for distinguishing between the two types of structures, one of these being the **pronoun copy test**.

Test yourself

1. Why is it sometimes difficult in a sign language to determine whether a sentence is an embedded clause or a main clause? What are possible clues?
2. What is the difference between factual and counterfactual conditional clauses? Illustrate your answer with examples from your own spoken language. How are they produced in sign languages?
3. What are the main differences between indirect and direct speech in sign language? Consider in your answer the indirect or direct representation of an utterance like "I don't feel well".
4. Please explain the semantic difference between a restrictive and a non-restrictive relative clause by providing examples from a spoken language. How can this difference be made clear in sign languages?

Assignments

1. Create two different types of complex sentences using the following DGS constituents:

    [TODAY], [LAST NIGHT], [POSS₁ FRIEND INDEX₃], [RESTAURANT WORK], [TIRED]

    You can – depending on the type of embedded clause – add grammatical elements (like a conjunction or a relative pronoun). Do not forget to indicate the non-manual markers.
2. The NGT sentence below is ungrammatical. Can you explain why? How should the sentence be constructed in order for it to be grammatical?

    *i-n-g-e INDEX₃ₐ POSS₁ BROTHER HOUSE WITH GARDEN BUY WANT.
    'Inge wishes that my brother buys a house with a garden.'
3. The following sentence exemplifies an ASL construction that includes a relative clause. Which type of relative clause is this? Please provide arguments for your answer.

    $$\overline{\phantom{\text{RECENTLY DOG CHASE CAT COME}}\ \ \text{re}}$$
    RECENTLY DOG CHASE CAT COME HOME.
    'The dog which recently chased the cat came home.'
4. Is the DGS construction below a combination of a main clause with an embedded clause, or a combination of two main clauses? Provide arguments and also describe the structure of the two sentences that are combined.

    $$\overline{\phantom{\text{INDEX₂ ALWAYS ON-TIME COME BUT POSS₂}}\ \ \text{hs}}$$
    INDEX₂ ALWAYS ON-TIME COME BUT POSS₂ BROTHER NEVER.
    'You always come on time, but your brother never.'

5. Please consider the two complex ASL sentences in (a) and (b). One of the sentences is ungrammatical. Which one? Motivate your answer.

    a. INDEX$_{3a}$ SLAP$_{3b}$ s-u-s-a-n, INDEX$_{3b}$ TELL MOTHER, INDEX$_{3a}$.
        'He slapped Susan and she told her mother.'

    b. YESTERDAY INDEX$_1$ DECIDE CHRISTMAS $_1$VISIT$_{3a}$ BROTHER INDEX$_1$
        'Yesterday I decided to visit my brother at Christmas.'

References and further reading

Properties of coordination and subordination in various sign languages are reviewed in Tang & Lau (2012); Pfau & Steinbach (2016) sketch how the study of subordination relates to issues in modality, typology, and discourse structure. Complement clauses in sign languages have been described for ASL by Liddell (1980) and Padden (1988), for NGT by Van Gijn (2004), for LIS by Geraci & Aristodemo (2016), and for TİD by Göksel & Kelepir (2016). The early study by Liddell (1980) is a reaction to Thompson (1977), who claimed that embedded clauses do not exist in ASL. Role shift in the context of direct speech has been studied by Engberg-Pedersen (1995), Lillo-Martin (1995), and Herrmann & Steinbach (2012); for a recent overview, see Lillo-Martin (2012). With regard to adverbial clauses, most studies focus on conditional clauses; see Coulter (1979) and Liddell (1986) for ASL and Dachkovksy (2008) for ISL. Wilbur (2016) provides a more general discussion of (the position of) adverbial clauses in ASL. The function and structure of wh-clefts in ASL is addressed in Wilbur (1996); as for the status of these constructions, Caponigro & Davidson (2011) offer an alternative account. Noonan (1985) and Thompson & Longacre (1985) are detailed typological studies on complement clauses and adverbial clauses, respectively, in spoken languages. Relative clauses have so far been described for ASL (Liddell 1978, 1980), LIS (Cecchetto et al. 2006; Branchini & Donati 2009), DGS (Pfau & Steinbach 2005), and TİD (Kubus 2014). Keenan (1985) offers a comprehensive survey of the typology of relative clauses in spoken languages. Only few studies have addressed the coordination of main clauses in sign languages. Waters & Sutton-Spence (2005) describe various possibilities to combine main clauses in BSL, and Davidson (2013) looks at conjunctive and disjunctive coordination in ASL. Cecchetto et al. (2015) and Jantunen (2013) describe characteristics of ellipsis in LIS and FinSL, respectively. Padden (1988) proposes a number of criteria to distinguish subordination from coordination in ASL.

Properties of complement clauses are exemplified by NGT examples from Van Gijn (2004) and TİD examples from Göksel & Kelepir (2016). The LSC examples illustrating differences between direct and indirect speech are from Quer (2005). Some of the DGS examples involving temporal adverbial clauses are from Happ & Vorköper (2006). The conditional clauses from ASL and ISL are taken from Coulter (1979) and Dachkovsky (2008), respectively; the Vai example is from Thompson & Longacre (1985). In the section on relative clauses, we use LIS examples from

Branchini & Donati (2009) and DGS examples from Pfau & Steinbach (2005). The Navajo example was found in Keenan (1985). Different types of coordination are illustrated by examples from Auslan (Johnston & Schembri 2007), HKSL (Tang & Lau 2012), BSL (Waters & Sutton-Spence 2005), and ASL (Davidson 2013). Examples involving ellipsis are from Liddell (1980 – ASL) and Cecchetto et al. (2015 – LIS). The ASL examples illustrating the pronoun copy test are taken from Padden (1988).

Chapter 8

Lexicon

Trude Schermer

8.1　Introduction

Throughout this book, when we refer to a sign, we use a gloss. For instance, when we talk about the signs for 'to walk' or 'to be used to', we use the glosses WALK and BE-USED-TO. These glosses do not provide information about the phonological form of a sign, as a transcription would do (see Section 1.7). The gloss is not (always) a strict translation of the sign, but is meant to reflect its meaning. The British Sign Language (BSL) sign glossed as JAW-DROP, for instance, could also be translated as 'surprise'. Hence, the gloss for that sign could also be SURPRISE. This illustrates that a gloss offers a possible translation. In concrete cases like CAT and CHAIR, the relation between the gloss and the translation is clear, but for many glosses, relations to various words are possible. Glosses are a convenient way to write down the meaning of a sign, but they do use another language to represent the sign and are thus often approximations to the actual meaning of the sign. The use of glosses is due to the fact that sign languages do not have a common written form. There are different notation systems (see also Sections 1.7 and 10.5), but these are highly complex and are therefore not suitable for the average sign language user. A related disadvantage of the use of glosses is that a gloss does not always do justice to the meaning of the sign. The Sign Language of the Netherlands (NGT) sign with the meaning 'I understand/I get it' is sometimes glossed as UNDERSTAND/GET-IT but also sometimes as VAN. This latter gloss is based on a Dutch mouthing that usually accompanies the sign, the Dutch word 'van'. The gloss VAN, however, does not provide an accessible indication of the sign's meaning.

In order to describe the lexicon of a sign language, it must be clear what can be considered a sign and what not; this aspect is discussed in Section 8.2. Subsequently, in Section 8.3, we address the relation between the form of signs and their meaning and go deeper into the – in comparison to spoken languages – high degree of iconicity attested in the lexicons of sign languages. In Section 8.4, we make a distinction between the 'frozen' lexicon' and the 'productive' lexicon. The latter can be considered as an inventory of phonological building blocks (handshapes, movements, etc. – see Chapter 11) from which the language user can make a selection to form new signs that

DOI 10.1075/z.199.08sch
© 2016 John Benjamins Publishing Company

do not (yet) belong to the 'frozen' lexicon. Sign language dictionaries are discussed in Section 8.5, in particular the differences between dictionaries for spoken languages and for sign languages. In Section 8.6, we will examine the meanings of signs and the relationships between these meanings. Finally, in Section 8.7, the use of metaphors and idioms in sign languages will be addressed.

8.2 What can be a sign?

In Section 1.4, we already mentioned that there is a difference between signs and gestures. Not all behavior that can be perceived visually can be called a sign and be part of the lexicon of a sign language, as becomes clear from the examples in (1).

(1) a. *Pantomime*   b. *Thai Sign Language*   c. *French Sign Language*

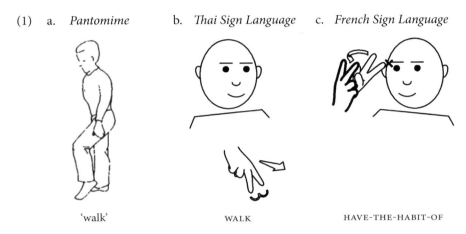

      'walk'   WALK   HAVE-THE-HABIT-OF

The drawing in (1a) depicts a man who is walking to express the meaning 'walk'. This movement of the whole body (or at least the legs) is pantomime and could not be a sign in any sign language. In order for a movement to classify as a sign, and not as pantomime, certain conditions must be met. One important condition is that a sign is made with the hand(s), sometimes in combination with a non-manual component (as already discussed in Section 1.2). The manual part of the sign minimally consists of a handshape, a location, an orientation (of palm and fingers), and a movement. The forms depicted in (1b) and (1c) meet this condition, while the form illustrated in (1a) does not. The sign in (1b) is from Thai Sign Language (ThaiSL) and means 'to walk', but the same form (or at least a very similar one) is used in many sign languages for the same concept. In (1c), we see a sign from French Sign Language (LSF), which means 'to have the habit of'. Both signs are composed of a clear handshape, location, and movement.

A second condition that must be met in order to be able to call a manual form a sign is that it must have a clearly described meaning. This is particularly true for lexical (content) signs, such as the ones in (1b,c), but there are also many function signs that have a clear meaning, such as conjunctions or the general question sign in Indopakistani Sign Language (see Chapter 5). The meaning of a sign is **conventional**; this means that sign language users have come to an agreement about the meaning of the sign.

8.3   Form and meaning: iconicity

Words have a form and a meaning. Generally, the relation between these two components is **arbitrary**. There is, for instance, nothing about the word *chair* that would reflect (part of) the meaning of the object it refers to; the word is arbitrarily chosen to represent the object – and this is why the the same object is referred to as *Stuhl* in German and as *sandalye* in Turkish. However, there are some exceptions in spoken languages. For example, the names of some birds are based on the sounds that they make, like *cuckoo*. Similarly, the 's' of *snake* could be argued to refer to the sound of a snake. Verbs referring to animal noises commonly imitate the sound of the action, and this is why a cat *meows*. Other examples are English words like *buzz* and *slither*: in both, we observe a relation between the phonological form of the verb and the actual sound of the action the verb refers to: the 'zz' in *buzz*, for instance, imitates the sound of a buzzer or a bee, while the 'sl' in *slither* refers to the noise such a movement makes. The words *sneeze*, *snort*, and *sniff* begin with the nasal cluster 'sn' that also refers to the sound that is made. In all cases, the relation is based on the similarity between the sound of the **referent** (that to which the word refers) and the pronunciation of the word. Words which are characterized by such a clear form-meaning relationship are called **onomatopoeia**. In the lexicons of most spoken languages, however, words of this type occur relatively infrequently.

In contrast, in the lexicons of sign languages, a relation between the form and the meaning of lexemes is much more frequently observed. This is a logical consequence of the fact that sign languages are visual-spatial languages. After all, it is much easier to visually imitate the form of a concrete object or an action than acoustically. As already discussed in Section 1.6, when there is a relation between the form of a sign and its meaning, we speak of an **iconic sign**. When there is no apparent relation between form and meaning, we speak of an **arbitrary sign**. In (2) to (4), we provide some more examples of iconic and arbitrary signs.

Signs differ in the degree to which they are iconic or non-iconic. Actually, it is often impossible to make a clear distinction between iconic and arbitrary signs; we are rather dealing with a continuum from highly iconic to completely arbitrary.

Even for someone who does not know any sign language, the meaning of sign (2a) is probably quite intuitive. The sign is made in front of the mouth, the shape of the hand indicates that the hand is holding a container, and the movement is towards the mouth. The combination of these three form elements is sufficient to enable the person to guess that the sign means 'to drink'. Such a sign is called **transparent**. In (2a), we specify that the sign is from Icelandic Sign Language, but given its transparent character, it is not surprising that the same form expresses the same meaning in many sign languages. Now consider the sign in (2b). This sign is also articulated in front of the mouth and has the same movement as sign (2a); its handshape, however, is different. Yet this sign also means 'to drink' in Brazilian Sign Language (Libras). Here the handshape has no relation with the holding of a glass, but rather reflects the shape of a water jar. Iconicity can thus be culturally bound. In both cases, the sign is also a conventional gesture in the respective country.

(2) a. *Icelandic SL*   b. *Brazilian SL*   c. *French SL*

DRINK   DRINK   CAT

The meaning of the LSF sign in (2c) is not as easily guessed if you know no sign language. However, once you are told that the sign means 'cat', you can see why: the sign refers to the whiskers of the cat. Often knowing the meaning is sufficient to be able to explain what the relation is between the form of the sign and its referent.

For sign (3a), it is more difficult to establish a relationship between form and meaning. The sign shows that something is turned in relation to something else, but what? The sign means 'coffee' in BSL. People who know that in the old days, coffee was ground in a coffee mill will now see the relationship between the sign and its meaning. For people who are unaware of this, the sign will remain arbitrary. The same is true for the sign THURSDAY in (3b) from Adamorobe Sign Language (AdaSL), a sign language used in a village in Ghana. In that village, Thursday is traditionally the day on which the villagers visit the local market to have their tools repaired. The action of hammering that is visible in the sign THURSDAY is connected to that. Without knowledge of this cultural fact, it is impossible to see the iconicity of the sign.

(3)   a.   *British Sign Language*

b.   *Adamorobe Sign Language*

COFFEE

THURSDAY

The signs in (3) thus illustrate that signs can change from iconic signs to less iconic or even arbitrary signs in the course of time. The signs shown in (4) are examples of such arbitrary signs. In (4a), we see the NGT noun WATCH, which refers to a timepiece. In the old days, the sign was articulated at the right of the stomach, in the area of the waistcoat pocket in which the watch was carried. The movement of the sign imitated the movement of taking the watch out of that pocket. In the course of time, the location of the sign has moved upwards towards the neck, and the movement has also changed, so that for new generations of sign language users, the relationship between the form of the sign and its meaning is no longer obvious; that is, the iconicity is lost. The same is true for the ASL sign HOME depicted in (4b). Originally, this sign was a compound composed of the iconic signs EAT (hand brings food to the mouth) and BED (flat hand next to cheek, head tilted towards hand as if you are sleeping). Over time, the form of the individual signs has been changed and reduced to the extent that we cannot actually speak of a compound anymore (see Section 9.3 for discussion of phonological changes in compounds). In the present sign HOME, the handshape of EAT is retained, and the hand performs a small movement from the mouth towards the ear. Again, the consequence of these changes is that the iconicity of the original sign has virtually disappeared.

(4)   a.   *SL of the Netherlands*

b.   *American Sign Language*

WATCH

HOME

In sum, we can say that, because of the possibilities afforded by the visual-spatial modality, iconicity is more prevalent in sign languages than it is in spoken languages. As a result of changes over time in the form of signs, the iconicity of a sign may be reduced and eventually even be lost. This aspect is discussed further in Sections 11.9 and 13.4.1.

8.4   The frozen and the productive lexicon

First and second language learners learn that there is a specific sign for a particular meaning, which is characterized by a fixed handshape, location, orientation, and movement (and possibly a non-manual part). Language learners must simply acquire these forms and at the right moment retrieve them from their mental lexicon. This part of the lexicon is called the **frozen lexicon** or established lexicon. The frozen lexicon is expandable and may undergo changes. In the past few years, the field of computer technology, for example, has been responsible for the emergence of many new terms. This has also led to new signs for concepts like 'computer', 'internet', 'e-mail', 'iPad', and 'Whatsapp'. In sign languages, there are various ways in which new signs can enter the lexicon (see Chapters 9 and 13). Two already existing signs can, for instance, be combined in a compound to form a new term (see Section 9.3). Moreover, signs can be borrowed from another sign language (see Section 13.5.3). The sign COMPUTER shown in (5a), for example, was borrowed into German Sign Language (DGS) from ASL. Signs can also be newly coined, often based on the form of an existing, semantically related sign. An example is the Italian Sign Language (LIS) sign E-MAIL (5b). This sign is related to the sign SEND through its movement. In both signs, a path movement combines with a handshape change: the fingers open while the hand moves away from the body. SEND, however, begins with a 🖐-hand while E-MAIL begins with a 🖐-hand (contact between thumb and index).

(5)   a.   *German Sign Language*   b.   *Italian Sign Language*

COMPUTER

E-MAIL

The three NGT signs for 'telephone' in (6) illustrate that an old sign can be replaced by a new sign when the iconic relation to the referent is changing or no longer present. The old-fashioned wind-up telephone was the basis for the sign in (6a). This sign was later replaced by a new sign for 'telephone', in which the handshape reflects the form of the handset of modern telephones (6b). The sign in (6c) means 'cell phone', and this is increasingly becoming the standard form used to refer to a telephone.

Sign Language of the Netherlands

(6)   a.   b.   c.

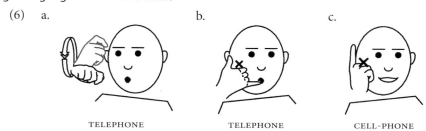

          TELEPHONE   TELEPHONE   CELL-PHONE

Phonological parameters of signs can also change over time for articulatory reasons, as we saw in the signs for WATCH (4a) and HOME (4b) (see also Chapter 13.4). For the present language user though, the signs in the frozen lexicon are fixed: there is only one way in which they can be made (except for phonetic variation, of course; see Chapter 10.4 for discussion).

In contrast, signs in a different part of the lexicon are not (yet) characterized by a fixed form or meaning. Just like signs in the frozen lexicon, these signs are composed from a set of handshapes, locations, movements, and non-manual components, but in contrast to these, they are often formed ad hoc. This part of the lexicon is called the **productive lexicon**. For instance, when telling a story about driving in a car, a Spanish Sign Language (LSE) signer could use the sign 'DRIVE (in a car)' shown in (7a). This sign has a fixed form and meaning and thus belongs to the frozen lexicon of LSE. However, at the moment that the storyteller wants to make clear that the engine of the car was failing, which caused the car to jerk ahead, he can modify the sign. By changing the movement pattern and the non-manual component, he creates a new sign that reflects the way the car is driving: the sign 'DRIVE (in a car, in a jerky way)' shown in (7b). This sign is created on the spot; it has no fixed form or meaning, but in the story about the car, the meaning is clear from the context. In another context, the same sign might be used to convey the meaning of driving over bumpy cobblestones. This sign is thus part of the productive lexicon.

Spanish Sign Language

(7) a.   b.

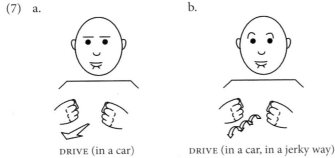

DRIVE (in a car)   DRIVE (in a car, in a jerky way)

The ASL sign GIVE is another example of a productive sign. In the choice of hand-shape and movement for this verb, the signer is taking into account the object that is being given. In (8a), the sign is articulated with a ⎰-hand, indicating that the object given is something that can be held on the palm of your hand. In (8b), the same sign is articulated with a ⎰-handshape that refers to something that is flat but can be held between fingers and thumb, for instance, a book. In (8c), two hands are used, indicating a larger flat object, and at the same time, the movement and the non-manual component (puffed cheeks) indicate that the object is heavy, that is, that it is given with effort.

American Sign Language

(8) a.   b.   c.

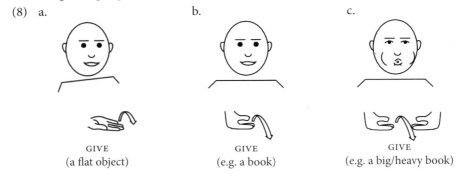

GIVE   GIVE   GIVE
(a flat object)   (e.g. a book)   (e.g. a big/heavy book)

Depending on the perspective of the signer, an object can also change form. A church tower, for example, which looks quite slender from a distance, may appear to be much broader when you stand in front of it. A sign language user can take this perspective into account in his choice of handshape, that is, he can refer to one and the same object by different forms.

It is possible that these kinds of signs, in specific combinations with other signs, have never been produced before. And yet, they are completely clear and full of meaning for other signers in that specific context. This is due to the fact that signers do not create new signs in an idiosyncratic way, but rather combine the components from the productive lexicon in a systematic way that is understood by other signers. Recent research indicates that productive forms are a much bigger part of sign language use than has previously been assumed. The assumption has been that productive forms appear with high frequency in stories and poetry, while they are rare in other contexts. This, however, appears not to be true; the productive lexicon is also frequently used in legal, medical, and other scientific conversations. Its use is a creative process: the language user creates, as it were, new signs that are necessary at that moment in order to make something clear. In Section 8.7, we will show that the productive lexicon is extensively used in metaphors.

Signs that have become part of the frozen lexicon usually have handshapes that are also used in the productive lexicon. This is illustrated by the examples in (9) from Libras. In the sign APARTMENT-BUILDING (9a), the flat hands refer to the flat sides of the building; the fists in the sign CAR (9b) reflect the way the steering wheel is held; and in the sign HORSE-RIDE in (9c), the handshape with two extended fingers refers to the two legs of a human (see also the sign WALK in (1b)).

Brazilian Sign Language

(9) a.   b.   c.

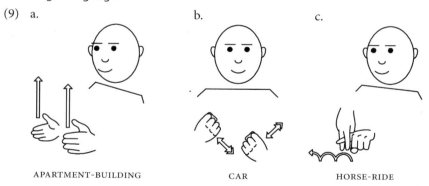

APARTMENT-BUILDING   CAR   HORSE-RIDE

These signs are all part of the frozen lexicon in Libras, so the handshapes are not dependent on the context. Here we observe that there is actually a continuum between the frozen and the productive lexicon. When productive forms are considered to form part of the lexicon, they can be included in a dictionary. When they are seen as morphologically modified forms (see Chapter 9), then they do not appear in a dictionary – just like morphologically modified words would not usually be included in the dictionary of a spoken language. Lexicographers differ in their view on whether or not the productive lexicon should be included in dictionaries.

8.5   Sign language dictionaries

So far, we have used the term 'lexicon' to refer to the collection of words from a spoken language or signs from a sign language. When these words or signs are listed, often together with a brief description, then we call these lists 'dictionaries'.

Dictionaries of spoken languages are made up of lemmas, as was briefly mentioned in Section 1.8. A **lemma** is the word or heading under which the meanings are listed that are connected to each other. The English word *awesome*, for instance, has several different related meanings and is listed as one lemma, whereas the word *steer* has two different meanings, namely 'to guide' and 'a young bovine animal', and thus constitutes two lemmas. There is no one-to-one relationship between word and meaning. A word can have multiple meanings, and one meaning can be listed under various words. Many sign language dictionaries, whether in book form or on DVD, list signs based on either their **gloss** or their translation from the spoken language to the sign language. Note that the gloss and the translation are often identical (e.g. ASL CAR – 'car') but they do not have to be, as is true for many compounds (e.g. DGS MONK^BOSS – 'abbott'; see Chapter 9.3). In any case, the lemmas in such bilingual dictionaries are thus words from the spoken language (see Section 1.8, Example (18), for an example from an ASL dictionary). This implies that the user can only search for an answer to the question "What is the sign for...?" but not to the question "I have seen a sign, but what does it mean?". Such dictionaries usually only include signs from the frozen lexicon, and then in their **citation form**, which is a form of the sign that is not influenced by the linguistic context, that is, that has not undergone any morphological or phonological changes.

In other words, the starting point in such dictionaries is the meaning of the words, not the meaning of the signs. By using glosses as opposed to translations as lemmas, some dictionary makers attempt to reduce the emphasis on the meaning of the word. In the introduction to this chapter, we already made clear that a gloss is not the translation of a sign, but a representation (or approximation) of its meaning in words. A disadvantage is that, since the gloss is a word from the spoken language, the word will continue to subconsciously play a role in the mind of dictionary users: the user might stick to the meaning of the word, even though it is represented in the form of a gloss. This can be overcome by making the gloss as specific as possible. For instance, the gloss can indicate differences in meaning, so instead of simply using the gloss BREAK, the gloss can specify either BREAK(INTERRUPTION) or BREAK(CRACK).

However, there are also sign language dictionaries that take the sign as the starting point. The signs are then ordered on the basis of the form of the sign. The users can look up a sign, for example, on the basis of its handshape and whether it is one- or two-handed. The very first sign language dictionary to be organized in this way was the ASL dictionary compiled by William Stokoe, the pioneer of linguistic research on ASL, and dates from 1965. Other examples are the first national NGT dictionary for parents of deaf children from 1988, the BSL dictionary from 1992, the Australian Sign Language

(Auslan) dictionary from 1998, and the Finnish Sign Language (FinSL) dictionary from 1998. All these early dictionaries were in book form and contained drawings or photographs of the signs. The rapid developments in information technology in the early 1990s made it possible to develop digital dictionaries in which the lemmas are citation movies. It is thus now possible in principle to create a monolingual dictionary in which the user can search for signs on the basis of their basic elements – handshape, location, palm and finger orientation, and movement – and where definitions and grammatical information are also presented in the respective sign language. No such dictionary has yet been produced. However, a number of bilingual sign dictionaries exist on DVD or online in which users can search for signs either on the basis of some or all the basic elements of a sign or by gloss. Such dictionaries have been compiled, for example, for Flemish Sign Language (VGT – online), for Auslan, and for NGT. The meaning of signs, however, is still conveyed using the written language.

There are huge differences in the way in which sign dictionaries are compiled, and with respect to the reliability of the information provided. Sometimes a dictionary is a reflection of the signs that the compilers themselves use, or the dictionary contains only signs from a certain area. Often very little information is provided about sign variation (see Chapter 12) or the way in which the signs were selected. This is in contrast to dictionaries for spoken languages, and it is an indication that sign language lexicography is still in its infancy. However, modern sign dictionaries in many countries, be they in digital or book form, are increasingly based on nationwide inventories of signs, the so-called corpus projects, and take into account regional and age-based variation, for instance (see also Chapter 12).

Sign language dictionaries differ also in terms of the information supplied with individual lemmas. In some dictionaries, there is only a one-to-one translation from word to sign. This is actually not a dictionary, but rather a glossary. Other dictionaries provide information on the form and use of the sign. Digital dictionaries in particular can contain more elaborate information, such as:

- extra information on the form of the sign, especially when a sign is presented in the form of a drawing or a picture;
- a movie of a sign instead of a drawing or picture;
- an example sentence in written language when the meaning of a word and a sign are not exactly the same, or (in digital dictionaries) a signed sentence;
- information about the word class and other grammatical information;
- information on regional variation;
- information about form and meaning relations with other signs.

When it comes to printed dictionaries of spoken languages, there is no relation whatsoever between the user of a dictionary and the person who has typed the word into the dictionary or the person who provided the information. For sign language dictionaries, the situation is different. All sorts of dictionaries may include pictures and drawings based on real people, and digital dictionaries generally contain movies showing actual people who are signing. Especially in pictures and video clips, it is usually easy to identify the signer, in particular for members of the Deaf community. It is therefore important that the presenters who are involved are accepted members of the Deaf community of the relevant country. The status of the presenters can influence the acceptance of a dictionary. In order to overcome this problem, it is possible to make use of a virtual animated signer, that is, an avatar (see Section 10.6). This technology is not yet used extensively, however. One on-line ASL dictionary uses an avatar, but it contains quite a limited list of signs. In this book, we use a combination of photographs of actual signers and drawings that are abstract and bear no relation to actual people.

8.6   Meaning and meaning relations

The DGS sign in (10a) reflects quite a common movement of the fingers. Depending on the context, this sign can have (at least) four meanings: (i) typing, (ii) keyboard, (iii) secretarial office, and (iv) ICT. Clearly, these meanings are related. This relation covers (i) the activity, (ii) the instrument used for the activity, (iii) the place where the activity commonly takes place, and (iv) the abstract subject area.

(10)   a.   *German Sign Language*   b.   *British Sign Language*

Similarly, the BSL sign in (10b) also has various interrelated meanings, namely (i) sick, (ii) sickness, (iii) invalid, and (iv) defective. For both the DGS and the BSL sign, the context will have to make clear which meaning is intended. These signs are examples of **polysemy**: there are multiple meanings, but these meanings are related to each other.

The BSL sign shown in (11) also has more than one meaning: (i) 'Belgium', (ii) 'Belgian', (iii) 'toilet', and (iv) 'maybe' – the last two meanings being regional. There is a clear relationship between the meanings (i) and (ii), but not between these two and (iii) and (iv). The latter type of relationship is called **homonymy**, which implies that mulitple signs happen to share the same form, but have no obvious meaning relationship (the same is true for the English word *steer* we mentioned in the previous section).

British Sign Language

(11)

Polysemy and homonymy can both cause **ambiguity**, that is, situations in which the intended meaning is unclear. However, as pointed out before, the context will usually shed light on the intended meaning. In some sign languages (like DGS and NGT), this ambiguity is often resolved by making use of a mouthing, the silent articulation of (a part of) a word simultaneously with a sign (see Chapter 11.6). Once a mouthing becomes a fixed part of a sign, that is, part of its phonological make-up, we are no longer dealing with one sign with different meanings. Rather, we are then dealing with different signs, and thus we cannot speak of polysemy or homonymy anymore.

As mentioned in Section 8.5, polysemy and homonymy are treated differently in dictionaries. In the case of polysemy, the connected meanings are presented under one lemma. In contrast, in the case of homonymy, the two (or more) meanings are presented as separate lemmas. That is, the BSL sign in (10b) would receive one dictionary entry, while the BSL sign in (11) would have three entries (with the additional information that two of these represent regional variants).

The three ASL signs in (12) do have a semantic relationship: SAD (12b) and JEAL-OUS (12c) are examples of FEELINGS (12a); that is, they are subordinate to the first sign, and this type of relationship defines a hyponym. **Hyponymy** relations are hierarchical relations between lemmas, and they occur occur in all languages. Examples in English are *animal – giraffe* and *furniture – chair*.

American Sign Language

(12)   a.   b.   c.

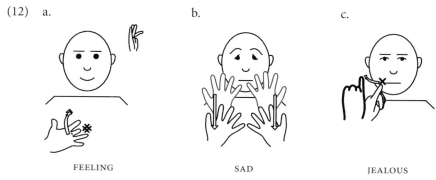

FEELING   SAD   JEALOUS

In (13), we provide three sign pairs from three different sign languages in which the members of each pair are semantically opposite; these pairs are thus cases of **antonymy**. In the NGT pair, DIFFICULT (13a) is the opposite of EASY (13b); in the ThaiSL pair, FAR (13c) is the opposite of NEARBY (13d); and in the VGT pair, ALIVE (13e) is the opposite of DEAD (13f).

(13)   *Sign Language of the Netherlands*

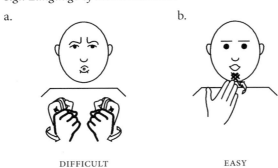

a.   b.

DIFFICULT   EASY

Thai Sign Language

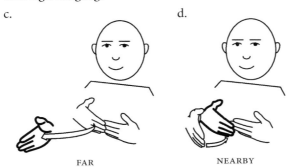

c.   d.

FAR   NEARBY

Flemish Sign Language

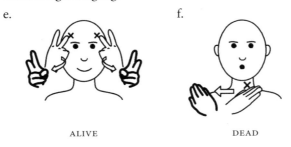

e.   f.

ALIVE   DEAD

Finally, the signs in (14) are examples of **synonymy**: two different signs with the same meaning. The two NGT signs in (14a) and (14b) both mean 'newspaper', the two BSL signs in (14c) and (14d) both mean 'begin'.

(14)   *Sign Language of the Netherlands*

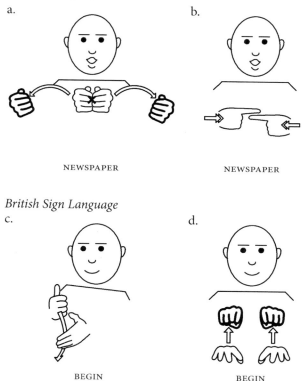

a.

b.

NEWSPAPER

NEWSPAPER

British Sign Language

c.

d.

BEGIN

BEGIN

It is important to note that synonyms are often not really fully equal in meaning, as one sign may be used in another context than the other sign. This is related to the fact that signs not only have a **denotation** (that which you can refer to) but also a **connotation**. Factors like emotional value, stylistic value, and social meaning of a sign may play a crucial role in selecting one sign over the other (see Section 12.4).

8.7   Metaphor and idiom

Both in spoken languages and in sign languages, users often refer to an entity or an action by comparing it to something else – this strategy is referred to as **metaphoric language use**. In the expression *the heart of the town*, for instance, the active center of the town is compared to the heart of a living being. In the expression *time flies*, a verb is used in a non-literal way. Obviously, time does not fly like a bird, but the verb evokes the impression of something passing quickly. We use such expressions very frequently in daily communication and in fact, they can become conventionalized to the extent that the original comparison is forgotten, as in *fork in the road* and *to be down*. A categorization of metaphors has shown that many languages use the same types of metaphors, including sign languages.

A large group of metaphors uses **spatial comparisons** (e.g. *up–down, front–back*). One of the features of sign languages is that they can make use of the space in front of the body. Research on various sign languages has shown that this space is indeed commonly employed in metaphoric language use. Many signs which express a positive meaning are characterized by an upward movement, as is illustrated by the examples in (15).

(15)   a.   *American Sign Language*   b.   *American Sign Language*

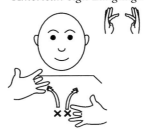

PRIDE   EXCITED

c.   *Chinese Sign Language*   d.   *SL of the Netherlands*

INCREASE   BETTER

In contrast, in signs with a negative meaning, we often see a downward movement, as is shown by the examples in (16). This metaphoric link between positive and upward, and negative and downward can also be observed in spoken languages, as the English examples in (17) show.

(16)   a.   *American SL*   b.   *Chinese SL*   c.   *SL of the Netherlands*

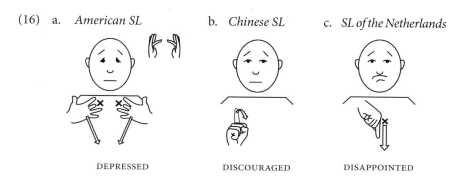

DEPRESSED   DISCOURAGED   DISAPPOINTED

(17)   a.   Upward metaphors: express positive values like happiness (*to be in high spirits*), consciousness (*to wake up*), health (*to be in top shape*), and high status (*at the peak of your career*)

   b.   Downward metaphors: express negative values like sadness (*feeling down*), unconsciousness (*to fall asleep*), illness and death (*to fall ill, to drop dead*), and low status (*a lower rank*)

In the signs in (15) and (16), the spatial metaphors are expressed by an upward or downward movement, in the examples in (17) by prepositions, adjectives, nouns, or verbs that imply up- or downward movement. In sign languages. these movements are considered to be part of the productive lexicon, as discussed in Section 8.4.

Similarly, expressions related to time are commonly expressed by means of spatial metaphors, both in spoken and in signed languages. In many spoken languages, the past is conceptualized as lying behind us while the future is seen as lying ahead of us, as the English examples in (18) show.

(18)   a.   Behind metaphors: refer to events in the past, e.g. *back in the old days, this lies behind us now*

   b.   Front metaphors: refer to events in the future, e.g. *years ahead, to look forward to*

The ThaiSL signs in (19) are all articulated at particular locations (and with particular movements) in the signing space. The signs in (19a–c), all of which refer to the past, are made above or behind the shoulder and involve a movement towards the back, while the signs that refer to the future in (19d–f) are made in front of the shoulder and are characterized by a a forward movement. Were a line to be drawn between these locations, we could see a continuous line from the back to front, with the extremes being the final location of LONG-AGO (19a) and the final location of IN-THE-FAR-FUTURE (19f). Such a line is often referred to as '**time line**'.

Thai Sign Language
(19) a.

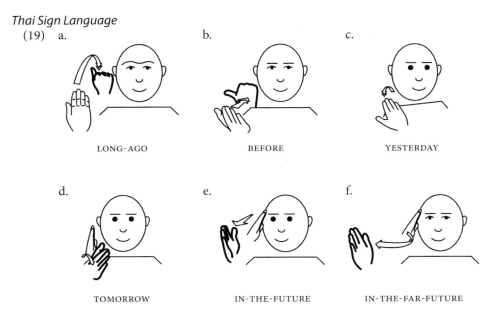

b.

c.

LONG-AGO

BEFORE

YESTERDAY

d.

e.

f.

TOMORROW

IN-THE-FUTURE

IN-THE-FAR-FUTURE

The pattern observed in (18) and (19) is conceptually linked to the idea that what is past lies behind you, and that which is yet to come lies before you. In other cultures, however, the relation between time reference and spatial locations is the reverse of what we have just described. In the Urubu-Kaapor Sign Language, a sign language used by Brazilian Indians, and also in AdaSL, the past is conceptualized as lying in front of the shoulder and the future above and behind the shoulder. This mapping reflects a world view according to which the past is known, and thus visible, while the future is unknown, that is, invisible. Given that the choice of metaphorical mapping is culture-dependent, it is not surprising that time reference is expressed in the same way in the surrounding spoken languages. The same is true for more spoken languages, for instance Malagasy, a language spoken on Madagascar. Interestingly, in spoken Chinese, some time expressions are motivated by a vertical time line with the future being down and the past up. This spatial metaphor is also visible in the equivalent time expressions in Hong Kong Sign Language (HKSL) and Chinese Sign Language (CSL); the sign NEXT-WEEK, for instance, involves a downward movement, while LAST-WEEK is signed with an upward movement.

Apart from the use of space, metaphors can also be expressed in sign languages through handshapes. For BSL, the 'emanate or emit metaphor' has been described. In signs in which this metaphor occurs, a closed ⍦- or ⍦-handshape changes to an open handshape with spread and slightly bent fingers. This handshape change is metaphorical as it refers to the emission of light (see Example (32b) in Chapter 10, the NGT sign LAMP) or the flowing away of water, for instance. In the BSL sign SPRING (20a), the metaphor reflects the sprouting of new life. A related metaphor is found in the LSF sign REJECT (20b), in which the handshape change indicates that an idea is thrown away, and again in the ASL compound MIND^DROP 'faint' (20c). Both these signs are examples of the 'abstract entities are objects' metaphor: an idea or the mind are conceptualized as concrete objects that can be manipulated by the hands (cf. the English expression *to grasp an idea*).

(20) a. *British SL*   b. *French SL*   c. *American SL*

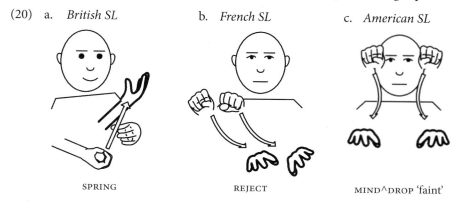

SPRING   REJECT   MIND^DROP 'faint'

Metaphoric language use in spoken languages is an important source for the development of **idioms**. Idiomatic expressions are expressions with a fixed form and a fixed meaning. This meaning cannot be literally deduced from the meaning of the words that make up the idiom. The example in (21a), for instance, means that someone passed away – no bucket is involved in this event. Idioms are characterized by clear restrictions on their form; they cannot be manipulated in the way other utterances can be manipulated. The passive sentence in (21b), intending the same meaning as (21a), is therefore unacceptable.

(21) a. He finally kicked the bucket.
      b. *The bucket was finally kicked by him.

Idiomatic expressions seem to be quite rare in sign languages. An example of an idiom is the sign EASY/PIECE-OF-CAKE in NGT. There are only few expressions involving multiple signs that have a fixed form and a fixed meaning which cannot be deduced from the meaning of the separate signs. In ASL, the idiom TRAIN GONE SORRY is used to indicate frustration with having to repeat too often; it can be translated as 'Sorry, you missed it and I am not going to repeat it'. Also, the combination FINISH TOUCH means 'I have already been there'. In VGT, the expression NOW TELEPHONE can be used to mean 'I am going to the toilet'.

Summary

Combinations of manual and non-manual components are considered to be signs when they meet certain criteria as to their form and meaning. The meaning of a sign is **conventional**, which means that a convention about the meaning of a sign has developed amongst the sign language users. Except for **onomatopoeia**, in spoken languages, the relation between form and meaning is generally **arbitrary**. A striking feature of visual-spatial languages is that their lexicons contain many **iconic signs**, that is, signs that are based on an iconic relation with the **referent**. Despite this iconicity, the relation between form and meaning often only becomes obvious once the meaning of the sign is known. When this relation is immediately clear, even to non-signers, such signs are called **transparent**. In contrast, signs that are not characterized by an iconic form-meaning relation are called **arbitrary signs**.

The lexicon of sign languages consists of the **frozen lexicon**, which contains signs with a fixed form, and the **productive lexicon**, which functions as a reservoir of morphemes for creating new signs. Dictionaries organize entries as **lemmas**, that is, entries under which the meanings of a word or sign are placed that are connected to each other. Many dictionaries use a word from the spoken language, or a **gloss**, to indicate the meaning of a sign, and they usually only include signs from the frozen lexicon in their **citation form**. Developments in information technology have made it more feasible to create dictionaries and databases in which lemmas are organized according to the form of the signs.

Just like words, signs can have various meaning relations to each other. When a sign has more than one meaning, but these meanings are related, this is called **polysemy**. We speak of **homonymy** when two signs have the same form, but differ in meaning. Both polysemy and homonymy can cause **ambiguity**, but in some sign languages, ambiguity is resolved by the use of mouthings. Other common meaning relations are **hyponymy**, **antonymy**, and **synonymy**. Even signs that are considered synonyms are often not fully equal in meaning, as there can be a difference between **denotation** and **connotation**. Factors like emotional and stylistic value play an important role in creating a different connotation.

In **metaphoric language use**, a referent is compared to something else. Our daily language is interspersed with metaphors, and similar metaphors are used across many unrelated languages. In many spoken and signed languages, **spatial comparisons** are frequently employed. Positive values, for instance, are conceptualized as involving an upward movement, and negative values as involving a downward movement. Reference to time may also be based on spatial comparison, and in sign languages, this is often expressed on a so-called **time line**. From metaphoric language use, **idioms** can be formed: fixed expressions with a fixed syntactic form. In sign languages, however, idioms appear to be rather infrequent.

Test yourself

1.   What constitutes a sign? Mention two criteria.
2.   What is a gloss and what are the disadvantages of using glosses?
3.   What is the difference between iconic and arbitrary signs?
4.   What is the frozen lexicon and what the productive lexicon?
5.   What is a lemma?

6. Describe the difference between a dictionary that uses glosses as entries, and one that is based on the form of a sign.
7. What is the difference between polysemy and homonymy?
8. How is this difference reflected in dictionaries?
9. What is hyponymy, antonymy, and synonymy?
10. What is the difference between metaphorical language use and idiom?

Assignments

1. Find in a dictionary or other source a sign where the relation between the gloss and the meaning is clear, and another sign where this is not the case. Describe in what respect the relationship is not clear.

2. There is a continuum between highly iconic and completely arbitrary signs. Place these four signs from South African Sign Language (SASL) on this continuum. Give arguments for your choices.

a. SASL WOMAN

b. SASL MAN

c. SASL AFTERNOON   d. SASL BUS

3. Give three signs from the frozen lexicon and three signs from the productive lexicon of any sign language. Explain why they are frozen or productive.

4. Find a dictionary that uses glosses as lemmas and one that organizes lemmas based on the form of signs. For both dictionaries describe the elements given below:
    –   the way in which the signs are visualized,
    –   the information that is provided about the signs,
    –   the items for which spoken language and for which sign language is used and the ratio of use of the two languages in the dictionary.

5. Give examples from a sign language you know of polysemy, homonymy, hyponymy, antonymy, and synonymy.

6. Describe the metaphors being used in the following signs (clips on www.spreadthesign.com).

a. DGS: DISAPPOINT

b. Polish SL: FAIL

c. Turkish SL: DIE

d. ASL: ADMIRE

References and further reading

A good introduction to the issue of iconicity and the frozen and productive lexicon, based on BSL data, can be found in Brennan (1992). Perniss, Thompson & Vigliocco (2010) provide an excellent overview of the role and use of iconicity in signed and spoken languages. The first study offering a detailed analysis of iconic devices (in ASL) is Mandel (1977). Pietrandrea (2002) discusses the topic for LIS, and Cuxac & Sallandre (2007) for LSF. A cross-linguistic and cross-cultural analysis of iconicity and transparency is provided by Pizzuto & Volterra (2000). Padden et al. (2013) present a comparative study on iconicity patterns in various sign languages. Information about morphemes that are used in the productive lexicon can be found in Supalla (1986). A more in-depth investigation of iconicity and metaphor, and their relation, in sign languages is to be found in Taub (2001, 2012). Meir (2010) discusses interesting constraints on the metaphorical extension of iconic forms. Different types of metaphors are described for ASL in Wilbur (1990) and Wilcox (2000), Grushkin (1998) focuses on metaphorical expressions of anger in ASL; see also Brennan (1992, 2001) for BSL, as well as a special issue of the journal *Sign Language Studies* edited by Wilcox (2005). The use of time lines is discussed for NGT by Schermer & Koolhof (1990) and for LSE by Cabeza Pereiro & Fernández Soneira (2004). An influential study on metaphors in spoken languages is Lakoff & Johnson (1980).

Research papers on sign dictionaries and databases are Brien et al. (1995), Schermer, Brien & Brennan (2001), Hanke, Konrad & Schwarz (2001), Johnston (2001a, 2003b), and Schermer (2003, 2004, 2006). The following is a selection of some of the many available sign language dictionaries: ASL: Stokoe, Casterline & Cronenberg (1965) and Valli (2005); Auslan: Johnston (1989, 2005); BSL: Brien (1992); FinSL: Malm (1998); HKSL: Tang (2007); LSE: Fundación CNSE (2003a); NGT: Schermer et al. (2006, 2014) and Schermer & Koolhof (2009); VGT: De Weerdt et al. (2004). Examples of online dictionaries can be found at: www.gebarencentrum.nl (NGT), www.auslan.org.au (Auslan), and www.gebaren.ugent.be (VGT). An (incomplete) overview of digital sign dictionaries is provided at www.yourdictionary.com/languages/sign.html. The ASL-lexicon in which signs are presented by an avatar can be found at http://signsci.terc.edu/SSD/about/animation.htm.

The AdaSL examples are taken from Nyst (2007), the ThaiSL examples from Wrigley et al. (eds.) (1990), the Libras examples from Capovilla & Raphael (2001), the NGT examples from Schermer et al. (2006), the ASL examples from Klima & Bellugi (1979) and Sandler (1996a), and the BSL examples from Deuchar (1984). The ASL TRAIN-GONE-SORRY example is mentioned in Hall (1989). The SASL examples are taken from the SASL dictionary by the National Institute of the Deaf (2011). Some of the examples of spoken language metaphors are from Lakoff & Johnson (1980).

Chapter 9

Morphology

Roland Pfau

9.1 Introduction

In many – but not all – spoken languages, it is possible to form complex words by combining morphemes. It is therefore not surprising that this possibility also exists in signed languages. In this chapter, we will examine various morphological processes attested in sign languages, and point out differences and similarities between spoken and signed languages.

In Section 9.2, we will begin by discussing the general nature of morphological processes. It appears that spoken and signed languages behave quite differently when it comes to the formation of complex words. In the next two sections, we will describe how vocabulary can be expanded in sign languages, by means of compounding (Section 9.3) and derivation (Section 9.4). Various inflectional processes – tense, aspect, agreement, and pluralization – are the topic of Section 9.5. Finally, two specific word formation strategies, which are not easily grouped with the types discussed in the previous sections, are described in Section 9.6: incorporation and classification.

9.2 Word formation: sequentiality versus simultaneity

In this section, we will discuss the nature of word formation processes in sign languages in general. Spoken languages vary in the ways in which complex words are formed. In fact, we can identify various morphological types, namely isolating, agglutinating, fusional, and polysynthetic languages. To which type would sign languages belong? Are they all of the same type?

Let us start by looking at an example. In Japanese Sign Language (JSL), as in many other sign languages, the citation form of the sign GIVE has a 👐-hand (palm orientation up), that moves away from the body in neutral space (1a). If one wants to express that a flat object, for example a book, is being given, the handshape changes into a ✍-hand, as shown in (1b) (for further discussion of such handshape modifications, see Section 9.6.2). But if the book is bigger, the non-dominant hand can be added, copying the handshape and the movement of the dominant hand. Through a change

DOI 10.1075/z.199.09pfa
© 2016 John Benjamins Publishing Company

in facial expression, it is possible to further indicate that the book is being given with great effort: the eyebrows are furrowed and the cheeks are puffed (1c).

The result of these different word formation processes is a verb with a highly complex meaning, namely 'give a large flat object (e.g. a book) to someone with great effort'. Note that almost a whole English sentence is required to translate that one sign.

Japanese Sign Language

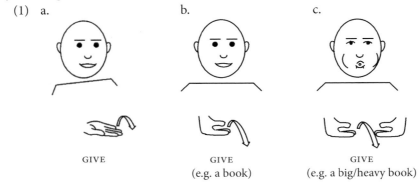

(1) a.	b.	c.
GIVE	GIVE (e.g. a book)	GIVE (e.g. a big/heavy book)

Similar phenomena are also attested in many spoken languages. In Turkish, for instance, it is quite common to combine a considerable number of morphemes, whereby each morpheme yields a specific change in meaning. A complex, but not uncommon, example is presented in (2). *Ev-* is the noun stem 'house', and this stem is followed by a number of grammatical suffixes: plural, possessive (first person plural), locative case, a so-called relative marker (indicating that it concerns someone at a certain location), and finally once again plural.

Turkish

(2)   ev-ler-imiz-de-ki-ler
      house-PL-1PL.POSS-LOC-REL-PL
      'those in our houses'

In this example, the resulting word also has a rather complex meaning, which in English requires a whole phrase to translate it. And yet the Turkish and the JSL examples are clearly different from each other. In languages with strictly agglutinating morphology, like Turkish, the morphemes are placed one after the other, and thus every morpheme makes the word a little bit longer. In contrast, the complex form in the JSL example (1c) is barely longer than the **underlying form (citation form)** in (1a) because all morphological operations are realized simultaneously. The morphologically complex form is only slightly longer than the citation form because the movement is tense and therefore a little slower; yet, the basic structure of the two signs – a location-movement-location sequence (see Chapter 11 for discussion) – is the same.

Spoken languages generally employ affixes in processes of word formation (in the Turkish example (2), only suffixes are involved). In that case, we speak of **sequential** word formation, because individual bound morphemes are organized in a linear way. However, the sequential combination of morphemes is not the only strategy available to spoken languages; there are also cases in which the change takes place within the word stem. Such cases exemplify **simultaneous** word formation. The next two examples from spoken languages illustrate this word formation strategy.

In English, the past tense is generally formed by the suffix -*ed*, as shown for the verb *walk* in (3a). But there are a number of exceptions where only the vowel in the stem changes, for instance the verb *win* (3b).

English

(3) a.   I walk   –   I walked
     b.   I win   –   I won

Occasionally, even phonological features can function as a morpheme. In tone languages, for example, a change in tone value can lead to a grammatical change (e.g. aspect marking). Yet, tone is not the only feature that can fulfil a morphemic function. In the Brazilian language Terena, for instance, the feature [nasal] marks first person singular. This phenomenon is illustrated in (4), where the symbol '~' indicates the nasality of a segment.

Terena

(4) a.   unae   →   ūnãẽ
          'boss'   'my boss'
     b.   emoʔu   →   ẽmõʔũ
          'word'   'my word'

What the examples in (3) and (4) have in common is the fact that a morphological operation occurs stem-internally, that is, simultaneously. In (3b), the operation affects the vowel of the stem, while in (4), the feature [nasal] is added to multiple vowels. Clearly, no linearly organized morphemes are involved in these cases; the segmental structure of the underlying and the derived words is the same.

As this discussion shows, simultaneous morphological processes are also attested in spoken languages, but in signed languages, simultaneity plays a far greater role. Moreover – and unlike spoken languages – it is possible, and even common, to realize various morphological modifications at the same time. This is possible as every phonological parameter (e.g. handshape, movement, and non-manual marking) may function as a morpheme, and multiple parameters can be changed simultaneously (see Chapter 11 for further discussion). In the JSL example in (1), the movement of the sign can be considered as the stem. The start and end locations of GIVE realize agreement and function as morphemes that determine the direction of movement of the sign.

The handshape (and the non-dominant hand) is a classifier that reflects properties of an argument and thus also a morpheme. Finally, the facial expression is a morpheme that signals the manner of the action. In the next sections, we will see that this way of forming words is very typical for sign languages, even though sequential word formation also occasionally occurs.

9.3 Compounding

In **compounds**, two or more words are combined into a complex word. Let us start by looking at an NGT example. In NGT, the sign for 'parents' is a combination of the two signs FATHER and MOTHER (5a). The signs are produced one after the other, but the movement is often reduced, and together they form the compound 'parents'. This is an example of a **coordinated compound**. In coordinated compounds, the combined words have equal status. That is, in compounds of this type, neither of the two elements has a modifying or specifying function; rather, the two separate meanings are, as it were, added, as, for instance, in English compounds like *bittersweet* or *fighter bomber*. In Mandarin Chinese, just as in NGT, the word for 'parents' is a coordinated compound which combines the hyponyms 'father' and 'mother' (6a), while the word for 'children' is a combination of the words 'sons' and 'daughters' (6b).

Sign Language of the Netherlands

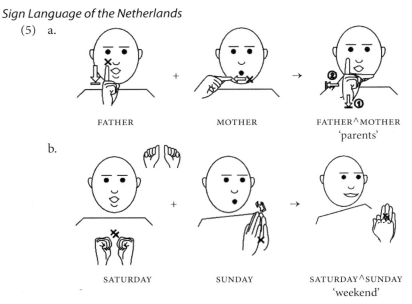

(5) a.

FATHER   MOTHER   FATHER^MOTHER
                                'parents'

b.

SATURDAY   SUNDAY   SATURDAY^SUNDAY
                                  'weekend'

Mandarin Chinese
(6) a. fùmǔ   'parents (father and mother)'
     b. zǐnǚ   'children (sons and daughters')'

The NGT sign for 'weekend' is also a coordinated compound, a combination of the two signs SATURDAY and SUNDAY (5b). But this compound has different characteristics than Example (5a): the two parts are not combined sequentially but simultaneously. SATURDAY and SUNDAY are both symmetrical two-handed signs; SATURDAY is made with two ⟨⟩-hands, SUNDAY with two ⟨⟩-hands. In the compound, the two handshapes are combined, one on the dominant hand, the other one on the non-dominant hand. The movement is that of SATURDAY, that is, the two hands make repeated contact with each other.

The next two examples differ from (5) because the function of the two signs in the compound is different. In Example (7) from German Sign Language (DGS), the two signs that are combined are of the same category (noun), just as in (5), but they have different status, as one sign modifies the other: MONK modifies BOSS to create the concept of MONK^BOSS 'abbot'.

German Sign Language

(7)

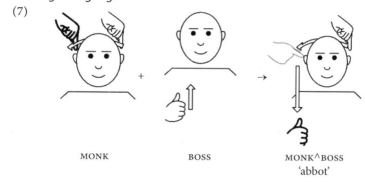

| MONK | BOSS | MONK^BOSS |
| | | 'abbot' |

In principle, words of all grammatical categories can be combined to form compounds, for instance, an adjective with a noun, as in the English compound *blackbird*. Such a combination can also be seen in Example (8) from American Sign Language (ASL), where the adjective BLACK modifies the noun NAME to yield the concept 'bad reputation'. This compound also exemplifies metaphorical language use, as the term BLACK expresses a negative value.

American Sign Language

(8)

| BLACK | NAME | BLACK^NAME |
| | | 'bad reputation' |

For compounds in many spoken languages, including English and German, the rule is that the right element in the compound determines the grammatical category of the compound; that is, the right element is the **head** of the construction. In the glosses in (7) and (8), the head is also on the right, whereas the left element has a modifying or specifying function. Compounds that consist of a head and a modifier are called **subordinated compounds**.

Sign language compounds often exhibit striking phonological changes in comparison to the single signs that make up the compound. Firstly, interesting rhythmic modifications can be observed, which influence the duration of the compound. A meticulous analysis of ASL compounds has revealed that signs in compounds are often reduced. If, for instance, one of the elements contains a repetition, this repetition is usually lost – as is true for the sign NAME in (8). As a consequence of such rhythmic changes, the duration of production of a compound consisting of two signs is much shorter than the combined duration of the same signs in a sentence. The duration of many compounds rather equals the duration of an individual sign.

In the DGS compound MONK^BOSS 'abbot' (7), for instance, we observe a change in the movement parameter: while the sign BOSS has an upward movement, in the compound MONK^BOSS, the movement is downward. This change in movement guarantees a smooth transition between the two parts of the compound (see also Section 11.8) which, again, reduces the duration. The DGS compound EAR^NOSE^THROAT^DOCTOR 'otorhinolaryngologist' is a loan compound from German (see Section 13.5.4), but in German, the word order in the compound differs, namely *Hals-Nasen-Ohren-Arzt* (literally 'throat-, nose-, ear-doctor'). In DGS, the order of the components is changed in order to allow for a continuous downward movement (as the last sign DOCTOR is articulated on the wrist of the non-dominant hand). Without this change, the movement would first proceed upwards (from throat to nose) and then downwards. Actually, there is a general tendency for downward movement in signed compounds.

Let us consider the compound RED^COMB 'rooster' from Swedish Sign Language (SSL) in (9), which consists of the signs RED and COMB-ON-HEAD. The first part, the sign RED, actually involves a repetition of movement; this is then lost in the compound as mentioned earlier. But a second, interesting change can be observed: in the compound both parts have the same handshape. This change is the result of **regressive handshape assimilation**. This means that the first sign RED adopts the handshape of the second sign COMB-ON-HEAD. Consequently, in the compound, only the parameter location of the first part (RED) is retained.

Swedish Sign Language
(9)

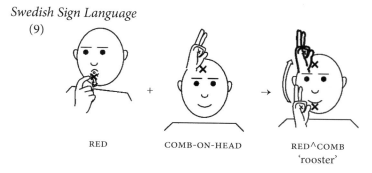

| RED | COMB-ON-HEAD | RED^COMB |
| | | 'rooster' |

In compounds where one of the parts is a two-handed sign, further changes may occur. As for the signs that make up the ASL compound BLACK^NAME 'bad reputation' (8), we see that in isolation BLACK is a one-handed sign, whereas NAME is produced with two hands. In BLACK^NAME, the non-dominant hand of NAME is already present in the signing space in front of the signer whilst BLACK is signed (but somewhat higher than usual). This phenomenon is called **weak hand spreading**, because the handshape of the non-dominant (weak) hand spreads to the first part of the compound.

Signs thus undergo a number of form changes in compounds: reduction, deletion, and change of movement, handshape assimilation, and spreading of the non-dominant hand. These changes cause the two (or more) signs to meld together, resulting in a complex sign the production of which barely takes longer than the production of a sign in isolation.

Moreover, compounds commonly involve changes in meaning that are often not predictable on the basis of the two parts. Consequently, they must be stored in the lexicon separately (see Chapter 8). It is therefore not a contradiction to combine the ASL compound BED^SOFT 'pillow' in one sentence with the sign HARD. The sentence MY BED^SOFT HARD actually does not mean 'my soft bed is hard' but rather 'my pillow is hard'.

9.4   Derivation

In contrast to compounds, in derivational processes a word (a free morpheme) is combined with a bound morpheme. In (10), we see the complex sign FEEL^ZERO from ASL. The first part of the sign is the verb FEEL; the second part – a one-handed sign where the fingers form a zero – is etymologically related to the two-handed sign ZERO. The meaning that is associated with the suffixed one-handed form is 'not at all'. So here, from the verb FEEL the morphologically complex sign FEEL^ZERO 'not feel at all' is derived.

American Sign Language
(10)

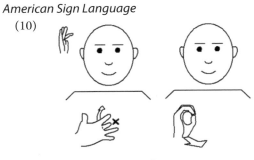

FEEL^ZERO

Other ASL verbs that can be combined with the suffix ZERO are SEE, EAT, SAY, TOUCH, and UNDERSTAND. When the sign to which the suffix is added has a movement, this movement is often shortened; FEEL, for instance, loses the repeated movement. Furthermore, the meaning of the resulting complex sign is not always fully predictable: SAY^ZERO, for example, means 'not mention' and TOUCH^ZERO means 'not use'. Remember that in Section 9.3, we described reduction/loss of movement and change in meaning as characteristics of sign language compounds. Why, then, is the complex form in (10) not considered a compound? Two properties, a categorial and a phonological restriction, make it likely that ZERO is actually a derivational affix: first, it can only be added to verbs; secondly, it can only combine with one-handed signs. Comparable restrictions are not observed in compounding. Consequently, ZERO is considered a derivational negative suffix.

Across spoken languages, sequential derivational processes, comparable to the one illustrated in (10), are very common. In general, under derivation, an existing word (or word stem) is combined with an element that is not (or no longer) a word by itself, and this morphological operation is capable of changing the category of a word. In the combination of the English word *eat* with the bound morpheme *-ery*, for instance, a noun is derived from a verb. In contrast, the sequential derivation in (10) does not change the word category, as is also true for the negation of verbs by means of the negative prefix *dis-* in English (e.g. *disrespect*, *disfavor*). Example (10) thus shows clearly that sequential **derivational processes** do exist in sign languages. Researchers have pointed out, however, that sequential derivation only accounts for a very small part of the word formation processes in sign languages.

In Section 5.4.1, we already presented an example of a simultaneous and category-changing derivational process in ASL: the derivation of nouns from verbs by means of movement changes and reduplication. Just like the derivation in (10), this change affects the manual component of the sign. But non-manual modifications can also play a role in derivation in sign languages, and these modifications are, of course, always simultaneous.

The diminutive and the augmentative are two simultaneous derivational processes that are related to each other and that do not change the category of the word. Both processes can be applied to many nouns in many sign languages, the former expressing the meaning 'little x', the latter carrying the meaning 'big x'. As can be seen in Example (11), in NGT, as in many other sign languages, both changes are realized by non-manual markers – the diminutive by sucking in the cheeks with pursed lips (marked by the symbol ')(' in (11a)), often in combination with showing the tip of tongue, the augmentative by puffed cheeks (glossed as '( )' in (11b)). These non-manual changes often go hand in hand with a manual change: in (11a), the sign HOUSE is articulated with a slightly smaller movement, while the movement of the sign BALL in (11b) is larger than usual.

Sign Language of the Netherlands

(11) a. $\overline{\hspace{2.5cm})(}$
       LAST WEEK, MY FRIEND HOUSE BUY.
       'Last week my friend bought a small house.'

      b. $\overline{\quad()\quad}$ $\overline{\hspace{2cm}/shhh/}$
       GARDEN$_{3a}$ BALL BE-PRESENT$_{3a}$.
       'There is a big ball in the garden.'

English and German also feature diminutive affixes, for instance, *-ie* in English, as in *sweetie*, and *-chen* in German, as in *Kätzchen* 'little cat' (from *Katze* 'cat') – the latter example illustrates that in German, suffixation often combines with a simultaneous, stem-internal change. The two languages do not have augmentative markers, which, however, are attested in many other spoken languages.

Simultaneous derivational processes do also occur in spoken languages, but far less often. Examples of simultaneous derivation in a spoken language are the English word pairs *the próduce / to prodúce* and *the pérmit / to permít*. In both cases, the noun and the verb only differ with respect to the stress pattern: the noun receives stress on the first syllable, the verb on the second. Moreover, many spoken languages feature derivational processes that are not phonologically marked at all; such processes are referred to as **conversion** (as e.g. in the English noun-verb pairs *love – to love* and *walk – to walk*). It seems that across sign languages, conversion is also very common. In NGT, for instance, the sign BIKE can be used as a noun and a verb without any phonological change that would signal the different word categories.

In this section, we looked at derivational word formation. We have seen that derivation by means of sequential affixation is quite rare in sign languages, unlike spoken languages, where derivational processes are predominantly sequential. In contrast, in sign languages, derivational processes are commonly realized by stem-internal changes that may affect manual and/or non-manual components (possibly in combination with reduplication).

9.5 Inflection

In contrast to derivation and compounding, inflectional word formation processes are determined by the grammatical structure of a sentence and/or by the interaction of two (or more) elements within a sentence. Compounding and derivation are often defined as word formation in the lexicon, whereas inflection is generally considered to be **syntactic word formation**. The different types of inflection addressed in this section are tense and aspectual inflection (Section 9.5.1), verb agreement (Section 9.5.2), and pluralization (Section 9.5.3). The relevant categories, tense, aspect, person, and number, are also called **grammatical** or **morpho-syntactic features**.

9.5.1 Tense and aspect

In the Flemish Sign Language (VGT) example in (12), we see that the verb STUDY has the same form in both sentences, although (12a) expresses an event that happened in the past while (12b) expresses a present tense event.

Flemish Sign Language
(12) a. YESTERDAY POSS$_1$ FRIEND THREE^HOUR STUDY.
          'Yesterday my friend studied for three hours.'
      b. TODAY WHOLE-DAY STUDY INDEX$_{3a}$.
          'Today he is studying all day long.'

In both cases, information about tense is contributed by an adverb. In fact, almost all sign languages described to date do not employ systematic morphological strategies for marking **tense** on verbs (comparable to English *walk – walked*). This may seem exceptional at first sight but actually the same is true for many spoken languages, for instance Chinese and Vietnamese. In the Vietnamese example (13), tense is specified by the adverb *hôm qua* 'yesterday', just as it is specified by the adverbs TODAY and YESTERDAY in the VGT sentences in (12). Moreover, Vietnamese does have an aspectual marker *dã*, which indicates that an action has finished (ANT = anterior). However, neither in VGT nor in Vietnamese are verbs inflected for tense.

Vietnamese
(13) **Hôm qua**, lúc   tôi gõ   cua,
      day   past moment I   knock   door
      thì   họ   **dã** ăn   com xong rôi.
      then   they ANT   eat rice finish already
      'Yesterday when I knocked at the door, they had already finished their dinner.'

There appear to be a few individual verbs in different sign languages that carry tense information. In NGT, this is only true for a single verb, the verb HAPPEN. This sign is produced with two 🖐-hands, palms oriented towards the body. When the two hands make a circular movement forwards, this indicates that something is happening now or will happen in the future. However, if a signer wants to express that something happened in the past, then the circular movement can be reversed such that the movement proceeds towards the signer's body (often the body also moves backwards a little bit). In this NGT example, the only difference is in the direction of the movement. The BSL signs WIN and WON, on the other hand, differ in various phonological aspects from each other. The present tense form WIN (14a) involves a turning movement of the wrist in front of the body with a simultaneous change in handshape from a 🖐-hand to a 👌-hand. In contrast, the past tense form WON (14b) is signed on the contralateral side of the chest, with a movement towards the body ending in contact; during the movement, the fingers make contact with the thumb. Clearly, these two examples must be seen as exceptions, as the relevant change only applies to a single sign; in other words, these forms are **lexicalized** and need to be included as separate entries in a dictionary (see Section 8.5).

British Sign Language
  (14)   a.   b.

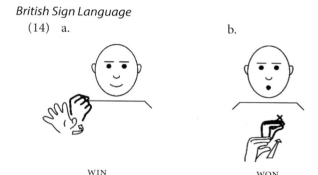

WIN   WON

Above, we mentioned that the past tense form of NGT HAPPEN may be accompanied by a slight backwards lean. A sign language for which a systematic non-manual tense marking strategy has been described is Italian Sign Language (LIS). The relevant non-manual marker is shoulder position: if the shoulders are tilted backward, then the event took place before the time of utterance (past tense); if the shoulders are straight, then the clause receives a present tense interpretation, and if the shoulders are tilted forward, then the event is assumed to take place after the time of utterance (future tense). This modification applies to all verbs, and it can thus be considered tense inflection.

While tense inflection appears to be rare across sign languages, sign languages are known to employ complex systems of **aspect** inflection. Just like tense, aspect is a grammatical category that is related to the concept of time. But while tense places an event on a time line in relation to another point in time (usually the time of speaking), aspect is related to the internal temporal structure of an event.

Let us compare the three forms of the ASL verb LOOK-AT in (15) to each other. In these three forms, we observe different movements. The citation form of the sign LOOK-AT is articulated with a short movement forward (15a). In (15b), we see a fast repetition of the movement, which yields the meaning 'looking at something habitually or regularly'. This is called the **habitual** form. The form in (15c) also has a repeated movement, but the movement characteristics are different: the movement is tense and at the endpoint of the movement, the hand is held in space for a brief moment, before moving back in an arched movement. This movement modification marks the **iterative**; the meaning of the modified verb is 'to look at something repeatedly'. Similar forms of aspectual marking have been described for other sign languages. Specifically, habitual and iterative aspect are commonly expressed by means of specific movement changes in combination with **reduplication** (repetition) of the base sign.

American Sign Language
(15)   a.   b.   c.

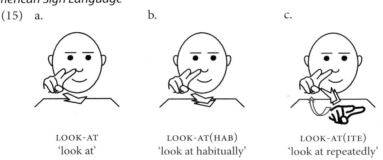

LOOK-AT	LOOK-AT(HAB)	LOOK-AT(ITE)
'look at'	'look at habitually'	'look at repeatedly'

In English, aspectual information is generally provided by adverbs. Still, English also features aspectual inflection, as shown in (16). Here, the event as a whole is placed in the past by means of tense inflection (the suffix -*ed*) on the main verb. In addition, the suffix -*ing* provides information about aspectual features of the singing event, namely that it takes place over a longer period of time – this aspect type is called **durative** (or continuative). The durative can also be expressed in sign languages, usually by adding a large circular movement and reduplication to the base sign.

English
(16)   Peter walk-**ed** down the street sing-**ing**.

When it comes to aspectual inflection, many spoken languages allow for more fine grained distinctions than English. The examples in (17) from Ewe (a Niger-Congo language spoken in Togo) illustrate three different aspectual categories, two of which are marked on the verb: the suffix -*a* expresses habitual aspect (17a), while the prefix *ga*- realizes iterative aspect (17b).

Ewe

(17) a. é-du-**a**   móli.   b. é-**ga**-du   móli.
          3SG-eat-HAB rice   3SG-ITE-eat rice
          'He/she usually eats rice.'   'He/she eats rice repeatedly.'

      c. é-du   móli **vo**.
          3SG-eat rice COMPL
          'He/she has finished eating rice.'

Hence, in the Ewe examples (17a) and (17b), just as in the ASL examples in (15), aspect marking is realized by a change affecting the verb (reduplication versus affixation). (17c) is different in this respect, as it involves a **free morpheme**. The sentence-final element *vo* signals that an action is completed – this type of aspect is called **completive**. Similar morphologically independent aspectual markers have also been identified in various sign languages. Israeli Sign Language (ISL), for instance, has a **perfective** marker, glossed as ALREADY, which expresses that an action has finished. Example (18) clearly shows that ALREADY is not a past tense marker, because it can also co-occur with temporal adverbs that express future tense. Such markers have also been described for other sign languages, although their use may differ somewhat from sign language to sign language. In NGT, for example, the sign READY has a comparable function. In Example (19), use of READY in the first clause indicates that the first action (the reading) must be finished, before the second action (the giving) can take place.

Israeli Sign Language

(18) WEEK FOLLOWING INDEX$_{(dual)}$ **ALREADY** MARRY.
      'Next week, they will already be married.'

Sign Language of the Netherlands

(19) INDEX$_1$ BOOK READ **READY**, INDEX$_1$ $_1$GIVE$_2$.
      'When I have read the book, I will give (it) to you.'

Both ALREADY in (18) and READY in (19) fulfil a grammatical function, as they add aspectual information. Yet both elements can also have a lexical function. The NGT adjective READY, for instance, can appear in a sentence like MY HOMEWORK READY 'My homework is done', where it functions as the predicate of the sentence. The lexical function of these signs is the original function. Such developments of grammatical markers from lexical elements are very common in signed and spoken languages, and are referred to as **grammaticalization** (see Section 13.4.2 for further discussion).

9.5.2 Agreement

Agreement can be defined as a match between two elements with regards to certain **features** like person, number, and gender. Agreement relations can be found in various domains. In Spanish, for instance, we find, on the one hand, gender agreement within the noun phrase, as in *una camisa roj-a* 'a red shirt' compared to *un zapato roj-o* 'a red shoe' – the former noun is feminine, the latter masculine, and the adjective agrees with the noun in gender by means of the suffix -*a/-o*. On the other hand, within the clausal domain, there is agreement between subject and verb with respect to person and number as in *El hombre habl-a* 'The man speaks' compared to *Los niños habl-an* 'The children speak'. In the remainder of this section, we will only be concerned with verb agreement. At the end of the section, we will add a cautionary note with respect to the nature of the phenomenon that we discuss here under the header 'agreement'.

In most sign languages that have been studied so far, agreement can be realized on certain verbs by means of **loci in the signing space**. These loci are either the actual locations of referents that are present in a discourse (the signer, the addresses, or present third persons) or arbitrary locations that were introduced for non-present referents. Locations are usually established by means of the pointing sign INDEX, but this can also be done by means of eye gaze direction or the use of a classifier (see Section 9.6.2). The example from Spanish Sign Language (LSE) in (20) illustrates the localization-by-INDEX strategy.

Spanish Sign Language
   (20)

    INDEX$_{3a}$ INDEX$_1$ SIBLING^FEMALE   WORK   LAWYER
    'My sister works as a lawyer.'

There is one present referent, the signer herself, and she talks about her sister, who is not present in the discourse setting. The signer starts her utterance by using the pointing sign INDEX$_x$, which points towards the arbitrary location '3a' at the ipsilateral side of the signing space, thereby localizing the sister at this locus (note that the signer's eye gaze also targets this locus; see also Section 5.5.1). This locus is abstract, as it does not carry spatial meaning: the sister is/was not to the right of the signer. The second pointing sign INDEX$_1$ is a first person possessive pronoun ('my') and points towards the signer's chest.

Across sign languages, some verb signs can change their form, dependent on these loci. The NGT examples in (21) illustrate this phenomenon. In (21a), there are two present referents, the signer and the addressee. The pointing sign INDEX$_2$ 'you' targets the addressee while the pointing sign INDEX$_1$ 'I' again points to the signer (both are optional; see Section 6.9 for discussion). The NGT **agreeing verb** GIVE is lexically specified for a movement away from the signer's body, just as in JSL (see (1a)). In (21a), this movement is reversed and goes from locus 2 (the location of the conversation partner) towards the signer's chest (locus 1). In (21b), the two non-present referents TEACHER and STUDENT are associated with different loci in the syntactic signing space – one ipsilateral (locus 3a), one contralateral (locus 3b) – by means of pointing signs. Note that in NGT, the localizing INDEX usually follows the noun, while in the LSE example in (20), it precedes the noun.

Sign Language of the Netherlands

(21) a.   INDEX$_2$ INDEX$_1$ WANT BOOK $_2$GIVE$_1$.
            'You want to give me a book.'
      b.   TEACHER INDEX$_{3a}$ STUDENT INDEX$_{3b}$ $_{3a}$CALL$_{3b}$.
            'The teacher calls the student.'

In contrast to GIVE, the NGT sign CALL involves no path movement, but a smaller repeated movement articulated at the wrist joint. In this case, the orientation is the relevant phonological parameter: the back of the hand 'points' in the direction of the subject, whilst the fingertips point towards the location of the object. In yet other verbs, e.g. the NGT verb VISIT, both movement and orientation are relevant. In all cases, the association between a referent and a locus in space is unambiguous. The same phenomenon has been described for many sign languages, including ASL, BSL, JSL, and LSE.

The forms of the two verbs in (21) are illustrated by means of video stills in (22); for the verb GIVE, we provide stills of the starting and end point of the movement.

Sign Language of the Netherlands

(22)

$_2$GIVE$_1$ $_{3a}$CALL$_{3b}$
'you give to me'   's/he calls him/her'

What is striking in these examples is that the agreeing verbs not only agree with the subject of the sentence, but also with the object, as the NGT examples in (21) demonstrate. This may seem exotic at first glance, but object agreement is actually a phenomenon that is attested in many spoken languages, too, for instance, in Itelmen, a language spoken on the peninsula Kamchatka (Eastern Russia). In both examples in (23), the transitive verb *to see* agrees with its subject (prefix) and its object (suffix).

Itelmen

(23)   a.   t'-əlčqu-ɣin.
            1SG-see-2SG.OBJ
            'I saw you.'

       b.   n-əlčqu-z-um.
            3PL-see-PRS-1SG.OBJ
            'They see me.'

However, across sign languages, the realization of agreement is more complex than the above examples suggest. Here, we will briefly address three complications. First, in the sign languages that have been studied, only a subset of all verbs can be modified to realize agreement in the way illustrated above. Actually, most verbs are **non-agreeing verbs** (***plain verbs***) and thus cannot change their direction of movement or orientation. This is true, for example, for body-anchored verbs such as the NGT verb UNDERSTAND in (24), which is signed in front of the forehead, or the LSE verb WANT, which is articulated on the chest (25). Both verbs are transitive but cannot detach from their body location in order to move towards the locus associated with the object.

Sign Language of the Netherlands

(24)   <u>   </u> ^{neg}
       INDEX$_1$ COLLEAGUE INDEX$_{3a}$ ASSIGNMENT UNDERSTAND.
       'My colleague does not understand the assignment.'

Spanish Sign Language

(25)

WANT

Secondly, there are a few agreeing verbs in which the movement does not proceed from the subject to the object, as in (21a), but in the opposite direction; these verbs are called **backward verbs**. In LSE, for instance, this group includes the verbs INVITE (26a) and

UNDERSTAND (26b). The stills in (26a) show that the movement goes from locus 1 to locus 3b. Based on what we explained above, one would thus expect that the meaning of the inflected verb is 'I invited her', but this is not the case. Rather, the meaning is 'She invited me', as the starting point is associated with the object and the end point with the subject. Without going into much detail, we wish to point out that some scholars have argued that it is actually not the grammatical roles subject/object that are relevant for agreeing verbs, but rather the semantic roles Source/Goal (see Section 6.4): in both regular and backward agreeing verbs, the movement proceeds from the Source to the Goal argument. Comparing the NGT example (24) to the LSE example (26b), it is also interesting to note that the verb UNDERSTAND belongs to different verb classes in the two languages, due to different phonological properties: in NGT it is a plain verb, in LSE it is a (backward) agreeing verb.

Spanish Sign Language

(26) a.

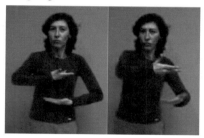

$_1$INVITE$_{3b}$
'She invited me.'

b.

$_2$UNDERSTAND$_1$
'I understand you.'

The third complication we address concerns the fact that some sign languages have developed alternative ways to express agreement: in combination with non-agreeing verbs and adjectival predicates, they make use of a dedicated **agreement auxiliary**. This auxiliary is semantically empty and only serves to express the agreement relation. Such elements have been described for a number of unrelated sign languages including

DGS, Taiwan Sign Language (TSL), Indopakistani Sign Language (IPSL), Greek Sign Language, and NGT. ASL and BSL, on the other hand, lack such an auxiliary. TSL is special in that it has three different agreement auxiliaries. In Example (28), the auxiliary AUX2 is used; it combines with the non-agreeing verb LOVE and occupies a preverbal position. Phonologically, it resembles the verb SEE (it is signed with a ⫚-hand, fingertips in direction of object), but has lost its original meaning, as is also evident from (28). This implies that we are, once again, dealing with a process of grammaticalization (from verb to auxiliary; see Section 13.4.2).

Taiwan Sign Language

(28) THIS WOMAN $_3$AUX2$_1$ LOVE.
      'This woman loves me.'

The NGT auxiliary, which generally appears in sentence-final position, is glossed as AUX-OP, because it is always accompanied by the mouthing /op/, a borrowing from Dutch (29). AUX-OP is signed with a ⫔-hand that performs a path movement from the locus of the subject to the locus of the object, the tip of the index finger being oriented towards the object. In (29), AUX-OP expresses agreement in the context of the (non-agreeing) adjectival predicate PROUD; it moves from in front of the signer's body to an ipsilateral position in the signing space, at which the referent BROTHER has been localized.

Sign Language of the Netherlands

(29) INDEX$_1$ BROTHER INDEX$_{3a}$ PROUD $_1$AUX-OP$_{3a}$. ‾‾‾‾‾/op/‾‾‾‾‾
      'I am proud of my brother.'

At this point, it is important to note that, while the type of agreement system sketched above is very common across sign languages, it is not the case that all sign languages feature such a system. Two sign languages that have been reported to not allow for the spatial modulation of verbs are Al-Sayyid Bedouin Sign Language (ABSL), a village sign language from Israel, and Kata Kolok, a village sign language from Bali. For instance, in ABSL, a signer would convey the meaning 'you give to me' by signing INDEX$_2$ GIVE INDEX$_1$, that is, the verb GIVE appears in its citation form, moving forward from the signer's body.

But what are the relevant features for agreement in sign languages? In the literature on sign linguistics, the status of verb agreement is hotly debated, and one of the central issues in the discussion is the role of person features. In most spoken languages, the relevant person distinctions are first, second and third person – actually, some scholars have suggested that this three-way distinction is a language universal. Sign languages, however, appear to behave differently. In fact, the only locus that is fixed is the locus for first person singular, while the loci for second and third person can vary. Given this pattern, some researchers have proposed that sign languages only distinguish between first (in front of or on the signer's body) and non-first (all other loci) person, which would imply that in this domain, sign languages violate a proposed language universal. Another challenge is posed by the fact that there are, in principle, an infinite number of loci for non-first person, depending on the discourse situation, which in turn implies that there are also an infinitive number of agreement markers. It is simply impossible to provide a fixed phonological form for the non-first person singular marker (in contrast to spoken languages where agreement markers have a fixed form, as e.g. English third person singular -*s*) – this complication is referred to as the '**listability problem**'.

In conclusion, we would like to point out that not all sign linguists would agree with the assumptions made in this section. We discussed the spatial modulation of verbs under the header 'agreement'. Our basis assumption was that loci in the syntactic space are an instantiation of agreement, in other words, that these loci are part of the grammatical system of sign languages. However, given the listability problem (and other challenges that we did not address), some researchers take it that these locations are not part of the grammar, but rather are gestural in nature. Given differences between the grammatical phenomenon agreement and the spatial modulation of sign language verbs, they therefore prefer to refer to the verbs that undergo such modulations as 'directional' or 'indicating' verbs. However, the patterns we introduced (e.g. distinction of verb types, existence of auxiliary-like element) are independent of the theoretical treatment of the phenomenon.

9.5.3 Pluralization

Just as other grammatical features can be expressed in many different ways, the realization of number also shows considerable variation. Across spoken languages, the main strategies for the **pluralization** of nouns are affixation, reduplication, and zero marking. But even within a single language, different strategies may be attested. In German, for instance, we find **affixation** – there are four different plural-suffixes, as shown in (30a–d) – and **zero-marking** (30e) ('ø' represents the zero-affix). Moreover, both affixation and zero-marking may be accompanied by a stem-internal change (umlaut), as illustrated in (30b) and (30e).

German

(30) a. Kino   →   Kino-s   b. Zahn   →   Zähn-e
          'cinema'   'cinemas'   'tooth'   'teeth'
      c. Tasche   →   Tasche-n   d. Kind   →   Kind-er
          'bag'   'bags'   'child'   'children'
      e. Mutter   →   Mütter-ø
          'mother'   'mothers'

The German system is thus fairly complex. Moreover, it is almost impossible to predict for a given noun which suffix it takes. In contrast, in other languages, the choice of suffix can be predicted on the basis of phonological features of the stem. This is true, for instance, for Turkish, where the choice between the two plural **allomorphs** *-ler* and *-lar* depends on the last vowel in the stem: following *e–i–ö–ü*, the suffix *-ler* is attached (31a–b), whereas after *a–o–u*, the suffix *-lar* is added (31c–d). This phenomenon is called 'vowel harmony', as the suffix vowel harmonizes with the stem vowel with respect to the feature [±back].

Turkish

(31) a. ev → ev-ler   b. gün → gün-ler
'house'   'houses'   'day'   'days'

c. adam → adam-lar   d. çocuk → çocuk-lar
'man'   'men'   'child'   'children'

Finally, in some spoken languages, plurality is realized by means of **reduplication**. In (32), we illustrate this strategy with two examples from the Australian language Warlpiri, where the whole stem is reduplicated.

Warlpiri

(32) a. kurdu → kurdu-kurdu   b. kamina → kamina-kamina
'child'   'children'   'girl'   'girls'

It appears that across sign languages, reduplication is an important pluralization strategy. This is not surprising given that by means of reduplication, plurality is expressed in an iconic way: one articulation of the sign refers to a single entity, repeated articulation refers to multiple entities. Interestingly, in DGS, we find two different forms of reduplication. In some one-handed nouns, such as CHILD (33a), the reduplication is executed with a sideward movement, while other nouns, such as the two-handed BOOK (33b), are reduplicated without a change of location (simple reduplication). Note that in both cases, the number of repetitions does not necessarily reflect the actual number of people or objects; that is, in (33a), the repetition does not indicate that there were three children, and in (33b), it does not necessarily indicate not that there were two or three books.

German Sign Language

(33) a.   b.

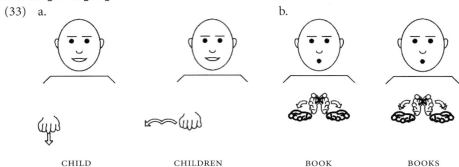

CHILD   CHILDREN   BOOK   BOOKS

However, not all nouns in DGS can be pluralized by means of reduplication. One important restriction that has been noted is that nouns that are already lexically specified for a repeated or complex movement cannot be reduplicated. Clearly, we are dealing here with a **phonological constraint**. Due to this constraint, the signs RESTAURANT (34a) and BICYCLE (34b), for instance, cannot be reduplicated, as they are both specified for repeated, alternating movement (straight or circular). That is, the plural form of these nouns is zero-marked. If the context does not make it clear that the plural is implied, the signer can make use of a numeral or a quantifier like MANY.

German Sign Language

(34)   a.   b.   c.

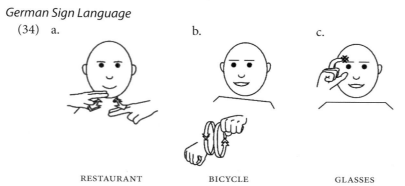

| RESTAURANT | BICYCLE | GLASSES |

These examples illustrate that DGS, unlike German or Turkish, does not employ plural affixes. And yet pluralization in DGS shows interesting parallels to patterns found in spoken languages. First, just as in Warlpiri (32), reduplication of a noun is an important strategy for pluralization. Second, whether or not this strategy is applicable to a particular noun depends on phonological properties of the stem – just as the choice of a Turkish plural suffix (31). Third, nouns that, due to a phonological constraint, cannot be reduplicated show zero-marking, just like certain nouns in German (30e).

Sign languages may also differ from each other in how they realize pluralization. In general, NGT behaves very similarly to DGS in this domain, but there are also differences. While body-anchored signs like GLASSES can be reduplicated in NGT, reduplication is excluded for the phonologically identical DGS sign GLASSES (34c) – and for body-anchored signs in general. Nouns in IPSL can never be reduplicated; in this language, we thus only find zero-marking (the only exception seems to be the sign CHILD).

Finally, we would like to point out that there is another strategy for pluralization in sign languages, namely by means of a **reduplicated classifier handshape** (see also Sections 5.4 and 9.6.2). The NGT examples in (35) show that this strategy is available for nouns that cannot be reduplicated (e.g. BICYCLE) as well as for nouns that can be reduplicated (e.g. BOOK). However, it is important to note that these are not 'pure' plural forms. Rather, in both cases, the classifier adds meaning, specifically information about the spatial location of objects – in the below examples 'next to each other'.

Sign Language of the Netherlands

(35)   a.

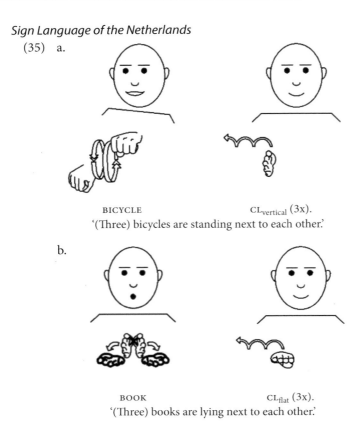

BICYCLE   CL~vertical~ (3x).
'(Three) bicycles are standing next to each other.'

b.

BOOK   CL~flat~ (3x).
'(Three) books are lying next to each other.'

Taken together, the discussion in this section reveals that sign languages have rather complex inflectional systems. Two important morphosyntactic processes that are commonly realized by reduplication (possibly in combination with other phonological changes) are aspect marking and pluralization. From a typological perspective, this is not so remarkable, since aspect and plurality are also expressed by means of reduplication in many spoken languages. Case and tense, on the other hand, appear to be rarely marked in sign languages – a gap that is paralleled in many spoken languages.

Further, we have seen that across sign languages, some verbs can agree with their subject and object by means of movement and/or orientation changes. A comparison of various sign languages reveals striking similarities when it comes to the realization of the inflectional processes addressed in this section – while this is clearly not the case in spoken languages. These similarities are probably due to the specific affordances made available by the visual-spatial modality. In other words: to date, no sign language has been discovered that would, for instance, realize aspect by means of a handshape change or plurality by means of a change of location.

9.6 Incorporation and classification

In the final section of this chapter, we address two special ways of word formation: incorporation and classification. Both phenomena also occur in spoken languages. We treat these two word formation processes in a separate section because it is – also for spoken languages – sometimes debated under which type of word formation they should be subsumed, or whether they possibly constitute entirely different types of word formation.

9.6.1 Incorporation

A term that one may often come across in the scientific literature on sign languages is **incorporation**. In this section, we shall first describe what incorporation actually is, and then turn to the description of a typical process of incorporation in sign languages, namely numeral incorporation.

Incorporation is an example of word formation in syntax. This means that, unlike in derivation and compounding, two elements are not combined in the lexicon, but within a syntactic structure (i.e. a sentence). In contrast to inflection, however, two free elements are combined. In spoken languages, the most common type of incorporation is noun incorporation, that is, incorporation of a direct object into a verb. This can be seen in the examples in (36) from the North American language Southern Tiwa. Whereas the direct object *seuan* 'man' in (36a) constitutes a separate word (and is accompanied by a specific nominal suffix), in the alternative structure in (36b), it is part of the verbal complex which includes the stem *mū* 'see'. The fact that the agreement prefix *ti-* in (36b) precedes the object makes clear that the object in this example is really part of the verbal complex (in the example, the subject ('I') is not expressed because Southern Tiwa allows pro-drop).

Southern Tiwa
(36) a. Seuan-ide ti-mū-ban.
        man-SUF   1SG-see-PST
        'I saw the man.'
    b. Ti-**seuan**-mū-ban.
        1SG-man-see-PST
        'I saw the man.'

An important characteristic of incorporation is that the two sentences in (36) are paraphrases of each other; both sentences thus express the same meaning. Some complex verbs in other spoken languages, like the Dutch verb *pianospelen* 'to piano-play' may look like incorporated structures (since *piano* is the object of the verb), but, unlike Southern Tiwa, it is impossible to say, for instance: **Ik pianospeelde gisteren* '*I piano-played yesterday'.

A comparable word formation process in sign languages is **numeral incorporation**. In many sign languages, it is possible to incorporate numerals (generally realized by a number of selected fingers) into temporal expressions like 'week', 'month', or 'year'. This is achieved by simply changing the handshape of the respective temporal sign; the numeral is then no longer signed separately. In the NGT example (37a), for instance, the numeral FOUR is incorporated into the temporal sign WEEK, whereas in Example (37b) from IPSL, the numeral THREE substitutes the handshape of the sign YEAR.

(37) a. *SL of the Netherlands*   b. *Indopakistani Sign Language*

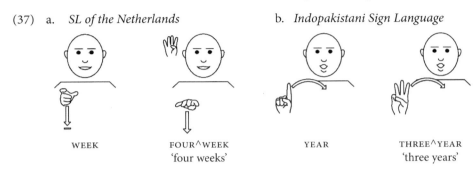

WEEK	FOUR^WEEK	YEAR	THREE^YEAR
	'four weeks'		'three years'

The fact that it is also possible to sign the two signs separately suggests that the changes in (37) are indeed the result of a process of incorporation; in NGT, for instance, a signer could choose to sign FOUR WEEK instead of FOUR^WEEK. Which number handshapes can be incorporated is language-specific; amongst other things, this depends on whether a sign language has a one-handed or a two-handed counting system. NGT and IPSL, just like ASL and many other sign languages, employ one-handed counting systems (yet, the systems are different from each other). In ASL, it is possible to incorporate numerals larger than 5, but this seems to be uncommon in NGT. Jordanian Sign Language (LIU) also has a one-handed counting system, but the signs for 7 and 8 involve movement, and thus cannot be incorporated (both have, just like the sign TWO, a 𝒱-handshape). In Chinese Sign Language, numbers higher than 10 can sometimes be incorporated, but this is rather unusual cross-linguistically. It thus appears that the application of numeral incorporation is highly restricted. Sign languages generally draw the line either at 5 or at 10, but even within these ranges, there may be exceptions due to phonological restrictions. Moreover, even within a sign language (e.g. ASL), the possibilities may vary from sign to sign.

Although numeral incorporation has been described for many sign languages, it is not attested in all sign languages. In Hausa Sign Language (Nigeria), for instance, there are far fewer possibilities than in the sign languages we just discussed. In this sign language, signs referring to time units cannot incorporate numerals. The only exception is the adverb YESTERDAY: the basic form of YESTERDAY is signed with the 𝒶-hand, but the handshape can change to express 'two/three/… days ago'.

9.6.2 Classification

Classification is a morphological process in which a bound morpheme reflects particular semantic or form characteristics of a noun, for instance, characteristics like animate, edible, liquid, or flat. **Classification** appears to occur, to varying degrees, in most sign languages studied so far. Yet, sign language classifiers do not combine with all verbs but are restricted to **verbs of motion or location**, in which they are realized by means of a handshape change (thus simultaneously).

We will illustrate the use of classifier handshapes by means of examples from DGS. In Example (38a), the motion verb MOVE combines with the classifier handshape for a human referent, the ⫣-hand (sometimes called 'person classifier'; we gloss this as CL: ⫣). The verb sign moves from right to left, and in combination with the sign STREET, this results in the meaning of 'crossing the street'. In (38b), the same verb is used, but now it is signed with a ⫣-hand (palm down), the DGS classifier for cars and other four-wheeled vehicles.

German Sign Language

(38)   a.   STREET, MAN ₍right₎MOVE-CL:⫣₍left₎.
           'The man crosses the street.'

       b.   STREET, CAR ₍next-to-body₎MOVE-CL:⫣₍neutral.space₎.
           'The car drives along the street.'

The sentences in (38) are intransitive (the locative STREET is an adjunct; see Section 6.2), and the classifier handshapes reflect form features of the subject of the verb. Such classifiers are called **entity classifiers**. What does the shape of the classifiers tell us about the form of the subject in (38)? A man – even if rather portly – is taller than he is wide, and this feature is reflected in the ⫣-hand. A car, on the other hand, has a larger surface but is less 'tall,' two characteristics that are applicable to the ⫣-hand.

Despite the fact that the relation between a referent and a classifier is usually rather iconic, entity classifiers may differ from sign language to sign language. In (39), this is illustrated for vehicle classifiers in three sign languages. Clearly, the handshape used in DGS (39a) is most faithful to the shape of the referent, while in ASL (39b) and LIU (39c), the relation between the handshape and the referent is less transparent (note that these classifiers are actually articulated with the palm oriented sideward). For ASL, it has been argued that the ⫣-handshape can be traced back to a classifier for ships, the extended thumb representing the funnel; yet its use has been extended to other vehicles like cars and trucks.

(39)   *German (a), American (b), and Jordanian Sign Language (c)*

a.   b.   c.

Another type of sign language classifier that is distinguished in the literature are **handle classifiers**. These reflect shape characteristics of an object in a transitive sentence. As was already illustrated in Example (1) at the beginning of this chapter, the verb GIVE may change its handshape, depending on the object being given. In the DGS example (40a), GIVE is articulated with a ✍-hand, the handle classifier for long and thin objects, whereas round objects require the ✊-handshape, as shown in (40b).

German Sign Language

(40)   a.   MAN INDEX₃ₐ WOMAN INDEX₃ᵦ FLOWER ₃ₐGIVE-CL:✍₃ᵦ.
       'The man gives the woman a flower.'

b.   MOTHER INDEX₃ₐ CUP ₃ₐGIVE-CL:✊₁.
       'My mother gives me a cup.'

We can characterize the difference between the two classifier types by stating (i) that entity classifiers refer directly to the shape of an entity: the hand *is* as it were the entity; while (ii) handle classifiers refer *indirectly* to the shape of an entity by showing how it is handled or manipulated. Note that further classifier types have been suggested in the literature (e.g. bodypart and instrument classifiers), but these shall not be considered here.

In Section 6.3, we already pointed out that occasionally, one and the same predicate may combine with different types of classifiers, thereby undergoing a valency change. Now, equipped with the relevant terminology, we can specify that in many sign languages, the verb root BREAK can combine either with an entity classifier (two ✌-hands) or with a handle classifier (two ✊-hands), yielding an intransitive clause (*The stick breaks*) in the first case, but a transitive clause (*Peter breaks the stick*) in the latter case.

Classifier morphemes are also attested in various spoken languages. The examples in (41) from Cherokee, a language spoken in North America, resemble the DGS examples in (40) in that classifier morphemes that reflect certain shape characteristics of a direct object combine with verb stems; the relevant property is liquid in (41a) and flexible in (41b). However, in contrast to DGS, the classifier morphemes are realized sequentially (Cherokee, too, is a pro-drop language; the prefix *gá-* expresses subject- and object agreement).

Cherokee
(41) a. Àma   gà-**nèèh**-nééʼa.
         water 3SG.SBJ/3SG.OBJ-CL(**liquid**)-give.PRS
         'She is giving him water.'
     b. Àhnàwo gà-**nvv**-nèèʼa.
         shirt   3SG.SBJ/3SG.OBJ-CL(**flexible**)-give.PRS
         'She is giving him a shirt.'

Similar to what we reported in Section 9.5.2 for agreement, there are different opinions concerning the analysis of classification in sign languages. Some researchers consider classification in sign languages a type of incorporation, which implies that the classifier is an incorporated argument (subject or object) – just as in the Southern Tiwa example in (36b). Other scholars, however, analyze classification as a special case of agreement since the choice of a classifier is determined by another element in the same sentence – similar to what characterizes other agreement processes. According to this analysis, the verb GIVE in (40) agrees with its object by means of a handshape change. There are even researchers that propose that classifiers are not part of the grammatical system of sign languages, but should rather be seen as non-linguistic gestures.

In conclusion of this section, we would like to point out that, although most sign languages studied so far make use of classifier handshapes, not all do. Research on Adamorobe Sign Language (AdaSL), a village sign language from Ghana, has revealed that motion verbs in AdaSL never combine with entity classifiers and only rarely with handle classifiers. Instead, AdaSL employs 'directionals', that is, a small group of signs with very general meaning that express directional motion, including FROM ('movement from a reference point'), TOWARDS ('movement towards a reference point'), and ENTER ('entering movement'). The first two meanings are illustrated in (42a). Crucially, both directionals have variable handshapes (for instance ☝- or 🖐-hand) that are articulated in a lax manner; moreover, they can be signed with one hand or two hands.

Adamorobe Sign Language
(42) a. INDEX FROM_{left} SOON AGAIN TOWARDS_{right}.
         'They went and came back soon afterwards.'
     b. TOWARDS_{head} FROM.
         'I put it on my head and go.'

In (42b), too, the two directionals co-occur. In contrast to (42a), however, the sign TOWARDS refers to the handling of an object in this example (a basket). Yet, no handle classifier is used. FROM expresses the movement of the subject in both examples, but here too, the handshape does not reflect shape features of the referent. To compare: in DGS and other sign languages, probably the ☝-hand would be used to express 'person moving' and two 🖐-hands for 'putting on basket'.

Summary

In basically all sign languages studied to date, morphemes can be combined in morphologically complex signs. An interesting, modality specific pattern is observed in complex signs: most morphological processes in sign languages are not **sequential** in nature but apply **simultaneously**; in spoken languages, simultaneous processes are the exception.

There are different ways to form **compounds**. **Coordinate compounds** have to be distinguished from **subordinate compounds** in which one of the components is the **head**. Characteristic form changes are observed in compounds in comparison with the signs that make up the compound: the movement is reduced or deleted, and **handshape assimilation** and **weak hand spreading** are common. Moreover, the meaning can change. Compounding is frequent in sign languages whereas **derivational processes** involving the combination of a stem with a (manual or non-manual) **bound morpheme** are quite infrequent. Rather, **conversion** appears to be rather common.

Inflectional processes on the basis of certain **morphosyntactic features** play an important role in sign languages. Different types of **aspect** can either be realized by means of **reduplication** and changes in movement (for instance, the **habitual**, **iterative**, and **durative**) or by **free morphemes** (e.g. the **completive** and **perfective**). Free aspectual markers are commonly **grammaticalized** from lexical signs. In contrast, **tense** is usually not morphologically marked on verbs.

In the realization of **agreement**, locations in the syntactic space play a crucial role. As for their agreement properties, different types of verbs have to be distinguished: **non-agreeing (plain) verbs** and **agreeing verbs** (which come as regular and **backward verbs**). Furthermore, some sign languages have **agreement auxiliaries** that can express agreement when the lexical verb is incapable of doing so. A challenge in the analysis of sign language agreement is the **listability problem**.

Pluralization of nouns is realized in many sign languages by means of **reduplication** or **zero-marking**, rather than by **affixation**. The choice of strategy appears to be determined by **phonological constraints**. As in some spoken languages, we may find plural **allomorphs**. Another option to express plurality is the use of **reduplicated classifier handshapes**.

Two special ways of word formation that have been described for numerous sign languages are **incorporation** and **classification**. In **numeral incorporation**, a number handshape substitutes the handshape of a noun. Classification affects **verbs of motion and location** and is realized by means of a change in handshape; the handshape reflects certain shape properties of an argument. Two important types of classifiers are **entity classifiers** and **handle classifiers**.

Test yourself

1. What is the difference between coordinate and subordinate compounds?
2. a. Mention two types of aspect and explain how these can be realized phonologically in a sign language.
   b. How could these same aspect types be realized in English?

3. a. How is agreement expressed in a sign language you know? Please mention different verb types.

    b. In what way does the agreement system of the sign language you know differ from that of the surrounding spoken language? Please discuss two aspects.

4. Name two types of sign language classifiers that can appear in verbs of motion and location and explain how they differ from each other.

Assignments

1. Please look carefully at the following individual signs and how they are combined in compounds: one example is from ASL (a), the other one from South African Sign Language (b). What changes can be observed in the compounds? Use the relevant terminology. (For the SASL compound, the beginning and end positions of the hands are shown.)

    a. *American Sign Language*

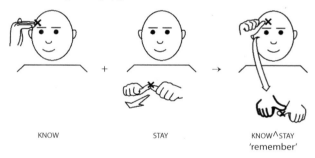

KNOW   STAY   KNOW^STAY
                                'remember'

    b. *South African Sign Language*

SAND   +   PLACE   →

SAND^PLACE 'desert'

2. How would you analyze the following signs from SASL in terms of the type of word formation? Motivate your answer.

MECHANIC^PERSON 'mechanic'

PIPE^PERSON 'plumber'

ELECTRICITY^PERSON 'electrician'

3. What would the plural forms of the following three DGS signs look like? Motivate your answer.

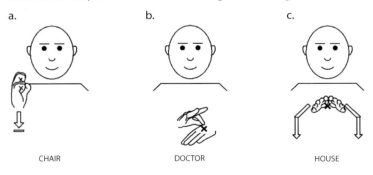

a.

b.

c.

CHAIR

DOCTOR

HOUSE

4. Why is word formation by means of simultaneous (stem-internal) changes in sign languages far more common than in spoken languages?

5. At the outset of Section 9.2, we asked the question to which morphological type sign languages could belong. However, we did not provide an answer. What do you think? Does the sign language you know belong to the isolating, agglutinating, fusional, or polysynthetic type? Or is the typology proposed for spoken languages not applicable to your sign language?

References and further reading

An interesting description of the characteristics and particularities of sign language morphology can be found in Aronoff, Meir & Sandler (2005); a recent overview is provided in Meir (2012). As for sketches of morphological processes in various sign languages, see Sutton-Spence & Woll (1999) for BSL, Johnston & Schembri (2007) for Auslan, Meir & Sandler (2008) for ISL. Compounds and their formational characteristics have been described in detail for ASL in Klima & Bellugi (1979), Liddell & Johnson (1986), and Vercellotti & Mortensen (2012), for SSL in Wallin (1983), for DGS in Becker (2003), and for Al-Sayyid Bedouin Sign Language (a young village sign language) in Meir et al. (2010a). In contrast, derivational processes – except for noun-verb pairs (see Chapter 5) – have only received little attention (but see Aronoff, Meir & Sandler 2005). Non-manual tense marking in LIS is the topic of the study by Zucchi (2009). Aspectual modifications are addressed in Klima & Bellugi (1979), Bergman & Dahl (1994), and Rathmann (2005); free aspectual markers are discussed in Fischer & Gough (1999[1972]) and Meir (1999). For an overview of tense and aspect marking, see Pfau, Steinbach & Woll (2012b). As for agreement, the different verb types were first distinguished in Padden (1988). Meir (2002) compares agreement in spoken and signed languages; Zwitserlood & van Gijn (2006) discuss properties of agreement in NGT. Recent overviews of the phenomenon, including discussion of the status of sign language agreement, are Lillo-Martin & Meier (2011), Mathur & Rathmann (2010, 2012), and Wilbur (2013). Descriptions of agreement auxiliaries (including their grammaticalization) can be found in Steinbach & Pfau (2007) and Sapountzaki (2012). Pfau & Steinbach (2006b) present a comparative study on DGS pluralization whereas Zwitserlood & Nijhof (1999) describe the phenomenon for NGT and Zwitserlood, Perniss & Özyürek (2012) for TİD. Numeral incorporation has been investigated by Liddell (1997) for ASL, and by Ktejik (2013) for JSL. The classical study on sign language classifiers is the one by Supalla (1986); convenient overviews are provided by Schembri (2003) and Zwitserlood (2012). For a comprehensive theoretical account of NGT classifiers see Zwitserlood (2003). Benedicto & Brentari (2004) discuss the interaction of classifiers with argument structure.

Examples of sign language compounds are taken from Klima & Bellugi (1979), Leuninger (2001), and Wallin (1983). The ASL negative suffix has been described by Aronoff, Meir & Sandler (2005). Sutton-Spence & Woll (1999) discuss the BSL signs WIN/WON, and Meir (1999) describes the use of the ISL aspect marker ALREADY. All LSE examples are taken from Costello (2015). The TSL auxiliaries are discussed by Smith (1990), while lack of agreement in ABSL and Kata Kolok is addressed by Aronoff et al. (2005) and Marsaja (2008), respectively. All DGS plural examples are taken from Pfau & Steinbach (2006b). For numeral incorporation, we found the IPSL example in Zeshan (2000) and the Hausa SL example in Schmaling (2000). All LIU examples mentioned in the text are from Hendriks (2004). AdaSL directionals are described in Nyst (2007). The SASL examples are taken from the SASL dictionary by the National Institute of the Deaf (2011). As for spoken language examples, the Terena examples are from Akinlabi (1996), the Vietnamese example from Đình-Hoà (1997), the Itelmen examples from Bobaljik & Wurmbrand (2002), the Warlpiri examples from Olsen (2014), the Southern Tiwa examples from Baker (1988), and the Cherokee examples from Aikhenvald (2000).

Chapter 10

Phonetics

Onno Crasborn & Els van der Kooij

10.1 Introduction

The most important and striking difference between spoken languages and signed languages is the **modality difference**. This is the difference in communication channel: words in spoken languages are produced by the speech organs and perceived through the ears, whereas signs are made with the upper body and perceived through the eyes. The entire **communication chain** in both types of language consists of three parts: the production of a **signal**, the signal itself, and the **perception** of the signal, as illustrated in (1a) for speech and in (1b) for signs.

The speech and sign chain

(1) a.

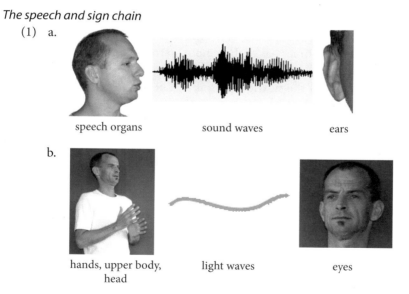

    speech organs   sound waves   ears

    b.

    hands, upper body,   light waves   eyes
         head

Within the science of linguistics, there are two disciplines that deal with this communication chain. **Phonetics** studies the physical properties of the process, while phonology (see Chapter 11) focuses on the parts of words and signs as they function in the system of a specific language. We assume that signers store one abstract form of each sign in their memory (the *phonological form*). Each time they produce the sign, it will look

DOI 10.1075/z.199.10cra

slightly different: the pronunciation, the *phonetic form*, is variable. Take, for example, the American Sign Language (ASL) sign SAY, as shown in (2). The movement in this sign could be described as follows: 'move an extended index finger from the chin in a forward direction'. The articulation is different each time the sign is used: sometimes the movement is 10 centimeters and takes half a second to produce; at other times, it may well be 30 centimeters, and will take somewhat longer.

American Sign Language
(2)   The ASL sign SAY, which is articulated with a forward movement from the chin of some 30 centimeters

Of course, the same is observed in spoken languages. The English vowel [u] in a word like 'zoom', for example, sometimes has slightly more lip rounding than at other times depending on the context.

In the course of this and the next chapter, it will become clear that phonetics and phonology cannot be studied entirely independently of each other. The physical boundaries to the process of production and perception constrain what is possible in sign language, and, as a result, the possible shapes of the abstract phonological forms. Signs that our hands are incapable of articulating obviously do not occur in sign languages, but in addition, as in spoken languages, easier forms are often preferred over difficult ones. Those difficult forms are 'marked' in the language system: they occur less frequently, and in fewer types of combinations with other forms (see also Chapter 3). Occasionally, a movement may be made in a somewhat less complex way because it is more efficient at that moment, for instance, if you are holding something in your hands. It has also been observed that less complex movements or handshapes occur more often in the fixed vocabulary of sign languages (the 'frozen lexicon', see Section 8.4) than more complex movements or handshapes.

In order to determine what is easy and what is difficult, it is important to distinguish the perspective of the signer from the perspective of the one being signed to (the perceiver). Their interests are often in conflict: a small movement of the little finger, for example, requires little energy on the side of the signer, but is relatively difficult to perceive and recognize. It is therefore not possible to state in any absolute sense that one sign is 'easier' than the other. It is thus important to determine independently of each other what is difficult and easy for the signer and the perceiver, respectively.

In the following, we first look at the production of signs (Section 10.2) and then at their perception (Section 10.3). Subsequently, we offer a detailed discussion of phonetic variation (Section 10.4). Finally, we briefly present various notation systems for signs that have been suggested (Section 10.5), and we address language technology, in the form of sign recognition and the development of virtual animated signing characters (Section 10.6). It will become clear that we still know fairly little about the phonetics of sign languages. Limited research has been done on this aspect of sign languages compared to the linguistic properties of sign languages discussed in other chapters of this book.

10.2 Production

10.2.1 Muscles, joints, and body parts

When a signer has determined what s/he wants to say, the **articulation** of the sign is initiated (see also Section 2.4). The muscles that are then contracted cause parts of the arm, hand, and fingers to move. These movements can be described at several levels: in terms of the **muscles** that are active, in terms of the **joints** at which movement takes place, or in terms of the **body parts** that move. The same process applies to the non-manual parts of the signs: the posture of the upper body, the position of the head, and the facial expression.

The articulation of the ASL sign SAY shown in (2), for instance, can be described as follows:

Muscles	The extensor muscle of the elbow contracts.
Joints	The elbow joint extends 60 degrees.
Body parts	The forearm, hand, and index finger move obliquely forwards/downwards away from the chin and make a 60 degree turn through space, rotating about the center point of the elbow.

This is a very concise description, and it only relates to the movement in the sign. At the same time as the movement is performed, a number of muscles are active to keep the forearm and hand elevated in space, while prior to this, other muscles made it possible for the initial position of the sign to be reached: in this case, touching the chin with the tip of the index finger while the other fingers are clenched. This movement towards the initial position of a sign is called a **transitional movement**; it does not belong to the sign proper and varies considerably depending on where the hand is located prior to the sign.

The articulation of facial expressions can be described along the same lines. The main difference to the movement of the hand and fingers is that only one joint in the face is involved: the lower jaw. This joint is primarily used in non-manual components, that is, in mouthings (derived from spoken words) and mouth gestures (not derived from spoken words; see Section 11.6). However, the complexity of the face as an articulator lies mainly in the vast number of muscles together with the flexibility of the skin. The movements of those dozens of muscles can be seen in the skin folds of the face: the lips, cheeks, eyelids, eyebrows, etc.

In addition to the facial muscles, breathing is also important. Facial expressions with puffed cheeks, for example, are not uncommon in many sign languages. To puff the cheeks, muscles contract in order to (almost) close the lips, and exhaled air blows out the cheeks. Most facial expressions, however, are simply formed by the facial muscles, which have an effect on the skin in our face. There are over thirty facial muscles, which together can form a large number of facial expressions. Two examples of facial expressions are shown in (3).

(3) a.   b.

face relaxed   raised eyebrows

The production of the facial expression (3b) can be described as follows:

Muscles	The inner and outer eyebrow muscles are contracted
Joints	–
Body parts	The eyebrows are raised and wrinkles appear on the forehead

In (4), the various joints of the arm and hand are depicted. There are a very large number of muscles that are responsible for moving these body parts and the possible movements are correspondingly diverse. Two important terms for describing the parts of the arm and hand are **proximal** (close-by) and **distal** (far away) (4). These are relative concepts, referring to whether a joint or a movement is closer to the torso or farther away from it. A movement of the wrist, for instance, is distal in comparison to an elbow movement, but proximal in comparison to a movement of a finger.

(4)   Joints and parts of the arm and hand

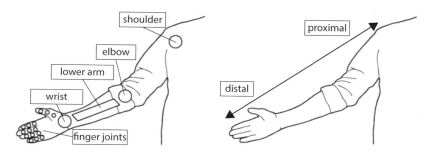

Generally speaking, a distal movement is easier to produce than a proximal movement, as it requires less energy to move the fingers than the entire arm. Still, as already mentioned in Section 3.3.2, for small children, proximal movements are easier because the fine motor control required to make distal movements takes time to develop. The use of both hands makes the difference between easy and difficult signs (from the signer's perspective) clearer. Many signs are lexically specified for articulation with both hands, with the two hands doing exactly the same thing. It is easier to produce these two-handed signs with one hand, and this is what regularly happens with most, if not all such signs, in informal conversations (see Section 12.4). This process is called **weak drop**: the weak hand sometimes disappears in the production. This process will be discussed further in Section 11.8.

The way our bodies are built restricts the possibilities of making signs. Extreme positions of the joints that are strenuous for the muscles and the tissue around the joints, for instance, rarely occur in sign languages. For a similar reason, sign languages across the world appear to make more use of handshapes in which only the index finger or little finger are extended than handshapes in which only the middle finger (5a) or ring finger (5b) are extended.

(5)   Handshapes that are highly unusual in the sign languages of the world

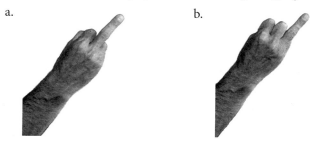

a.

b.

Of course, the extended middle finger is a taboo gesture in many western cultures, which also explains why it is little used in some sign languages. Nevertheless, there is also a physical restriction since the middle finger (5a) and ring finger (5b) do not have their own extensor muscle, whereas the index finger and little finger do. In order to extend the middle or ring finger, one therefore has to use the extensor muscle for all fingers, while simultaneously contracting the flexor muscles of the other three fingers to keep them out of the way. Moreover, it is impossible to extend the ring finger and middle finger as far as the index finger or little finger without also extending the other fingers. Consequently, across sign languages, it is more common for the middle finger or ring finger to be flexed while the other fingers are extended.

The movement of the wrist is also constrained and influences the form of signs. Because the tendons of the muscles that extend the fingers run from the forearm along the wrist, the fingers are automatically slightly extended when the wrist moves: there is not much flexibility in the muscles, and as the distance from the forearm to the fingertips increases, the fingers are extended unless they are prevented by a flexor muscle. Conversely, when the fingers of the hand are rapidly clenched into a fist, the wrist will extend a bit. This physiological tendency can be seen in the phonetic and phonological systems of sign languages: closing or opening movements of the fingers often occur simultaneously with a movement of the hand. An example of such an interaction can be seen in the Polish Sign Language sign SHOWER: while the fingers extend (i.e. open), there is a movement which affects the orientation of the palm of the hand (towards the head). This movement is often articulated by only bending the wrist.

Polish Sign Language
   (6)   Opening of the fingers in combination with movement of the wrist
          in the sign SHOWER (initial position, final position)

10.2.2 Symmetrical articulators: the two hands

One of the most obvious differences between the production of spoken languages and signed languages is that we have one mouth, but two hands. That is, signers have at their disposal two symmetrical articulators. In a one-handed sign, such as SHOWER, it does not matter whether the sign is made with the left or right hand. We have a **hand**

preference for all sorts of manual actions, such as writing, eating soup with a spoon, and so forth. Most people are right-handed, with a small minority being left-handed, and a very small proportion has no clear hand preference (these people are 'ambidextrous'). Signers, too, usually make one-handed signs with their preferred hand, in which case we speak of their **dominant hand**. For communication, this does not make any difference – as far as we know, deaf people can understand left-handed signers as well as right-handed signers.

In sign languages, there are many situations in which signers use their two hands simultaneously. First of all, there are two-handed signs, that is, signs that are lexically specified for articulation with two hands, such as the examples from Finnish Sign Language in (7). Besides these, there are different kinds of morphosyntactic constructions with classifiers involving two hands (see Section 9.6.2 for classifiers and Section 11.7 for further discussion of two-handed signs). Generally speaking, it is not easy for us to move our two hands entirely independently of each other (musicians, such as violinists and drummers, are clear exceptions). This is not due to a physical problem at all; after all, the two hands are not connected to each other by muscles or tendons. Rather, the limitation lies in the brain, as the **coordination** of the movements by the motor system is restricted. Consequently, the two hands can move simultaneously only if they are doing more or less the same thing; in this case, the movement may be **synchronous**, as in PARTY (7a), or **alternating**, as in CYCLE (7b). When the two hands are not moving in more or less the same way, one hand has to remain stationary, while the other hand moves, as is true in the sign in (7c), which may mean THING, OBJECT, or STORY.

Finnish Sign Language

(7)   a.   b.   c.

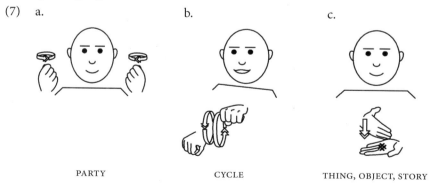

        PARTY   CYCLE   THING, OBJECT, STORY

In sum, we have seen that the production of signs is a complex phenomenon, involving muscles, tendons, and joints. Some movements are easier to articulate than others as a result of the construction of our body. In the following section, we will discuss the extent to which there are also easy and difficult forms when it comes to the perception of signs, and how this can influence the form of signs.

10.3 Perception

Just as in production, the way in which hand movements are perceived limits the possible form of signs. It goes without saying that signs will usually not be articulated behind the signer's back – unless of course the conversation partner is standing behind the signer – as it would be impossible to perceive them. Very small movements will also not readily be used in signs, as they are difficult to perceive.

Usually, when watching the signer, the conversation partner will not be continually tracking the movement of the hand(s) with his/her eyes. Rather, the **eye gaze** will be fixated on a point near or on the face. Research indicates that eye gaze patterns differ between native signers and second language learners: the former tend to look at the eyes of the signer while the latter focus more on the mouth (8).

   (8)   Center and periphery of the visual field

In **visual perception** in general, more details can be picked up in the center of the **visual field** than in its periphery (see large circle in (8)). It can thus be expected that small movements and subtle differences in the location of the fingers can be perceived better near the face than, for example, near the stomach. This, in turn, is expected to have an influence on the shape of signs in that more subtle differences in location and movement should be attested in signs that are articulated near or on the face. As far as the location parameter is concerned, this seems indeed to be the case. In the phonological system of Sign Language of the Netherlands (NGT), for instance, the locations [mouth], [chin], and [cheek] function as three different locations, although for the perceiver these locations are very close to each other. In (9), we provide examples of signs articulated at these three locations: the sign RED is made near the mouth (9a), DADDY on the chin (9b), and DAY on the cheek (9c).

Sign Language of the Netherlands

(9)   a.   b.   c.

RED   DADDY   DAY

In contrast, on the upper body, only the locations [chest], [belly] and [shoulders] are distinctive, and these are much more distant from each other. Constraints imposed by the visual field clearly play a role here but in addition, it is also the case that the face has more striking features (such as the mouth and the nose) that facilitate the recognition of small differences in location. These differences can also have an impact on diachronic changes in the form of signs (see Section 13.4).

Visual perception is specialized in processing various types of simultaneous information, in contrast to auditory perception. We are therefore able to process signals from different information channels at the same time, such as facial expression, the position of the head and the upper body, the handshape, and the orientation of the fingers in space. Chapters 6 and 7 on the syntax and Chapter 9 on the morphology of sign languages already showed that the grammars of sign languages regularly exploit this possibility. In the area of morphology, for instance, sign languages clearly make more use of simultaneous morphemes than spoken languages do. In other words, many units of meaning are articulated simultaneously instead of sequentially (see Section 9.2).

In a perceptual description of signs, no reference needs to be made to joints. In the case of the ASL sign SAY in (2), for instance, a perceptual description could be as follows: 'the tip of the index finger starts from contact with the chin and moves forward'. This description, too, refers to a part of the articulator (the fingertip), but it focuses on what deaf people recognize as a sign, that is, the information that is required for the correct recognition of the sign. In the next section, we discuss variation in the pronunciation of signs, and it will become clear that in many pronunciation variants, the abstract perceptual features of signs remain constant.

10.4 Phonetic variation

As in spoken languages, there is considerable variation in the way signs are articulated. When an English word like *collect* is pronounced clearly, one can hear a distinct [ʋ] sound in the first syllable. When the word occurs in a sentence and is pronounced more quickly, that [ʋ] usually changes into a 'silent e' ([ə], also known as schwa); in fact, this phenomenon is observed with many unstressed vowels.

Similar **phonetic variation** occurs in the pronunciation of signs. Take, for instance, the two-handed ASL sign DECEASED. This sign is sometimes articulated with a curved path movement of the hands through space, executed at the elbow joints (10a), but it can also be reduced by only rotating the forearms (10b). The sign remains the same, but the pronunciation differs. While the former version (10a) is the citation form, the latter pronunciation (10a) has reduced the curved movement – a change that is comparable to the change from [ʋ] to [ə] in *collect* because the mouth does not open as widely in the reduced version.

American Sign Language

(10)   a.   b.

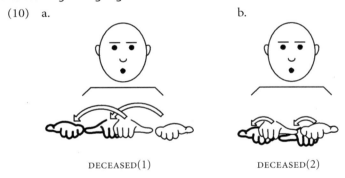

DECEASED(1)   DECEASED(2)

Similar to variation in word choice (lexicon) and sentence structure (syntax), such phonetic variation is partially related to **social factors**: women speak differently than men, there are differences between ethnic groups, and moreover, each human being has his own style of speaking and signing (see Section 12.4). At the phonetic level, differences can be seen in the speed or size of the movements, the number of repetitions of a movement, etc. As yet, little is known for any sign language about exactly which phonetic properties may vary and how the variation correlates with specific sociolinguistic groups or personal style.

We will now focus on **linguistic factors** causing variation in pronunciation. For instance, when signs are used in a sentence, the form of the preceding or following sign may have an influence: this phenomenon is known as **coarticulation**. Sometimes such coarticulation may lead to a change of the phonological building blocks of a sign (see Chapter 11). For instance, as mentioned previously, signs that are normally two-handed may sometimes be articulated with one hand (weak drop). This is an instance of **deletion**: there is no gradual adjustment of the pronunciation of a sign, but rather a component of a sign is *deleted* (so that it is articulated with one hand). A phonological feature of a sign can also change under the influence of a neighbouring sign; this process is known as **assimilation**. Thus, within a sentence, a sign may, for instance, adopt the handshape of the preceding sign (similar to what we described in Section 9.3 for compounds). To give an example: if the ASL sign DECEASED (10) was followed by a first person pronoun, then the pronoun might be articulated with a -hand instead of a -hand.

Apart from such rather clear-cut categorical changes, it is becoming increasingly clear that also at a lower, phonetic, level, variation is extremely common. Only a detailed phonetic notation or articulatory or visual measurements will reveal this type of variation. An example of such small, phonetic, variation relates to the exact curving of the fingers. Signs that involve a handshape characterized by the phonological feature 'curved fingers', as is true for the -hand in the German Sign Language signs COMPUTER (11a) and TEA (11b), are not always pronounced with an exact 30 degree angle of all the finger joints; sometimes the fingers are stretched more. The two examples indicate that such phonetic variation may affect the dominant hand (11a) as well as the non-dominant hand (11b).

German Sign Language

(11) a.   b.

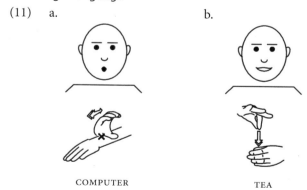

          COMPUTER   TEA

There is an even greater variation in the articulation of stretched fingers. Whereas the most distal finger joints are almost always fully extended, the bending of the first finger joint may vary greatly. There are strong indications that this joint, just like the wrist and other arm joints, has no clear phonological function in distinguishing different meanings, but simply adjusts itself to facilitate the pronunciation of other phonological aspects. In the NGT sign VISIT, for instance, the bending of the first finger joints depends on the direction of the movement: the signer makes sure that the fingertips always point in the direction of the movement. In 'I visit you', the direction is forward and the most 'economical' way of also pointing the fingers forward is by fully extending both the wrist and the fingers (12a). In the inflected form 'you visit me', on the other hand, the fingertips point towards the body of the signer (12b). To achieve this, the signer might try to have his fingers fully extended (including the first finger joint) and only bend the wrist. This, however, is virtually impossible: the wrist is simply not flexible enough, and one would have to move one's elbows far forward to achieve the desired orientation of the fingertips towards the signer. The easy way to have the fingertips point towards one's own body is to bend the fingers at the first finger joint as well as the wrist, as is shown in (12b).

Sign Language of the Netherlands

(12)   a.   Extended wrist and finger joints   b.   Bent first finger joints and wrist

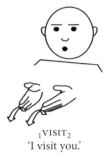   

₁VISIT₂   ₂VISIT₁
'I visit you.'   'You visit me.'

As mentioned above, the pronunciation of a sign can be influenced by phonological features of the preceding or following sign. In (13a), the citation form of the NGT sign COURSE is shown; note that it is articulated rather high next to the face. In (13b), where COURSE is preceded by SIGN (in the compound 'sign language course'), it is articulated slightly lower and farther away from the body. This change results from the fact that SIGN is articulated at a lower location. In this coarticulation, or phonetic assimilation, the pronunciation changes a little, but the original location of COURSE (level to the face, see (13a)) is not completely replaced by the location of SIGN (level to the diaphragm). In other words, despite the phonetic assimilation, there is no risk of a perceiver mistaking the sign for a different phonological form with a different meaning.

Sign Language of the Netherlands

(13)   a.   b.

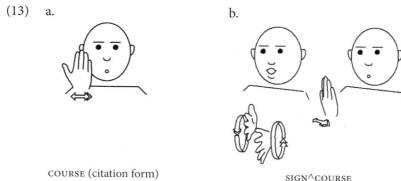

COURSE (citation form)   SIGN^COURSE

In sign language conversations, there is often a tendency for the articulation of signs to be smaller than in their citation forms. Smaller movements cost less energy, and as long as the perceiver receives enough information from the context to recognize the sign, a smaller movement creates no problems. Movement reduction is usually achieved by using more distal (i.e. less proximal) joints. Thus, the ASL sign SAY in (2) is usually articulated by an extension at the elbow joint, but it is also possible to articulate the sign by only extending the more distal wrist joint (14). There is a large amount of variation in joint selection, which can be related to discourse factors (e.g. the expression of emotion) as well as sociolinguistic factors (see Section 12.4).

American Sign Language

(14)

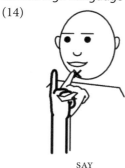

SAY

Such pronunciation differences clearly exemplify the conflict of interests that exists between the signer and perceiver. When the perceiver is close-by, a small movement executed at the wrist may suffice, but at a distance of 30 metres, a more pronounced movement is required in order to ensure that the sign is recognized. In the example, this larger movement can either be realized by making the movement at the wrist very large (for instance, by extending the wrist 120 degrees) or by using more proximal joints such as the elbow and shoulder joint. The latter change in particular increases the duration of the sign and enlarges the forward movement of the fingertip. In other words: while the signer may have a preference for smaller movements (ease of articulation), the addressee may be helped by larger movements (ease of perception).

10.5 Notation systems for sign languages

In their daily lives, deaf people do not write in their sign language. When they want to write something down, they will use the script of the spoken language they know – so Spanish deaf people write Spanish sentences using the Spanish alphabet. There is no standard **writing system** for individual signs and signed sentences. Although modern techniques make it possible to measure hand movements and facial expressions, most researchers have used one of several **transcription** or **notation systems** to record the form of signs. For other forms of movement, such as dance, notation systems have also been developed, which attempt to record the form of articulation as accurately as possible, for instance, by describing the position of all joints. Most existing notation systems for sign language are based on the first phonological analysis of signs proposed by William Stokoe in 1960. Such notation systems describe the various aspects of the hand: the handshape, the location of the hand in space or on the body, and the movement of the fingers or hand. Categories such as handshape, location, and movement come closer to the perceptual properties of signs, and do not include a detailed description of the articulation at the various joints of the arm and hand.

Several notation systems are being used in research. They mainly differ in the possibilities they offer to record small details of the pronunciation of signs. Obviously, such details are very important for phonetic research, but in the creation of dictionaries, for instance, it is more crucial that users are able to search for more global properties of signs. A user of a computer dictionary, for example, may want to look up a sign that was articulated 'somewhere on the head', having forgotten where exactly the hand made contact with the face. On the other hand, for a linguist who wants to know how the location of a sign can be influenced by the signs preceding and following it, it becomes very important to be able to distinguish between 'high on the cheek' and 'low on the cheek'. A system like HamNoSys (Hamburg Notation System for signs) allows you to choose between abstraction and detail, thus making it extremely useful for research purposes. In that way, it is similar to the International Phonetic Alphabet (IPA) for spoken languages, which can be used for the description of speech sounds on various levels of detail. In (15), we give two possible transcriptions of the English words 'time' and 'language' using the IPA system, in (15a) a broader, less detailed transcription and in (15b) a narrow, more detailed transcription which also contains information on stress, duration, and aspiration.

(15) a. broad transcription   b. narrow transcription

['taɪm]   ['tʰaɪ:m]

['læŋwɪdʒ]   ['læ̃:ŋwɪdʒ]

The example in (16) shows the NGT sign SOD-OFF (a rather impolite sign for telling someone to go away). In (17a), this sign is presented in HamNoSys transcription and compared with its transcription using the Dutch KOMVA notation system (17b). Both of these include considerable detail while the American Stokoe system (17c) offers a broader transcription. It is noteworthy that HamNoSys is not bound by conventions from one particular country or sign language, as it does not make use of alphabetic letters for handshapes occurring in the local manual alphabet (see Section 1.4). As can be seen in (17), the KOMVA and Stokoe systems specify the handshape as '1' and 'G', respectively, while HamNoSys employs a handshape symbol. Also, HamNoSys has a computer font.

Sign Language of the Netherlands

(16)

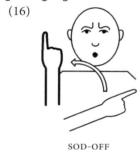

SOD-OFF

(17) a.   b.   c.

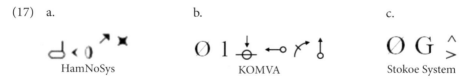

HamNoSys   KOMVA   Stokoe System

An important difference between the KOMVA and HamNoSys transcriptions, on the one hand, and the Stokoe transcription, on the other, is that the Stokoe system offers fewer possibilities for representing detail on the orientation of the hand. This system only distinguishes two orientations: the forearm can be rotated inwards ('prone'; palm downwards), or outwards ('supine'; palm upwards). In contrast, the KOMVA and HamNoSys systems allow for a distinction between the orientation of the palm and that of the fingers. For both, there are a great number of values available, which may not only depend on the rotation of the forearm, but also on the state of the wrist and elbow. The fingers, for example, can point exactly to the left (as in the initial position of SOD-OFF), or upwards (as in the final position). With HamNoSys, even more detail can be represented than with KOMVA. Both the Stokoe and KOMVA notation systems were mainly directed at describing signs in dictionaries, whereas the HamNoSys system was designed for multiple purposes, including phonetic and phonological research.

The notations in the systems discussed above only cover the manual aspects of isolated signs; in most notation systems, it is impossible to capture the non-manual aspects of signs. While various conventions have been developed to transcribe non-manual aspects of signed utterances – such as the position of the eyebrows and the configuration of the lips – these conventions are mainly used when transcribing entire sentences (see the examples in Chapters 6 and 7). A code may either indicate the *function* of the non-manual marker (like 'y/n' for a yes/no question or 'neg' for negation) or its *form* (such as 're' for raised eyebrows or 'hs' for headshake). Such cases are not phonetic transcriptions, but rather syntactic classifications – an important distinction to make.

Besides these linguistic notation systems, writing systems are being developed and are becoming increasingly popular. The aim is to use a clear visual form of the sign, easy to write and read. For an effective writing system, it is extremely important to leave out as many details as possible and to ensure that the written form abstracts away from all possible pronunciations. One such system is SignWriting, which is used in various places in the world, but is by no means a standard system in any deaf community yet. Below, we illustrate how the Japanese Sign Language sign DANCE (18a) and the Indopakistani Sign Language sign ABSTRACT (18b) are written in SignWriting.

(18)   a. *Japanese Sign Language*   b. *Indopakistani Sign Language*

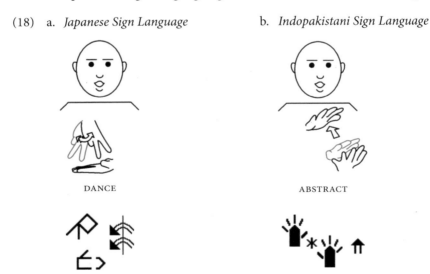

DANCE   ABSTRACT

In sum, there is a clear difference in use and form between notation systems and writing systems. Writing systems make it easy for the language users to write the words of their language, such as the various scripts that exist for spoken languges. Notation systems are similar, but they are capable of describing the form of signs (or words) more precisely, even including the details of a specific articulation of a sign. Depending on the purpose of the notation, more or less phonetic detail can be added to the notation.

10.6 Language technology

Rapid developments are being made in **language technology**, such as, for example, computers that can speak, listen, and translate. The help lines of, for instance, telephone companies are often manned by a computer rather than a person, and this computer is (to a limited extent) able to react to spoken utterances. However, everyone who has used such a computerized service has probably had the experience that this may sometimes lead to misunderstandings: the computer repeats continuously 'I have not understood you clearly. Please, repeat your choice', although the speaker is convinced that s/he has clearly articulated the instruction. **Speech recognition** can sometimes be a solution for Repetitive Strain Injury by pre-empting the use of a mouse or keyboard: verbal commands are given to the computer or the text to be written is read aloud. The computer must, of course, be equipped with software that is capable of recognizing a target word irrespective of its many possible pronunciations (that is, phonetic variants).

In fact, one of the challenges in the development of technological applications for language is the fact that there is considerable variation in how words and sentences are pronounced. While human beings have no problem whatsoever in dealing with this kind of 'noise', it is very difficult for computers to filter it out. Apart from these phonetic problems, the **automatic translation** from (the written form of) one language to another is also challenging. Websites such as 'Babelfish' or 'Google Translate' make it possible to access automatic translations on the Internet, but they have great problems with words with multiple meanings and fixed expressions. For instance, the English word *organ* has two meanings, one referring to a musical instrument and the other to a body part. Currently, when appearing in the sentence *The musician needs an organ*, this word is translated by Google Translate as body part in other languages, although the context should make it clear which meaning is intended. The idiomatic expression *I need a hand*, which means 'I need assistance', is currently translated literally into other languages, which is obviously not very helpful. In comparison, human language users constantly use the context to interpret the meaning of utterances and the intentions of speakers.

Efforts are being made to develop comparable software for recognition and automatic translation for sign languages – and these are faced with the same problems. Some people, for instance, welcome the idea that a computer could take over the function of an (expensive, stressed) sign language interpreter. Others, however, may experience a speaking or listening computer as rather cold and impersonal.

In the past, text telephones were commonly used by deaf people but are being replaced more and more by video chat on computers and mobile phones. It is possible that in the future, the screen will no longer show a video image of a real person but rather a virtual animated signer, a so-called **avatar**, that produces signs computed by a translation program. As difficult as automatic translation between two languages may be, in the case of sign languages, there is the added challenge of making the animated figure produce smooth sign movements. The image in (19) shows a picture of Tessa, such a virtual signer or avatar.

(19)

In order to make an avatar move smoothly, we need to know what the movements look like in real signers. To that end, the precise phonetic properties of the articulation must be studied. Although there are rapid developments in this area, present-day sign language animations still clearly reveal the lack of such phonetic knowledge about sign languages. In fact, the movements produced by the avatar seem rather stiff and awkward. But what exactly causes this awkward impression has so far eluded researchers. Is the speed of the movement the reason? Is it the rhythm of the signs? Are, for instance, the transitions between the signs not long enough? Or are the facial expressions not natural enough? Questions like these show that our phonetic knowledge of sign languages is still in its infancy. It is therefore clear, that a naturally signing virtual sign language interpreter will not be available in the near future.

Summary

Phonetics studies the articulation and perception of speech and signs, and it is therefore focussed on the **modality difference** between visual-spatial and oral-aural languages. In both types of languages, a distinction is made in the **communication chain** between the **articulation**, the **signal**, and the **perception** of that signal. In the **visual perception** of signs, **eye gaze** plays an important part, since it determines where the center of the **visual field** is: in that area, finer details can be perceived. In sign languages, articulation can be described in terms of the various **body parts** that are involved, such as the arm, the hand, and the fingers. Signs that are easy to pronounce are often more difficult to perceive, and vice versa; these differences can be understood by looking at **joints** and **muscles** that play a role in the articulation. The movements that are required in order to move the articulators to the starting position of a sign are called **transitional movements**.

Signs, just like words, are not always articulated in exactly the same way; they may, for instance, sometimes be articulated with more care than at other times. Consequently, there is considerable **phonetic variation** in sign language. Some variants can be described in terms of the size of the movement, which may vary depending on whether more **proximal** or more **distal** joints are used. Signers usually have a **hand preference** for one-handed signs; their preferred hand is called the **dominant hand**. In two-handed signs in which both hands move, the **coordination** between the two hands may vary: the movement may be **synchronous** or **alternating**. Variation may also involve **deletion** of the non-dominant hand in two-handed signs; this phenomenon is called **weak drop**. When the form of a sign is influenced by a sign in the linguistic context, this is called **coarticulation**. When parts of a sign adapt to the form of a preceding or following sign, we speak of **assimiliation**. Apart from such **linguistic factors** determining the phonetic form, **social factors** may also be involved.

The phonetic form of different variants of signs can be represented for research purposes by means of several **transcription/notation systems**. A **writing system** has been developed for more general use, but it is not commonly used. All these aspects of phonetic knowledge are also of importance in the development of **language technology**, such as **speech recognition** (i.e. software that can recognize and process (sign) language), **automatic translation**, and virtual signers or **avatars**.

Test yourself

1. In the two articulations of the NGT sign BOOK depicted below, identify where the articulation differs. Which phonetic properties are identical in the two signs?

    a.   b.

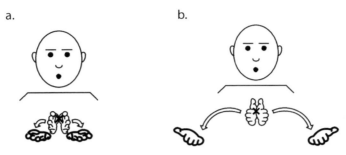

2. Do you think the two forms below have the same meaning? Motivate your answer.

    a.   b.

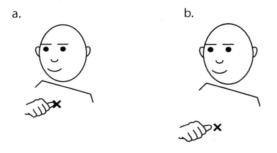

Assignments

1. Try to find five, but at least three, different pronunciations of the same (frequent) sign in a specific sign language on DVDs, CD-ROMs, or the Internet. Use, for instance, the fables told by signers from three different sign languages, which can be downloaded from http:// sign-lang.ruhosting.nl/echo. Describe the articulation of these signs in terms of the joints involved.

2. Provide three examples – real or hypothetical – from the sign language you know best in which the form of a sign changes under the influence of a preceding or following sign. Try to find examples in which different parameters are affected and describe what exactly happens.

3. Left-handed people usually make one-handed signs with their left hand, whereas right-handed people articulate them with their right hand. Could you also call this a variation of pronunciation? Motivate your answer.

References and further reading

A more extensive (and more technical) overview of sign language phonetics is provided by Crasborn (2012). Detailed information about the anatomical structure and movements of the arm and hand can be found in Luttgens, Deutsch & Hamilton (1992). Facial expressions and their transcription are described in detail in Ekman, Friesen & Hager (2002). Siple (1978), Mandel (1979), Ann (1993), and Crasborn (2001) have investigated the influence of perception and production limitations on the form of signs. Lindblom (1990) studied the competition between ease of articulation on the side of the speaker and ease of perception on the side of the listener in spoken language. Phonetic variation in sign language is discussed in detail in Crasborn (2001) and for the parameter location by Mauk & Tyrone (2012). Coarticulation in sign language is addressed in studies by Tyrone & Mauk (2010) and Grosvald & Corina (2012); handshape assimilation is the subject of a study by Corina (1990). Limitations on two-handed signs were first discussed in Battison (1978); weak drop has been investigated for ASL by Battison (1974) and Brentari (1998), and for NGT by Van der Kooij (2001).

The HamNoSys transcription system is described in Prillwitz et al. (1989) and can be found at www.sign-lang.uni-hamburg.de/hamnosys. The KOMVA transcription system is described (in Dutch) in Stroomberger & Schermer (1988). Frishberg, Hoiting & Slobin (2012) provide a detailed overview of existing notation systems. Information on the Visicast project and the virtual signer Tessa can be found at www.visicast.co.uk. Automatic translation services on the internet include Babelfish (www.babelfish.org) and Google Translate (http://translate.google.com). Signwriting is further explained at www.signwriting.org.

Chapter 11

Phonology

Els van der Kooij & Onno Crasborn

11.1   Introduction

Phonology studies those elements used to form words and their possible combinations. In the phonology of spoken languages, the sounds of a specific language are analyzed and how these sounds are combined into syllables and words. Not all languages use the same set of sounds, and not every combination is possible. The word *tlaak*, for instance, is not a possible English word. However, there is at least one language, Tlingit (spoken in southeast Alaska) in which the word *tlaak* is well-formed and part of the lexicon – it means 'being wet'.

It is important to distinguish well-formedness from the property of having meaning. Any English speaker knows that *tlaak* cannot be an English word: the combination of /t/ followed by /l/ cannot occur at the beginning of an English word. On the other hand, the nonsense word *blim* could well be an English word: the combination of /b/ followed by /l/ is possible in English (e.g. *blue*). Both nonsense forms do not exist in English, but, in contrast to *tlaak*, *blim* could in principle be an English word.

In sign languages, the same distinction applies. It is not possible to do just anything with your hands and for that to be a possible sign in a given sign language. A sign with a handshape in which only the ring finger is extended (see (5b) in Chapter 10) could never be part of the vocabulary of, for instance, Sign Language of the Netherlands (NGT), as this handshape is not part of the handshape inventory of NGT. In (1), we see a sign that does not exist in BSL and that would be considered as 'foreign' by British signers. As it happens, this sign does exist in a different sign language: it is the sign for SHOULD in Chinese Sign Language (CSL).

Chinese Sign Language
(1)

SHOULD (**X**-hand → **e**-hand)

DOI 10.1075/z.199.11koo

Generally speaking, this impression of a sign being 'foreign' either results from a form being used that does not exist in that sign language, such as the extended ring finger in NGT, or from a combination of forms that is not possible. Taking the CSL sign in (1), both the initial handshape (⚊-hand) and the final handshape (⚊-hand) do exist in BSL, but they cannot be used in sequence within one sign.

The CSL sign for IMPERIALISM (2a) is a possible sign in French Sign Language (LSF), but it does not happen to have a meaning. It is a well-formed sign, since all the form elements can be used in LSF: the two ⚊-handshapes, the crossing of the arms on the chest, and the position of the hands with the palms oriented towards the body. Actually, it resembles a form that does happen to have a meaning in LSF: the LSF sign AUSTRIA (2b).

Chinese Sign Language (a) and French Sign Language (b)

(2)   a.   b.

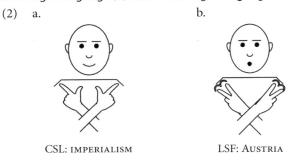

CSL: IMPERIALISM   LSF: AUSTRIA

In order to find out which form elements occur in a language and which do not, we need to carry out a phonological analysis. In spoken languages, we distinguish vowels and consonants. In sign languages, handshapes, locations, and movements are contrasted; these building blocks are often referred to as **parameters** (see Section 1.2).

The distinctive sounds of a language are called **phonemes**. The size of the phoneme inventory can differ between spoken languages: the number of **distinctive** sounds used in a specific spoken language can be quite small but also very large. A phonological analysis is required to establish which of the attested sounds actually are phonemes. The sounds *m* and *b*, for example, distinguish the English words *make* and *bake*. Those two words have different meanings in English. They form a **minimal pair**, as they are identical except for their initial sound. Therefore, we can conclude that the sounds /m/ and /b/ are phonemes of English. We can understand the distinctiveness of these sounds at different levels. When looking more closely at the properties of the sounds /m/ and /b/, they are in fact alike: they are both bilabials and voiced. The sole difference is that the exhalation of air passes through the nose when articulating /m/ but through the mouth when articulating /b/. It is thus the feature [nasal] which is responsible for the difference in meaning between the words *make* and *bake*. Such a feature is called a **distinctive feature**. Distinctiveness can be a property of the phonemes (the succession of sounds) as well as of the features that make up those phonemes. In order to determine the distinctive features of a sign language, an analysis of the language's entire system of form elements is required. We need to know which form elements are capable of distinguishing meaning. Moreover, we need to find out how the form elements are articulated. As we saw in Section 10.4, signs, just like words, can be articulated slightly differently depending on the context in which they appear. Predictable variants of phonemes (i.e. form elements that distinguish meaning) are called **allophones**. For instance, in English, plosive consonants are articulated with aspiration [pʰ], but after /s/, there is no aspiration. The sounds [pʰ] and [p] are then allophones of the phoneme /p/ in English.

Minimal pairs occur in all sign languages. In British Sign Language (BSL), the two signs in (3) form a minimal pair: (3a) means CRUEL, (3b) means SWEET. All parameters of the two signs are the same except for the location. Both signs are articulated with a χ-handshape which makes a turning movement. However, the location of the sign CRUEL is the throat while SWEET is articulated at the side of the mouth. In other words, these two locations are distinctive, they are part or the phonological inventory of BSL.

British Sign Language

(3)   a.   b.

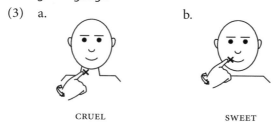

CRUEL   SWEET

In the following sections, we will discuss the various parameters in turn: the handshape (Section 11.2), location (Section 11.4), and movement (Section 11.5) of the hand(s). In a more restricted set of signs, the orientation of the hand (Section 11.3) and certain non-manual aspects (Section 11.6) also play a role in distinguishing meaning. As already discussed in Section 10.2, an important property of signs is whether they are articulated by one or by two hands; this property will be further explored in Section 11.7. Section 11.8 focuses on the adjustments of form in phonological processes, and Section 11.9 discusses the role of iconicity within phonology. While Sections 11.2–11.9 focus on the phonological structure of signs, in Section 11.10, we broaden our perspective by addressing phonology at the sentential level, that is, aspects of sign language prosody.

11.2   Handshape

Of the different parameters, the **handshape** seems to have the largest number of distinctive possibilities. We still know relatively little about the phonology of many sign languages but in those that have been studied, the number of distinctive handshapes appears to be larger than the number of distinctive locations and movements. The size of the handshape inventory may differ from one sign language to another, but there does not seem to be as much variation as in the sound inventories of spoken languages. The study of many sign languages has resulted in lists of those handshapes that frequently occur, but a systematic analysis of allophones has not been conducted yet. This makes it hard to compare languages, although we can give examples of differences between languages. For instance, Finnish Sign Language (FinSL) has the handshape shown in (4) which does not occur as a phonemic handshape in NGT. This handshape, however, does exist as an allophone of the handshape 𝄽 in NGT (see (16)).

Finnish Sign Language

(4)

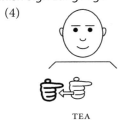

TEA

In order to determine which handshapes should be in the handshape inventory of a specific sign language, we have to consider finer aspects of handshapes and the features that describe them. An important distinction in the division of these features is that between the selection and the position of the fingers (Section 11.2.1). In Section 11.2.2, we address the frequency of handshapes and the notion of markedness. Finally, we will look at the allophones that exist within the handshape parameter (Section 11.2.3).

11.2.1   Selection and position of fingers

When describing the characteristics of handshapes, a distinction is made between the selection of fingers and the position of the fingers. We explain this distinction by means of the five handshapes shown in (5).

(5)

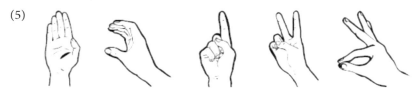

The **selected fingers** are the 'active' or 'foregrounded' fingers. In the ✋- and the ✋-hand-shapes, all four fingers are selected, in the ✋-hand, the index finger, and in the ✋-hand, the index finger and the middle finger. The selected fingers are often extended (e.g in ✋, ✋ and ✋), but in the ✋-handshape (which is used e.g. in the NGT sign LIVE; see the illustration in assignment 4), the middle finger, ring finger, and little finger are extended, although they are not the selected fingers. In order to determine which fingers are selected, the following criteria are used.

(6) Selected fingers
– can make contact with the body, the head, or the other hand and arm;
– can adopt a special position (curved, bent, closed, spread);
– can move (open and close).

When we look at the handshapes that are attested in a variety of sign languages, it appears that not all finger combinations can be selected. Handshapes that hardly ever occur are shown in (7); these are handshapes with extended ring and middle finger (7a), handshapes with extended ring and little finger (7b), handshapes with extended index and ring finger (7c), and handshapes with extended little, index, and middle finger (7d).

(7) a.   b.   c.   d.

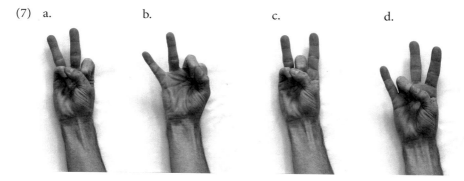

This does not mean that we are unable to produce these handshapes, but they are clearly more difficult in their articulation. Furthermore, within and across sign languages, not all handshapes are used with the same frequency. It appears that the most frequent handshapes have either one or all fingers selected. When two fingers are selected, these are usually the index and middle finger. Handshapes with three fingers selected appear to be exceptional across sign languages.

As mentioned above, the selected fingers are usually extended. However, the position of the selected fingers can be modified by a finger position feature. The ✋-hand and the ✋-hand both have four selected fingers, but in the former, the fingers are fully extended (open) while in the latter, they are curved. Sometimes the selected fingers are spread, as in the ✋-handshape. The ✋-hand and the ✋-hand only differ from each other in the spreading of the fingers. Furthermore, handshapes can be distinguished from each other on the basis of an aperture feature specifying the relation between the selected finger(s) and the thumb. In the -hand, the thumb and index finger make contact. This contact is represented using the feature 'closed'. Pairs of open and closed handshapes are shown in (8).

(8) Open and closed handshapes

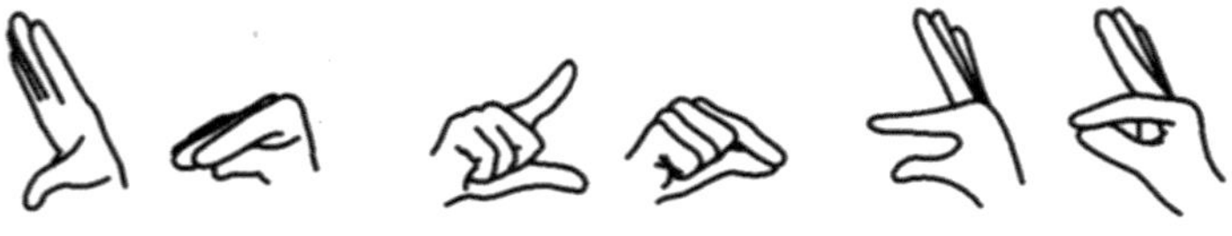

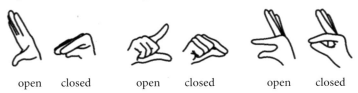

open closed open closed open closed

When the position of the fingers changes during the articulation of a sign, then we are usually dealing with a change from open to closed or vice versa. Apparently, the position of the fingers can change within a sign, but the selected fingers cannot (see Section 11.5). In NGT, the 'open' handshapes shown in (8) only occur in signs in combination with their 'closed' counterparts. Examples of NGT signs that involve these pairs of open and closed handshapes are given in (9).

Sign Language of the Netherlands

(9) a.

TALK

b.

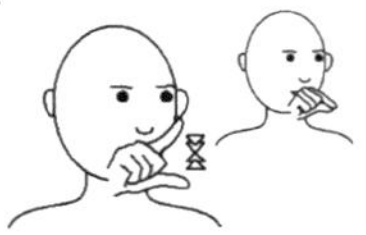

CHICKEN

c.

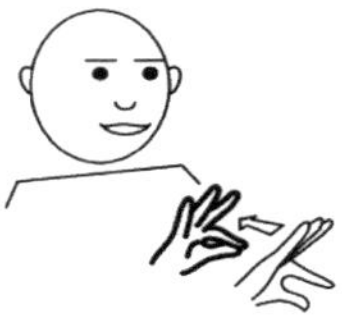

CHOOSE

The **position** of the selected fingers can be described using three position features (10). All finger positions are described by means of aspects of these three groups. These position features always refer to the selected fingers.

(10) Position features of the fingers
- curving of the fingers (for example in the -hand);
- spreading of the fingers (for example in the -hand);
- an aperture relation between the thumb and the selected fingers (for example in the 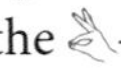-hand).

11.2.2 Frequency and markedness

The handshapes that relatively occur most frequently in most known sign languages are presented in (11).

(11)   a.

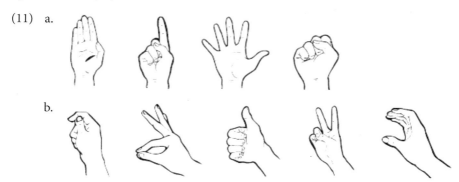

b.

The handshapes in (11a) occur in many sign languages and in many signs and are referred to as **unmarked** handshapes. Unmarked handshapes are easy to produce (ease of articulation; see Section 10.2), and are quite distinct in terms of perception (ease of perception; see Section 10.3). They are also the first to be acquired by children (see Section 3.3.2). Furthermore, unmarked handshapes combine best with other parameters, such as location. That is to say, we find these unmarked handshapes at more different locations than **marked** handshapes. The handshapes in (11b), while also quite frequent across sign languages and across signs, are more complex and more marked. Some highly marked, and much less frequent, handshapes are depicted in (12). The ⵥ-handshape, for instance, is a marked handshape in NGT and does not occur in combination with the various locations on the head and the body. However, this constraint does not hold for all sign languages. As has been shown in (1), in CSL the ⵥ-hand can be used in combination with a location below the chin. Another feature of marked handshapes is that they never occur on the passive or non-dominant hand in two-handed signs, unless the non-dominant hand has the same handshape as the dominant hand (see Section 11.7 for further discussion). In contrast, the unmarked ⵥ-handshape can be found in combination with all locations, and it frequently occurs on the non-dominant hand in two-handed signs.

(12)

A phonological description of the handshapes can help us understand why children usually acquire the unmarked handshapes before the marked handshapes. The descriptions of the unmarked handshapes ⑂ and ⑃ in (11a) look rather simple, as they require only one feature: a feature specifying finger selection, as is shown in (13). In contrast, the description of the more marked ⑄ -handshape in (11b) requires more features and is thus more complex.

(13)   Features of marked and unmarked handshapes

	Handshape	Description
Unmarked	⑂	finger selection: [4]
	⑃	finger selection: [1]
Marked	⑄	finger selection: [4] flexing: [curved] aperture: [open]

For the description of really unusual handshapes, we often need exceptional features, that is, features which are not otherwise used in the description of handshapes. The feature [crossed], for example, which indicates that the middle finger is crossed over the index finger, is only needed for the description of the ⑁-handshape. It seems that handshapes that are characterized by exceptional features, such as the crossing of the fingers in ⑁, often have special functions and, unlike other handshapes, in fact carry some referential meaning. These meaningful handshapes can be subdivided into three categories: classifier handshapes, handshapes representing a letter, or handshape representing a number.

Classifiers have already been discussed in Section 9.6.2. Remember that classifier handshapes are handshapes that either refer to a group of nouns which share certain form features, or they represent how some object is handled or manipulated. Some handshapes are only, or at least most frequently, used with a classifier function; three examples of such handshapes are given in (14).

(14)

Handshapes may also be used to refer to a letter of the manual alphabet which is used for fingerspelling words from a particular spoken language (see Section 1.4) or to represent the numbers of the manual counting system. Signs that contain an alphabet handshape which refers to the initial letter of a word from a spoken language are called **initialized signs**. Another group of signs frequently containing handshapes from the manual alphabet is the group of name signs. Examples of NGT handshapes referring either to letters or numbers are given in (15). Except for the leftmost handshape, these handshapes are rarely used besides for fingerspelling and initialization or counting and numeral incorporation.

(15)

| letter C | letter I | letter W | number 3 | number 4 |

11.2.3 Allophonic handshapes

Some handshapes are different phonetically but not phonologically. If the exact context in which either of the variants occurs can be described, then these handshapes are allophones. We will illustrate this allophonic relation by means of the bending of the fingers. Fingers can be flexed in two ways. All of the finger joints can be flexed (this is called 'curved'), or the fingers can be flexed only at the knuckles at the base of the fingers. This last feature is called 'bent'. The -hand is an example of a handshape with curved fingers. Two examples of bent handshapes are shown in (16).

(16)   Bent handshapes

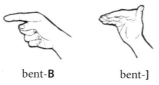

bent-**B**   bent-]

These bent handshapes are possible handshapes of the inventory of a sign language since they are visually distinct from their counterpart with extended fingers (i.e. the - and -hands). However, the occurrence of these bent handshapes is often predictable on the basis of other phonological or phonetic features of the sign (see Chapter 10.4). The bent handshapes in (16) can therefore be considered **allophones** or **phonetic variants** of the - and -hand, respectively. As illustrated by the NGT verb VISIT, discussed in Section 10.4 and repeated below in (19), in the inflected form expressing the meaning 'you visit me', the tips of the selected fingers make contact with a location on the upper body. Contact with the upper body is one of the factors that motivate the use of an allophonic bent hand. The orientation of the fingertips – pointing towards the body – determines the bending of the fingers. In order to clarify the allophonic relationship between the handshapes with straight fingers and their bent counterparts, we first have to discuss the orientation of the hand.

11.3   Orientation

The NGT signs for SUPPOSE-THAT and EASY shown in (17) form a minimal pair; they only differ in the **orientation** of the hand. We can describe their orientation by looking at the direction in which the palm and fingers point. In both signs, the fingers points upwards. In the sign for EASY (17a), however, the palm points towards the body while in the sign for SUPPOSE-THAT, it points to the left (17b).

Sign Language of the Netherlands

(17)   a.   b.

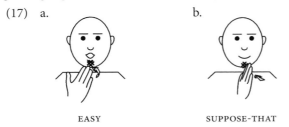

         EASY   SUPPOSE-THAT

Another, and as we shall see better, way to describe orientation is by identifying the part of the hand that points towards the location of the sign. In the sign EASY, it is the palm that points towards the location (the chin), and in the sign SUPPOSE-THAT, it is the thumb side of the hand that points towards the same location. We now actually do not say anything about the orientation of the fingers, but assume that the easiest way for the palm or thumb side of your hand to make contact with the chin is with your fingers pointed (more or less) upwards.

The advantage of this description of orientation is that it can help us in dealing with the considerable variation in articulation that exists both between signs and signers. If we were to describe orientation on the basis of the absolute direction of the palm and the fingers, then we would have to say that the NGT sign ALSO as articulated in (18a) has a phonological orientation value different from that of its variant in (18b). This is undesirable for a phonological description, as the phonological representation focuses on the essence of the form; this essence is always the same, irrespective of the exact articulation of the sign. What generally remains constant in various articulation variants is the side of the hand that points towards the location, as can clearly be seen in the two articulation variants of the NGT sign ALSO.

Sign Language of the Netherlands

(18)   a.   b.

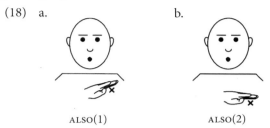

ALSO(1)   ALSO(2)

In both variants of ALSO, the thumb side of the hand makes contact with the chest, while the orientation of the palm and fingers varies. The description 'thumb side of the hand points towards the location' is accurate for all articulation variants of the sign ALSO. Consequently, the orientation features that we can distinguish correspond to the sides of the hand that can either point towards a location or make contact with the location: that is, the palm, the back of the hand, the thumb side (radial side), the little finger side (ulnar side), the wrist side, and the tips of the fingers.

By describing orientation as a relation between a part of the hand and a location, we can also uniformly describe the different forms of verbs that inflect spatially (see Section 9.5.2 for discussion). Consider the two forms of the NGT verb VISIT in (19) that were already discussed in Section 10.4.

Sign Language of the Netherlands

(19)   a.   b.

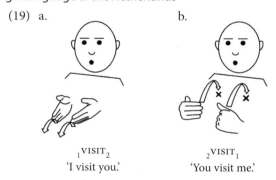

$_1$VISIT$_2$ $_2$VISIT$_1$
'I visit you.'   'You visit me.'

In all conjugations of the verb VISIT, the fingertips point towards the person or thing that is being visited. As we can see in this example, the handshape adjusts to the direction of the fingertips. In $_1$VISIT$_2$ (19a), the fingertips point towards the addressee, and the fingers are extended. In contrast, in $_2$VISIT$_1$ (19b), the base joints of the ⁀-hand are flexed, as this is the easiest way to articulate the relative orientation value [fingertips] in combination with the final location [chest]. This example thus shows that by means of **relative orientation**, we can formulate clear conditions for the occurrence of the bent handshape allophones ✑ and ✑, discussed in Section 11.2.3: when a sign articulated on the chest has the orientation value [fingertips], then both the ∤-hand and the ∤-hand will be realized in their bent variants.

11.4 Location

As has already been demonstrated by the minimal pair in (3), the **location** where a sign is articulated is one of the features that may distinguish the meaning of signs. In BSL, a rotated index finger near the side of the mouth means SWEET, whereas the same movement articulated with the same handshape near the throat means CRUEL. This minimal pair thus provides evidence that these two locations (side of the mouth and throat) belong to two different phonological categories in that sign language.

We can distinguish roughly four major location categories in every sign language: the head, the upper body, the non-dominant (or weak) hand, and the neutral space. The two BSL signs just mentioned are both made near the head, while the NGT sign ALSO in (18) is articulated on the upper body. The subdivision of the parameter location into these four groups is motivated. When a sign makes contact at the beginning and end of the movement (a so-called double contact sign), the two locations always fall into the same major location. The double-contact sign DEAF from Brazilian Sign Language (Libras) in (20) illustrates this: the hand moves from the ear to the cheek, both of which belong to the location group 'head'. There are, however, no mono-morphemic signs that begin, for example, at a location on the head and end on the weak hand.

Brazilian Sign Language
(20)

DEAF

In fact, a closer look at double contact signs reveals that the movement does not only stay within one of the four location groups, but actually remains within an even smaller area within a major location. The location phonemes seem to be small areas rather than points. The Libras sign DEAF then has 'cheek' as its location and is specified for a double-contacting movement within that area. For morphologically simple (i.e. non-compound) signs, a location is an area within which the hand can move. This implies that we will, for example, not find mono-morphemic signs in the location group 'head' in which the hand moves from the forehead to the cheek, or from the nose to the chin.

The restriction on major location does not always apply to multi-morphemic signs such as compounds or signs that originally were compounds (see Section 9.3). For example, in the complex ASL sign REMEMBER, the hand moves from the forehead (head) to the weak hand (21c). This is possible because REMEMBER is originally a compound sign that is made up of the individual signs KNOW (21a) and STAY (21b).

American Sign Language

(21) a.   b.

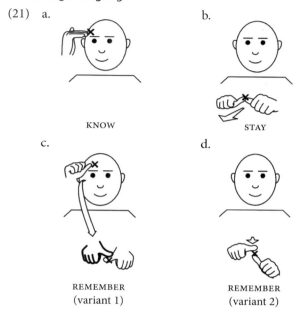

c.   d.

        KNOW   STAY

    REMEMBER   REMEMBER
    (variant 1)   (variant 2)

Interestingly, a second variant of this sign has developed (21d). While in variant 1 (21c), the hand moves between the two original locations of KNOW and STAY, variant 2 (21d) has only one location, the weak hand, taken from STAY. This variant of the compound has lost its special phonological feature (i.e. two major locations), which marked it as a compound, and thus resembles morphologically simple (non-compound) signs (see Section 13.4.1 for a discussion of phonological change).

This phonological analysis of locations as areas within which the hand moves has the advantage that fewer locations are needed to describe a sign language. And there is yet another advantage: the movement does not only stay within a phonemic location, it also seems to make optimal use of it. Broadly speaking, the articulator always moves from one side of the location (area) to the other. To some extent, this allows us to predict what the relative size of a movement will be: movements on the chin are smaller than movements on the chest, and movements on the arm are bigger than movements on the cheek.

The largest number of distinctive locations are found within the location group 'head'. Common areas found in sign languages are the forehead, the temple (the side of the forehead), the cheek, the ear, the nose (the center of the face), the mouth, and the chin. As mentioned in Section 10.3, when people are looking at signs, they actually focus on the face of the signer. This focus makes it easier to distinguish the numerous different locations on the face than the different distinct locations on the chest. Furthermore, the head features a number of prominent visual points, such as the eyes, nose, and mouth. Taken together, there are several phonetic reasons to expect more phonological location distinctions on the head than, for instance, on the upper body.

These prominent visual points or 'landmarks' that function as locations on the head are commonly related to specific meaning aspects of signs. The location of the sign is often predictable on the basis of its meaning when this meaning contains a clear reference to the function of one of those 'landmarks'. Thus, all signs related to 'eating' or 'talking' are produced near the mouth (see Section 8.3 on iconicity).

In contrast, we do not find many locations that distinguish meaning on the upper body. An exception is formed by the lower half of the upper body. In signs made there the location is often related to their meaning. In many sign languages, the signs HUN-GRY, GIVE-BIRTH, and URINATE, for example, are made on the lower part of the upper body. The NGT sign for KIDNEY is articulated at a location which is not used for any other sign (22). The Hong Kong Sign Language (HKSL) sign TAIL is made on the lower back and again, this location is not used for any other sign. In these cases, the meaning of the sign determines a more specific location on the body.

Sign Language of the Netherlands
(22)

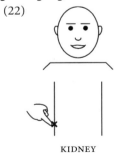

KIDNEY

The specific location of the hand on the body can also be related to the orientation of the hand (i.e. which side of the hand makes contact with the body, see Section 11.3). In the one-handed NGT signs ALSO (18) and BROTHER (27a), the thumb side of the hand makes contact with the body. To facilitate articulation, the location of the hand is more on the 'opposite' side of the body (the contralateral side) than the side from which the hand comes (the ipsilateral side).

In principle, we could distinguish many different locations in the space in front of the body, the so-called 'neutral' signing space. It seems that these locations are not used to distinguish signs in the lexicon though. Rather, the space in front of the body seems to be used primarily for other grammatical functions, such as localization of referents and verb inflection (Section 9.5.2). Similar to signs on the upper body, some signs in the neutral space are articulated with the hands in a relatively high or low position. This is usually related to the meaning of the signs as well. For example, in many sign languages, the signs SUN, SHOWER, and ATTIC are made relatively high in neutral space.

Finally, as we have seen, the non-dominant hand can also be used as a location. We will discuss two-handed signs and the phonological constraints related to them in Section 11.6.

11.5   Movement

Movement has been considered to be one of the phonological parameters since Stokoe's phonological description of ASL. There are two types of movements: movements of the fingers and the wrist (**hand-internal movements** and **orientation changes**) and movements of the entire hand (**path movements**). An example of a sign with a long path movement is the ASL sign REMEMBER in (21c), in which the hand moves from the forehead to the weak hand. But the small movement of the entire hand in the NGT sign ALSO (18) is also considered a path movement. NGT signs with a hand-internal movement – a handshape change from open to closed handshape – have been illustrated in (9). Apart from signs with only a path movement or only a hand-internal movement, there are also signs in which a path and a hand-internal movement are combined. An example of this is the NGT sign HUNDRED (23): the path movement proceeds from a central position towards the ipsilateral side, and during the movement, the hand closes.

Sign Language of the Netherlands

(23)

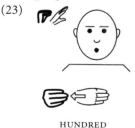

HUNDRED

One of the reasons to consider the movement in HUNDRED a more complex movement is that children acquiring a sign language often at first omit one of the two simultaneously occurring movement components. Thus, a child acquiring NGT would either

produce the sign HUNDRED by using only the final handshape and the path movement, or by making the closing hand-internal movement first, followed by the path
movement.

The change in aperture between the thumb and the selected fingers, as in (9) and
(23), is the most frequent hand-internal movement. We could describe this movement
as a transition from one handshape to another. The problem with such a description is
that any sequential combination of two handshapes should theoretically be a possible
hand-internal movement. This makes it hard to explain why in practice this is not the
case. For example, a sign in which a ⚲-hand closes to a ⚲-hand, as shown in (24),
has not been found in any sign language to date.

(24)   An impossible hand-internal movement

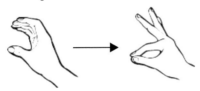

In hand-internal movements that are attested, only the position of the fingers appears
to change, but not the finger selection. This is true for the sign HUNDRED in (23) as well
as for the signs TALK, CHICKEN, and CHOOSE in (9). This constraint on hand-internal
movements is called the '**selected finger constraint**'.

Apart from path movements and hand-internal movements, there are also movements that result from an orientation change by means of a rotation of the lower arm.
Examples of this are the BSL signs CRUEL and SWEET in (3). As is the case with hand-
internal movement, an orientation change can be simultaneously combined with a path
movement, as is illustrated by the NGT sign RECOGNITION in (25).

Sign Language of the Netherlands

(25)

RECOGNITION

A complex movement usually does not consist of a hand-internal movement in combination with an orientation change, although there are a few cases (see e.g. the BSL sign
WIN in Section 9.5.1). As we have seen, both can be combined with a path movement
though. In (26), we provide an overview of the different movement types and their
possible combinations.

(26)   Simple and complex movements

Simple movements	Complex movement
Path movement	
Hand-internal movement	path movement + hand-internal movement
Orientation change	path movement + orientation change

Movements in lexical signs can usually be described as transitions between the initial and the final location; that is, almost all lexical movements can be predicted when the initial and the final position of the hand are known. Thus, (predictable) straight movements, as, for example, in FinSL TEA (4) or ASL STAY (21b) do not require a phonological description. In contrast, circular movements, as in FinSL CYCLE (Chapter 10, Example (7b)), require further specification of the shape of the movement.

Just as with location, the movement parameter of a sign can often be related to its meaning. The FinSL sign CYCLE, for instance, imitates the moving of the feet on the bicycle pedals. Moreover, signs depicting negative emotions often involve a downward movement, as is true for the ASL sign DEPRESSED and the NGT sign DISAPPOINTED, and vice versa: signs referring to positive emotions are often specified for an upward movement, as in, for example, the BSL sign HAPPY (see Sections 8.3 and 8.7).

11.6 Non-manual aspects in the lexicon

While most phonological properties of signs relate to the articulation by the hand(s), there is also a role for non-manual aspects in lexical items (as already mentioned in Section 1.2). By **non-manual aspects**, we mean form elements that relate to the posture of the body and the head, facial expressions, and certain movements or configurations of the mouth. As detailed in previous chapters, they play a more significant role in prosody, relating to the syntax and discourse of sign languages (see Section 11.10). Also, given that parts of the face can function as separate 'articulators', non-manual aspects are also found as bound morphemes. An example of a non-manual marker functioning as a bound morpheme are puffed cheeks that add the meaning 'thick' when articulated simultaneously with, for example, the nouns SWEATER or COAT (see Section 5.4.2).

Here, however, we are interested in non-manual aspects that fulfil a phonological function, that is, that are lexically specified. Non-manual aspects play a rather modest role in the lexicon. Broadly speaking, we can distinguish the upper and the lower part of the face. The lower part of the face, especially the cheeks and the mouth, play the biggest role as part of lexical signs. As set out in Section 1.2, within the lexicon, movements of the mouth are subdivided into **mouthings** and **mouth gestures**. Mouthings are loan elements that are derived from the articulation of words in spoken languages, whereas mouth gestures are not. Both can play a role in distinguishing meaning. The NGT sign in (27a,b) can mean either 'brother' or 'sister', depending on whether it is accompanied by the mouthing 'broer' (27a) or 'zus' (27b). The Dutch word is in fact often greatly reduced. Not all sign languages use mouthings in the same way: Saudi Arabian Sign Language, for example, has a separate sign SIBLING and indicates gender by adding another sign. It does not rely on mouthing in this case. Also, some sign languages appear to make less use of mouthings than others.

Sign Language of the Netherlands

(27)   a.   b.   c.

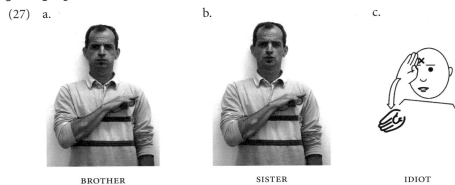

BROTHER   SISTER   IDIOT

The NGT sign IDIOT (27c) illustrates the use of a lexically specified mouth gesture. The mouth gesture consists of a lax tongue hanging slightly out of the mouth while some air is being blown out. Mouth gestures, in contrast to mouthings, do not have an independent meaning.

11.7 Two-handed signs

An important and unique feature of sign languages is that, in contrast to spoken languages, they have multiple active articulators. Apart from the mouth, which can be seen as an independent articulator, we have two hands, which can move largely independently from each other. To an extent, this also happens in signed utterances. For instance, while one hand is held in space to refer to a referent, the other hand can keep on signing. In lexical signs, however, there are far fewer possibilities of using the two hands. In Chapter 10, we saw that this is partly due to limitations in motor control. However, motor limitations cannot be the only reason: after all, certain complex interactions of the two hands that do not occur in lexical signs are attested in utterances. This suggests that, apart from motor limitations, there are also linguistic constraints which apply in the lexicon, but not, for example, in syntactic constructions.

The limitations on **two-handed signs** were originally formulated for ASL, but subsequent studies on various other sign languages indicate that they hold for all sign languages. This suggests that the constraints originate in articulatory limitations or cognitive restrictions. Two important constraints have been identified. The first one, the so-called **Symmetry Condition**, applies to signs in which both hands are moving (28a); the second one, the **Dominance Condition**, constrains the form of signs in which only one hand is moving while the other hand functions as a location (28b).

(28) a. *Symmetry Condition*
          When both hands are moving, they have the same handshape and orientation
          and they make the same or an alternating movement.
      b. *Dominance Condition*
          When the hands have different handshapes, one hand will be the weak hand
          (also called non-dominant or passive hand) and will not move. The handshape
          of the weak hand comes from a limited set (in ASL, that set consists of the
          handshapes 🖐, 👆, 🖖, 👌, ✌, and 👆).

In (29), we provide three examples of symmetric signs (i.e. signs which meet the Symmetry Condition) from different sign languages; in (30), three examples are given of signs that comply with the Dominance Condition.

Sign Language of the Netherlands (a), British Sign Language (b),
and Saudi Arabian Sign Language (c)

(29) a.   b.   c.

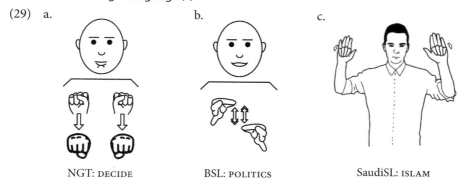

NGT: DECIDE   BSL: POLITICS   SaudiSL: ISLAM

Sign Language of the Netherlands (a), British Sign Language (b), and Japanese Sign Language (c)

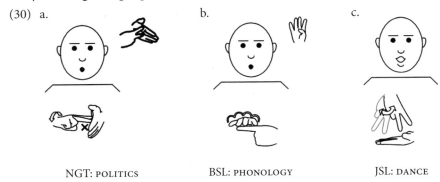

NGT: POLITICS   BSL: PHONOLOGY   JSL: DANCE

These two conditions constitute an important restriction on phonetically possible signs, but, as mentioned previously, this restriction only applies to lexical signs. It explains why, in the sign languages studied to date, we will not find signs like the one shown in (31), which combines a ⋔-handshape on the right hand and a ⋞-handshape on the left hand, the two hands performing an alternating up- and downward movement.

A non well-formed sign

(31)

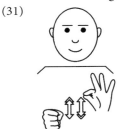

In some signs, two-handedness is a distinctive feature. This means that some pairs of signs can be found that only differ from each other by the presence of the second hand.

11.8 Phonological processes

Phonology does not only study the inventory of form elements that distinguish meaning, but it also aims to describe the form adjustments or **assimilations** that occur when words or signs are strung together in utterances, as already mentioned in Section 10.4. As we saw in Section 9.3, such assimilations are very common in compounds. Another example of assimilation can be seen in the movement direction of the NGT sign POST, when it appears in the compound POST^LAMP 'lamppost', which is built up from the signs POST and LAMP. When occurring on its own, the sign POST is specified for a downward movement (32a). However, when it is followed by the sign LAMP, which is articulated somewhat higher in the signing space (32b), POST is articulated with an upward movement (32c).

Sign Language of the Netherlands

(32)   a.   b.   c.

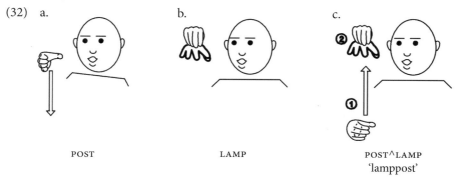

POST   LAMP   POST^LAMP
                                                          'lamppost'

Another example of a phonological process is **reduction**. Reduction implies that lexically specified phonological information gets lost in the pronunciation (see Section 10.4). The application of such a reduction process in a spoken language can be exemplified by the English word *banana*. The vowel in the first syllable is produced as schwa: /bənana/. A condition for this process to apply is that the schwa cannot be in a stressed position of the word. Phonological information can also be completely lost: in the same word *banana,* the whole first syllable /ba/ can be deleted resulting in /nana/, a form often used with and by children. In sign languages, certain signs that are lexically specified for articulation with two hands may sometimes be produced with only one hand. This **deletion** of one hand in a two-handed sign is called 'weak drop', as was already mentioned in Section 10.2. The weak hand can easily be omitted in symmetrical signs, such as those in (29). Also, the 🖐-hand in asymmetrical signs can often be omitted. As symmetry and the presence of the 🖐-hand are phonological features of the sign, we can consider weak drop as a phonological reduction (or deletion) process.

11.9   Iconicity and phonology

Signs are commonly characterized by iconic features, which implies that parts of the form resemble (parts of) the meaning (see Section 8.3 for discussion). In spoken languages, relationships between form and meaning occur only incidentally as, for example, in the onomatopoetic English word *hiss*. Iconic motivation of the form occurs, however, very frequently in all sign languages studied so far. Whereas phonemes or distinctive features of spoken language are generally meaningless, we find iconic elements at all levels of the phonological organization in sign languages.

When we consider so-called iconic signs more closely, we see that the iconic motivation of signs is often connected to one or more specific phonological parameters. This is illustrated by the Turkish Sign Language (TİD) sign SAY in (33a) and the German Sign Language (DGS) sign EAT in (33b). The location of the signs (the mouth) is connected to the fact that both speaking as well as eating involve the mouth, and it is used iconically in most sign languages for such actions.

Turkish Sign Language (a) and German Sign Language (b)

(33)   a.   b.

TİD: SAY   DGS: EAT

Handshapes are also often used **iconically**. As we saw in Section 8.3, the Libras verb DRINK uses the ⸙-handshape to represent the flask being drunk out of. In the same sign language, the ⸙-handshape is also used to represent the shape of a plane (its wings) in the sign AIRPLANE. The handshape of the Estonian Sign Language sign HEARING-AID (34b) represents the shape of the object it refers to. Equally, the handshape of NGT CHICKEN (9b) represents the beak of the bird.

Movements in a sign can also be iconic. We have already mentioned the circular movements of the hands in the FinSL sign CYCLE. The movement in the Japanese Sign Language sign DANCE (30c) also represents the action of dancing (while the ⸙-handshape refers to the legs of the dancer).

Iconicity can lead to infrequent (exceptional) form elements. The locations used in the NGT sign KIDNEY (22) and the HKSL sign TAIL do not usually occur in those respective sign languages. Such exceptionality is particularly common for the location parameter, as the body may function as an absolute location. This also explains the unusual location used in the sign COCHLEAR-IMPLANT, which in Estonian Sign Language (as in many other sign languages) is articulated above and behind the ear, where the real device is located (34a), although this location is not otherwise used. The same applies to the sign HEARING-AID (34b).

Estonian Sign Language

(34) a.   b.

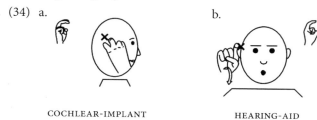

   COCHLEAR-IMPLANT   HEARING-AID

11.10 Prosody

In all previous sections, we have been concerned with the phonological structure of signs, that is, their phonological building blocks and the changes they may undergo in certain contexts. However, phonology also plays an important role at the level of the sentence, where (sometimes subtle) phonological differences can signal important meaning nuances. Sentence-level phonology is referred to as **prosody**. The domain of prosody is usually taken to include intonation, stress, and rhythm, but in the following, only the first two phenomena will be briefly addressed.

   In spoken languages, intonational contours consist of sequences of high and low tones that associate with tone-bearing units (for the most part, vowels). **Intonation** thus constitutes a layer on top of the segmental layer, that is, a **suprasegmental** layer. In (35), we repeat examples from Section 6.7.1 that illustrate the prosodic marking of yes/no questions. In Hindi, an SOV language, a yes/no question is distinguished from the corresponding declarative clause only by means of the intonational contour: in (35a), it is the rising intonation, realized as a high tone on the verb, that signals that we are dealing with an interrogative clause.

Hindi (a) and Indopakistani Sign Language (b)

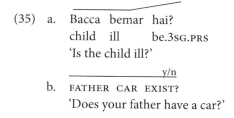

(35) a.   Bacca bemar hai?
            child   ill   be.3SG.PRS
            'Is the child ill?'

      b.   FATHER CAR EXIST?
            'Does your father have a car?'

Indopakistani Sign Language (IPSL) is also an SOV language, and (35b) illustrates that this word order is maintained in a yes/no question. Only the non-manual marker – a combination of eyes wide open and a forward head tilt – indicates that the utterance has to be interpreted as a question. Sign linguists therefore commonly assume that certain non-manual markers fulfil a prosodic function by adding a grammatically determined intonation contour to (part of) a clause; in (35), this is a question intonation. The same argument could be made for other constructions discussed in Chapter 6, for instance, topics and imperatives.

In (35b), the non-manual marker extends over the whole clause (it may, however, increase in intensity towards the end). Besides this, intonation patterns may also serve to prosodically structure sentences. The DGS example in (36) is a wh-question with a topicalized noun phrase. Prosodically, the topic POSS$_2$ DOG and the question NAME WHAT are clearly separated: they both constitute their own **intonational phrase** (IP). This is marked in the following ways: First, both IPs come with their own non-manual marker; as these markers extend over the whole prosodic constituent, they are referred to as **domain markers**. Secondly, the right boundary of both IPs is marked by a prosodic **boundary marker**, an eye blink ('b') – blinks have been found to commonly coincide with prosodic boundaries. Thirdly, IPs may also be manually marked, for instance, by a prosodic break (a pause) during which the IP-final sign may be held longer than usual.

German Sign Language

$$\overline{}^{\text{b}} \qquad \overline{}^{\text{b}}$$
$$\overline{}^{\text{t}} \quad \overline{}^{\text{wh}}$$

(36)   [POSS$_2$ DOG]$_{\text{IP}}$, [NAME WHAT]$_{\text{IP}}$?
       'Your dog, what was his name again?'

The second component of prosody we briefly address is **stress**. Stress is commonly used to highlight information, for instance, to emphasize a constituent in a clause or to contrast it with information that has previously been provided in the discourse. In spoken languages, this is commonly achieved by an increase in loudness, pitch, and/or vowel lengthening. For sign languages, it has been observed that stressed signs may undergo various manual and non-manual changes. Depending on the phonological form of the sign (for instance, whether it involves path movement or not), one or more of the following features may characterize stressed signs: increased size, duration or speed, a sharp boundary, repetition, higher location in space, and non-manual behaviors such as raised eyebrows, puffed cheeks, body lean, or head nod. Some of these features are observed in the NGT example in (37), which was uttered as a reply to a wh-question. Material that provides the answer to a wh-question is generally in focus, as it provides new information (see Section 4.6.2), and focused words often receive a stressed articulation. In (37), the fingerspelled sequence 'a-s-l' is in focus. Since fingerspelled letters do not involve path movement, certain modulations, such as increase in size or speed, cannot apply. However, it was found that the height of articulation of 'a-s-l' was elevated compared to other fingerspelled words produced by the same signer (indicated in the gloss by '↑'). Also, the fingerspelled sequence was accompanied by a brow raise.

Sign Language of the Netherlands
(37)   *Context: Which language did your brother learn?*

$$\overline{}^{\text{br}}$$

INDEX₃ a-s-l(↑) LEARN.
'He learned ASL.'

Taken together, the prosodic structure of signed utterances may be marked by manual and non-manual cues. Such cues may signal the sentence type (e.g. question intonation), may prosodically structure complex constructions, and may be used to highlight individual signs.

Summary

Similar to words in spoken language, signs can be constructed of form elements which are meaningless in themselves but which have the capacity to distinguish meaning; that is, these form elements are **distinctive**, just as **phonemes** are in spoken language. The phonological building blocks that have been identified for sign languages – handshape, orientation, location, and movement – are referred to as **parameters**. Signs that only differ in one of these parameters are called **minimal pairs**; predictable variants of parameter values are called **allophones** or **phonetic variants**.

Handshapes can be described by two groups of **distinctive features**, one describing the **selected fingers** and the other one specifying the **position** of selected fingers. Frequently used, **unmarked** handshapes require a less complex description than infrequent, **marked** handshapes. The parameter **orientation** is often taken to include orientation of the palm and of the fingers, but a phonological description of signs profits from the notion of **relative orientation**. In all sign languages, roughly four major **location** categories have to be distinguished: head, upper body, non-dominant hand, and neutral space. Distinctive locations are areas rather than points. As for the movement parameter, **hand-internal movements** and **orientation changes** can combine with **path movements**. Hand-internal movements (handshape changes) are subject to the **selected finger constraint**. Apart from these manual building blocks, **non-manual aspects** can also play a role in the phonology of sign languages. At the lexical level, mouth movements, for instance, can play a distinctive role. We distinguish mouth movements that originate from spoken language, the so-called **mouthings**, and mouth movements that do not, the so-called **mouth gestures**. The specification of handshapes and movement in **two-handed signs** is constrained by the **Symmetry Condition** and the **Dominance Condition**.

Similar to spoken languages, form adjustments or **assimilations** are often observed when signs are produced consecutively; also **reduction** or **deletion** of phonological features can occur, as, for instance, deletion of the non-dominant (weak) hand in **weak drop**. In contrast to phonemes in spoken languages, form elements in sign language, such as handshapes that are used as classifiers and in **initialized signs**, are not always meaningless. In fact, all parameters bear **iconically** motivated elements.

Important components of **prosody** are **intonation** and stress. As for the former, in sign languages, **domain** and **boundary markers** commonly flag **intonational phrases**; when these markers are realized non-manually, they constitute a **suprasegmental** layer. **Stress** may be signalled by manual and non-manual cues.

Test yourself

1. Which parts of the sign (groups of distinctive features) can be distinguished?
2. Give an example of a minimal pair in a sign language. In what respect does it differ from the English minimal pair *sell – tell*?
3. Handshapes are described in terms of finger selection and finger position. Why? Name a feature for both of them.
4. What groups of exceptional handshapes can be distinguished? What makes them exceptional?
5. What is the advantage of giving a relative description of orientation over an absolute description?

Assignments

1. Describe the following handshapes with the help of the handshape features introduced in Section 11.2.

Which handshape is the least 'marked' and why is this?
2. Argue that the ⌾-hand and the bent version of it (⌾-hand) are/could be allophones. Make use of the information on pronunciation variance in Chapter 10.

3. Children that grow up with Brazilian Sign Language (Libras) acquire handshapes in the following order:

     Which features are acquired here in the various stages?

4. Why is the phonological description of the handshape in the Chinese Sign Language sign for TOPIC (a) not identical to that of the handshape in the NGT sign LIVE (b)?

     a.   b.

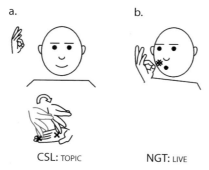

        CSL: TOPIC   NGT: LIVE

5. In the sign DELICIOUS from Khmer Sign Language, the handshape changes from ∂-hand to ∂\-hand. What makes the hand-internal movement in this sign unusual? Why do you think it is still possible?

     KSL: DELICIOUS

References and further reading

When starting to analyze a (new) sign language, it is useful to look at Klima & Bellugi (1979, Chapter 2), which is still an excellent introduction to the phonology of sign languages. Brennan et al. (1984) contains an analysis of the form elements of BSL and gives a good though somewhat more complicated introduction. The first phonological analysis of a sign language by Stokoe (1960) is still a very accessible classic. A more recent overview of the phonology of sign languages can be found in Brentari (2012). Comprehensive analyses of the phonological systems of individual sign languages are available for ASL (Sandler 1989; Brentari 1998), NGT (Van der Kooij 2002), and VGT (Demey 2005). All of these studies contain a great deal of information, but cannot be read without some theoretical background knowledge. The studies by Van der Kooij and Demey offer a detailed discussion of the iconic motivation of phonological parameters. Nyst (2007) includes an investigation of the phonological system of AdaSL. The emergence of phonological structure in homesign and in a young sign language is described in Brentari et al. (2012) and Sandler et al. (2011), respectively.

For an analysis of handshapes, we refer the reader to Van der Hulst (1993, 1995), Sandler (1996a), Brentari (1998), and Van der Kooij (2002). The notion of orientation as discussed in this chapter originates in Crasborn & Van der Kooij (1997, 2003). The parameter movement is addressed by Sandler (1996b) and Hansen (2011). Concerning the function of the mouth, we refer to the studies on various sign languages compiled in Boyes Braem & Sutton-Spence (2001), as well as to Nadolske & Rosenstock (2007) on ASL, Bank (2014) on NGT, and Crasborn et al. (2008) for a comparison of NGT, BSL, and SSL. Limitations on two-handed signs were first described in Battison (1978); more recently, these limitations have been investigated for Kenyan Sign Language by Morgan & Mayberry (2012). More on the phonological representation of two-handed signs can be read in Sandler (1993) and Van der Hulst (1996). For references on assimilation and weak drop, see Chapter 10. Aspects of sign language prosody are discussed in Sandler (1999), Brentari & Crossley (2002), and Dachkovsky & Sandler (2009); for an overview, see Sandler (2012). Wilbur & Schick (1987) investigated the realization of stress in ASL.

The examples from Tlingit are derived from Ladefoged & Maddieson (1996). The CSL signs are taken from the standard lexicon of Yau (1977). Information on Saudi Arabian Sign Language was found in the study by Kozak & Tomita (2012). In the section on prosody, the Hindi example is from Zeshan (2004b), the IPSL example from Zeshan (2003b), the DGS example from Herrmann (2010), and the NGT example from Crasborn & van der Kooij (2013). Finally, the Libras acquisition data are from Karnopp's (1999) dissertation.

Chapter 12

Language variation and standardization

Trude Schermer

12.1 Introduction

In the United Kingdom, deaf people from Birmingham sign differently from deaf people in Leeds or Durham. Deaf Brazilians from Florianopolis sign differently from deaf people in Sao Paolo. And in the Netherlands, deaf people from Groningen sign differently from deaf people in the West of the Netherlands.

Sign Language of the Netherlands

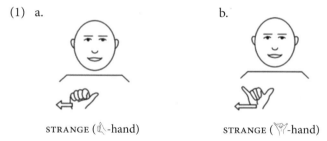

(1) a.

STRANGE (🖐-hand)

b.

STRANGE (🤙-hand)

The two signs in (1) are very similar to each other, and they both mean 'strange' in Sign Language of the Netherlands (NGT). The place of articulation and movement are the same; the only difference is the handshape (or, to be more precise, the position of the pinky). The sign in (1a) is made with a 🖐-hand while the sign in (1b) is articulated with a 🤙-hand. The first sign is used mainly in the West of the Netherlands, the second one mainly in the North – in other words: the signs are regional variants. In this case, they exemplify phonological variation, as they differ only in handshape and not in meaning (see also Section 10.4). The sign in (1b) is one of the two standard NGT signs for STRANGE.

All adult language users are more or less familiar with regional differences in their own language, and this is, of course, also true for sign language users. In this chapter, we will look at what constitutes a standard language in a sign language (Section 12.2) and what constitutes a dialect (Section 12.3). In Section 12.4, we discuss the different types of variation that can occur in a language. The status of a sign language and the official recognition are dealt with in Section 12.5, while language politics and policy are considered in Section 12.6. Finally, in Section 12.7, we explain in some detail the process of standardization.

DOI 10.1075/z.199.12sch

12.2   What constitutes a standard language?

It is possible to describe a **standard language** as a language which can generally be used in the public domain, that is, in all important sectors of public life, such as the government, the administration, the administration of justice, education, and the media. Words, expressions, forms of pronunciation, or constructions which are standard can, in principle, therefore be used in the sectors and situations mentioned above. This does not mean, however, that the standard language has a fixed, static form. Rather, what is considered to be standard language changes over time, and variety is also found in the standard language at any given moment. Sometimes two or more words, expressions, or constructions exist to express (more or less) the same thing, and in addition, some words can be pronounced in different ways. A standard language is therefore a language which is clearly described. This is the case for French in the form prescribed by the *Académie Française*. Standard English, however, can refer to many different varieties: Standard American English, Standard British English, etc. The absence of a standard form and a written form has contributed significantly to the linguistic variation found in many (sign) languages.

12.3   What counts as a dialect in sign languages?

Discussion about the difference between a language and a **dialect** has never led to a clear definition of what constitutes a language and what constitutes a dialect. There are no linguistic arguments that can be put forward for classifying a system as the one or the other.

It seems as though the difference between language and dialect has more to do with a difference in status. In Western societies, a language frequently has more status than a dialect. In Europe, there has been considerable debate as to which minority languages should be officially recognized as such. With recognition as a language can come the right to use the variety in education and the administration of justice.

Research into the language of deaf people started in the 1950s, but the breakthrough only came after 1960, when the basic phonological building blocks of signs were identified (see Section 1.2 and Chapter 11). Initially, researchers were mainly interested in the differences and similarities between spoken languages and sign languages. This focus was for the most part motivated by the need to demonstrate that sign languages are independent, natural languages and not derivative forms of spoken languages. As a result, only little attention was paid to the possible differences and similarities between different sign languages in the seventies and eighties. Researchers mainly considered whether or not a sign language was a language. Consequently, the question of whether a specific sign language might perhaps be a dialect did not arise.

Research into possible relationships between sign languages did not get underway until around the turn of the century. Until the late 1990s, British Sign Language (BSL), Australian Sign Language (Auslan), and New Zealand Sign Language (NZSL) were therefore almost always described as independent languages, although it had already been established that Auslan and NZSL originated from BSL. In this case, however, research has clearly shown that it is not linguistically justified to consider these three sign languages as three different languages. Rather, they are different varieties of one language: there is a large degree of similarity between the three languages, at least in terms of the lexicon. This is due to the fact that BSL users emigrated to Australia and New Zealand in the eighteenth century and introduced BSL there.

Many people think that BSL and American Sign Language (ASL) must be related to each other because spoken English is used in both countries. This is not the case. ASL is in fact related to French Sign Language (LSF). A deaf Frenchman, Laurent Clerc, went to Hartford (Connecticut) in the nineteenth century to teach at the first school for the deaf in the United States (1817), and in so doing introduced French signs (see also Section 14.3.1). The political situation is also important: Hong Kong Sign Language (HKSL), for instance, developed from a dialect of Chinese Sign Language (CSL) but is now considered a separate language.

In spite of regional variety, we still talk about *the* American Sign Language, *the* British Sign Language, *the* Italian Sign Language (LIS), and so forth. The most important criterion seems to be that few grammatical differences between regional variants exist. In the 1980s, this was the basis for the decision that *the* Sign Language of the Netherlands exists, as it was for South African Sign Language (SASL) at the turn of the century. There are indeed lexical differences between the varieties but usually few differences in terms of morphology and syntax. The same is true in other countries, such as the United States, Britain and Brazil, where lexical differences between regional sign languages have been identified. However, because in these cases, too, researchers identified a shared morphological and syntactic structure, we still talk about the American, British, and Brazilian Sign Languages. In this book, the term dialect is used to indicate regional variety in the context of sign languages.

12.4 Variation in sign languages

As in spoken languages, variation may occur at different levels in all sign languages, that is, we find lexical, phonological, morphological, and syntactic variation. In comparison with spoken languages, it seems that variation occurs more frequently in the lexicon of sign languages. However, there certainly are differences between sign languages in the extent to which this variation occurs. It seems that ASL is more uniform than sign languages such as SASL and LIS. An explanation for this might be that the American

School for the Deaf in Hartford played a central role in early deaf education at the end of the nineteenth century. Basically everyone who used signs in deaf education in the United States was educated in Hartford. The signs could thus be easily disseminated by the teachers who had been trained there. Contrast this with the situation, present or past, in many countries, where no national center of education for deaf teachers exists, where no signs are used in education, and where little exchange takes place between deaf people. In Italy, for example, there was in the past little contact between deaf people from different regions. Consequently, clear differences can be found in the lexicon of deaf language users from the north of Italy and the middle and south.

As in spoken languages, variation in sign languages has to do with social differences between language users. As we have already seen, the place or region where the sign comes from is an important source of variation in the lexicon. The sign language user's background also has an influence, in particular the parents' language and the type of education the person has followed. Furthermore, variation can be related to the age, gender, race/ethnic group, and social class of the language user. In addition to factors which have to do with the language user himself, the context in which the language is used can also play a role. The different factors which contribute to language variation are discussed in the following two subsections.

12.4.1 Factors related to the language user

By far and away the most research into **lexical variation** in sign languages has focused on **regional** variation. This variation can be related to geographical dispersal but also commonly results from the organization of education. This is the case in the Netherlands and in Flanders, where variants of NGT and Flemish Sign Language (VGT), respectively, arose at the different deaf schools. It also appears to be true in Spanish Sign Language (LSE), where three variants of the verb ASK are found: the variants depicted below are from Valencia (2a), the Basque Country (2b), and Madrid (2c).

Spanish Sign Language

(2)   a.   b.   c.

Three variants of LSE ASK

Surprisingly, in some sign languages that are used in large geographical areas, relatively little variation is found; this has been described, for instance, for Inuit Sign Language (IUR) and Indopakistani Sign Language (IPSL). Still, it is true that regional differences are found in the lexicons of most sign languages. This has only been extensively re-searched and documented for a handful of sign languages, such as NGT, VGT, Danish Sign Language, German Sign Language (DGS), British Sign Language (BSL), Auslan, and ASL. Sometimes lexical differences can be found between sign language users from cities and sign language users from villages. Therefore, in the Nigerian Hausa Sign Language, new signs are mainly used in the cities, and the signs used in the cities also have a higher status than those from the villages.

Morphological variation and **syntactic variation** can also occur, although these types of variation are less frequent than lexical variation. In Russian Sign Language (RSL), for instance, the sign meaning SELF, as used in the regions of Moscow and Omsk, cannot agree in space with a referent and is always articulated on the body, even if it refers to the addressee or a third person (3a). In contrast, in Murmansk in the North West of the Russian Federation, the sign can be spatially modified, thus inflecting for person; in Example (3b), the sign agrees with a third person referent at the ipsilateral side of the signing space by orienting the fingertips towards this locus.

Russian Sign Language

   (3) a.   The sign SELF as non-inflecting form

       b.   The sign SELF as inflecting form (third person)

The **background** of a sign language user, for instance, the **type of education** followed, also has an influence on language use: deaf children in an oral education system will use few or no school language signs, as will be further discussed in Chapter 14. Deaf children in a bilingual education system, on the other hand, learn to use both the sign language and the spoken language in different situations and will also develop and use a school sign language. Deaf children who pursue a standard education or attend a school for children with hearing impairments will hardly or never use their sign language at school because their classmates do not know that language. Obviously, this has an influence on the children's language use, particularly at the lexical level. Deaf children at a school in Nigeria (Tudin Maliki School), for example, have hardly any contact with the deaf community but created their own wealth of school language signs. In Hausa Sign Language, it is possible to find examples of signs which are not used by deaf people among themselves, but are used exclusively by hearing impaired and hearing people in communication with deaf people.

Usually languages are passed on from one generation to the next. For sign languages, however, this is only true to a very limited extent because 95% of deaf children have hearing parents. As a consequence, deaf children generally do not learn a sign language as a matter of course from their parents. This unusual acquisition situation leads to considerable inter-generational changes in the language. In addition to this, each generation of language users has its own typical vocabulary, as is also the case with spoken language users. In fact, variation related to **age** is mainly found in the lexicon. In those countries where deaf people go to boarding schools, certain signs ended up typifying a specific generation from a certain school. The education system can change to involve more signing, or sometimes less signing, as in Turkey. Again, this influences the language use of different generations. Where boarding education has been reduced, as in Britain, variation also decreases amongst the younger signers since they are more frequently exposed to signs in more general use.

Highly local signs can develop into a general standard sign. The sign for the city of Veenendaal in the Netherlands, depicted in (4), was originally the sign for a teacher at one of the deaf schools. This teacher's last name was Veenendaal, and he had a long pointed nose. His name sign is now the sign for the city of Veenendaal.

Sign Language of the Netherlands

(4)

VEENENDAAL

The extent to which the spoken language has an influence on the sign language also results in variation. Due to the impact of oral education, the sign language of older deaf people in different countries in Europe is often more strongly influenced by the spoken language than is the language of the generation which enjoyed a bilingual education. Examples of this can be found in Germany, the Netherlands, Greece, and Italy. There are, for instance, signs in these sign languages which can only be distinguished from one another through the mouthing. The BSL sign depicted in (5) is an example of this: the manual form can mean HUSBAND and WIFE, but the meaning can be disambiguated by means of an accompanying mouthing corresponding to the English word (see also the NGT signs in Section 11.6).

British Sign Language

(5)

HUSBAND/WIFE

In some sign languages, clear differences are found between signs which are used by men and those which are used by women. Differences related to **gender** mainly concern the lexicon (see Section 13.4.1 for an LSE example). Once again, the educational system plays an important role. In Irish Sign Language, for instance, major differences used to exist between the signs that were used at the school for deaf girls and at the school for deaf boys in Dublin. It is interesting to note that no problems arose during communication between the boys and girls because the girls adapted themselves to the boys. In contact situations with the boys, they used the boys' signs, but used their own signs among themselves. For ASL, researchers have described differences at the meaning level between homosexual and heterosexual signers. For example, the question whether the other person is homosexual – 'Are you one?' – was interpreted by most heterosexual signers as meaning 'Are you alone?'.

Differences have also been observed between white and black signers in the United States as a result of, among other things, segregated education. **Ethnic** differences can be found at the phonological level. Many variants of English are related to ethnic differences, as is true for Jamaican English, for example. A similar phenomenon has been described for ASL: white ASL signers make certain signs centrally in front of the body, while black signers articulate the same signs somewhat lower and closer to the body. There does indeed seem to be a form of 'black signing', but how exactly this can be distinguished from the 'white' form of ASL is still the subject of research.

Social class can also have an influence on language variation. Major class differences exist within certain cultures which are characterized, among other things, by a difference in language use. The difference between the upper class and the lower class in Great Britain exemplifies this. Another example is the caste system found in India, Pakistan, and Bangladesh. A caste system is a centuries-old system which divides people into different groups. These groups have a certain position and role within society. Vocations, rights, and duties are tightly linked to castes. More specifically, the manner in which people are expected to behave, what they must eat, which language they speak, whom they marry, and the type of work they do are determined by the caste to which they belong. The question is, however, whether the same class differences exist within the deaf community as in the surrounding hearing culture. In most countries, deaf people have little opportunity to pursue a higher education because they are unable to satisfy the entrance requirements. As a result of this, deaf people are hardly ever found in vocations which enjoy a higher social status. In the United States, there might even be talk of a class difference between the deaf people who have been educated at, for example, Gallaudet University or the National Technical University for the Deaf in Rochester, and people who have not had such an education. The question is: Can a difference in sign language use be found which is attributable to this sort of class difference?

12.4.2 Factors related to the context of language use

The **topic of conversation**, the **conversation partner**, and the **context** in which the discussion takes place can also have an influence on the linguistic form that is used. As in spoken languages, there is a difference in style between formal and informal situations, although little research on sign languages has been done in this area. In spoken languages, it is more common for the standard variants of a language to be used in formal situations. In the case of sign language users, we sometimes find differences in the lexicon used, as is true for the two variants of NGT TEA in (6), one of which (6a) is more formal than the other (6b).

Sign Language of the Netherlands

(6) a.   b.

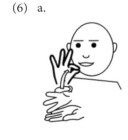

TEA (formal)   TEA (informal)

However, differences in the manner of signing are more frequently observed. Informal signs are frequently characterized by bigger movements, more facial expression, and the use of only one hand in two-handed signs ('weak drop; see Section 11.8). In (7a), we see the informal, one-handed version of the LSE sign SIBLING, while the picture in (7b) shows the formal two-handed version (7b). It is interesting to note that in the one-handed version, the movement between the two hands (the two index fingers contacting each other) is taken over by a hand-internal movement, a wiggling movement of the middle and index fingers.

Spanish Sign Language

(7) a.   b.

SIBLING (informal)   SIBLING (formal)

For HKSL, it is reported that mouth gestures can be used in informal contexts with no manual component at all; that is, the sign only consists of a non-manual part. Such 'non-handed' signs can express, for instance, the meanings FINISHED (8a) or NOT-HAVE (8b).

Hong Kong Sign Language

(8)   a.   b.

FINISHED   NOT-HAVE

Lexical differences can also be found as a result of who is signing to whom: in NGT, there is a sign ANGRY, which is only used with children and not with adults – compare (9a) and (9b). The sign BANANA also has one variant for adults and another one for children, as (9c) and (9d) demonstrate.

Sign Language of the Netherlands

(9) a.   b.

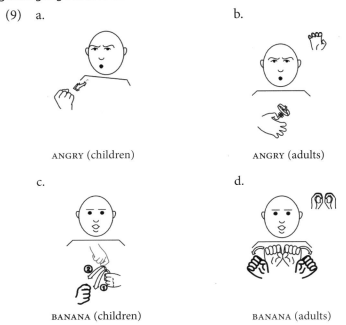

ANGRY (children)   ANGRY (adults)

c.   d.

BANANA (children)   BANANA (adults)

Finally, a clearly modality-specific factor that may lead to language variation is the **hearing status** of the conversation partner: a deaf person signs differently to a hearing person than to a deaf sign language user. That is to say, deaf sign language users adapt themselves to a hearing sign language user by, for example, making more use of their voice.

Language use which is appropriate in a specific situation and to a specific group of speakers is called a **register**. Different groups have their own characteristic language use: football players, scientists, doctors, etc. Such registers also occur in sign languages. Kata Kolok, the sign language of the Balinese village of Bengkala, thus has an extensive set of signs which have to do with agriculture and trade, while IUR has a rather considerable vocabulary related to fishing.

12.5   Status and recognition of sign languages

The **status** of a sign language is closely related to the status of deaf people in a society, the historical background, and the role that a sign language plays in deaf education (see also Section 14.3). Whenever sign language is prohibited as the language of instruction in deaf education, the language clearly occupies a minority position which is closely linked to the minority position occupied by its users. There are also a few scattered communities in which deaf people are less marginalized and where a considerable number of hearing community members also uses the local sign language. Examples of such communities are the island of Martha's Vineyard (off the coast of Massachusetts, US), the village of Bengkala in Bali, the village of Adamorobe in Ghana, and a village in Yucatan (Mexico) (see also Section 1.3).

The status of sign languages has changed enormously since the 1960s. The emancipation of deaf people is partly due to the fact that linguistic research has shown that sign languages are natural languages and that deaf sign language users can be said to have their own particular culture. While until the middle of the twentieth century, sign languages had been generally regarded as inferior to spoken languages, in the twenty-first century, people no longer doubt that they are in fact fully-fledged, natural languages. When measured against the national spoken languages, the status of sign languages is, in the majority of European countries, comparable to that of a minority language. ASL is the fourth language of the United States, a clear indication that ASL cannot be considered a small minority language.

As early as 1953, UNESCO had already established the importance of the mother tongue as the language of instruction. Until the 1980s, the prevailing view within deaf education in Europe and parts of other continents was that the spoken national language was the mother tongue of deaf children and should therefore be the language of instruction. This view, however, changed under the influence of results of scientific research into sign languages and as a consequence of the poor education results achieved by deaf children who receive instruction in their spoken national language. In 1981, Sweden became the first country in the world where the government made the sign language (Swedish Sign Language) mandatory in deaf education. In the majority of European countries, such as Norway, Sweden, Finland, Portugal, Spain, Germany, Denmark, England, Austria, Belgium (Flanders), Hungary, Finland, Estonia, Latvia, Lithuania, Poland, France, and Greece, the local sign languages have been recognized as an official language. Outside the European Union, countries such as the Russian Federation, Uruguay, Brazil, Uganda, Thailand, Vietnam, Mexico, South Africa, the United States, and Canada have also given **recognition** to their national sign language.

This recognition, however, does not necessarily imply that rights have been awarded for the use of sign language. In the Russian Federation, for example, official recognition of RSL was achieved in 2012, but this has had little impact so far on the use of RSL in education. There is also no legal basis for a minority language policy in the European Union (EU). This means that the EU has no right to compel member states to carry out measures that have political or legal consequences. Nevertheless, the EU does have a policy on minority languages, including since 1992 an official European Charter on Regional or Minority Languages. Since 2003, sign languages have been recognized within the European Union as minority languages, but the implications for rights for interpreting, education, and so on vary considerably from one country to another.

Deaf people are found in all sorts of communities but not all deaf people organize themselves in the same way. Some deaf communities are well organized and have a common sign language and culture. The American and Scandinavian deaf communities are two such examples. However, there are also places in Brazil and Mexico, for example, where deaf people are ignored or marginalized by the hearing society, and still do not form a real community among themselves, simply because they live too far away from each other and thus have too little contact. Education plays an important role in the formation of a community and the development of a common sign language and culture. Paradoxically enough, oral deaf education in boarding schools in Europe has contributed to the development and preservation of sign languages. Boarding schools are a place where deaf children meet and interact and thus learn a sign language from each other. In places where the deaf community has been able to develop into a language community, we can talk about a deaf community as a **minority language group**.

12.6 The politics of language and language policy

Language policy or **language planning** implies that active intervention is undertaken in the natural process of the development of a language. Language planning can cover two areas: the internal structure of a language (corpus planning) or the status of a language (status planning). Corpus planning activities comprise aspects like the development of a written form for a language, spelling reform, the making of a lexical inventory, and the writing of grammar books. Sign languages have no written form comparable to the written form of spoken languages. As pointed out previously, there are indeed different ways of transcribing signs, but there is no commonly used written form of any of the world's sign languages (see Sections 1.7 and 10.5). The grammars of some sign languages have indeed been documented and published, ASL being the sign language that has been described most comprehensively. Still, the grammar of a great many sign languages has either only been partly researched and described, or has not been investigated at all.

The **standardization** of a language plays a central role in corpus planning. By this we mean the codification of a language's linguistic norm. Languages can vary from non-standardized (such as the majority of languages for which there is no written form, including sign languages) to modern standard languages such as Dutch, English, and Spanish, which are used in all communicative situations.

12.7 Standardization

Standardization can take place in an indirect way as a result of exposure to the language, or it can take place in a more directed way. The availability of material, such as dictionaries, and the extent to which this material is disseminated, plays an important role in indirectly leading to the standardization of a language. Which signs are included in a dictionary, for example, can be interpreted as reflecting the fact that they are the standard signs (see Section 12.7.1).

Where authorities wish to actively direct standardization, this is, in general, a highly controversial subject for any community, particularly because the concept of standardization is frequently, but erroneously, interpreted in terms of right and wrong lexemes. For a deaf community in particular, a language policy that is imposed from above by hearing people is seen as a major invasion of its own language and culture. This view is partly the result of an age-old suppression of sign language by hearing people. The Netherlands is an example of a country where the government has clearly intervened in the natural process of standardization of a sign language. The way this was implemented will be briefly described in Section 12.7.2. For purposes of education, pressure is often exerted by authorities for a choice to be made between signs, thus creating a standard. The size of the country is not always relevant: standardization was carried out in the Netherlands, a small country, but in the neighboring Flanders region of Belgium, which is even smaller, people explicitly spoke out against any form of standardization.

New signs come into being wherever there is a need. The lexicon of many sign languages is, however, often less extensive than that of the surrounding spoken languages. In many instances, this can be attributed to the fact that those sign languages are not used, or cannot be used, in all communication situations. Most European sign languages were not used in primary schools until the mid-1990s. Since the emancipation of deaf people, the recognition of sign languages as natural languages, and the introduction of bilingual education for the deaf, the need for signs for school subjects and signs in work situations, for example, has increased in many countries. As a result of this, new signs for many different kinds of concepts have quickly emerged. This process can be both non-directed and directed.

12.7.1 Non-directed standardization: the role of sign language dictionaries and the media

The availability of material (such as **dictionaries**) and the extent to which this material is disseminated plays an important role in making a language more uniform. One of the first descriptions of a sign language is often a dictionary of signs. Numerous dictionaries were compiled in the 1970s and 1980s, but many of these compilations should in fact better be described as lexical lists: in the majority of cases, these are lists of words that are paired with an equivalent sign but with little structural information. In addition, it is often unclear just how representative of the sign language most of the signs included in these dictionaries or word lists are (see Chapter 8), since the authors do not specify how many regions have been consulted. Several countries have set up a center responsible for dictionary work, particularly in relation to the official recognition of the sign language in that country. The recording of signs, even if it is in a very rough form with just a photo or a drawing with a translation alongside, does have a standardizing effect, but little systematic research has been carried out into how much influence dictionaries actually have on a language.

The use of sign language in the **media**, that is, on television and the internet, also has an important influence on the dissemination of signs among users. In many countries, sign language interpreting is available for at least some television programs, particularly the news. Specific programs aimed at the Deaf community are also influential. For example, the BBC program *See Hear!* has been hugely influential in Britain because a number of leading British deaf personalities have appeared as presenters.

New signs are needed when a new concept emerges or when a sign language starts to be used in a new context. For instance, when the internet became commonplace, there was a need for a new sign INTERNET. In ASL, three different signs were being used in the beginning but currently only one of these is in common use. This is an example of a natural process of standardization.

12.7.2 The directed standardization process

To date, there are only few examples of a direct standardization process for sign languages. Since the various steps in the Netherlands have been well documented, this process will be discussed with particular reference to the situation in the Netherlands.

In 1998, the Dutch government wished to support the introduction of bilingual education for deaf children and to that end wished to achieve standardization of NGT in order to ensure that educational materials were available in one form of the language only. A covenant was signed involving various organizations for the deaf. There were objections from sign language researchers and the deaf community on the grounds that non-directed standardization should still be allowed to take place.

Nevertheless, a working group was formed comprising deaf people from different regions, who were highly proficient in NGT, two hearing linguists, and two bilingual (NGT/Dutch) hearing people. The working group not only developed guidelines for establishing standard signs but also laid down guidelines for the development of new signs. The premise underlying the standardization of signs in the lexicon was that no one regional variant would become the standard variant for all signs. An important reason for not doing this was that no linguistic arguments could be found to corroborate the choice of one region.

It was vitally important that this project be supported by the entire deaf community. For this reason, as many deaf people as possible throughout the country were involved in the project. Altogether some 5,000 signs were involved, many of which were also new signs. The designation of a sign as 'standard' implied that the sign should be used nationwide in education and family guidance. At the same time, however, it was made explicit that signs which are not standardized are not 'incorrect' or 'wrong'.

The linguistic guidelines for establishing standard signs have their origins in the lexicographic work. Some of these guidelines are mentioned below.

i.   A sign is considered to be a standard sign if it has the same meaning in all the regions, is made in the same manner in all the regions, and is recognized in all the regions.
ii. If a sign for a particular concept exists in only one region, and the other regions have no sign for that concept, then this sign is included as a standard sign.
iii. The morphological connection between signs which are semantically related to each other must be preserved.

As an example of the application of guideline (iii), consider the sign ELECTRICITY (10a), which is made with a ⁀-hand. Consequently, the choice for the standard form of semantically related signs such as PLUG (10b), CURRENT, SOCKET, and BATTERY is partly determined by the fact that those signs are all made with a ⁀-handshape.

Sign Language of the Netherlands

(10)   a.   b.

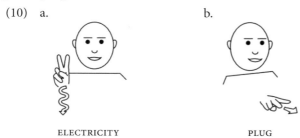

ELECTRICITY   PLUG

Another example of signs that belong together in terms of their meaning are the signs YESTERDAY and TOMORROW. The signs that have their origin in Amsterdam both have a ⌕-handshape, while the signs that have their origin in Groningen are both articulated with a ⌕-handshape. Clearly, it would be confusing, and thus undesirable, to choose one sign from one region and the other sign from the other region.

Finally, there are also a few signs for which it proved impossible to reach a standard on the basis of the above criteria. In those cases, both variants were included in the standard dictionary as synonyms. There are therefore synonyms for the signs PAPA, PARENTS, and TEACH.

In some countries, active steps are taken to create new signs, as opposed to borrowing them from other sign languages (Section 13.5.3). Obviously, newly created signs should respect the phonological constraints of the respective sign language (see Chapter 11). In the Netherlands, in the process of standardization, only deaf signers were allowed to create new signs. Many new NGT signs for concepts needed in the teaching of school subjects thus came into being. For example, for the area of physics, the signs DIVERGENT (11a) and ADHESION (11b) were developed.

Sign Language of the Netherlands

(11)   a.   b.

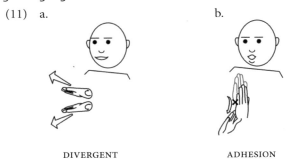

DIVERGENT   ADHESION

In other countries, too, explicit efforts have been made to develop new signs. In Germany, for example, a DGS dictionary for terms from psychology was compiled, and this involved developing new signs for some concepts. Such signs are often put into one large database that forms the basis for educational tools and sign language dictionaries (see Section 8.5).

Occasionally, a sign may exist for a certain concept but nevertheless a new sign is developed because, for some reason, deaf people no longer want to use the existing sign. In NGT, for example, the existing signs for certain days of the week and months of the year were based on fingerspelling, that is, they were derived from Dutch. Deaf sign language users, however, preferred to have signs that were more typical of NGT. Examples of newly created standard signs are TUESDAY and WEDNESDAY (12a,b) and JANUARY and FEBRUARY (12c,d).

Sign Language of the Netherlands

(12)   a.   b.

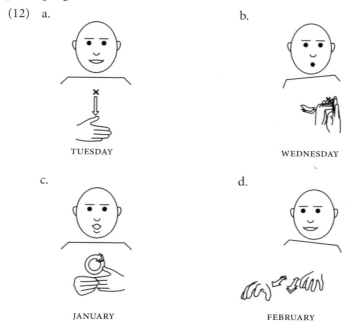

      TUESDAY   WEDNESDAY

   c.   d.

      JANUARY   FEBRUARY

Finally, signs are sometimes modified because they are experienced as being discriminatory (see Section 13.4 for more discussion on language change). For that reason, the older NGT sign for JEWISH, which refers to a hooked nose, is no longer used in the Netherlands; the sign pictured in (13) is used instead.

Sign Language of the Netherlands

(13)

      JEWISH

Summary

Much variation can be found in sign languages, just as in spoken languages. There are **standard languages** but also **dialects**. However, it is often unclear what exactly is meant by a sign language dialect. Variation can be found at all linguistic levels: phonological, **morphological, syntactic,** and **lexical variation** – with variation of the latter type being most significant in the majority of sign languages. At all levels, variation is commonly related to social differences between the language users, such as the **region,** the sign language user's **background** (e.g. **type of education), age, gender, ethnic background,** and **social class.** In addition, the **topic of conversation,** the **conversation partner,** and the **context** in which the language is used may have an influence. The **hearing status** of the conversation partner is of particular importance. Signs which belong to a specific subject and a specific group of users constitute a **register.**

Sign languages can be regarded as minority languages. The **status** of a sign language is closely related to the historical background and educational situation of the deaf community in a country. Not every deaf community constitutes a **minority language group.** This only occurs when the deaf community has been able to evolve into a language community. Some countries have given **recognition** to their national sign language.

Standardization of sign languages is a part of **language planning** or language policy. The need for uniformity and a standard form has resulted in the directed standardization of the lexicon in some countries. Linguistic criteria can underpin the decision to opt for signs for the basic lexicon. **New signs** come into being as a matter of course and are developed in response to a need. **Dictionaries** and **media** such as television and internet play an important role in the indirect standardization of a sign language.

Test yourself

1. What is the difference between a dialect and a standard language?
2. What factors influence language variation?
3. Give a possible explanation for the lexical variation found in sign languages.
4. Why is it important for sign languages to be recognized as languages?
5. When does a deaf community constitute a minority language group?
6. What types of language planning are there?
7. What does standardization mean?
8. Why is the standardization of sign languages often controversial?
9. What was the purpose of the standardization project in the Netherlands?
10. What criteria were applied in the Dutch standardization project?
11. Why do many sign languages have gaps in their lexicons?
12. How can dictionaries and the media contribute to the standardization of a sign language?

Assignments

1. Name four factors that can play a part in variation in sign languages and give an example for each of the four factors.

2. Give two examples of phonological variation involving two different parameters in a sign language you know or by using a search on the internet.

3. The following variants of the sign DOG occur in HKSL. They are used at two different schools for the deaf. What does this tell us about the factors influencing variation in sign languages?

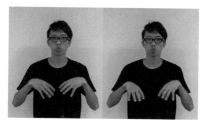   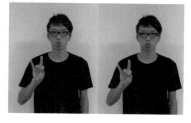

DOG(1)   DOG(2)

4. What kind of forms of recognition are there for sign languages, and what are their effect?

5. Does youth culture have a different effect in Deaf communities compared to its effect in spoken language communities?

6. There are two different signs for 'caribou' in IUR: one from Rankin Inlet (left) and one from Toloyoak (right). What kind of variation does this exemplify? Do you think this variation leads to problems in communication? Provide arguments for your answer.

CARIBOU (Rankin Inlet)   CARIBOU (Toloyoak)

References and further reading

The chapters by Lucas et al. (2001b), Lucas & Bayley (2010), and Schembri & Johnston (2012) provide convenient overviews of all aspects of variation in sign languages. Also, the volumes edited by Lucas (1989, 1995) compile articles on various aspects of variation in different sign languages. Lexical variation in BSL is addressed in Stamp et al. (2014) and Sutton Spence & Woll (1999), and Schembri et al. (2010) add to the picture Auslan and NZSL. The relationship between BSL, Auslan, and NZSL is investigated in Johnston (2003a). As for different factors motivating variation, gender variation is addressed in Leeson & Grehan (2004), regional variation in Schermer (2004) and Vanhecke & De Werdt (2004), and ethnic variation (African American signing) in Lucas et al. (2001a) and McCaskill et al. (2011). Lucas (2003) discusses the role of variation in lexicography, and Lucas (2013) provides an overview of methodological issues in variation research.

Nyst (2012) sketches the unique sociolinguistic characteristics of 'deaf villages'; for an evaluation of these characteristics, see also Kusters (2010). An overview of language policy in the European Union with respect to sign languages is provided by Krausneker (2000, 2001), while Schermer (2012) addresses various aspects of language planning. Language planning and standardization is discussed further for Auslan in Johnston (2003b) and for NGT in Schermer (2003). The influence of the media is reported in Allsop, Woll & Sutton-Spence (1990).

Information on Hausa Sign Language is from Schmaling (2000) and on SASL from Aarons & Akash (1992). The IUR examples are taken from Schuit (2013), the LSE examples from Minguet Soto (2001) and the LSE-Sign database (Gutierrez-Sigut et al. 2015). The ASL 'Are you one?' example was found in Rudner & Butowsky (1981), and examples from HKSL were provided by the Chinese University at Hong Kong. The NGT standardization examples are taken from Schermer (2003, 2004).

Chapter 13

Language contact and change

Trude Schermer & Roland Pfau

13.1   Introduction

Like all spoken languages, sign languages undergo diachronic change, and just as in spoken languages, such changes may be motivated by external factors (e.g. language contact) or internal factors (e.g. ease of articulation). Obviously, there is a clear relation between language variation, as discussed in Chapter 12, and language change. At some point in time, two or more variants – be they lexical or grammatical in nature – may co-exist, but at a given moment, one variant may dominate and the other one will thus disappear, resulting in language change.

In fact, many changes in a language can be attributed to processes that evolve over a longer period of time. In current English, for example, the word *ask* is not only a verb but is also being used as a noun, as in *that is a big ask*. This nominalization was unknown fifty years ago. In this chapter, we address changes in sign languages that cannot be attributed to the factors discussed in Chapter 12 (such as age, sex, and ethnicity).

We start by briefly describing the history of sign languages (Section 13.2) and the existence of sign language families (Section 13.3). Language change that occurs in languages over a longer period of time, that is, diachronic change, is the topic of Section 13.4. In this context, we will address instances of language change at different linguistic levels (Section 13.4.1), as well as processes of grammaticalization (Section 13.4.2) and lexicalization (Section 13.4.3). In Section 13.5, we examine various phenomena that have to do with language contact, such as the relationship between sign languages and spoken languages. We discuss forms of signing such as Signed English (Section 13.5.1), code-switching, and code-mixing (Section 13.5.2). Finally, we also address ways in which sign languages can influence one other (Section 13.5.3) as well as ways in which surrounding spoken languages can have an impact on sign languages (Section 13.5.4).

DOI 10.1075/z.199.13sch

13.2   Sign languages in historical perspective

In order to be able to establish what changes have taken place in a sign language, you need to know what earlier forms of signing looked like. Sign languages have been around just as long as Deaf communities have been in existence, and references to the use of signs by the Deaf can, for example, already be found in Plato in Ancient Greece. There are even scholars who hypothesize that sign languages might be older than spoken languages, that is, that manual communication preceded vocal communication; this is sometimes referred to as 'the gestural theory of language origin'. Linguistic research into older forms of sign languages, however, is impossible for the simple reason that sign languages have no script and that hardly any materials or descriptions exist. From roughly the eighteenth century onwards, some written descriptions and drawings are available, but generally, these only illustrate the form of individual signs and are therefore not sufficient to explore, for example, the grammar of a sign language. Only with the advent of film, it became possible to document signed utterances and natural conversations.

In the eighteenth century, it was recognized that deaf people could be taught with the help of signs. In a book on educating deaf children, the French cleric Abbé Charles-Michel de L'Épée described the use of signing. He distinguished natural signs (which hearing people also produce, that is, gestures), the signs made by his deaf pupils, and the signs that he devised himself in order to be able to create a visual form of French grammar. We would now call the latter a form of spoken French with supporting signs, or Signed French. De L'Épée's teaching method has had immense influence on other European countries and also on the United States of America. Traces of this influence of old French signs can still be found in the lexicon of American Sign Language (ASL), as well as in Sign Language of the Netherlands (NGT). For example, the sign for GOOD in ASL and a dialect of NGT is derived from the old French sign with the same meaning.

As mentioned previously, the descriptive material available for most sign languages is of very recent origin so that it is almost impossible to get a historical perspective on a specific sign language. For ASL, there are a few films dating from the early twentieth century, produced by the National Association of the Deaf to preserve early ASL on film. The NAD was concerned at that time that "pure" sign language might disappear under the pressure of oralism. These films turned out to be valuable sources for diachronic studies on ASL. Also, there are some translations of old ASL films from the period around 1870 as well as descriptions of single signs from the eighteenth and nineteenth centuries. For Finnish Sign Language (FinSL), some photographs of signs dating from the nineteenth century are available in the Døves Museum in Helsinki. These photographs were extremely progressive for their time since they include arrows to indicate the movement in the sign. Some historical material also exists for Spanish Sign Language (LSE), and it is possible to compare the 1981 LSE dictionary with a 2003 glossary. It is important to remember that the history of sign languages is closely related to the history of the Deaf community in which that language is used and to the education of deaf people (see also Chapter 14).

13.3 Sign language families

Sign languages are not related to or derived from spoken languages, but there are relationships between different sign languages. Current research indicates that there are **language families** of sign languages, just as there are in spoken languages. Research on sign language families started only fairly recently, as it requires descriptions of many different sign languages in order to be able to establish connections between them. Initially, however, studies focused on individual sign languages. From a political perspective, it was also extremely important for every Deaf community to have its own sign language and thus the right to use that language. It was not until the 1990s that research into the relationship between different sign languages really started.

As in comparative work on spoken languages, a comparative study of the lexicons, or a lexicostatistical study, is commonly used to establish the relationship between languages. This method is frequently applied to languages for which there is barely any description. The extent to which the lexicon of one language is related to that of another language is established on the basis of a list of concepts. A list that is often used is the Swadesh list of 100 words, which was compiled by the American linguist Morris Swadesh (1909–1967). He attempted, by means of a **lexicostatistical comparison**, to establish how closely related one language is to another. Thus, if 81–100% of the lexical items corresponding to the concepts on the list is the same, then both languages are regarded as varieties of one language. If there is an overlap of between 36% and 81% in the lexicon of both languages, then the two languages are separate but are to be seen as belonging to the same language family.

The relationship between ASL and French Sign Language (LSF) had already been clearly demonstrated in the 1970s. Applying the original Swadesh list to sign languages, however, is not without problems. Crucially, some of the concepts included in the list (e.g. 'tree', 'see', and 'two') are likely expressed by iconic signs. That is, the fact that two sign languages use similar or identical signs for these concepts does not necessarily imply that they belong to the same sign language family. Rather, the similarity probably results from the iconic potential afforded by the visual-spatial modality. Therefore, scholars have come up with an adapted list that is considered more appropriate for sign languages. Based on this adapted list, it has recently been demonstrated that some Vietnamese Sign Languages are related to LSF and that Modern Thai Sign Language (ThaiSL) is closely related to ASL. Because ASL and LSF also belong to the same language family, some Vietnamese Sign Languages can show a very close relationship to ThaiSL.

Australian research has established that the lexicons of Australian (Auslan), British (BSL) and New Zealand (NZSL) Sign Languages overlap to a large extent. Therefore, the three sign languages should not be considered different sign languages but rather varieties of the same language, that is, BSL (occasionally, the group of three sign languages is therefore referred to by the acronym BANZSL). This conclusion is further supported by the fact that BSL, Auslan, and NZSL also show a great deal of similarity in their grammars. It is interesting to note that some varieties of BSL bear a greater similarity to Auslan than to each other. Obviously, the similarity between these geographically distant languages is related to the emigration of deaf people from the United Kingdom to Australia and New Zealand in the nineteenth century.

We also see influences from Western sign languages in some countries in Africa. This is often the result of signing used by European or North American missionaries involved in the education of deaf children. ASL has therefore had some influence on South African Sign Language (SASL), and on sign languages in Kenya, Tanzania, and Ghana. On the other hand, BSL has had very little influence on Indopakistani Sign Language (IPSL), since most deaf children did not attend schools for the deaf at which BSL was used in colonial times.

13.4 Diachronic change

There are different ways of looking at language change. **Synchronic linguistics** studies changes which take place at a given point in time, possibly as a result of synchronic variation. **Diachronic linguistics**, on the other hand, looks at how the language changes over time by comparing the findings from different synchronic studies. In English, for example, the verb *do* was used in Old and Middle English as a lexical verb meaning 'to act'. Only later, the verb took on other, more grammatical functions, being used, for instance, in emphatic contexts (e.g. *He does sleep*) and negative constructions (e.g. *She doesn't like dogs*). Also, historical documents reveal that basic constituent order in English has changed from SOV to SVO.

Grammatical changes can also occur in sign languages. On the basis of the historical evidence, it appears that the most frequent constituent order in ASL used to be SOV (just as in LSF), while in contemporary ASL, the SVO word order is more commonly used (see also Section 6.5). This change may well be the result of the influence of spoken American English. Changes are also observed in the lexicon, where words can take on new meanings. *Cool*, for instance, originally meant 'close to cold' but nowadays carries the additional meaning of 'modern' or 'trendy'. Similarly, signs can disappear from the sign language lexicon or take on another meaning (see also Chapter 8). Actually, across sign languages, changes in the lexicon appear to be very common. A major factor contributing to this tendency is the fact that 95% of sign language users have hearing parents and do not learn signs from their parents as a matter of course. In Chapter 12, we briefly discussed how, in some sign languages, the lexicon is supplemented by devising new signs. In this chapter, we are mainly concerned with the non-directed changes that occur in the lexicon. As with spoken languages, a number of factors may trigger or influence changes at different linguistic levels.

13.4.1 Changes at different linguistic levels

As mentioned in Section 13.2, research on historical change in sign languages is complicated by the fact that only little historical material is available. Until now, historical change – mostly phonological change – has only been studied in detail for ASL and BSL, as some historical documents exists for these two sign languages.

Scholars have, for instance, compared Old French signs from the beginning of the nineteenth century, as documented by drawings, with ASL signs from 1918 and subsequently with ASL signs from the 1970s. In this way, they were able to identify trends in the changes affecting individual ASL signs. An example is the general tendency for signs to develop from iconic symbols into more arbitrary symbols. A similar trend has also been found in BSL. Obviously, iconicity is an important factor in coining signs, but at a later stage, other factors may override iconicity (see below). Body movements that iconically represent an action, for instance, are frequently replaced by hand (-internal) movements. In Russian Sign Language (RSL), the older sign READ included a non-manual component, namely a sideways movement of the head, representing the following of the lines in a book; in the modern sign, the head movement is substituted by a side-to-side movement of the hands. The iconicity is thus reduced – after all, it is less likely that the hands move while reading.

In cases of **lexical change**, one can also observe 'iconic shifts'. In this case, the newer sign is as iconic as the older sign, but it is iconic in a different way. Often, such shifts are motivated by technical advancements. The older sign TELEPHONE in BSL (and probably other sign languages) was a two-handed sign, as telephones used to be a two-piece apparatus with an earpiece and a mouthpiece. Later, the sign was one-handed, with the 🤙-handshape mirroring the shape of the receiver next to the ear. Nowadays, the handshape reflects how a mobile phone is held. In other sign languages, the new form has a 👌-handshape, which reflects the shape of the phone as a whole – but this may also change as the extended index finger represents an antenna, and modern cell phones don't have antennas anymore (see also Chapter 8.4). However, technical changes do not always lead to lexical changes. The NGT sign COFFEE, for instance, still represents the grinding of coffee in a coffee mill.

In NGT, lexical change has affected the sign for the concept 'citizen'. In contrast to the previous examples, this concept was originally expressed by a compound: CITY^PERSON. The first part of the compound has now been substituted by the sign WRITE, yielding the compound WRITE^PERSON. This change was motivated by a change of rules: every Dutch citizen has to be registered at the city, a law which came into practice when every citizen was required to have a valid identification card. The older sign can still be used, but only in a historical context; it is not appropriate when referring to modern-day citizens of the Netherlands.

As mentioned in the introduction, where there used to be lexical variation, one sign can emerge as the most commonly used. In Spain, education of deaf children was often organized in separate schools for boys and girls. For some concepts, there used to be different signs used in the two types of school. So, for example, the LSE sign for WEDNESDAY was different for girls (1a) and boys (1b) (see Chapter 12). Usually, the sign used by the boys later became the standard sign.

Spanish Sign Language
(1)   a.   b.

WEDNESDAY (girls)   WEDNESDAY (boys)

Lexical change always involves **phonological change** (for instance, in the phonological parameters movement or handshape in the above examples). However, changes may also occur at a phonological level. Such changes are, in a way, more "purely" phonological in nature, as they are usually motivated by ease of articulation and/or perception, rather than by loss of iconicity or technical advancements. Take, for example, the ASL sign DEPEND, as shown in (2).

American Sign Language

(2) a. 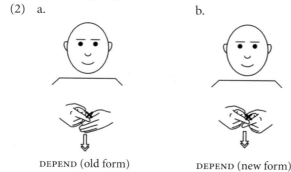 b.

DEPEND (old form)   DEPEND (new form)

In the old form, we see two different handshapes, the -hand on the non-dominant hand and the -hand on the dominant hand. In the new form, however, the two hands have the same handshape, the -hand. There appears to be a trend towards symmetry of handshape in two-handed signs in many sign languages, a change that is motivated by ease of articulation, an internal factor motivating change. Similarly, complex movements tend to become simpler over time, and in the case of BSL, a tendency towards more one-handed signs has been identified. Above, we also pointed out that (whole) body and head movements may be substituted by hand(-internal) movements. Again, these changes contribute to ease of articulation. Consider, for instance, the Saudi Arabian Sign Language sign ISLAM in Section 11.7. It seems likely that in this sign, a whole body movement (upper body bending forward) has been substituted by a hand-internal movement (from -hand to -hand).

We observe another type of change at the phonological level in the ASL sign FEEL in (3).

American Sign Language

(3) a. 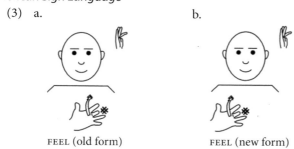 b.

FEEL (old form)   FEEL (new form)

When comparing the two signs, it is obvious that the location of the sign has shifted from the contralateral side of the body to the center of the body. It may well be the case that the new form is easier to articulate, as it does not require the hand to cross the midline. In addition, however, it may also facilitate perception. As already pointed out in Section 10.3, signers look at each other's faces while communicating and not, for example, at the hands. The new form of FEEL in (3b) is closer to the interlocutor's focus of attention and thus easier to perceive. For the same reason, we observe a shift from a central location in front of the face to the side of the head in other signs. This shift is motivated by a tendency for the face to be clearly visible. As argued in previous chapters, in sign languages, important grammatical information is expressed on the face, which therefore should not be covered by the hand(s). Furthermore, examples studied thus far suggest that signs made near the face will be made with one hand, while signs made further away from the face will be made with two hands.

An important trend to have emerged from the study of historical changes in ASL and other sign languages is the tendency towards assimilation and fluency. Clear examples of this tendency are found in compounds such as ASL INFORM. This sign was originally a sequential combination of the one-handed sign KNOW and the two-handed sign BRING. The current sign INFORM, however, appears like a single sign. The first part became two-handed (both hands at forehead), and the two parts have been merged into one fluent movement from the forehead to in front of the body (see Chapter 9.3 for discussion of compounds). When assimilation cannot take place, a part of the compound may disappear. The ASL sign BIRD was originally a compound of BEAK and WING, but in its present form, only the component BEAK is retained (4).

American Sign Language
(4)

BIRD

Some **morphological changes** have also been observed. In BSL and NGT, for example, the verb PHONE used to be a non-directional (plain) verb with a lexically specified place of articulation close to the ear. In current usage, the sign is frequently inflected for person, thus moving from one location to another in order to express, for instance, the complex meaning 'You called me' (see Section 9.5.2 for this type of spatial modification). Material from LSE (5) reveals that phonological and morphological changes do not necessarily go hand in hand. The two-handed sign ACCOMPANY was originally articulated with two 𝄠-hands moving forward (5a), but is now signed with two 🖐-hands moving forward (5b). Interestingly, the LSE sign TOGETHER, in which the hands make contact once in front of the body, has undergone the same handshape change (5c,d). Since the signs ACCOMPANY and TOGETHER are semantically related, it is probably no coincidence that the same handshape change is observed in both signs.

The older sign TOGETHER formed the basis of a nominalization with the meaning 'colleague/mate' (5e), which is characterized by repeated movement (see Section 9.4). The nominalized form, however, retained its handshape, that is, the phonological change did not affect the derived noun.

Spanish Sign Language

(5) a.

ACCOMPANY (1851)

b.

ACCOMPANY (2008)

c.

TOGETHER (1989)

d.

TOGETHER (2008)

e.

COLLEAGUE/MATE (2008)

At present, not very much can be said about syntactic changes since too little evidence is available. Remember, however, that we pointed out above that constituent order in ASL has changed from SOV to SVO.

Studies on the recent emergence of a sign language in Nicaragua have offered some fascinating insights into language emergence and change. In 1977, a school for the deaf was established in Nicaragua's capital Managua, at which deaf kids from scattered villages came into contact with deaf peers for the first time. None of the kids knew a sign language, but they soon started to communicate with each other by means of the gestures they had used in their families/villages. Within a relatively short period of time, a more complex communicative system emerged. Children who entered the school later were thus exposed to a more complex system; their input was more language-like, and they further developed the system. In research on **Nicaraguan Sign Language** (ISN), one therefore often speaks of 'cohorts', with cohort membership being defined by the year of entry into the school. From cohort to cohort, the communication system became more complex. All of this happened under the advertent eye of linguistics. The birth of ISN and the subsequent changes that it underwent have therefore been extensively documented and analyzed. Obviously, this is a unique situation – a linguist's dream, as it were – as language emergence cannot usually be witnessed in real time.

As for the form of signs, it was found that the signs used by the first cohort were rather big and frequently symmetrical, while signs used by later cohorts are somewhat smaller, more limited to the triangle in front of the body and, in the case of two-handed signs, also more frequently asymmetrical. This is an interesting finding, as it suggests that complex phonological structure emerges gradually. As argued in the context of Example (2), at a later stage, complexity might be sacrificed again for ease of articulation. Grammatical structure has also been found to emerge over time. This includes the use of space for grammatical purposes, as reflected in pronouns and directional verbs. In other words, besides phonological change, we also observe morphological change.

13.4.2 Grammaticalization

In the preceding sections, we have seen that signs can be subject to phonological and morphological change over time. Besides this, signs can also change their function. We will discuss two sorts of functional changes, grammaticalization and lexicalization, in this and the following section.

Grammaticalization is defined as the diachronic change of a lexical element – a noun, verb, or adjective – into a grammatical element such as a pronoun, auxiliary verb, or preposition. Grammaticalization is an extremely common phenomenon in spoken languages where, for instance, a noun can develop into a personal pronoun or a verb can acquire an aspectual function. In an ancestor of English, Gothic, for example, there existed a full lexical noun *leik* 'body', which occurred on its own but also in compounds.

The compound *sildaleiks* literally meant 'strange body', but gradually took on a more abstract meaning, namely 'strangely'. The noun *leik* thus gradually developed into a suffix indicating manner and eventually became the adverbial suffix *-ly* in current English.

Grammaticalization may proceed in two steps. In the first grammaticalization step in (6), a lexical element turns into a grammatical element; this element is still an independent word, but has gained an additional grammatical function. Also, in the process, it may undergo **phonological reduction**. In the second step, the grammatical element can be further reduced and become a bound element, an affix (as is true for the suffix *-ly*). The development of a lexical element via a grammatical element into an affix is called a **grammaticalization path**; three cross-linguistically common pathways are illustrated in (6).

(6)

	①		②
LEXICAL ELEMENT →	GRAMMATICAL ELEMENT	→	AFFIX
Noun →	personal pronoun	→	agreement
Verb →	adverb	→	tense affix
Noun →	adposition	→	case affix

It is interesting to see that similar grammaticalization paths are attested in sign languages. We will discuss two examples. In both cases, we will juxtapose an example from a spoken language with an example from a sign language to make clear that many of these developments are indeed modality-independent.

The first example involves the change of a noun into a conjunction. In German Sign Language (DGS), the noun REASON can also function as a conjunction which introduces an adverbial clause (as explained in Chapter 7). The lexical function of this element is illustrated in (7a) and its grammatical function in (7b). In both signs, the ⟨⟩-hand (finger slightly bent) makes contact with the palm of the non-dominant hand, but while the movement is repeated in the noun, the conjunction comprises only a single movement. The grammatical element is therefore phonologically reduced, a phenomenon that – as pointed out above – is characteristic of grammaticalization.

German Sign Language

$$\overline{\qquad\qquad\text{neg}}$$

(7) a. **REASON** INDEX₁ UNDERSTAND.
        'I don't understand the reason.'

 b. INDEX₁ SAD **REASON** POSS₁ GRANDMOTHER DIE.
        'I'm sad because my grandmother has died.'

We find a similar phenomenon in English, where the conjunction *because* has come into being as a result of a combination of the copula verb *be* with the noun *cause*.

The second example comes from ASL and illustrates the development of an aspectual marker from a verb. In ASL, the verb FINISH (8a) can also function as a completive marker (see also Chapter 9.5.1). That is to say: while FINISH functions as a lexical verb in (8a), it is combined with another lexical verb in (8b) and thus functions as an aspectual auxiliary which contributes the meaning that an action has been completed.

American Sign Language

(8)   a.   CLASS ALMOST **FINISH**.
           'The class is almost done.'

      b.   STORY, INDEX₁ **FINISH** WRITE.
           'I wrote the story.'

Exactly the same grammaticalization path has been described for Rama, an Amerindian language from Nicaragua. Just like FINISH in ASL, the verb *atkul* 'finish', the use of which is illustrated in (9a), can be combined with other verbs to express the fact that an action has been completed (9b). Note, however, that in contrast to ASL, this development also involves step ② in (6), that is, in its aspectual use, *atkul* is a verbal suffix, as is evident from the fact that tense inflection follows the completive marker.

Rama

(9)   a.   tabulaak   tkeeruk   nsu-**atkul**-u.
           evening   grave   1PL-finish-TNS
           'We finished (digging) the grave in the evening.'

      b.   dor   y-aakang-**atkul**-u
           door 3SG-close-COMPL-TNS
           'She shut the door tight.'

The previous examples illustrate what we consider to be modality-independent grammaticalization paths. However, there are also intriguing grammaticalization phenomena that appear to be modality-specific. Given the fact that they are visual-spatial languages, sign languages have the unique possibility of integrating gestures into their grammatical systems. In Section 6.8, we have already seen that in many sign languages, a headshake may function as the sole marker of sentential negation. Of course, headshakes are also commonly used as co-speech gestures in the hearing community, but in sign languages, their use and distribution is tightly linked to the structure of the sentence and is subject to language-specific grammatical constraints. This clearly indicates that the headshake has taken on a linguistic function in many sign languages, that is, it has grammaticalized.

Manual gestures may grammaticalize, too. An illustrative example is the pointing gesture, which frequently accompanies spoken utterances. Across sign languages, pointing signs are used for various grammatical functions (see Section 5.5.1), and it is thus likely that we are dealing with a pathway from gesture to grammatical element (e.g. a pronoun). Here we provide yet another example, the 'palm up' gesture. In spoken discourse, this gesture is commonly used to present a referent or, at a more metaphorical level, an idea to the interlocutor. In NZSL, the sign PALM-UP (which may be articulated with one or two hands) can fulfil various related discourse functions: amongst other things, it may be used sentence-initially as a discourse particle (comparable to sentence-initial "Well …" in English), as a conjunction linking two clauses, and as a sentence-final question particle. The latter two functions are illustrated in (10). Note that in (10a), PALM-UP is accompanied by the mouthing /so/. For the use in (10b), it could be argued that the signer in a way presents his question to the addressee; in this sense, PALM-UP marks the end of a turn in this example.

New Zealand Sign Language

/so/

   (10) a. THERE NOTHING THERE **PALM-UP** ME THERE NEXT THIS FRIDAY.
          'They didn't have any, so I said I'd come back the next Friday.'
      b. WHERE JAY **PALM-UP?**
          '(So) where's Jay?'

13.4.3 Lexicalization

While in a typical grammaticalization process, grammatical categories are created from lexical material, **lexicalization** refers to the creation of conventionalized lexemes with a specific meaning from a construction with a more general meaning. We illustrate this phenomenon in (11), using two examples from the North American languages Cayuga (11a) and Mohawk (11b).

Cayuga (a) and Mohawk (b)
   (11) a. te-ká:-the
          DUAL-it-fly.off.HAB
          'airplane' (lit. 'it habitually flies off')
      b. t-ahuht-a-né:kv
          DUAL-ear-INCR-to.be.side.by.side
          'rabbit' (lit. 'two ears side by side')

In both cases, it is clear that morphologically complex word forms – that is, verb stems in combination with number and aspectual affixes or an incorporated noun – have taken on a more specific meaning. The complex word in (11a), for example, could, in principle, also refer to another object (with two wings) which flies away, but the construction has nevertheless been associated with the specific meaning 'airplane' and has been stored in the lexicon with that meaning. Similarly, the literal meaning 'two ears side by side' in (11b) could refer to any animal with two ears (as ears usually appear side by side), but the lexicalized form only refers to rabbits.

    We also find lexicalization processes in sign languages. It has even been suggested that this functional change is much more common in sign languages than it is in spoken languages. Such processes often involve **classifier constructions** that have acquired a specific lexical meaning over time. The process can be illustrated by the two Auslan examples in (12). In (12a), we see a contour sign (a size-and-shape specifier). In Auslan (as in other sign languages), this sign has a very general meaning and can specify the form of many different objects (for example, a window, a mirror, etc.). In spite of this, it still also has a specific lexical meaning, namely that of IMAGE/PAINTING.

Australian Sign Language
(12)   a.   b.

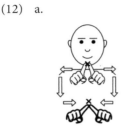   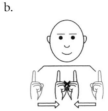

IMAGE/PAINTING	MEET
(lit. 'square on vertical plane')	(lit. 'two long thin entities move towards each other')

(12b) involves another sort of classifier construction, namely a combination of two entity classifiers (see Section 9.6.2). The original compositional meaning of this construction is 'two long thin entities (persons, for example) move towards each other'. This construction comprises at least three morphemes: (i) a movement morpheme, (ii) a classifier handshape, and (iii) the non-dominant hand (which exhibits the same movement and handshape characteristics). However, in its lexical meaning, MEET, the sign is no longer interpreted as morphologically complex. The sign can then also represent a meeting of more than two people, or a meeting of two groups. It can even be used to refer to a meeting that does not involve any movement (for example, 'we met each other on the internet').

If we compare grammaticalization with lexicalization, we can state, in very general terms, that grammaticalization involves the development of a grammatical from a lexical element, while the converse is true for lexicalization, which can be characterized as the development of a lexical element from a grammatical construction.

The above examples demonstrate that, from a cross-linguistic point of view, the patterns of language change attested in sign languages are quite similar to those identified for spoken languages. In other words: diachronically, sign languages follow the same paths as spoken languages. Lexical elements can take on grammatical functions and morphologically complex constructions can be stored in the lexicon with a more specific meaning. Remember, however, that we also argued that the development of grammatical markers from gestures constitutes a modality-specific diachronic phenomenon.

13.5 Language contact

13.5.1 Signed and spoken languages

In the first period of research into sign languages (from 1965 until the late 1970s), linguists tried to describe language varieties which resulted from contact between a sign language and a spoken language. Some researchers described this contact in terms of a **diglossia situation**, that is, a situation in which a particular language variety is always used in formal situations (e.g. the media, schools, government, church) while another language variety is always used in informal situations (e.g. at home, on the street, in shops). There is a large difference between the varieties in terms of standing or status. To some researchers, the American situation, in which deaf people used either ASL or Signed English, initially seemed to closely resemble that of diglossia. Signed English was regarded as the language variety for formal situations and ASL as the language variety for use in informal situations. In line with this reasoning, ASL would not then be a separate, independent language – something which researchers later contested. They showed that ASL is not a variety of English, but an independent language with its own grammar and its own lexicon. In order to describe the different language varieties which are neither a sign language nor a spoken language, some American researchers proposed that a series of possibilities (that is, a **continuum**) exists between spoken English on the one hand and ASL on the other hand within which hybrid forms are possible. In this view, spoken languages and sign languages are indeed regarded as separate languages, as can be seen in the example continuum in (13).

(13)   Spoken English -------------- Pidgin Sign English -------------- ASL

In the 1970s, the form of language in which spoken English is supported with signs from ASL was considered to be a Pidgin language, given the name *Pidgin Sign Language*. The term 'pidgin' is used for situations in which two groups of language users are in contact who each have their own mother tongue and do not know each other's language. It is, however, highly unlikely that today deaf ASL users would have no knowledge of English (at least in its written form), and therefore the term Pidgin Sign English is no longer considered appropriate, nor is the continuum regarded as an appropriate manner to represent the relationship between a spoken language and a sign language.

We can also look at the relationship between a sign language and a spoken language supported by signs in another way. A sign system like Signed English is a combination of a spoken language and a signed language. These languages can be described as **domains**, as can be seen in (14), whereby each language has its own grammar, lexicon, and group of users.

(14)   Domains

If there is contact between the users of both languages, a hybrid or 'contact language' can come into being, as can be seen in (15).

(15)   Domains

This is indeed what has happened in the case of many sign languages. These **contact languages** are then often, but not always, called Signed English, Signed Russian, etc. This seems quite clear and simple; however, the spoken language and the sign language involved are quite different in terms of modality, users, grammar, and status. Spoken languages are perceived via hearing, and this has consequences for their grammatical structure. As discussed in previous chapters, spoken languages are thus mainly organized sequentially: sounds and words are articulated one after another and are perceived in the same way. In contrast, sign languages are visual languages which have a tendency to organize certain grammatical aspects based on visual principles. These principles are fundamentally different from the principles of spoken languages. One of these principles is the principle of simultaneity, which implies that phonological and morphological building blocks can be expressed at the same time. The differences in modality and grammar between spoken and signed languages will always lead to clashes when trying to produce both languages at the same time: certain non-manual and spatial features of a sign language, for example, are likely to be deleted. That is why the combination of a spoken and a signed language in any form cannot be considered to be a language.

The mixing of the two languages can also take place in different ways. By way of illustration, we can describe contact languages as having three forms on a spectrum. Form 1 most closely resembles the spoken language, while Form 3 most closely resembles the sign language. In Form 2, both languages are more or less 'in balance', and both languages are used 'equally frequently'. The characteristics of these forms are broadly set out in (16).

(16)   Forms of contact languages

Form 1	Form 2	Form 3
Spoken language	Spoken language	Spoken language, but sometimes formulated in the same way as the sign language
Signs from the sign lexicon	Signs from the sign lexicon	Signs from the sign lexicon
Grammatical features of the spoken language	Grammatical features of the sign language (localization, facial expression, verbs)	Extensive use of grammatical features of the sign language (oral components, classifiers, localization, facial expression, role shift)
One-to-one relationship between the spoken words and the signs accompanying them	One-to-one relationship where possible	Word order mainly from the spoken language, but no one-to-one relationship
All signs with a spoken mouth pattern	Most signs with a mouth pattern	Some signs without a mouth pattern

Somewhat confusingly, the term 'sign language' is sometimes used as an umbrella term for different sub-varieties of the contact language; as mentioned previously, the choice of the specific variety is dependent on many factors (see Chapter 12). The term '**contact signing**' is also used in the literature to refer to all the varieties of signing that can occur as a result of contact between a spoken language and a signed language.

13.5.2 Code-switching, code-mixing, and code-blending

A switch in language variety during a conversation in response to, for instance, a changed situation or topic of discussion is called **code-switching**. This term is used for both the switching between language varieties within one language and for the switching between two or more languages. The following is an example of such a code-switch, here from Dutch to English: *Gisteren was ik in Amsterdam. We had a nice dinner with friends from Spain* ('I was in Amsterdam yesterday. We had …'). Typically, such a combination of sentences will be used in a conversation between two friends with a good command of both English and Dutch. When a switch is made within a sentence, we speak of **code-mixing**. Bilingual or multilingual people make frequent use of code-switching and code-mixing for all sorts of reasons. Both are also important mechanisms in the language use between deaf and hearing people. Research into code-switching between sign languages and spoken languages has revealed that not only is the situation an important factor, but also the degree of command a participant has of the languages.

A crucial difference between code-switching involving two spoken languages and code-switching involving a spoken and a signed language is that in the former case, elements from the two languages cannot be used simultaneously. In contrast, given the different articulators, signs and spoken words are easily combined simultaneously. This type of combination is referred to as **code-blending**. Various studies have indicated that code-blending is a very common strategy in this case, while sequential code-mixing appears to be relatively rare. As was suggested in (16), one language may be more dominant than the other. In (17), we provide examples of various types of code-blending between NGT and Dutch (for the sake of simplicity, the Dutch words are glossed in English). (17a) is a very simple sentence, and both languages are used equally. In (17b), the spoken language is dominant, whereas in (17c), the sign language is dominant – both examples contain only one element from the other modality. The sentence in (17d) is an interesting case: every sign is accompanied by a Dutch word, but what is expressed in the two languages is not exactly the same. Note that the NGT verb SHOOT is more specific than the Dutch word *kill*; at the same time, however, shooting does not necessarily imply killing. Consequently, in this example, neither language is dominant.

Code-blending: Sign Language of the Netherlands and Dutch

(17)	a.	Signed	BOOK FETCH
		Spoken	book fetch
		Meaning	'I am going to fetch the book.'
	b.	Signed	FALL
		Spoken	it going to fall
		Meaning	'It is going to fall.'
	c.	Signed	INDEX COAT BLUE
		Spoken	blue
		Meaning	'He has a blue coat.'
	d.	Signed	POLICE OTHER PEOPLE SHOOT
		Spoken	police other people kill
		Meaning	'The police shot the other people dead.'

Such variations in code-blending occur frequently in this bilingual situation, which is commonly referred to as **bimodal bilingualism**.

13.5.3 Contact between sign languages

Throughout this chapter, we have seen that languages do not stand alone, and that they are not a static medium. Rather, they are subject to change, and such changes can occur as a result of contact with other languages. A sign language can be influenced by other sign languages, but also by the spoken language of the area where the sign language is used.

Changes resulting from contact with other languages are mainly found in the lexicon, and this is what we focus on in this and the next section. The lexical integration of elements from another language is referred to as **borrowing**. Borrowed elements, or loan words, are frequently recognizable by their unusual pronunciation; it may, for instance, be the case that the loan word contains a sound which is not part of the phonological system of the borrowing language. So the English term *think-tank* has been borrowed into many other languages, but the *th*-sound often does not form part of the sound system and consequently, the word is easily identifiable as a loan word. Still, over time, loan words may undergo phonological changes such that their foreign origin is no longer transparent. The English word *fact*, for example, is derived from the Latin *factum*, but has become an integral part of the lexicon of English.

Borrowing is also attested between sign languages, and thus, sign languages also have **loan signs**. One such example is the Swedish sign for 'language' which has been adopted by BSL. Another example is the ASL sign TREE (18a), which has been borrowed into many different sign languages, often co-existing alongside the original sign. The Hong Kong Sign Language (HKSL) sign PINEAPPLE was borrowed from Taiwan Sign Language (18b); European sign languages have not borrowed this sign, which emphasizes the importance of regional contact.

American Sign Language (a) and Hong Kong Sign Language (b)

(18) a.   b.

TREE (ASL)   PINEAPPLE (HKSL)

The LSE sign CONFIDENCE (19a) would appear to be borrowed from BSL (19b), since it is phonologically very similar. Interestingly, the LSE sign contains the handshape corresponding to the fingerspelled letter C () even though the Spanish word for 'confidence' is *autoestima*, which does not begin with a C. Some LSE signers are starting to produce the sign with the handshape corresponding to fingerspelled letter E (from the Spanish word *estima*), which suggests lexical integration of the borrowed form (although the ⟨-hand is, of course, part of the phonological system of LSE).

Spanish Sign Language (a) and British Sign Language (b)

(19)   a.   b.

CONFIDENCE (LSE)   CONFIDENT (BSL)

Loan signs which are borrowed from other sign languages, but whereby the form is partially modified, are a special type of loan signs. As for the manual part, the sign HETERO in FinSL is identical to the sign STRAIGHT in ASL. The non-manual part is, however, different: in the Finnish sign, the mouth configuration corresponds to the Finnish word for 'hetero'.

Deaf education has been a considerable source of language contact and thus loan signs, as was discussed earlier in relation to BSL, Auslan, and NZSL. DGS signs have been borrowed into Israeli Sign Language due to the influence of the German teacher Marcus Reich (see Section 14.3). Loan signs from Japanese Sign Language entered the lexicon of Taiwan Sign Language (TSL) since deaf schools were introduced in Taiwan under Japanese rule. In fact, it is estimated that there is more than 40% overlap in the lexicons of these two sign languages. Later, Taiwan was under the influence of China, and consequently, signs from Chinese Sign Language were also introduced into the TSL lexicon.

Inuit Sign Language (IUR), the sign language used in part of Nunavut, Canada's Arctic territory, has been influenced by ASL due to the fact that ASL is now used in deaf education in that part of Canada. In (20), we see the IUR signs BOY and WATER both of which are identical to the ASL versions.

Inuit Sign Language

(20)   a.   b.

BOY   WATER

In some cases, the original sign language has suffered from language erosion due to intense contact. This is true for IUR, for example, which is suffering from erosion due to the increased use of ASL in Canadian schools for the deaf. In Jamaica, the local sign language has all but disappeared, again due to the use of ASL in schools. In the extreme case, contact may thus even lead to language death.

International Sign is increasingly used at international gatherings where users of different sign languages come together. This language variety is a mixture of different sign languages whereby the ASL lexicon is usually dominant, but signs from BSL and other sign languages are also commonly used. Signs for countries and cities, for instance, which are used in the sign language of the country in question, are frequently borrowed. For example, the Greek Sign Language sign for GREECE in (21) is used in International Sign. As for its grammar, it has been observed that International Sign makes use of fewer mouthings, but enhances the use of mouth gestures for adverbials. Also, the signing space is often larger.

Greek Sign Language
(21)

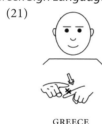

GREECE

Contrary to what many people think, there is no such thing as one International Sign Language. Rather, International Sign is dependent on the lexicon that the signer draws on. Hardly any research has been carried out into the grammar of International Sign, and we currently know too little to assess the extent to which International Sign makes use of grammatical rules from, for example, ASL or BSL, or the extent to which one can speak of an own grammar. In 2007, at the general assembly in Madrid, the World Federation of the Deaf determined that International Sign is not a language, in the sense that it is not a natural language with its own lexicon and its own grammar. Still, it is an increasingly common means of communication that deaf people from different countries use whenever it is necessary or desirable.

13.5.4 Sign languages in contact with spoken languages

Signs are not only borrowed from other sign languages. Loan signs also come into being through the influence of spoken languages. Take, for example, the NGT sign BLUE depicted in (22).

Sign Language of the Netherlands

(22)

BLUE

This sign is derived by means of **fingerspelling** from the Dutch word *blauw* 'blue': the initial hand is the -hand (representing the letter B) which then changes into a -hand (representing L). The remaining letters are not represented by handshapes, but the wrist rotation which characterizes the letter U from the NGT manual alphabet is seen in the transition from B to L. Like other loan signs, loan signs based on fingerspelling are usually adapted to the phonological system of the sign language in question. This can be done through:

- the omission of one or more fingerspelled letters;
- a change in position, movement, orientation;
- a change in one or more handshapes;
- the addition of a second hand;
- the addition of a non-manual component.

As for borrowing from a writing system, it has been shown that TSL makes use of so-called 'character signs', that is, signs that mimic the shape of Chinese characters. The character 人, for instance, means 'person', and the corresponding TSL sign is thus formed by two -hands that make contact at the fingertips. Signs that are based on fingerspelling can also undergo a change in meaning. Thus the ASL sign NO, which is made by a combination of the fingerspelled letters N and O, is not used as a particle meaning 'no', but rather as a verb meaning 'say-no'. Note that the two-letter sequence is heavily reduced such that we are actually dealing with a single form in which the index and middle finger make contact with the thumb.

The spoken language itself can also have an influence on a sign. This influence is obvious in the use of **mouthings**, that is, lip or mouth movements which directly reflect (a part of) a spoken word from the surrounding spoken language – for example, the mouthing 'fs' which accompanies the BSL sign FINISH, or 'off' in the BSL sign SWITCH-OFF (see Section 11.6 for a discussion of the functions of mouthings). An interesting situation emerges when a sign language is used in an environment where more than one spoken language is used. Amongst the Inuit, for example, both Inuktitut and English are commonly used and consequently, IUR signs can be accompanied by mouthings from either of the two languages.

Finally, there are many examples of **loan translations**, that is, instances where a form from the spoken language is translated into a sign language. Thus, in HKSL, the sign for 'jeans' is a translation of a Chinese compound which consists of 牛 'cow', 仔 'boy', and 裤 'trousers'. The pictures in (23) reveal that the second part of the original compound has not been borrowed; yet, the HKSL compound COW^TROUSERS is clearly based on Chinese.

Hong Kong Sign Language

(23)

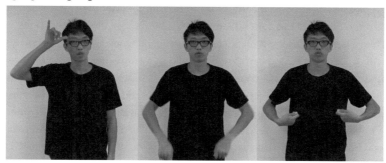

COW   TROUSERS

Taken together, we have seen that sign languages can change as a result of contact with other sign languages, but also as a result of contact with spoken languages. It is important to note that the influence of the surrounding spoken language(s) may differ from sign language to sign language. A stronger influence is often the result of the oral method employed in deaf education (see Section 14.3).

Summary

Sign languages have been around just as long as deaf communities. However, it is not until the eighteenth century that we find descriptions of French signs that were used in education. From the nineteenth century onwards, photos and films of different signs are available for some sign languages. Just as in spoken languages, there are **language families**. The relationship between languages can be established with the help of **lexicostatistical comparison**. Sign languages change over time, and change may be triggered by various factors. There are various ways of looking at language change: **diachronic linguistics** looks at how language changes over time while **synchronic linguistics** occupies itself with the language system at a particular moment in time. Changes take place at different linguistic levels: **lexical changes** may be the result of technical advancements; **phonological changes** are commonly motivated by ease of articulation or perception. **Morphological changes** are also attested. Interesting instances of language change have been described for **Nicaraguan Sign Language**, a recently emerged sign language.

Signs can also change their function over time. **Grammaticalization** characterizes the change from lexical element to grammatical element. The development that a word or sign undergoes is called **grammaticalization path**; along this path, the word/sign may undergo **phonological reduction**. The opposite development, from grammatical construction into a lexical element, is referred to as **lexicalization**; in sign language, this process often involves **classifier constructions**, which take on a more specific meaning.

There are different views on the relationship between sign languages and spoken languages: from a **diglossia situation** to a **continuum** to overlapping **domains**. The resulting form of language is often referred to as **contact language** or, in the case of sign languages, as **contact signing**. When a language user switches language variety or code within a discourse, we talk of **code-switching**. Code-switching can take place within a language, but also between two (or more) languages. When code-switching occurs within a sentence, we speak of **code-mixing**. The simultaneous combination of signs and words is called **code-blending**, a phenomenon that is often observed in **bimodal bilingualism**. Changes as a result of contact with other sign languages are frequently found in the lexicon: **loan signs** are an example of this. Sometimes signs are **borrowed** from another sign language in their entirety, but they may also be partly modified. **International Sign** is a means of communication between signers who speak different sign languages; it includes signs borrowed from different sign languages and is not usually considered a natural sign language. Contact with (the written form of) a spoken language can also have an influence on the sign language lexicon. This is seen in signs that are based on **fingerspelling**, in signs that are accompanied by **mouthings**, and in **loan translations**.

Test yourself

1. What is the difference between diachronic and synchronic linguistic change?
2. Why do BSL, Auslan, and NZSL belong to the same language family but ASL and BSL do not?
3. What factors play a role in language change?
4. What is the difference between code-switching and code-blending?
5. Why is International Sign not called International Sign Language?

Assignments

1. Signed Russian has a higher status in Russia than RSL. Why do you think this is the case?
2. Look up signs on http://www.spreadthesign.com/ and find some examples of what you think could be cases of borrowing between sign languages. What are your arguments?
3. In the United States, there are different signs used by white signers and Afro-American signers. Why do you think this is the case?

4. In HKSL, some signs have changed over several generations. Describe the precise changes that have taken place in the sign FISH (from stage 1 to stage 4). At what linguistic level has the sign changed?

Stage 1

Stage 2

Stage 3

Stage 4

5. In LSE, there are two signs for TIME: one used by younger signers (left) and one used by older signers (right). Is this variation likely to lead to a change in LSE in the future?

References and further reading

The topic of language families is discussed in relation to sign languages in McBurney (2012). More information about the relationship between BSL, Auslan, and NZSL can be found in McKee & Kennedy (2000) and Johnston (2003a). The relationship between NGT and VGT is investigated in Schermer & Vermeerbergen (2004). Woodward (2000) compares the sign language in Vietnam and Modern Thai Sign Language. For a critical discussion of the use of the Swadesh list in sign language comparisons, also see Hendriks (2008).

The general evolution of sign languages, including the gestural theory of language origin, is discussed in Armstrong & Wilcox (2007) and Pfau (2012). Historical changes are addressed for ASL in Fischer (1975), Frishberg (1975), and Rimor et al. (1984), for BSL in Woll (1987), and in general in Schembri & Johnston (2012). The emergence of Nicaraguan Sign Language, as well as specific changes in its lexicon and grammar, is described in Senghas (1995) and Kegl, Senghas & Coppola (1999); Sandler et al. (2005) and Senghas (2005) report on the emergence of Al-Sayyid Bedouin Sign Language. For emerging sign languages, see also Meir et al. (2010b).

Grammaticalization and common grammaticalization paths are described for spoken languages in Hopper & Traugott (1993) and Heine & Kuteva (2002a). Grammaticalization in sign languages is discussed specifically for ASL in Sexton (1999); Pfau & Steinbach (2006a, 2011) provide an overview of patterns from various sign languages and also compare the attested diachronic changes with those described for spoken languages. The grammaticalization of gestures is addressed in Wilcox (2004) and Van Loon, Pfau & Steinbach (2014), while Pfau (2015) focuses on the grammaticalization of headshake. Lexicalization is discussed in Johnston & Schembri (1999), Zeshan (2003a), and Zwitserlood (2003). For grammaticalization and lexicalization, see also Janzen (2012).

Language contact is described for ASL in Lucas & Valli (1989), for NGT in Schermer (1990), for JSL/TSL in Sasaki (2007), for ISL in Meir & Sandler (2008), and more generally in Adam (2012). Chapters in Brentari (2001) address foreign vocabulary in various sign languages. Diglossia in sign languages is discussed in Stokoe (1970); Woodward (1973a) describes the sign language – spoken language continuum, and Woodward (1973b) introduces the term 'pidgin' to describe the relationship between a sign language and a spoken language. Details of the situation in Taiwan are provided in Smith (2005). Characteristics of International Sign are described in Adam (2012) and, from an interpreting perspective, in Stone (2012).

The examples from ASL are taken from Frishberg (1975), Klima & Bellugi (1979), Baker & Cokely (1980), and the Gallaudet Dictionary of ASL (Valli 2005). Those from NGT come from Schermer (2003) and Schermer et al. (2006). LSF examples are adapted from L'Epée (1784); BSL examples are taken from Kyle & Woll (1985), Woll (1987), and Vinson et al. (2008). The example of FinSL comes from Vivolin-Karén & Kaisa (2003). LSE examples are taken from the LSE glossary for mental health terms (Fundación CNSE 2003b) and from Minguet Soto (2001) based on historical examples from Fernandez Villabrille (1851). The DGS grammaticalization examples are adapted from Pfau & Steinbach (2011), the ASL grammaticalization examples come from Isenhath (1990), and the NZSL examples from McKee & Wallingford (2011). The Auslan lexicalization examples are taken from Johnston & Schembri (1999). The examples of code-blending are translated from Dutch/NGT examples reported by Baker & van den Bogaerde (2008). The HKSL examples were provided by the Chinese University of Hong Kong. TSL character signs are discussed by Ann (1998). As for spoken languages, the Rama example is from Heine & Kuteva (2002b), the Cayuga example from Zeshan (2003a), and the Mohawk example from Zwitserlood (2003).

Chapter 14

Bilingualism and deaf education

Beppie van den Bogaerde, Marjolein Buré & Connie Fortgens

14.1 Introduction

Ildefonso was born in Mexico. His parents, brothers, and sisters were hearing, just like all other people around him. He, however, was deaf and, in contrast to his siblings, did not go to school. When he went to the United States as an adult, he could not read and barely knew how to sign. There had been no one who could have taught him; so he was a man without language. That changed when Ildefonso went to school and met a sign language interpreter who took the trouble to teach him a sign language. It took a while before Ildefonso understood that things have a name, that there is language.

Ildefonso's fate was not uncommon for most deaf people in the old days. For many deaf people in the non-Western world, this is probably still true. In countries where education is not common for all children, and especially where there are no schools for the deaf, deaf and hard-of-hearing people often grow up in isolation. The fact that these subjects have little or no opportunity to acquire a language and to develop may lead to language deprivation (see also Section 3.2).

In this chapter, we address deaf education. The focus is on bilingual education for the deaf. Section 14.2 will look at bilingual communities in general, leading on to the discussion of bilingual education of the deaf in Section 14.3, where both the history of deaf education and the forms bilingual education can take will be described.

14.2 Bilingual deaf communities

People who regularly use two languages are called bilingual. There are various types of **bilingual communities**. Generally, we can distinguish the three types depicted in (1).

(1) Schematic representations of three types of bilingual communities.

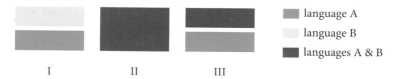

      language A
      language B
      languages A & B

    I   II   III

DOI 10.1075/z.199.14bog

Schema (1) shows that there are communities in which two or more languages are used, but almost everyone is monolingual (type I). Such a situation, exists, for instance, in Belgium, which officially is multilingual, but where most people either use Dutch or French or German. In other bilingual communities, however, almost everybody is bilingual (type II). A clear example is South Africa, where almost all inhabitants regularly use more than one language. Finally, there are communities where part of the people are bilingual and the other part is monolingual (type III). Australia is such a country, because even if most inhabitants speak English, there are also many groups which use other languages as well, for instance an Aboriginal language or Italian.

In communities where the deaf regularly meet, we usually find a type III situation. The majority, for example, of the people in a country like France are monolingual in French, but a minority – including most deaf – are bilingual in French and French Sign Language (LSF). On the Indonesian island of Bali, there is a village where the majority of the hearing population is bilingual (in the local spoken language and the local sign language, Kata Kolok) while most of the deaf inhabitants are monolingual. That is, we are dealing with a different kind of Type III situation. This situation has arisen because there are so many deaf in this village. The deaf villagers do not go to school, however, and therefore most of them do not learn the spoken language, while the hearing community members are in regular contact with deaf people and thus learn to sign. On the island of Martha's Vineyard (US), there used to be a type II situation. Deafness was so common at one time, that everybody – deaf and hearing – knew the local sign language, Martha's Vineyard Sign Language (which is now extinct). Besides this sign language, the deaf and the hearing also used English.

In a conversation with another bilingual, hearing bilinguals can choose to use the one language or the other. This is different for the deaf who use a sign language and a spoken language. They can effortlessly use the sign language with another deaf person, but obviously, this is not the case for the spoken language, since a spoken language is hardly accessible to them. Still, deaf people, in conversation with other bilinguals, do not always exclusively choose a sign language. Just like hearing people who are fluent in a sign language, they regularly make use of code-blending as discussed in Section 13.5.2.

Deaf children usually grow up bilingual but their situation is different from hearing bilingual children. Hearing children commonly learn their first language from their parent(s), and in many cultures, this is above all their mother. That is why the first language is often also called the mother tongue or the native language. In most cases, the first language is the language a person knows best or is most comfortable using. Bilingual children can either grow up with two languages they are exposed to equally, or they can learn one language later than the other. Because many deaf children do not learn sign language from their (hearing) parents (see Chapter 3), the term **preferred**

language is more applicable to their situation. Usually, this is a sign language. The second language for the deaf child is the spoken language of the community in which the deaf child is born. As mentioned above, acquiring this second language is difficult for deaf children because it is far less accessible to them. Studies have revealed that only roughly a third of spoken sounds are visible on the lips or the mouth. Most deaf children have to learn the language of their country in written form. For them, this is much more difficult than for hearing children since they have little basis for making a connection between sounds (which they cannot hear) and letters that represent these sounds.

In order to learn two languages well, a rich language environment is needed. Deaf children often grow up in a poorer language environment than hearing bilingual children. The majority of deaf children (90–95%) have hearing parents who still have to learn the sign language – if they take this effort at all. Consequently, the young deaf child has little contact with people who can sign, and even less contact with native signers. There are thus far fewer opportunities to receive sign language input, be it child-directed input or language used in the environment of the child.

14.3   Deaf education

14.3.1 History of deaf education

Most of what we know about the history of deaf education comes from European sources. In the 16th century, the first teacher of the deaf was probably Pedro Ponce de León (1520–1584; see (2)). He and his successors taught deaf members of the Spanish family De Velasquez. The focus in their education was on learning how to speak, because in those days, someone who could not speak did not have any rights in the eyes of Spanish law. As the Velasquez family did not want to lose their estates, their heirs had to be recognized as legal persons, and thus had to learn how to speak.

(2)   Pedro Ponce de León (1520–1584)

This emphasis on speech was still present a century later when the Swiss doctor Johann Conrad Amman (1669–1724) claimed that learning to speak was essential within a Christian tradition, since man is shaped after God's image; only speech makes an individual a true man. Some signing was used at this time but mostly in the form of fingerspelling and in order to support the learning of the spoken language.

From the second half of the eighteenth century, deaf schools were founded and curricula developed in the whole of Europe. Deaf education was one of the first forms of special education in Europe. The teachers of the deaf who founded schools were often motivated by Christian values like charity, and their main goal was to raise children as Christians and to teach them a trade. In the period of European colonization and religious missionary work, the prevalent forms of deaf education were spread across the globe from Europe.

Since deaf education began, there has been a **war of methods**, continuing to the present day. Do deaf children benefit most from purely oral education, where they learn how to speech-read and speak? Or should signing play a role in their education?

In the eighteenth century, education in European schools for the deaf was predominantly characterized by the use of signs, but still, signs were generally used for the purpose of learning to speak, read and write in the local spoken language. The 'French method' of Charles Michel de l'Épée (1712–1789), who around 1760 founded a school for deaf children in Paris, was used for more than a century in most schools for the deaf. He developed a system of signs (see also Section 1.4) which combined LSF signs with invented signs to make different aspects of the grammar of the French language visible. In addition, he made use of the manual alphabet. De l'Épée received visitors from other countries in Europe and even from the United States. He was willing to share his method with others, contrary to teachers from other deaf schools, who preferred to keep their methods a secret. After a visit to Paris, Henri Daniel Guyot (1753–1828) founded the first school for the deaf in the Netherlands in 1790, and Thomas Hopkins Gallaudet (1787–1851; see (3)) in the United States in 1816.

The fact that both Guyot and Gallaudet had contact with De l'Épée probably explains the relationship of Sign Language of the Netherlands (NGT) and American Sign Language (ASL) with older forms of French Sign Language; De l'Épée's deaf ex-student Louis Laurent Marie Clerc, who had been brought to the USA by Gallaudet and became head teacher in his school, certainly was of influence here (see also Section 13.3). In those days, deaf adults often played a role in education as teacher or assistant, and served as language role models for the children.

Outside Europe, educational organization often mirrored European developments. As mentioned earlier, education was brought to many countries by European or American religious missionaries. In South Africa, for example, Irish, Dutch and German priests and ministers combined oral and manual methods in the schools they

(3)   Thomas Hopkins Gallaudet (1787–1851) and Alice Cogswell
      (statue by Daniel Chester French)

founded. Such situations led to the introduction of methods from elsewhere but also to language contact (see Section 13.5.3). In Israel, deaf education was started under the influence of a Jewish German teacher, Marcus Reich. Reich had established a school for Jewish deaf children in Germany in 1873, and teachers from his school opened a school for deaf children in Jerusalem in 1932. Signs from DGS and other immigrant sign languages were used as well as sign systems, but, again, primarily with the goal of teaching the spoken language. In Taiwan, deaf schools were introduced under Japanese rule at the end of the nineteenth century with the use of signs from Japanese Sign Language, as is still reflected in the lexicon of Taiwan Sign Language.

Despite the enthusiastic adoption and dissemination of the 'French method', there were, at the time, also advocates for a more oral or even strictly oral approach. The German Samuel Heinicke (1723–1790) had a lively correspondence with De L'Épée about what was the best method to be used in deaf education. Heinicke and other Germans wanted to teach the deaf to speak without taking recourse to signing. This so-called 'German method' attracted more and more supporters in the course of the nineteenth century. The *Second International Congress of Teachers of Deaf-Mutes*, better known as the Milan 1880 conference, marked a temporary end to the dispute about methods. It was generally accepted that signs would hamper the learning of speech.

Following this congress, for about a hundred years, the oral method, or 'pure method of speech', dominated in the education of deaf children. They had to learn the spoken language of their country, and learn to read and write its written form.

After a hundred years of relative tranquility, deaf education in Europe and the USA began to change in the last decades of the previous century. The causes for this movement were manifold: disappointing results in oral deaf education, changes in society, and scientific developments. Within the field of general linguistics, sign languages received more and more attention. Sign languages were demonstrated to be natural languages, and not just an elaborate form of pantomime (see Chapter 1). Also, evidence accumulated which clearly showed that sign language acquisition was similar to spoken language acquisition (Chapter 3).

Within the fields of pedagogy and psychology, there was an increasing interest in the role of early interaction between parents and children. For that reason, the quality of interaction was more and more emphasized in parent counseling, rather than the linguistic form of the interaction. For a healthy social-emotional development of a child, good contact between parents and child is of paramount importance, and any means should be used to obtain this. Research indicated that most children could learn two languages from an early age without problems, which lead to an increasing acceptance of bilingualism in general. It was also established that the majority of deaf people grow up to be bilingual. Assuming that deaf children do not have a language problem per se, they therefore also have the capacity to grow up bilingual (see Section 14.3.2).

Around the same time, the emancipatory movement of minority groups changed the view that deaf people are handicapped. Deaf people increasingly viewed themselves as a **cultural minority**, with the local sign language as their mother tongue. Just like other minorities, they claimed the right to use their own, preferred language and the right to receive education in their sign language.

These developments had a considerable influence on the education of deaf children in many places in the world. In the 1970s, Total Communication (TC) emerged as a new approach in the United States. This approach was based on the idea that deaf children have a normal developmental potential and that a strong and natural interaction between the child and the environment is a first prerequisite for successful education. In order to achieve that interaction, good communication is essential, and thus all forms of communication were allowed: the use of voice, facial expressions, fingerspelling, writing, pictures, supporting signs and gestures, sign systems, and sign language. In the context of the TC approach, signs were slowly (re-)introduced into deaf education. The goal was to achieve optimal skills in (speaking and) writing the country's spoken language, and to that end primarily sign *systems* were used (see Section 1.4). It was thought that in this way, the structure of the spoken language was made visible, thus making it more accessible for the deaf child. Although signs were being used, deaf education in the TC approach remained in fact monolingual in its general approach: learning the spoken language of the country was the goal of education, and sign systems were only used to support the learning of that spoken language.

Despite the high expectations of these changes in deaf education, school results still turned out to be disappointing within the TC approach. In particular, reading skills did not improve. There was a positive influence on the social-emotional development, however, although this could also have been a result of the increasing attention paid to the counseling of hearing parents and their young deaf child at that time (see also Chapter 3).

Around the 1980s, more support came for the view that deaf education should be bilingual, that is, that both the spoken (written) and the sign language should have a place in the curriculum. Sweden took a leading role, and in 1981, the Swedish government officially recognized that deaf children have a right to education in their first language, that is, Swedish Sign Language; they would then learn (written) Swedish as a second language. Bilingual education was adopted as a national policy as well in Denmark. Within Europe, to date few countries have followed the Scandinavian example.

The international picture remains in fact very mixed and is complicated by the technical developments since the 1990s. Increasing numbers of deaf children, at increasingly younger ages, are receiving a cochlear implant (CI, see also Section 3.5.4). The discussion in many countries is now focusing on the role of a sign language after implementation: Should a sign language be offered to these young children in a bilingual setting, or should they grow up with only a spoken language? Should a sign language be offered as a second language? Offering both a spoken language and a sign language ensures that deaf children can develop age-appropriately. Moreover, it offers the children the opportunity to have contact with the deaf community and make their own choices later in life. This may be very important for those children who do not benefit fully from their CI. On the other hand, when young children can hear sufficiently thanks to the CI, they are not always motivated to acquire a sign language.

General trends and changes in educational policy also have an influence on deaf education. Some countries have ascribed to the idea that all children with special needs have the right of **inclusive** education, that is, to be in the **mainstream**. Parents can thus choose a mainstream school for their deaf child with financial support or specific facilities, as is the case, for example, in Norway and the Netherlands. All children who have special educational needs can attend mainstream education, usually with the support from a center of expertise. In Great Britain and Italy, mainstreaming has had the effect that almost all deaf schools have closed. In Greece, where Greek Sign Language was officially recognized in 2000, almost all deaf children are in mainstream education, with or without support, although occasionally interpreters are available. More often than not, only the spoken language is the means of communication in mainstream education and no sign language is taught.

In other countries, schools for the deaf remain, but the language policies adopted at these schools are diverse. In Flanders, for example, most schools for the deaf are oral with some using limited signing. In the Russian Federation, one monolingual oral school in Moscow started some bilingual classes in 1995, while the remaining schools remain oral, even though Russian Sign Language (RSL) was officially recognized in 2012. In South Africa, there are bilingual schools but also oral schools, even within the same province.

In countries where CIs are less common for financial reasons, there are initiatives to develop bilingual education. This is happening, for example, in Uganda, Tanzania, and Brazil. Usually, this is the result of initiatives of parents of deaf children or of the deaf community.

14.3.2 Bilingual education

As has become obvious from the discussion in the previous section, the forms of deaf education are extremely varied and are changing rapidly. Although deaf children are predominantly bilingual, this does not mean that **bilingual education** is offered everywhere. The term 'bilingual education' implies that in the curriculum, there is a place for both the sign language as well as the spoken/written language of the country, also as subjects to be studied as such. The are many forms of bilingual education for hearing children but the choices for deaf children are even more complex.

One of the two languages in bilingual deaf education is a spoken language, that is, a language which is not easily accessible, or even inaccessible, to deaf children. One of the basic decisions that must be taken is the **role of the spoken language**. An important question is whether skills related to oral performance are required, such as speech and speech reading, or whether proficiency in the written form (reading and writing) is considered sufficient. In the deaf schools in Sweden, in the early 1980s, the emphasis was on reading and writing. It was argued that learning to speak and to speech-read demanded too much time in the curriculum and usually yielded poor results. Moreover, it was assumed that for integration in society, perceptive and productive fluency in spoken Swedish was not a prerequisite, since deaf people could use interpreters of Swedish Sign Language. The training of speech fluency only occurred on a voluntary basis. In many other countries (such as the Netherlands, USA, Hong Kong, and South Africa), a different choice has been made. Speech fluency has a place in the curriculum, alongside reading and writing. This choice is based on the argument that the use of spoken language supports participation in society, also because interpreters are often not available. Moreover, a higher level of speech fluency seems to have a positive influence on learning to read, although it is not a necessary requirement. Sweden has in fact changed its policy in recent years, and now includes speech fluency in the curriculum. The increasing numbers of children with a CI also has an important influence since these children have better access to the spoken language and need speech fluency training.

Once the choice is made to include the spoken language, it is then necessary to choose which **form of the spoken language** should be used. This choice is, of course, quite specific to deaf education. In principle, it would be possible to use the spoken language without any supporting signs (see Sections 13.5.1 and 13.5.2), but in practice, this hardly ever happens. As mentioned before, the accessibility of spoken language is very limited, certainly for young deaf children, so that speaking only is not efficient. Consequently, spoken utterances are usually supported by signs but follow the structure of the spoken language, that is, they pattern like Form 1 in table (16) in Chapter 13. This form of a sign system is intended to increase the children's chances of learning the spoken language, in particular for children who have residual hearing and or/a CI.

Other choices that bilingual schools for the deaf have to make are similar to those for bilingual schools for the hearing. The two languages can be employed in different ways. The one person – one language system means that there are two teachers in the classroom, with the signing teacher being responsible for input and education in the sign language, and the hearing teacher in the spoken language. Alternatively, one teacher can use both languages, which implies that the pupils have to decide which language to use when communicating with that person. It is, of course, imperative that the teacher is highly proficient and can teach in and about both languages.

The two languages can also be introduced at different points in the curriculum, for instance, beginning with sign language and adding the spoken language later. If the spoken language is only to be offered in the written form, this **sequential approach** is more appropriate. Alternatively, the spoken language can be introduced first, and then the sign language. This choice is motivated by the need to devote as much time as possible to the spoken language. Some school systems take the approach that the sign language will then only be introduced for those pupils who do not become proficient in the spoken language. Sign language is then only a last resort to provide pupils with one language at least. The alternative to the sequential approach is the **simultaneous approach**: both languages are from the very start part of the curriculum. The advantages of this approach are that the pupils receive accessible language input and education (in sign language) early on and that the development and use of possible residual hearing is stimulated at a young age as well (in the spoken language). One form taking a simultaneous approach is **co-enrolment**. In this system, deaf and hearing pupils are taught in the same class and both learn the spoken and sign language. Hong Kong has experimented with this system in both a primary and secondary school and reports good results thus far.

Finally, the **language of instruction** also has to be decided upon. Which language will be used by the teacher in class to teach the pupils? Should one language be used, for example, in the mornings and the other in the afternoon? Or is one language used for one subject and the other language for another subject? How much is dependent on the situation, the pupil, and the fluency of the teacher?

As we have seen, bilingual deaf education can take many forms. Whichever form is chosen, one thing is a constant: the total number of teaching hours. It is rarely the case that bilingual schools have more teaching hours than monolingual schools. Bilingual education, however, adds another subject, sign language, to the curriculum, thus leaving less time for other subjects. Bilingual deaf education also requires enough skilled teachers who are fluent in sign language. Trained deaf teachers are often scarce: deaf people constitute a small percentage of the whole population, and few manage to follow higher education. Sometimes good speech fluency is a requirement for admission to teacher training, which forms a further barrier for deaf people. Hearing teachers – unless they have deaf, signing parents – learn a sign language as a second language making it more difficult for them to become fluent. Sign language training is also not always provided at a high level.

Whatever choices are made in the form of bilingual education, it is necessary to evaluate the educational outcomes. What are the comparison groups? Deaf children attending mainstream schools may not be comparable to those in special education because of a form of pre-selection. Those children who have a better speech fluency may, for example, be more frequently represented in mainstream classes. Moreover, research objectives and variables often are quite different from one study to the next, making outcomes difficult to compare. Comparisons between countries are also more or less impossible for the same reasons and because of differences in teachers' competence, school hours, curriculum, etc.

We will briefly summarize here the trends in the results obtained to date. The use of sign language as the language of instruction seems to help deaf pupils acquire a language faster than when they are only offered instruction in a spoken language or a sign system. They are better able to communicate with each other, to learn from each other, and to process the information. Pupils are more involved in lessons where a sign language is used than where a sign system is used. The influence of bilingual deaf education where speech fluency is included in the curriculum on the degree of involvement is not yet clear. Reading ability seems to correlate with speech fluency in deaf children, but research results also show that there is a correlation between signing skills and skills in reading, writing, and even speech fluency. However, from the few studies that have been conducted to date, it is not clear what the impact is of the type of reading program.

Deaf (bilingual) education is clearly very diverse. Professionals are still trying to find the best methods to improve the educational outcomes of deaf children.

Summary

There are different types of **bilingual communities** in the world. Most communities with both deaf and hearing groups belong to type III: a part is monolingual (hearing people using the spoken language) and another part is bilingual (deaf people using the spoken and the sign language). A major difference between hearing and deaf bilinguals is that the spoken language is far less accessible for deaf people. Because sign languages are fully accessible, they are often considered to be the first language or **preferred language** of the deaf. The role that signing should play in deaf education is an issue of hot debate (**war of methods**). The systems that have been used since the beginning of deaf education have moved from being more oral to more bilingual including signing (and sometimes back again). Reasons for the move towards a greater use of signing are, amongst others, the disappointing results of oral education, the recognition that sign languages are natural languages, the knowledge that the deaf usually grow up bilingual (even when they follow oral education), insights in the importance of smooth communication in early interaction, and the fact that many deaf consider themselves to be a member of a **cultural minority**. Technical developments such as cochlear implants and the changing view of **inclusion** in education has led to more **mainstreaming** of deaf children; this has led to a decline in the amount of special education provision for deaf children.

For the organization of **bilingual deaf education**, decisions have to be made, in particular regarding the **role of the spoken language** and **the form of spoken language** input. The language policy of a school determines whether the children are offered a sign language and a spoken language **sequentially** or **simultaneously** and what the **language of instruction** will be. Some countries are experimenting with **co-enrolment** where hearing and deaf children are taught in the same class.

Test yourself

1. What was the subject of the war of methods? Which two fractions can be distinguished?
2. Name three reasons why so many schools for the deaf have adopted bilingual education.
3. How do bilingual deaf schools differ from bilingual schools for hearing pupils in the choices they have to make?

Assignments

1. Is it realistic to expect, somewhere in the world, a type I community, consisting of hearing and deaf people? Please give arguments for your answer.

2. On Bali, there is a village with an unusually high percentage of deaf people. Most hearing villagers are bilingual. The deaf are not bilingual, and use only the local sign language. If more deaf children would attend the deaf school elsewhere on the island, what would change?

3. Describe your own ideal form of bilingual education. Provide arguments for your choices and describe the advantages and disadvantages of your choices.

References and further reading

A useful introduction to bilingualism can be found in Grosjean (2010). Bilingual communities in Bali and on Martha's Vineyard (USA) are described in Marsaja (2008) and Groce (1985), respectively. A more extensive review of bilingualism and deaf education has been written by Plaza-Pust (2012). Johnson, Liddell & Erting (1989) provide a critique of Total Communication and sketch principles for achieving access in deaf education. The impact of sign language research on deaf education is sketched in Hansen (2002). Moores (2010) offers an overview of the history of language and communication issues in deaf education. General information on deaf education can be found in Marschark (2007) and Lang (2011). Marschark, Tang & Knoors (2014) provide a recent overview of all aspects of bilingual education for the deaf. Good descriptions of the life of deaf people and, amongst other things, the consequences of oral education are provided by Sacks (1989) and Lane (1984). See also Tellings (1995) about different ideologies in deaf education (including the war of methods). The consequences of a CI for the education of deaf children have been described from different perspectives in Schauwers, Govaerts & Gillis (2005) and Thoutenhoofd (2006). The form of bilingual education in Brazil has been described by Skliar & de Quadros (2005). A recent publication on literacy in deaf pupils is Wauters & De Klerk (2014).

An initial description of the co-enrolment program in Hong Kong is available at http://www.cuhk.edu.hk/cslds/jcslco/introduction_en.html. The picture of Pedro Ponce de Léon is taken from the website http://www.istc.cnr.it/mostralis/eng/pannello08.htm; the photo of Gallaudet comes from http://pr.gallaudet.edu/GallaudetHistory/.

Appendix 1

Notation conventions

In this appendix, we explain the conventions used in this book for the presentation of sign language and spoken language examples. Firstly, we present the conventions for the transcription of sign language examples both in sign drawings and in glossed examples. Secondly, we provide lists with the sign language acronyms used in the text as well as the abbreviations for grammatical categories used in interlinear translations of spoken language examples.

1. Transcription of sign language examples

1.1 Sign language examples in *Salute*

For many examples, we have used drawings composed with the drawing program *Salute*, a program which unfortunately is not available anymore. The following symbols specify movement properties of signs.

⇐	Movement to the right – the arrow indicates the direction and size of the movement.
⌒↗	Arc movement – the arrow indicates the direction and size of the movement.
⇚	The movement is repeated once or several times.
↻ ◊	Circular movement – the arrow indicates the direction and size of the movement.
✕	The hand(s) make(s) contact once with the head, arm, or torso, or the hands make contact once with each other.
✲	The hand(s) make(s) repeated contact with the head, arm, or torso, or the hands make repeated contact with each other.
⌒⌒⌒	All the fingers wiggle.
▭	Movement ends in an abrupt stop whereby the hand remains for a moment in the final position.
① ②	Part 1 and part 2 of the sign.

Sometimes the handshape is depicted separately in the top right hand corner of an image for the sake of clarity.

In the text, we make use of a handshape font to indicate the relevant handshapes. In other publications, it is common to refer to handshapes by means of the role they play in the manual alphabet (e.g. T-hand). This strategy, however, is problematic for two reasons: first, handshapes referring to the same letter may differ between manual alphabets (the handshape representing the letter T, for instance, is different in ASL, DGS, and NGT – to give just one example); second, some handshapes are not included in the manual alphabet.

1.2   Sign language examples in glosses

Signs or sign sentences are often represented in the form of glosses in small caps. These glosses do not provide any information about the phonological form of the sign(s). We will illustrate our glossing conventions by means of the following two examples; we address first the conventions for manual glosses before explaining the conventions for non-manual markers.

(1)   a. $\overline{ \text{y/n}}$
TWO-DAYS-AGO INDEX$_2$ s-u-e IX$_{3a}$ FLOWER $_2$GIVE-CL: 🖐$_{3a}$?
'Did you give Sue a flower two days ago?'

   b. $\overline{ \text{neg}}$
POSS$_1$ FATHER^MOTHER BOOK++ READ.
'My parents don't read books.'

SIGN	A gloss (i.e. the translation of a sign in a spoken language) is indicated in small capital letters, for example FLOWER in (1a); in this book, all signs are glossed in English.
SIGN++	Reduplication of a sign (used, for example, to express plurality and certain aspectual categories) is indicated by a plus symbol (+), for example BOOK++ 'books' in (1b).
SIGN-----	Indicates either that a sign overlaps with a sign produced by a conversation partner, or that a part of a sign is held in space while the other hand continues signing.
SIGN^SIGN	Signs combined in a compound are linked using a circumflex (^), for example FATHER^MOTHER 'parents' in (1b). The same convention is used for numeral incorporation.
SIGN-SIGN	If several words are needed to gloss a single sign, then these words are linked by a hyphen, for example TWO-DAYS-AGO in (1a).
CL$_{XX}$, CL:X	If a classifier handshape is used, this is indicated by the abbreviation 'CL' in combination with either a subscript referring to the referent, for example CL$_{car}$ or CL$_{book}$, or with a symbol from the handshape font, for example CL: 🖐 in (1a).

INDEX$_x$/IX$_x$	A pointing sign (usually a ⫞-hand) that may fulfil various functions: it may, for instance, function as a personal pronoun, such as INDEX$_2$ 'you' in (1a), or to localize a non-present referent in the signing space, e.g. IX$_{3a}$ in (1a). The subscript numbers refer to specific locations in the signing space: 1 = close to the signer's chest; 2 = in the direction of the addressee; 3a/3b = towards the right or left of the signing space. Sometimes a specific location is indicated (for example, for a present referent) to which the INDEX points, for example INDEX$_{mother}$.
POSS$_x$	A possessive pronoun, in many sign languages signed with a]-hand, targeting a locus in space; e.g. POSS$_1$ in (1b), which is articulated on the signer's chest.
$_x$SIGN$_Y$	Verb sign that moves from one location to another and thus indicates agreement between the verb and the subject and/or object; the subscripts indicate the locations (as explained above with INDEX). In (1a), for example, the verb GIVE moves from the location of the addressee (2) to the location introduced for Sue (3a).
PU	Palm-up sign, which may fulfil various grammatical and discourse functions.
s-i-g-n	Fingerspelled elements are indicated in lower case letters which are linked by hyphens to each other or to a sign, for example 's-u-e' in (1a) or MAKE-s.
SIGN.	The end of the sentence is indicated by a full stop.
SIGN,	In those cases in which the end of a constituent (for example, a topic) is marked by a pause or a lengthening of the sign, the end is indicated by a comma.
"xxxx"	Gestures are indicated in lower case letters between quotation marks, for example "away".

Lines above the gloss indicate the extension (that is, the beginning and end) of a specific non-manual marker – this is also referred to as the *scope* of a non-manual marker. In (1a), the non-manual interrogative marker extends over the whole sentence, in contrast to (1b), where the scope of the negative non-manual is restricted to the verb phrase (the object BOOK++ and the verb READ). Non-manual markers can have various linguistic functions at the phonological, morphological, syntactic, and pragmatic levels. We use the following abbreviations and symbols (further specific abbreviations are introduced in the text):

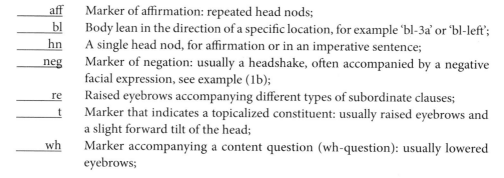

<u>aff</u>	Marker of affirmation: repeated head nods;
<u>bl</u>	Body lean in the direction of a specific location, for example 'bl-3a' or 'bl-left';
<u>hn</u>	A single head nod, for affirmation or in an imperative sentence;
<u>neg</u>	Marker of negation: usually a headshake, often accompanied by a negative facial expression, see example (1b);
<u>re</u>	Raised eyebrows accompanying different types of subordinate clauses;
<u>t</u>	Marker that indicates a topicalized constituent: usually raised eyebrows and a slight forward tilt of the head;
<u>wh</u>	Marker accompanying a content question (wh-question): usually lowered eyebrows;

_____y/n	Marker accompanying a yes/no question: usually raised eyebrows, sometimes in combination with head forward, see example (1a);
_____/xxx/	Phonological marker: either a mouth gesture, for example /shhhh/ with the sign BE-PRESENT, or a mouthing (i.e. the silent articulation of (a part of) the corresponding spoken word), for example /vava/ with the sign VACATION;
_____)(or ()	Sucked in cheeks that add the meaning 'small' to the sign; blown out cheeks that add the meaning 'big' to the sign.

2. Abbreviations

2.1 Sign language acronyms

We regularly refer to individual sign languages by means of acronyms that are conventionally used in the international literature. Some acronyms are based on the English name of a sign language (for example, CSL for Chinese Sign Language), while others are based on the name of the sign language used in the respective country (for example, DGS for German Sign Language). In the latter case, we also indicate the local name of the sign language between brackets in the following list.

ABSL	Al-Sayyid Bedouin Sign Language
AdaSL	Adamorobe Sign Language (Ghana)
ASL	American Sign Language
Auslan	Australian Sign Language
BSL	British Sign Language
CSL	Chinese Sign Language
DGS	German Sign Language (*Deutsche Gebärdensprache*)
FinSL	Finnish Sign Language
GSL	Greek Sign Language
HKSL	Hong Kong Sign Language
IPSL	Indopakistani Sign Language
ISL	Israeli Sign Language
ISN	Nicaraguan Sign Language (*Idioma de Señas Nicaragüense*)
IUR	Inuit Sign Language (*Inuit Uukturausingit*)
Libras	Brazilian Sign Language (*Língua de Sinais Brasileira*)
LIS	Italian Sign Language (*Lingua Italiana dei Segni*)
LIU	Jordanian Sign Language (*Lughat il-Ishaara il-Urdunia*)
LSC	Catalan Sign Language (*Llengua de Signes Catalana*)
LSE	Spanish Sign Language (*Lengua de Signos española*)
LSF	French Sign Language (*Langue des Signes Française*)
LSQ	Quebec Sign Language (*Langue des Signes Québécoise*)
NGT	Sign Language of the Netherlands (*Nederlandse Gebarentaal*)
NS	Japanese Sign Language (*Nihon Syuwa*)

NZSL	New Zealand Sign Language
ÖGS	Austrian Sign Language (*Österreichische Gebärdensprache*)
RSL	Russian Sign Language
SASL	South African Sign Language
SaudiSL	Saudi Arabian Sign Language
SSL	Swedish Sign Language
ThaiSL	Thai Sign Language
TİD	Turkish Sign Language (*Türk İşaret Dili*)
TSL	Taiwan Sign Language
VGT	Flemish Sign Language (*Vlaamse Gebarentaal*)

2.2 Abbreviations in interlinear translations

In interlinear translations of examples from spoken languages, we follow the conventions of the Leipzig Glossing Rules and use the following abbreviations for grammatical markers.

ACC	accusative
ASP	aspect marker
CL	classifier
COMPL	completive aspect
COND	conditionial
DAT	dative
F	feminine
FUT	future tense
HAB	habitual aspect
ITE	iterative aspect
LOC	locative
M	masculine
NOM	nominative
OBJ	object
PL	plural
POSS	possessive
PRS	present tense
PST	past tense
Q	question particle
REC	reciprocal marker
REL	relative marker
SG	singular
TNS	tense marker
TOP	topic marker

Appendix 2

Examples of manual alphabets

1. Sign Language of the Netherlands: one-handed alphabet

Note that the manual alphabets of, for example, ASL and DGS are very similar. Different one-handed alphabets are used, for instance, in RSL and Ethiopian Sign Language (Carmel 1982; Duarte 2010).

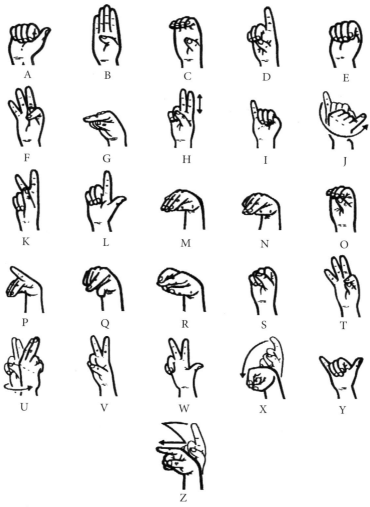

(source: www.effathaguyot.nl)

2. British Sign Language: two-handed alphabet

Note that the same manual alphabet is used in Auslan and NZSL. A different two-handed alphabet is used, for instance, in TİD (Taşçı 2013).

(source: http://www.deafblind.com/deafsign.html)

References

Aarons, Debra. 1996. Topics and topicalization in American Sign Language. *Stellenbosch Papers in Linguistics* 30, 65–106.

Aboh, Enoch O., Roland Pfau & Ulrike Zeshan. 2005. When a wh-word is not a wh-word: The case of Indian Sign Language. In: T. Bhattacharya (ed.), *The Yearbook of South Asian languages and linguistics 2005*, 11–43. Berlin: Mouton de Gruyter.

Adam, Robert. 2012. Language contact and borrowing. In: R. Pfau, M. Steinbach & B. Woll (eds.), *Sign language. An international handbook*, 841–862. Berlin: De Gruyter Mouton.

Adam, Robert, Eleni Orfanidou, James M. McQueen & Gary Morgan. 2011. Sign language comprehension: Insights from misperceptions of different phonological parameters. In: R. Channon & H. van der Hulst (eds.), *Formational units in sign languages*, 87–106. Berlin & Nijmegen: De Gruyter Mouton & Ishara Press.

Ahlgren, Inger. 1990. Deictic pronouns in Swedish and Swedish Sign Language. In: S. D. Fischer & P. Siple (eds.), *Theoretical issues in sign language research. Vol.1: Linguistics*, 175–190. Chicago: University of Chicago Press.

Aikhenvald, Alexandra Y. 2000. *Classifiers. A typology of noun categorization devices.* Oxford: Oxford University Press.

Akinlabi, Akinbiyi. 1996. Featural affixation. *Journal of Linguistics* 32, 239–289. doi:10.1017/S0022226700015899

Alibašić Ciciliani, Tamara & Ronnie B. Wilbur. 2006. Pronominal system in Croatian Sign Language. *Sign Language & Linguistics* 9, 95–132. doi:10.1075/sll.9.1-2.07ali

Allsop, Lorna, Bencie Woll & Rachel Sutton-Spence. 1990. Sign language varieties in British television. A historical perspective. In: S. Prillwitz & T. Vollhaber (eds.), *Current trends in European sign language research. Proceedings of the 3rd European Congress on Sign Language Research*, 61–72. Hamburg: Signum.

Anderson, Diane. 2006. Lexical development of deaf children acquiring sign languages. In: B. Schick, M. Marschark & P. E. Spencer (eds.), *Advances in the sign language development of deaf children*, 135–160. Oxford: Oxford University Press.

Ann, Jean. 1993. *A linguistic investigation into the relation between physiology and handshape.* PhD dissertation, University of Arizona.

Ann, Jean. 1998. Contact between a sign language and a written language: Character signs in Taiwan Sign Language. In: C. Lucas (ed.), *Pinky extension and eye gaze: Language use in Deaf communities*, 59–99. Washington, DC: Gallaudet University Press.

Antzakas, Klimis. 2006. The use of negative head movements in Greek Sign Language. In: U. Zeshan (ed.), *Interrogative and negative constructions in sign languages*, 258–269. Nijmegen: Ishara Press.

Armstrong, David F. & Sherman E. Wilcox. 2007. *The gestural origin of language.* Oxford: Oxford University Press. doi:10.1093/acprof:oso/9780195163483.001.0001

Aronoff, Mark, Irit Meir, Carol Padden & Wendy Sandler. 2005. Morphological universals and the sign language type. *Yearbook of Morphology 2004*, 19–39. doi:10.1007/1-4020-2900-4_2

Aronoff, Mark, Irit Meir & Wendy Sandler. 2005. The paradox of sign language morphology. *Language* 81, 301–344. doi:10.1353/lan.2005.0043

Baddeley, Alan D & Robert H. Logie. 1999. Working memory: the multiple-component model. In: A. Miyake, & P. Shah (eds.), *Models of working memory. Mechanisms of active maintenance and executive control*, 28–61. Cambridge: Cambridge University Press. doi:10.1017/CBO9781139174909.005

Bahan, Ben, Judy Kegl, Robert G. Lee, Dawn MacLaughlin & Carol Neidle. 2000. The licensing of null arguments in American Sign Language. *Linguistic Inquiry* 31, 1–27. doi:10.1162/002438900554271

Baker, Anne & Beppie van den Bogaerde. 2006. Eyegaze in turn-taking in sign language interaction. Paper presented at *Child Language Seminar*, July 2006, Newcastle, UK.

Baker, Anne & Beppie van den Bogaerde. 2008. Codemixing in signs and words in input to and output from children. In: C. Plaza Pust & E. Morales Lopez (eds.), *Sign bilingualism: Language development, interaction, and maintenance in sign language contact situations*, 1–27. Amsterdam: John Benjamins. doi:10.1075/sibil.38.04bak

Baker, Anne & Beppie van den Bogaerde. 2012. Communicative interaction. In: R. Pfau, M. Steinbach & B. Woll (eds.), *Sign language. An international handbook*, 489–512. Berlin: De Gruyter Mouton.

Baker, Anne & Beppie van den Bogaerde. 2014. KODAs: A special form of bilingualism. In: D. Quinto-Pozos (ed.), *Multilingual aspects of signed language communication and disorder*, 211–234. Bristol: Multilingual Matters.

Baker, Anne, Beppie van den Bogaerde & Onno Crasborn (eds.). 2003. *Cross-linguistic perspectives in sign language research. Selected papers from TISLR 2000*. Hamburg: Signum.

Baker, Anne, Beppie van den Bogaerde & Bencie Woll. 2005. Methods and procedures in sign language acquisition studies. *Sign Language & Linguistics* 8, 7–59. doi:10.1075/sll.8.1-2.03bak

Baker, Charlotte. 1977. Regulators and turn-taking in ASL discourse. In: L. A. Friedman (ed.), *On the other hand. New perspectives on American Sign Language*, 215–241. New York: Academic Press.

Baker, Charlotte & Dennis Cokely. 1980. *American Sign Language. A teacher's resource text on grammar and culture*. Silver Spring, MD: T. J. Publishers.

Baker, Mark C. 1988. *Incorporation. A theory of grammatical function changing*. Chicago: Chicago University Press.

Bank, Richard. 2014. *The ubiquity of mouthings in NGT. A corpus study*. PhD dissertation, Radboud University Nijmegen. Utrecht: LOT [http://www.lotpublications.nl/Documents/376_fulltext.pdf].

Battison, Robbin. 1974. Phonological deletion in American Sign Language. *Sign Language Studies* 5, 1–19. doi:10.1353/sls.1974.0005

Battison, Robbin. 1978. *Lexical borrowing in American Sign Language*. Silver Spring, MD: Linstok Press.

Baus, Cristina, Eva Gutiérrez-Sigut, Josep Quer & Manuel Carreiras. 2008. Lexical access in Catalan Signed Language (LSC) production. *Cognition* 108, 856–865. doi:10.1016/j.cognition.2008.05.012

Baus, Cristina, Manuel Carreiras & Karen Emmorey. 2013. When does iconicity in sign language matter? *Language and Cognitive Processes* 28(3), 261–271. doi:10.1080/01690965.2011.620374

Bavelier, Daphne, Elissa L. Newport, Matt Hall, Ted Supalla & Mrim Boutla. 2008. Ordered short-term memory differs in signers and speakers: Implications for models of short-term memory. *Cognition* 107, 433–459. doi:10.1016/j.cognition.2007.10.012

Becker, Claudia. 2003. *Verfahren der Lexikonerweiterung in der Deutschen Gebärdensprache*. Hamburg: Signum.

Benedicto, Elena & Diane Brentari. 2004. Where did all the arguments go?: Argument-changing properties of classifiers in ASL. *Natural Language & Linguistic Theory* 22, 743–810. doi:10.1007/s11049-003-4698-2

Bergman, Brita & Östen Dahl. 1994. Ideophones in sign language? The place of reduplication in the tense-aspect system of Swedish Sign Language. In: C. Bache, H. Basbøll & C.-E. Lindberg (eds.), *Tense, aspect and action: Empirical and theoretical contributions to language typology*, 397–422. Berlin: Mouton de Gruyter.

Bishop, Michelle & Sherry Hicks (eds.). 2009. *Hearing, father mother deaf. Hearing people in deaf families*. Washington, DC: Gallaudet University Press.

Bobaljik, Jonathan D. & Susi Wurmbrand. 2002. Notes on agreement in Itelmen. *Linguistic Discovery* 1(1). doi:10.1349/PS1.1537-0852.A.21

Bogaerde, Beppie van den. 2000. *Input and interaction in deaf families*. PhD dissertation, University of Amsterdam. Utrecht: LOT [www.lotpublications.nl/Documents/35_fulltext.pdf].

Bonvillian, John D. & Raymond J. Folven. 1993. Sign language acquisition: Developmental aspects. In: M. Marschark & M. D. Clark (eds.), *Psychological perspectives on deafness*, 229–268. Hillsdale, NJ: Lawrence Erlbaum.

Bonvillian, John D. & Theodore Siedlecki. 2000. Young children's acquisition of the formational aspects of American Sign Language. Parental report findings. *Sign Language Studies* 1, 45–64. doi:10.1353/sls.2000.0002

Bos, Heleen F. 1993. Agreement and prodrop in Sign Language of the Netherlands. In: K. Hengeveld & F. Drijkoningen (eds.), *Linguistics in the Netherlands*, 37–47. Amsterdam: John Benjamins. doi:10.1075/avt.10.06bos

Bos, Heleen F. 1995. Pronoun copy in Sign Language of the Netherlands. In: H. Bos & T. Schermer (eds.), *Sign language research 1994: Proceedings of the Fourth European Congress on Sign Language Research*, 121–147. Hamburg: Signum.

Boudreault, Pierre & Rachel I. Mayberry. 2006. Grammatical processing in American Sign Language: Age of first-language acquisition effects in relation to syntactic structure. *Language and Cognitive Processes* 21(5), 608–635. doi:10.1080/01690960500139363

Boyes Braem, Penny. 1990. Acquisition of handshape in American Sign Language: A preliminary analysis. In: V. Volterra & C. J. Erting (eds.), *From gesture to language in hearing and deaf children*, 107–127. Berlin: Springer Verlag. doi:10.1007/978-3-642-74859-2_10

Boyes Braem, Penny & Rachel Sutton-Spence (eds.). 2001. *The hands are the head of the mouth: the mouth as articulator in sign languages*. Hamburg: Signum.

Branchini, Chiara, Anna Cardinaletti, Carlo Cecchetto, Caterina Donati & Carlo Geraci. 2013. WH-duplication in Italian Sign Language (LIS). *Sign Language & Linguistics* 16(2), 157–188. doi:10.1075/sll.16.2.03bra

Branchini, Chiara & Caterina Donati. 2009. Italian Sign Language relatives: A contribution to the typology of relativization strategies. In: A. Liptàk (ed.), *Correlatives cross-linguistically*, 157–191. Amsterdam: North Holland. doi:10.1075/lfab.1.07bra

Brennan, Mary. 1992. The visual world of British Sign Language: an introduction. In: D. Brien (ed.), *Dictionary of British Sign Language/English*. London: Faber and Faber.

Brennan, Mary. 2001. Encoding and capturing productive morphology. *Sign Language & Linguistics* 4, 47–62. doi:10.1075/sll.4.1-2.06bre

Brennan, Mary, Martin D. Colville, Lillian K. Lawson & Gerry Hughes. 1984. *Words in hand. A structural analysis of the signs of BSL*. British Deaf Association.

Brentari, Diane. 1998. *A prosodic model of sign language phonology*. Cambridge, MA: MIT Press.

Brentari, Diane (ed.). 2001. *Foreign vocabulary in sign languages. A cross-linguistic investigation of word formation*. Mahwah, NJ: Lawrence Erlbaum.

Brentari, Diane (ed.). 2010. *Sign languages (Cambridge Language Surveys)*. Cambridge: Cambridge University Press. doi:10.1017/CBO9780511712203

Brentari, Diane. 2012. Phonology. In: R. Pfau, M. Steinbach & B. Woll (eds.), *Sign language. An international handbook*, 21–54. Berlin: De Gruyter Mouton.

Brentari, Diane, Marie Coppola, Laura Mazzoni & Susan Goldin-Meadow. 2012. When does a system become phonological? Handshape production in gestureres, signers, and homesigners. *Natural Language & Linguistic Theory* 30, 1–31. doi:10.1007/s11049-011-9145-1

Brentari, Diane & Laurinda Crossley. 2002. Prosody on the hands and face: Evidence from American Sign Language. *Sign Language & Linguistics* 5(2), 105–130. doi:10.1075/sll.5.2.03bre

Brien, David (ed.). 1992. *Dictionary of British Sign Language/English*. London: Faber and Faber.

Brien, David, Mary Brennan, Trude Schermer, Rita Harder & Robert Bakker. 1995. Creating a sign language database: The SIGNBASE project. In: H. Bos & T. Schermer (eds.), *Sign language research 1994. Proceedings of the Fourth European Congress on Sign Language Research, Munich*, 339–346. Hamburg: Signum.

Brunelli, Michele. 2011. *Antisymmetry and sign languages: A comparison between NGT and LIS*. PhD dissertation, University of Amsterdam. Utrecht: LOT [www.lotpublications.nl/Documents/284_fulltext.pdf].

Cabeza Pereiro, Carmen & Ana Fernández Soneira. 2004. The expression of time in Spanish Sign Language (SLE). *Sign Language & Linguistics* 7(1), 63–82. doi:10.1075/sll.7.1.06cab

Campbell, Cindy. 2001. *The application of speech act theory to American Sign Language*. PhD dissertation, State University of New York at Albany.

Campbell, Ruth, Mairéad MacSweeney & Dafydd Waters. 2008. Sign language and the brain: A review. *Journal of Deaf Studies and Deaf Education* 13, 4–20.

Capek, Cheryl M., Giordana Grossi, Aaron J. Newman, Susan L. McBurney, David Corina, Brigitte Roeder & Helen J. Neville. 2009. Brain systems mediating semantic and syntactic processing in deaf native signers: Biological invariance and modality specificity. *Proceedings of the National Academy of Sciences of the USA (PNAS)* 106(21), 8784–8789.

Caponigro, Ivano & Kathryn Davidson. 2011. Ask, and tell as well: Clausal question-answer pairs in ASL. *Natural Language Semantics* 19(4), 323–371. doi:10.1007/s11050-011-9071-0

Capovilla, Fernando C. & Walkiria D. Raphael (eds.). 2001. *Dicionário enciclopédico ilustrado trilingüe da Lingua de Sinais Brasileira. Vol. I. Sinais de A a L*. São Paulo: Editora da Universidade de São Paulo.

Carmel, Simon J. 1982. *International hand alphabet charts*. Published by author.

Carroll, David W. 2004. *Psychology of language*. Belmont, CA: Wadsworth.

Cecchetto, Carlo. 2012. Sentence types. In: R. Pfau, M. Steinbach & B. Woll, (eds.), *Sign language. An international handbook*, 292–315. Berlin: De Gruyter Mouton.

Cecchetto, Carlo, Alessandra Checchetto, Carlo Geraci, Mirko Santoro & Sandro Zucchi. 2015. The syntax of predicate ellipsis in Italian Sign Language (LIS). *Lingua* 166, 214–235. doi:org/10.1016/j.lingua.2014.12.011.

Cecchetto, Carlo, Carlo Geraci & Sandro Zucchi. 2006. Strategies of relativization in Italian Sign Language. *Natural Language & Linguistic Theory* 24, 945–975. doi:10.1007/s11049-006-9001-x

Chen Pichler, Deborah. 2008. Views on word order in early ASL: Then and now. In: J. Quer (ed.), *Signs of the time. Selected papers from TISLR 8*, 293–315. Hamburg: Signum.

Chen Pichler, Deborah. 2011. Sources of handshape error in first-time signers of ASL. In: D. J. Napoli & G. Mathur (eds.), *Deaf around the world. The impact of language*, 96–121. Oxford: Oxford University Press.

Chen Pichler, Deborah. 2012. Acquisition. In: R. Pfau, M. Steinbach & B. Woll (eds.), *Sign language. An international handbook*, 647–686. Berlin: De Gruyter Mouton.

Chen Pichler, Deborah & Helen Koulidobrova. 2015. Acquisition of sign language as a second language. In: M. Marschark (ed.), *The Oxford handbook of deaf studies: Research, policy, and practice*, 218–230. Oxford: Oxford University Press.

Chen Pichler, Deborah, James Lee & Diane Lillo-Martin. 2014. Language development in ASL-English bimodal bilinguals. In: D. Quinto-Pozos (ed.), *Multilingual aspects of signed language communication and disorder*, 235–260. Bristol: Multilingual Matters.

Clark, Eve V. 2009. *First language acquisition (2nd edition)*. Cambridge: Cambridge University Press. doi:10.1017/CBO9780511806698

Coates, Jennifer & Rachel Sutton-Spence. 2001. Turn-taking patterns in Deaf conversation. *Journal of Sociolinguistics* 5, 507–529. doi:10.1111/1467-9481.00162

Coerts, Jane. 1992. *Nonmanual grammatical markers: An analysis of interrogatives, negations and topicalisations in Sign Language of the Netherlands*. PhD dissertation, University of Amsterdam.

Conlin, Kimberley E., Gene R. Mirus, Claude Mauk & Richard P. Meier. 2000. The acquisition of first signs: place, handshape, and movement. In: C. Chamberlain, J. P. Morford & R. I. Mayberry (eds.), *Language acquisition by eye*, 51–69. Mahwah, NJ: Lawrence Erlbaum.

Corina, David P. 1990. Handshape assimilations in hierarchical phonological representation. In: C. Lucas (ed.), *Sign language research. Theoretical issues*, 27–49. Washington, DC: Gallaudet University Press.

Corina, David P. 1999. On the nature of left hemisphere specialization for signed language. *Brain and Language* 69, 230–240. doi:10.1006/brln.1999.2062

Corina, David P. & Nicole Spotswood. 2012. Neurolinguistics. In: R. Pfau, M. Steinbach & B. Woll, (eds.), *Sign language. An international handbook*, 739–762. Berlin: De Gruyter Mouton.

Cormier, Kearsy. 2012. Pronouns. In: R. Pfau, M. Steinbach & B. Woll (eds.), *Sign language. An international handbook*, 227–244. Berlin: De Gruyter Mouton.

Costello, Brendan. 2015. *Language and modality: possible effects of the use of space on Spanish Sign Language (LSE)*. PhD dissertation, University of Vitoria (Spain) & University of Amsterdam. Utrecht: LOT.

Coulter, Geoffrey R. 1979. *American Sign Language typology*. PhD dissertation, University of California at San Diego.

Crasborn, Onno. 2001. *Phonetic implementation of phonological categories in Sign Language of the Netherlands*. PhD dissertation, University of Leiden. Utrecht: LOT [www.lotpublications.nl/Documents/48_fulltext.pdf].

Crasborn, Onno. 2012. Phonetics. In: R. Pfau, M. Steinbach & B. Woll (eds.), *Sign language. An international handbook*, 4–20. Berlin: De Gruyter Mouton.

Crasborn, Onno & Els van der Kooij. 1997. Relative orientation in sign language phonology. In: J. Coerts & H. de Hoop (eds.), *Linguistics in the Netherlands* 1997, 37–48. Amsterdam: John Benjamins. doi:10.1075/avt.14.06cra

Crasborn, Onno & Els van der Kooij. 2003. Base joint configuration in Sign Language of the Netherlands: phonetic variation and phonological specification. In: J. van de Weijer, V. J. van Heuven & H. van der Hulst (eds.), *The phonological spectrum. Volume 1: Segmental structure*, 257–287. Amsterdam: John Benjamins. doi:10.1075/cilt.233.15cra

Crasborn, Onno & Els van der Kooij. 2013. The phonology of focus in Sign Language of the Netherlands. *Journal of Linguistics* 49(3), 515–565. doi:10.1017/S0022226713000054

Crasborn, Onno, Els van der Kooij, Dafydd Waters, Bencie Woll & Johanna Mesch. 2008. Frequency distribution and spreading behavior of different types of mouth actions in three sign languages. *Sign Language & Linguistics* 11(1), 45–67. doi:10.1075/sll.11.1.04cra

Cuxac, Christian & Marie-Anne Sallandre. 2007. Iconicity and arbitrariness in French Sign Language (LSF): Highly iconic structures, degenerated iconicity and diagrammatic iconicity. In: E. Pizzuto, P. Pietrandrea & R. Simone (eds.), *Verbal and signed languages. Comparing structures, constructs, and methodologies*, 13–33. Berlin: Mouton de Gruyter.

Dachkovsky, Svetlana. 2008. Facial expression as intonation in Israeli Sign Language: the case of neutral and counterfactual conditionals. In: J. Quer (ed.), *Signs of the time. Selected papers from TISLR 2004*, 61–82. Hamburg: Signum.

Dachkovsky, Svetlana & Wendy Sandler. 2009. Visual intonation in the prosody of a sign language. *Language and Speech* 52 (2/3), 287–314. doi:10.1177/0023830909103175

Davidson, Kathryn. 2013. 'And' or 'or': General use coordination in ASL. *Semantics & Pragmatics* 6, 1–44. doi:10.3765/sp.6.4

De Weerdt, Kristof, Mieke Van Herreweghe, Katrien Van Mulders & Myriam Vermeerbergen. 2004. *Woordenboek Nederlands – Vlaamse Gebarentaal / Vlaamse Gebarentaal – Nederlands* [http://gebaren.ugent.be/].

Demey, Eline. 2005. *Fonologie van de Vlaamse Gebarentaal: Distinctiviteit & iconiciteit*. PhD dissertation, Ghent University.

Deuchar, Margaret. 1984. *British Sign Language*. London: Routledge & Kegan Paul.

Đình-Hoà, Nguyễn. 1997. *Vietnamese*. Amsterdam: John Benjamins. doi:10.1075/loall.9

Dively, Valerie L. 1998. Conversational repairs in ASL. In: C. Lucas (ed.), *Pinky extension & eye gaze: Language use in deaf communities*, 137–169. Washington, DC: Gallaudet University Press.

Donati, Caterina, Gemma Barberà, Chiara Branchini, Carlo Cecchetto, Carlo Geraci & Josep Quer. In press. Searching for imperatives in European sign languages. In: S. Heinold & D. Van Olmen (eds.), *Imperatives and other directive strategies*. Amsterdam: John Benjamins.

Duarte, Kyle. 2010. The mechanics of fingerspelling: Analyzing Ethiopian Sign Language. *Sign Language Studies* 11(1), 5–21. doi:10.1353/sls.2010.0004

Dye, Matt W. G. 2012. Processing. In: R. Pfau, M. Steinbach & B. Woll (eds.), *Sign language. An international handbook*, 687–711. Berlin: De Gruyter Mouton.

Ekman, Paul, Wallace V. Friesen & Joseph C. Hager. 2002. *Facial action coding system (FACS)*. Salt Lake City, UT: Research Nexus.

Emmorey, Karen. 2002. *Language, cognition, and the brain. Insights from sign language research*. Mahwah, NJ: Lawrence Erlbaum.

Emmorey, Karen. 2007. The psycholinguistics of signed and spoken languages: how biology affects processing. In: M. G. Gaskell & G. Altman (eds.), *The Oxford handbook of psycholinguistics*, 703–722. Oxford: Oxford University Press.

Emmorey, Karen, Helsa B. Borinstein, Robin Thompson & Tamar H. Gollan. 2008. Bimodal bilingualism. *Bilingualism: Language and Cognition* 11(1), 43–61. doi:10.1017/S1366728907003203

Emmorey, Karen & Margaret Wilson. 2004. The puzzle of working memory for sign language, *Trends in Cognitive Sciences* 8, 521–523. doi:10.1016/j.tics.2004.10.009

Engberg-Pedersen, Elisabeth. 1995. Point of view expressed through shifters. In: K. Emmorey & J. Reilly (eds.), *Language, gesture, and space*, 133–154. Hillsdale, NJ: Lawrence Erlbaum.

L'Epée, Charles Michel Abbé de. 1784. *La véritable manière d'instruire les sourds et muets*. Paris: Nyon l'aîné.

Fernández Villabrille, Francisco. 1851. *Diccionario usual de mímica y dactilología: útil a los maestros de sordo-mudos, a sus padres y a todas las personas que tengan que entrar en comunicacíon con ellos*. Madrid: Imprenta del Colegio de Sordo-mudos y Ciegos. (full text available at: www.cervantesvirtual.com/nd/ark:/59851/bmc154h5).

Ferreira Brito, Lucinda. 1990. Epistemic, alethic, and deontic modalities in a Brazilian Sign Language. In: S. D. Fischer & P. Siple (eds.), *Theoretical issues in sign language research. Vol.1: Linguistics*, 229–260. Chicago: University of Chicago Press.

Fischer, Susan. 1975. Influences on word order change in American Sign Language. In: C. N. Li (ed.), *Word order and word order change*, 3–25. Austin, TX: University of Texas Press.

Fischer, Susan & Bonnie Gough. 1999[1972]. Some unfinished thoughts on FINISH. *Sign Language & Linguistics* 2, 67–77. doi:10.1075/sll.2.1.08fis

Foley, William A. 1991. *The Yimas language of New Guinea*. Stanford, CA: Stanford University Press.

Frajzyngier, Zygmunt. 2001. *A grammar of Lele*. Stanford, CA: CSLI.

Frishberg, Nancy. 1975. Arbitrariness and iconicity: historical change in American Sign Language. *Language* 51, 696–719. doi:10.2307/412894

Frishberg, Nancy, Nini Hoiting & Dan I. Slobin. 2012. Transcription. In: R. Pfau, M. Steinbach & B. Woll (eds.), *Sign language. An international handbook*, 1045–1075. Berlin: De Gruyter Mouton.

Folven, Raymond J. & John D. Bonvillian. 1991. The transition from nonreferential to referential language in children acquiring American Sign Language. *Developmental Psychology* 27(5), 806–816. doi:10.1037/0012-1649.27.5.806

Fromkin, Victoria A. 1971. The non-anomalous nature of anomalous utterances. *Language* 47(1), 27–52. doi:10.2307/412187

Fromkin, Victoria A. 1988. Grammatical aspects of speech errors. In: F. J. Newmeyer (ed.), *Linguistics: The Cambridge survey. Vol.II: Linguistic theory: Extensions and implications*, 117–138. Cambridge: Cambridge University Press.

Fundación CNSE. 2003a. *Diccionario normativo de la Lengua de Signos Española*. Madrid: Fundación CNSE.

Fundación CNSE. 2003b. *Glosario temático de la Lengua de Signos Española. Salud: Psicologia*. Madrid: Fundación CNSE.

Geraci, Carlo. 2005. Negation in LIS (Italian Sign Language). In: L. Bateman & C. Ussery (eds.), *Proceedings of the North East Linguistic Society (NELS 35)*, 217–229. Amherst, MA: GLSA.

Geraci, Carlo & Valentina Aristodemo. 2016. An in-depth tour into sentential complementation in Italian Sign Language. In: R. Pfau, M. Steinbach & A. Herrmann (eds.), *A matter of complexity: Subordination in sign languages*, 95–150. Berlin: De Gruyter Mouton.

Geraci, Carlo, Marta Gozzi, Costanza Papagno & Carlo Cecchetto. 2008. How grammar can cope with limited short-term memory: Simultaneity and seriality in sign languages. *Cognition* 106, 780–804. doi:10.1016/j.cognition.2007.04.014

Gijn, Ingeborg van. 2004. *The quest for syntactic dependency. Sentential complementation in Sign Language of the Netherlands*. PhD dissertation, University of Amsterdam. Utrecht: LOT [www.lotpublications.nl/Documents/89_fulltext.pdf].

Glück, Susanne, Daniela Happ, Jörg Keller, Gerald Koblitz, Helen Leuninger & Roland Pfau. 1997. Zur phonologischen Beschreibung von Gebärden: Vergebärdler. *Das Zeichen* 40, 240–257.

Göksel, Aslı & Meltem Kelepir. 2016. Observations on clausal complementation in Turkish Sign Language. In: R. Pfau, M. Steinbach & A. Herrmann (eds.), *A matter of complexity: Subordination in sign languages*, 65–94. Berlin: De Gruyter Mouton.

Goldin-Meadow, Susan. 2003. *The resilience of language. What gesture creation in deaf children can tell us about how all children learn language*. New York: Psychology Press.

Goldin-Meadow, Susan. 2012. Homesign: gesture to language. In: R. Pfau, M. Steinbach & B. Woll (eds.), *Sign language. An international handbook*, 601–625. Berlin: De Gruyter Mouton.

Grice, H. Paul. 1975. Logic and conversation. In: P. Cole & J. Morgan (eds.), *Studies in syntax and semantics III: Speech acts*, 183–198. New York: Academic Press.

Groce, Nora E. 1985. *Everyone here spoke sign language. Hereditary deafness on Martha's Vineyard*. Cambridge, MA: Harvard University Press.

Groeber, Simone & Evelyne Pochon-Berger. 2014. Turns and turn-taking in sign language interaction: A study of turn-final holds. *Journal of Pragmatics* 65, 121–136. doi:10.1016/j.pragma.2013.08.012

Grosjean, François. 2010. *Bilingual: life and reality*. Boston: Harvard College. doi:10.4159/9780674056459

Grosvald, Michael & David Corina. 2012. The perceptibility of long-distance coarticulation in speech and sign: A study of English and American Sign Language. *Sign Language & Linguistics* 15(1), 73–103. doi:10.1075/sll.15.1.04gro

Grushkin, Donald A. 1998. Linguistic aspects of metaphorical expressions of anger in ASL. *Sign Language & Linguistics* 1, 143–168. doi:10.1075/sll.1.2.04gru

Gutierrez-Sigut, Eva, Brendan Costello, Cristina Baus & Manual Carreiras. 2015. LSE-Sign: a lexical database for Spanish Sign Language. *Behavior Research Methods*, online first. doi:103758/s13428-014-0560-1

Hall, Stephanie. 1989. Train-gone-sorry: The etiquette of social conversations in American Sign Language. In: S. Wilcox (ed.), *American Deaf culture. An anthology*, 89–102. Burtonsville, MD: Linstok Press.

Hanke, Thomas, Reiner Konrad & Arvid Schwarz. 2001. GlossLexer: A multimedia lexical database for sign language dictionary compilation. *Sign Language & Linguistics* 4, 171–189. doi:10.1075/sll.4.1-2.12han

Hansen, Britta. 2002. Bilingualism and the impact of sign language research on Deaf education. In: D. F. Armstrong, M. A. Karchmer & J. V. Van Cleve (eds.), *The study of signed languages. Essays in honor of William C. Stokoe*, 172–189. Washington, DC: Gallaudet University Press.

Hansen, Kathryn L. 2011. ASL movement phonemes and allophones. In: R. Channon & H. van der Hulst (eds.), *Formational units in sign languages*, 285–314. Berlin & Nijmegen: De Gruyter Mouton & Ishara Press.

Happ, Daniela & Marc-Oliver Vorköper. 2005. Einige Bemerkungen zur syntaktischen und morphologischen Repräsentation von Numerus in Deutscher Gebärdensprache. In: H. Leuninger & D. Happ (eds.), *Gebärdensprachen: Struktur, Erwerb, Verwendung* (Linguistische Berichte Special Issue 15), 87–110. Hamburg: Buske.

Happ, Daniela & Marc-Oliver Vorköper. 2006. *Deutsche Gebärdensprache. Ein Lehr- und Arbeitsbuch*. Frankfurt: Fachhochschulverlag.

Heine, Bernd & Tania Kuteva. 2002a. On the evolution of grammatical forms. In: A. Wray (ed.), *The transition to language. Studies in the evolution of language*, 376–397. Oxford: Oxford University Press.

Heine, Bernd & Tania Kuteva. 2002b. *World lexicon of grammaticalization*. Cambridge: Cambridge University Press. doi:10.1017/CBO9780511613463

Hendriks, Bernadet. 2004. *An introduction to the grammar of Jordanian Sign Language*. Salt (Jordan): Al-Balqa Applied University.

Hendriks, Bernadet. 2008. *Jordanian Sign Language: Aspects of grammar from a cross-linguistic perspective*. PhD dissertation, University of Amsterdam. Utrecht: LOT [www.lotpublications.nl/Documents/193_fulltext.pdf].

Herrmann, Annika. 2007. The expression of modal meaning in German Sign Language and Irish Sign Language. In: P. Perniss, R. Pfau & M. Steinbach (eds.), *Visible variation: Cross-linguistic studies on sign language structure*, 245–278. Berlin: Mouton de Gruyter.

Herrmann, Annika. 2010. The interaction of eye blinks and other prosodic cues in German Sign Language. *Sign Language & Linguistics* 13(1), 3–39. doi:10.1075/sll.13.1.02her

Herrmann, Annika & Markus Steinbach. 2012. Quotation in sign languages: A visible context shift. In: I. Buchstaller & I. van Alphen (eds), *Quotatives. Cross-linguistic and cross-disciplinary perspectives*, 203–228. Amsterdam: John Benjamins. doi:10.1075/celcr.15.12her

Hickok, Gregory, Ursula Bellugi & Edward S. Klima. 2001. Sign language in the brain. *Scientific American*, June 2001, 42–49.

Hohenberger, Annette, Daniela Happ & Helen Leuninger. 2002. Modality-dependent aspects of sign language production: Evidence from slips of the hands and their repairs in German Sign Language. In: R. P. Meier, K. A. Cormier & D. G. Quinto-Pozos (eds.), *Modality and structure in signed and spoken languages*, 112–142. Cambridge: Cambridge University Press.

Hohenberger, Annette & Helen Leuninger. 2012. Production. In: R. Pfau, M. Steinbach & B. Woll (eds.), *Sign language. An international handbook*, 711–738. Berlin: De Gruyter Mouton.

Hopper, Paul J. & Elisabeth C. Traugott. 1993. *Grammaticalization*. Cambridge: Cambridge University Press.

Hulst, Harry van der. 1993. Units in the analysis of signs. *Phonology* 10, 209–241. doi:10.1017/S095267570000004X

Hulst, Harry van der. 1995. The composition of handshapes. *University of Trondheim Working Papers in Linguistics* 23, 1–17.

Hulst, Harry van der. 1996. On the other hand. *Lingua* 98, 121–143. doi:10.1016/0024-3841(95)00035-6

Hunger, Barbara. 2006. Noun/verb pairs in Austrian Sign Language (ÖGS). *Sign Language & Linguistics* 9, 71–94. doi:10.1075/sll.9.1-2.06hun

Isenhath, John O. 1990. *The linguistics of American Sign Language*. Jefferson, NC: McFarland.

Jantunen, Tommi. 2007. *On topic in Finnish Sign Language*. Manuscript, University of Jyväskylä, Finland. [http://users.jyu.fi/~tojantun/articles/JAN_topic_ms.pdf].

Jantunen, Tommi. 2013. Ellipsis in Finnish Sign Language. *Nordic Journal of Linguistics* 36(3), 303–332. doi:10.1017/S0332586513000292

Janzen, Terry. 2012. Lexicalization and grammaticalization. In: R. Pfau, M. Steinbach & B. Woll (eds.), *Sign language. An international handbook*, 816–841. Berlin: De Gruyter Mouton.

Janzen, Terry, Barbara O'Shea & Barbara Shaffer. 2001. The construal of events: Passives in American Sign Language. *Sign Language Studies* 1, 281–310. doi:10.1353/sls.2001.0009

Johnson, Robert E., Scott K. Liddell & Carol J. Erting. 1989. Unlocking the curriculum: Principles for achieving access in deaf education. *Gallaudet Research Institute Working Paper* 89–3. Gallaudet University, Washington, DC.

Johnston, Trevor. 1989. *Auslan dictionary: a dictionary of Australian Sign Language (Auslan)*. Adelaide: TAFE National Centre for Research and Development.

Johnston, Trevor. 2001a. The lexical database of Auslan (Australian Sign Language). *Sign Language & Linguistics* 4, 145–169. doi:10.1075/sll.4.1-2.11joh

Johnston, Trevor. 2001b. Nouns and verbs in Australian Sign Language: An open or shut case? *Journal of Deaf Studies and Deaf Education* 6(4), 235–257. doi:10.1093/deafed/6.4.235

Johnston, Trevor. 2003a. BSL, Auslan and NZSL: three signed languages or one? In: A. Baker, B. van den Bogaerde & O. Crasborn (eds.), *Cross-linguistic perspectives in sign language research. Selected papers from TISLR 2000*, 47–69. Hamburg: Signum.

Johnston, Trevor. 2003b. Language standardisation and signed language dictionaries. *Sign Language Studies* 3, 431–469. doi:10.1353/sls.2003.0012

Johnston, Trevor. 2005. *Auslan Signbank*. Sydney: Catalyst Communications & Training, Pty Ltd. [www.auslan.org.au].

Johnston, Trevor & Adam Schembri. 1999. On defining lexeme in a signed language. *Sign Language & Linguistics* 2, 115–185. doi:10.1075/sll.2.2.03joh

Johnston, Trevor & Adam Schembri. 2007. *Australian Sign Language. An introduction to sign language linguistics*. Cambridge: Cambridge University Press. doi:10.1017/CBO9780511607479

Johnston, Trevor, Myriam Vermeerbergen, Adam Schembri & Lorraine Lesson. 2007. 'Real data are messy': Considering cross-linguistic analysis of constituent ordering in Auslan, VGT, and ISL. In: P. Perniss, R. Pfau & M. Steinbach (eds.), *Visible variation: Cross-linguistic studies on sign language structure*, 163–205. Berlin: Mouton de Gruyter.

Karnopp, Lodenir. 1999. *Aquisição fonológica na língua brasileira de sinais: estudo longitudinal de uma criança surda*. PhD dissertation, Porto Alegre Pontifícia: Universidade Católica do Rio Grande do Sul.

Karnopp, Lodenir. 2002. Phonological acquisition in Brazilian Sign Language. In: G. Morgan & B. Woll (eds.), *Directions in sign language acquisition*, 29–53. Amsterdam: John Benjamins. doi:10.1075/tilar.2.05kar

Keenan, Edward L. 1985. Relative clauses. In: T. Shopen (ed.), *Language typology and syntactic description. Vol. II: Complex constructions*, 141–170 Cambridge: Cambridge University Press.

Kegl, Judy, Ann Senghas & Marie Coppola. 1999. Creation through contact: sign language emergence and sign language change in Nicaragua. In: M. DeGraff (ed.), *Language creation and language change: creolization, diachrony, and development*, 179–237. Cambridge: MIT Press.

Kimmelman, Vadim. 2009. Parts of speech in Russian Sign Language: the role of iconicity and economy. *Sign Language & Linguistics* 12, 161–186. doi:10.1075/sll.12.2.03kim

Kimmelman, Vadim. 2012. Word order in Russian Sign Language: An extended report. *Linguistics in Amsterdam* 5, 1–56 [www.linguisticsinamsterdam.nl/].

Kimmelman, Vadim. 2014. *Information structure in Russian Sign Language and Sign Language of the Netherlands*. PhD dissertation, University of Amsterdam. [http://dare.uva.nl/record/1/432175]. doi:10.1093/oxfordhb/9780199642670.013.001

Kimmelman, Vadim & Roland Pfau. In press. Information structure in sign languages. In: C. Fery & S. Ishihara (eds.), *The Oxford handbook on information structure*. Oxford: Oxford University Press.

Klima, Edward & Ursula Bellugi. 1979. *The signs of language*. Cambridge, MA: Harvard University Press.

Kooij, Els van der. 2001. Weak drop in Sign Language of the Netherlands. In: V. Dively, M. Metzger, S. Taub & A. M. Baer (eds.), *Signed languages: Discoveries from international research*, 27–42. Washington, DC: Gallaudet University Press.

Kooij, Els van der. 2002. *Phonological categories in Sign Language of the Netherlands. The role of phonetic implementation and iconicity*. PhD dissertation, University of Leiden. Utrecht: LOT [www.lotpublications.nl/Documents/55_fulltext.pdf].

Kooij, Els van der, Onno Crasborn & Wim Emmerik. 2006. Explaining prosodic body leans in Sign Language of the Netherlands: Pragmatics required. *Journal of Pragmatics* 38, 1598–1614. doi:10.1016/j.pragma.2005.07.006

Kozak, L. Viola & Nozomi Tomita. 2012. On selected phonological patterns in Saudi Arabian Sign Language. *Sign Language Studies* 13(1), 56–78. doi:10.1353/sls.2012.0027

Krausneker, Verena. 2000. Sign languages and the minority language policy of the European Union. In: M. Metzger (ed.), *Bilingualism and identity in deaf communities*, 142–158. Washington, DC: Gallaudet University Press.

Krausneker, Verena. 2001. Sign languages of Europe – future chances. In: L. Leeson (ed.), *Looking forward: EUD in the 3rd millennium – the deaf citizen in the 21st century*, 64–73. Coleford: McLean Publisher.

Ktejik, Mish. 2013. Numeral incorporation in Japanese Sign Language. *Sign Language Studies* 13, 186–210. doi:10.1353/sls.2013.0003

Kubus, Okan. 2014. *Relative clause constructions in Turkish Sign Language*. PhD dissertation, University of Hamburg.

Kusters, Annelies. 2010. Deaf utopias? Reviewing the sociocultural literature on the world's "Martha's Vineyard situations". *Journal of Deaf Studies and Deaf Education* 15(1), 3–16.

Kyle, Jim & Bencie Woll. 1985. *Sign language. The study of deaf people and their language*. Cambridge: Cambridge University Press.

Ladefoged, Peter & Ian Maddieson. 1996. *The sounds of the world's languages*. Oxford: Blackwell.

Lakoff, George & Mark Johnson. 1980. *Metaphors we live by*. Chicago: University of Chicago Press.

Lane, Harlan. 1984. *When the mind hears: a history of the deaf*. Harmondsworth: Penguin Books.

Lang, Harry G. 2011. Perspectives on the history of deaf education. In: M. Marschark & P. E. Spencer (eds.), *Oxford handbook of deaf studies, language, and education (2nd edition)*, 7–17. Oxford: Oxford University Press.

Leeson, Lorraine & Carmel Grehan. 2004. To the lexicon and beyond: The effect of gender on variation in Irish Sign Language. In: M. Van Herreweghe & M. Vermeerbergen (eds.), *To the lexicon and beyond. Sociolinguistics in European deaf communities*, 39–73. Washington, DC: Gallaudet University Press.

Leeson, Lorraine & John I. Saeed. 2012a. *Irish Sign Language. A cognitive linguistic account*. Edinburgh: Edinburgh University Press.

Leeson, Lorraine & John I. Saeed. 2012b. Word order. In: R. Pfau, M. Steinbach & B. Woll (eds.), *Sign language. An international handbook*, 245–265. Berlin: De Gruyter Mouton.

Leuninger, Helen. 1989. *Neurolinguistik. Probleme, Paradigmen, Perspektiven*. Opladen: Westdeutscher Verlag.

Leuninger, Helen. 2001. Das Projekt RELEX: Ein ökumenisches Lexikon religiöser Gebärden. In: H. Leuninger & K. Wempe (eds.), *Gebärdensprachlinguistik 2000: Theorie und Anwendung*, 171–192. Hamburg: Signum.

Leuninger, Helen, Annette Hohenberger, Eva Waleschkowski, Elke Menges & Daniela Happ. 2004. The impact of modality on language production: Evidence from slips of the tongue and hand. In: T. Pechmann & C. Habel (eds.), *Multidisciplinary approaches to language production*, 219–277. Berlin: Mouton de Gruyter.

Li, Charles N. & Sandra A. Thompson. 1987. Chinese. In: B. Comrie (ed.), *The world's major languages*, 811–833. New York: Oxford University Press.

Liddell, Scott K. 1978. Nonmanual signals and relative clauses in American Sign Language. In: P. Siple (ed.), *Understanding language through sign language research*, 59–90. New York: Academic Press.

Liddell, Scott K. 1980. *American Sign Language syntax*. Den Haag: Mouton.

Liddell, Scott K. 1986. Head thrust in ASL conditional sentences. *Sign Language Studies* 52, 243–262.

Liddell, Scott K. 1997. Numeral incorporating roots & non-incorporating prefixes in American Sign Language. *Sign Language Studies* 92, 201–225.

Liddell, Scott K. & Robert E. Johnson. 1986. American Sign Language compound formation processes, lexicalization, and phonological remnants. *Natural Language and Linguistic Theory* 4, 445–513. doi:10.1007/BF00134470

Lieberman, Amy M. & Rachel I. Mayberry. 2015. Studying sign language acquisition. In: E. Orfanidou, B. Woll & G. Morgan (eds.), *Research methods in sign language studies: A practical guide*, 281–299. Oxford: Wiley-Blackwell.

Lillo-Martin Diane. 1986. Two kinds of null arguments in American Sign Language. *Natural Language and Linguistic Theory* 4, 415–444. doi:10.1007/BF00134469

Lillo-Martin, Diane. 1995. The point of view predicate in American Sign Language. In: K. Emmorey & J. Reilly (eds.), *Language, gesture, and space*, 155–170. Hillsdale, NJ: Lawrence Erlbaum.

Lillo-Martin, Diane. 2012. Utterance reports and constructed action. In: R. Pfau, M. Steinbach & B. Woll (eds.), *Sign language. An international handbook*, 365–387. Berlin: De Gruyter Mouton.

Lillo-Martin, Diane & Deborah Chen Pichler. 2006. Acquisition of syntax in sign languages. In: B. Schick, M. Marschark & P.E. Spencer (eds.), *Advances in the sign language development of deaf children*, 231–261. Oxford: Oxford University Press.

Lillo-Martin, Diane & Richard P. Meier. 2011. On the linguistic status of 'agreement' in sign languages. *Theoretical Linguistics* 37, 95–141.

Lillo-Martin, Diane & Ronice M. de Quadros. 2008. Focus constructions in American Sign Language and Lingua de Sinais Brasileira. In: J. Quer (ed.), *Signs of the time. Selected papers from TISLR 8*, 161–176. Hamburg: Signum.

Lindblom, Björn. 1990. Explaining phonetic variation: a sketch of the H&H theory. In: W.J. Hardcastle & A. Marchal (eds.), *Speech production and speech modeling*, 403–439. Dordrecht: Kluwer Publishers. doi:10.1007/978-94-009-2037-8_16

Loon, Esther van, Roland Pfau & Markus Steinbach. 2014. The grammaticalization of gestures in sign languages. In: C. Müller, A. Cienki, E. Fricke, S.H. Ladewig, D. McNeill & S. Tessendorf (eds.), *Body – language – communication: An international handbook on multimodality in human interaction*. Berlin: De Gruyter Mouton, 2133–2149.

Lucas, Ceil (ed.). 1989. *The sociolinguistics of the Deaf community*. San Diego, CA: Academic.

Lucas, Ceil (ed.). 1995. *Sociolinguistics in Deaf communities*. Washington, DC: Gallaudet University Press.

Lucas, Ceil. 2003. The role of variation in lexicography. *Sign Language Studies* 3, 322–340. doi:10.1353/sls.2003.0009

Lucas, Ceil. 2013. Methodological issues in studying sign language variation. In L. Meurant, A. Sinte, M. Van Herreweghe & M. Vermeerbergen (eds.), *Sign language research, uses and practices: Crossing the views on theoretical and applied sign language linguistics*, 285–307. Berlin & Nijmegen: De Gruyter Mouton & Ishara Press.

Lucas, Ceil & Robert Bayley. 2010. Variation in American Sign Language. In: D. Brentari (ed.), *Sign languages (Cambridge Language Surveys)*, 451–476. Cambridge: Cambridge University Press. doi:10.1017/CBO9780511712203.021

Lucas, Ceil, Robert Bayley, Ruth Reed & Alyssa Wulf. 2001a. Lexical variation in African American and white signing. *American Speech* 76, 339–360. doi:10.1215/00031283-76-4-339

Lucas, Ceil, Robert Bayley, Clayton Valli, Mary Rose & Alyssa Wulf. 2001b. Sociolinguistic variation. In: C. Lucas (ed.), *The sociolinguistics of sign languages*, 61–111. Cambridge: Cambridge University Press. doi:10.1017/CBO9780511612824.006

Lucas, Ceil & Clayton Valli. 1989. Language contact in the American Deaf community. In: C. Lucas (ed.), *The sociolinguistics of the Deaf community*, 11–40. San Diego: Academic Press.

Luttgens, Kathryn, Helga Deutsch & Nancy Hamilton. 1992. *Kinesiology: scientific basis of human motion*. Madison, WI: Brown & Benchmark.

MacLaughlin, Dawn. 1997. *The structure of determiner phrases: Evidence from American Sign Language*. PhD dissertation, Boston University.

MacSweeney, Mairéad, Bencie Woll, Ruth Campbell, Philip K. McGuire, Anthony S. David, Steven C. R. Williams, John Suckling, Gemma A. Calvert & Michael J. Brammer. 2002. Neural systems underlying British Sign Language and audio-visual English processing in native users. *Brain* 125(7), 1583–1593. doi:10.1093/brain/awf153

Makharoblidze, Tamar. 2015. Indirect object markers in Georgian Sign Language. *Sign Language & Linguistics* 18(2), 238–250.

Malm, Amja (ed.). 1998. *Suomalaisen viitomakielen perussankirja*. Helsinki: Libris Oy.

Mandel, Mark. 1977. Iconic devices in American Sign Language. In: L. A. Friedman (ed.), *On the other hand: New perspectives on American Sign Language*, 57–107. New York: Academic Press.

Mandel, Mark A. 1979. Natural constraints in sign language phonology: data from anatomy. *Sign Language Studies* 24, 215–229. doi:10.1353/sls.1979.0006

Marsaja, I Gede. 2008. *Desa Kolok – A deaf village and its sign language in Bali, Indonesia*. Nijmegen: Ishara Press.

Marschark, Marc. 2007. *Raising and educating a deaf child (2nd edition)*. New York: Oxford University Press.

Marschark, Marc, Gladys Tang & Harry Knoors. 2014. *Bilingualism and bilingual deaf education*. Oxford: Oxford University Press. doi:10.1093/acprof:oso/9780199371815.001.0001

Martinez, Liza B. 1995. Turn taking and eye gaze in sign conversation between deaf Filipinos. In: C. Lucas (ed.), *Sociolinguistics in deaf communities*, 272–306. Washington, DC: Gallaudet University Press.

Mather, Susan M. 1987. Eye gaze and communication in a deaf classroom. *Sign Language Studies* 54, 11–30. doi:10.1353/sls.1987.0008

Mather, Susan M. 1994. Classroom turn-taking mechanism: effective strategies for using eye gaze as a regulator. In: C. Erting (ed.), *The deaf way: perspectives from the International Conference on Deaf Culture*, 627–632. Washington, DC: Gallaudet University Press.

Mathur, Gaurav & Christian Rathmann. 2010. Verb agreement in sign language morphology. In: D. Brentari (ed.), *Sign languages (Cambridge Language Surveys)*, 173–224. Cambridge: Cambridge University Press. doi:10.1017/CBO9780511712203.010

Mathur, Gaurav & Christian Rathmann. 2012. Verb agreement. In: R. Pfau, M. Steinbach & B. Woll (eds.), *Sign language. An international handbook*, 136–157. Berlin: De Gruyter Mouton.

Mauk, Claude & Martha E. Tyrone. 2012. Location in ASL: Insights from phonetic variation. *Sign Language & Linguistics* 15(1), 128–164. doi:10.1075/sll.15.1.06mau

Mayberry, Rachel I. 1993. First language acquisition after childhood differs from second language acquisition: The case of American Sign Language. *Journal of Speech and Hearing Research* 36, 1258–1270. doi:10.1044/jshr.3606.1258

McBurney, Susan. 2002. Pronominal reference in signed and spoken language: Are grammatical categories modality-dependent? In: R. P. Meier, K. A. Cormier & D. G. Quinto-Pozos (eds.), *Modality and structure in signed and spoken languages*, 329–369. Cambridge: Cambridge University Press.

McBurney, Susan. 2012. History of sign languages and sign language linguistics. In: R. Pfau, M. Steinbach & B. Woll (eds.), *Sign language. An international handbook*, 909–948. Berlin: De Gruyter Mouton.

McCaskill, Carolyn, Ceil Lucas, Robert Bayley & Joseph Hill. 2011. *The hidden treasure of black ASL – its history and structure.* Washington, DC: Gallaudet University Press.

McKee, David & Graeme Kennedy. 2000. Lexical comparison of signs from American, Australian, British, and New Zealand Sign Languages. In: K. Emmorey & H. Lane (eds.), *The signs of language revisited: An anthology to honor Ursula Bellugi and Edward Klima*, 49–76. Mahwah, NJ: Lawrence Erlbaum.

McKee, Rachel L. & Sophia Wallingford. 2011. 'So, well, whatever': Discourse functions of *palm-up* in New Zealand Sign Language. *Sign Language & Linguistics* 14(2), 213–247. doi:10.1075/sll.14.2.01mck

Meier, Richard P. 1990. Person deixis in American Sign Language. In: S. D. Fischer & P. Siple (eds.), *Theoretical issues in sign language research. Vol.1: Linguistics*, 175–190. Chicago: University of Chicago Press.

Meier, Richard P. 2000. Shared motoric factors in the acquisition of sign and speech. In: K. Emmorey & H. Lane (eds.), *The signs of language revisited: An anthology to honor Ursula Bellugi and Edward Klima*, 333–356. Mahwah, NJ: Lawrence Erlbaum.

Meier, Richard P. 2002. The acquisition of verb agreement: Pointing out arguments for the linguistic status of agreement in signed languages. In: G. Morgan & B. Woll (eds.), *Directions in sign language acquisition*, 115–141. Amsterdam: John Benjamins. doi:10.1075/tilar.2.08mei

Meier, Richard P. & Diane Lillo-Martin. 2013. The points of language. *Humana.Mente – Journal of Philosophical Studies* 24, 151–176.

Meir, Irit. 1999. A perfect marker in Israeli Sign Language. *Sign Language & Linguistics* 2, 43–62. doi:10.1075/sll.2.1.04mei

Meir, Irit. 2002. A cross-modality perspective on verb agreement. *Natural Language & Linguistic Theory* 20, 413–450. doi:10.1023/A:1015041113514

Meir, Irit. 2010. Iconicity and metaphor: Constraints on metaphorical extension of iconic forms. *Language* 86(4), 865–896.

Meir, Irit. 2012. Word classes and word formation. In: R. Pfau, M. Steinbach & B. Woll (eds.), *Sign language. An international handbook*, 77–112. Berlin: De Gruyter Mouton.

Meir, Irit, Mark Aronoff, Wendy Sandler & Carol Padden. 2010a. Sign languages and compounding. In: S. Scalise & I. Vogel (eds.), *Cross-disciplinary issues in compounding*, 301–322. Amsterdam: John Benjamins. doi:10.1075/cilt.311.23mei

Meir, Irit & Wendy Sandler. 2008. *A language in space. The story of Israeli Sign Language.* New York: Lawrence Erlbaum.

Meir, Irit, Wendy Sandler, Carol Padden & Mark Aronoff. 2010b. Emerging sign languages. In: M. Marschark & P. E. Spencer (eds.), *Oxford handbook of deaf studies, language, and education.* Volume 2, 267–280. Oxford: Oxford University Press.

Miles, Michael. 2000. Signing in the Seraglio: mutes, dwarfs and jestures at the Ottoman court 1500–1700. *Disability & Society* 15(1), 115–134. doi:10.1080/09687590025801

Mindess, Anna. 2006. *Reading between the signs: intercultural communication for sign language interpreters (2nd edition).* Yarmouth, ME: Intercultural Press.

Minguet Soto, Amparo (coordinator). 2001. *Signolingüística: introducción a la linguistica de la LSE*. Valencia: FESORD.

Morford, Jill P., Angus B. Grieve-Smith, James MacFarlane, Joshua Staley & Gabriel Waters. 2008. Effects of language experience on the perception of American Sign Language. *Cognition* 109, 41–53. doi:10.1016/j.cognition.2008.07.016

Moores, Donald F. 2010. The history of language and communication issues in deaf education. In: M. Marschark & P. E. Spencer (eds.), *Oxford handbook of deaf studies, language, and education*. Volume 2, 17–30. Oxford: Oxford University Press.

Morgan, Gary. 2006. The development of narrative skills in British Sign Language. In: B. Schick, M. Marschark & P. E. Spencer (eds.), *Advances in the sign language development of deaf children*, 314–343. Oxford: Oxford University Press.

Morgan, Gary, Sarah Barrett-Jones & Helen Stoneham. 2007. The first signs of language: phonological development in British Sign Language. *Applied Psycholinguistics* 28, 3–22. doi:10.1017/S0142716407070014

Morgan, Hope E. & Rachel I. Mayberry. 2012. Complexity in two-handed signs in Kenyan Sign Language: Evidence for sublexical structure in a young sign language. *Sign Language & Linguistics* 15(1), 147–174. doi:10.1075/sll.15.1.07mor

Mosel, Ulrike & Even Hovdhaugen. 1992. *Samoan reference grammar*. Oslo: Scandinavian University Press.

Nadolske, Marie & Rachel Rosenstock. 2007. Occurrence of mouthings in American Sign Language: A preliminary study. In: P. Perniss, R. Pfau & M. Steinbach (eds.), *Visible variation: Comparative studies on sign language structure*, 35–61. Berlin: Mouton de Gruyter.

Napoli, Donna Jo & Rachel Sutton-Spence. 2014. Order of the major constituents in sign languages: implications for all language. *Frontiers in Psychology* 5, Article 376. doi:10.3389/fpsyg.2014.00376

National Institute of the Deaf. 2011. *South African Sign Language dictionary on DVD*. Worcester, Western Cape, SA: National Institute of the Deaf.

Neidle, Carol, Judy Kegl, Dawn MacLaughlin, Ben Bahan & Robert G. Lee. 2000. *The syntax of American Sign Language. Functional categories and hierarchical structure*. Cambridge, MA: MIT Press.

Newkirk, Don, Edward S. Klima, Carlene C. Pedersen & Ursula Bellugi. 1980. Linguistic evidence from slips of the hand. In: V. A. Fromkin (ed.), *Errors in linguistic perfomance: Slips of the tongue, ear, pen and hand*, 165–197. New York: Academic.

Newport, Elissa L. & Richard P. Meier. 1985. The acquisition of American Sign Language. In: D. I. Slobin (ed.), *The cross-linguistic study of language acquisition*, 881–933. Hillsdale, NJ: Lawrence Erlbaum.

Nijen Twilhaar, Jan & Beppie van den Bogaerde. 2016. *Concise lexicon for sign linguistics*. Amsterdam: John Benjamins.

Nonhebel, Annika. 2002. *Indirecte taalhandelingen in Nederlandse Gebarentaal. Een kwalitatieve studie naar de non-manuele markering van indirecte verzoeken in NGT*. MA thesis, University of Amsterdam.

Noonan, Michael. 1985. Complementation. In: T. Shopen (ed.), *Language typology and syntactic description. Vol. II: Complex constructions*, 42–140. Cambridge: Cambridge University Press.

Nyst, Victoria. 2007. *A descriptive analysis of Adomorobe Sign Language*. PhD dissertation, University of Amsterdam. Utrecht: LOT [www.lotpublications.nl/Documents/151_fulltext.pdf].

Nyst, Victoria. 2012. Shared sign languages. In: R. Pfau, M. Steinbach & B. Woll (eds.), *Sign language. An international handbook*, 552–574. Berlin: De Gruyter Mouton.

Olsen, Susan. 2014. Delineating derivation and compounding. In: R. Lieber & P. Štekauer (eds.), *The Oxford handbook of derivational morphology*, 26–49. Oxford: Oxford University Press.

Ormel, Ellen, Daan Hermans, Harry Knoors & Ludo Verhoeven. 2009. The role of sign phonology and iconicity during sign processing: the case of deaf children. *Journal of Deaf Studies and Deaf Education* 14(4), 436–448. doi:10.1093/deafed/enp021

Ortega, Gerardo. 2013. *Acquisition of a signed phonological system by hearing adults: the role of sign structure and iconicity*. PhD dissertation, University College London. Available at: http://discovery.ucl.ac.uk/1416826/.

Padden, Carol A. 1988. *Interaction of morphology and syntax in American Sign Language*. New York: Garland Publishing.

Padden, Carol, Irit Meir, So-One Hwang, Ryan Lepic, Sharon Seegers & Tory Sampson. 2013. Patterned iconicity in sign language lexicons. *Gesture* 13(3), 287–308. doi:10.1075/gest.13.3.03pad

Park, Young-Me. 1997. Topikalisierung im Koreanischen: Eine Folge von Basisgenerierung oder Move-alpha? *Frankfurter Linguistische Forschungen* 21, 34–44.

Perniss, Pamela, Roland Pfau & Markus Steinbach (eds.). 2007. *Visible variation: Cross-linguistic studies on sign language structure*. Berlin: Mouton de Gruyter. doi:10.1515/9783110198850

Perniss, Pamela, Robin L. Thompson & Gabriella Vigliocco. 2010. Iconicity as a general property of language: evidence from spoken and signed languages. *Frontiers in Psychology* 1:227. doi:10.3389/fpsyg.2010.00227

Petitto, Laura A. & Paula F. Marentette. 1991. Babbling in the manual mode: Evidence for the ontogeny of language. *Science* 251, 1493–1496. doi:10.1126/science.2006424

Petronio, Karen. 1993. *Clause structure in American Sign Language*. PhD dissertation, University of Washington.

Petronio, Karen & Diane Lillo-Martin. 1997. WH-movement and the position of Spec-CP: Evidence from American Sign Language. *Language* 73, 18–57. doi:10.2307/416592

Pfau, Roland. 2002. Applying morphosyntactic and phonological readjustment rules in natural language negation. In: R. P. Meier, K. A. Cormier & D. G. Quinto-Pozos (eds.), *Modality and structure in signed and spoken languages*, 263–295. Cambridge: Cambridge University Press.

Pfau, Roland. 2008. The grammar of headshake: A typological perspective on German Sign Language negation. *Linguistics in Amsterdam* 2008(1), 37–74.

Pfau, Roland. 2011. A point well taken: On the typology and diachrony of pointing. In: D. J. Napoli & G. Mathur (eds.), *Deaf around the world. The impact of language*, 144–163. Oxford: Oxford University Press.

Pfau, Roland. 2012. Manual communication systems: evolution and variation. In: R. Pfau, M. Steinbach & B. Woll (eds.), *Sign language. An international handbook*, 513–551. Berlin: De Gruyter Mouton. doi:10.1515/9783110261325

Pfau, Roland. 2015. The grammaticalization of headshakes: From head movement to negative head. In: A. D. M. Smith, G. Trousdale & R. Waltereit (eds.), *New directions in grammaticalization research*, 9–50. Amsterdam: John Benjamins. doi:10.1075/slcs.166.02pfa

Pfau, Roland & Josep Quer. 2007. On the syntax of negation and modals in Catalan Sign Language and German Sign Language. In: P. Perniss, R. Pfau & M. Steinbach (eds.), *Visible variation: Cross-linguistic studies on sign language structure*, 129–161. Berlin: Mouton de Gruyter. doi:10.1515/9783110198850

Pfau, Roland & Markus Steinbach. 2003. Optimal reciprocals in German Sign Language. *Sign Language & Linguistics* 6, 3–42. doi:10.1075/sll.6.1.03pfa

Pfau, Roland & Markus Steinbach. 2005. Relative clauses in German Sign Language: Extraposition and reconstruction. In: L. Bateman & C. Ussery (eds.), *Proceedings of the North East Linguistic Society (NELS 35), Vol. 2*, 507–521. Amherst, MA: GLSA.

Pfau, Roland & Markus Steinbach. 2006a. *Modality-independent and modality-specific aspects of grammaticalization in sign languages* (Linguistics in Potsdam 24). Potsdam: Universitäts-Verlag. [http://opus.kobv.de/ubp/volltexte/2006/1088/].

Pfau, Roland & Markus Steinbach. 2006b. Pluralization in sign and in speech: A cross-modal typological study. *Linguistic Typology* 10, 135–182. doi:10.1515/LINGTY.2006.006

Pfau, Roland & Markus Steinbach. 2011. Grammaticalization in sign languages. In: H. Narrog & B. Heine (eds.), *The Oxford handbook of grammaticalization*, 683–695. Oxford: Oxford University Press.

Pfau, Roland & Markus Steinbach. 2016. Complex sentences in sign languages: Modality – typology – discourse. In: R. Pfau, M. Steinbach & A. Herrmann (eds.), *A matter of complexity: Subordination in sign languages*, 1–35. Berlin: De Gruyter Mouton.

Pfau, Roland, Markus Steinbach & Bencie Woll (eds.). 2012a. *Sign language. An international handbook (HSK – Handbooks of Linguistics and Communication Science)*. Berlin: De Gruyter Mouton. doi:10.1515/9783110261325

Pfau, Roland, Markus Steinbach & Bencie Woll. 2012b. Tense, aspect, and modality. In: R. Pfau, M. Steinbach & B. Woll (eds.), *Sign language. An international handbook*, 186–204. Berlin: De Gruyter Mouton. doi:10.1515/9783110261325

Pietrandrea, Paola. 2002. Iconicity and arbitrariness in Italian Sign Language. *Sign Language Studies* 2(3), 296–321. doi:10.1353/sls.2002.0012

Pizzuto Elena & Virginia Volterra. 2000. Iconicity and transparancy in sign languages: A cross-linguistic cross-cultural view. In: K. Emmorey & H. Lane (eds.), *The signs of language revisited: an anthology to honor Ursula Bellugi and Edward Klima*, 261–286. Mahwah, NJ: Lawrence Erlbaum.

Plaza Pust, Carolina. 2012. Deaf education and bilingualism. In: R. Pfau, M. Steinbach & B. Woll (eds.), *Sign language. An international handbook*, 949–979. Berlin: De Gruyter Mouton.

Poizner, Howard & Judy Kegl. 1992. Neural basis of language and motor behaviour: Perspectives from American Sign Language. *Aphasiology* 6, 219–256. doi:10.1080/02687039208248595

Poizner, Howard, Edward S. Klima & Ursula Bellugi. 1987. *What the hands reveal about the brain*. Cambridge, MA: MIT Press.

Prentice, David John. 1987. Malay (Indonesian and Malaysian). In: B. Comrie (ed.), *The world's major languages*, 913–935. London: Croom Helm.

Prillwitz, Siegmund, Regina Leven, Heiko Zienert, Thomas Hanke, Jan Henning, et al. 1989. *Ham-NoSys version 2.0. Hamburg notation system for sign languages: an introductory guide*. Hamburg: Signum.

Quadros, Ronice M. de. 1999. *Phrase structure in Brazilian Sign Language*. PhD dissertation, Pontifíca Universidade Católica do Rio Grande do Sul, Porto Alegre.

Quadros, Ronice M. de, Deborah Chen Pichler, Diane Lillo-Martin, Carina Rebello Cruz, L. Viola Kozak, Jeffrey Levi Palmer, Aline Lemos Pizzio & Wanette Reynolds. 2015. Methods in bimodal bilingualism research: Experimental studies. In: E.. Orfanidou, B. Woll & G. Morgan (eds.), *Research methods in sign language studies: A practical guide*, 250–281. Oxford: Wiley-Blackwell.

Quer, Josep. 2005. Context shift and indexical variables in sign languages. In: E. Georgala & J. Howell (eds.), *Proceedings from Semantics and Linguistic Theory* 15, 152–168. Ithaca, NY: CLC Publications.

Quinto-Pozos, David (ed.). 2014. *Multilingual aspects of signed language communication and disorder*. Bristol: Multilingual Matters.

Rankin, Miako N. P. 2013. *Form, meaning, and focus in American Sign Language.* Washington, DC: Gallaudet University Press.

Rathmann, Christian. 2005. *Event structure in American Sign Language.* PhD dissertation, University of Texas at Austin.

Reilly, Judy. 2006. How faces come to serve grammar: The development of nonmanual morphology in American Sign Language. In: B. Schick, M. Marschark & P. E. Spencer (eds.), *Advances in the sign language development of deaf children*, 262–290. Oxford: Oxford University Press.

Richmond-Welty, E. Daylene & Patricia Siple. 1999. Differentiating the use of gaze in bilingual-bimodal language acquisition: A comparison of two sets of twins with deaf parents. *Journal of Child Language* 26, 321–328. doi:10.1017/S0305000999003803

Rimor, Mordechai, Judy Kegl, Harlan Lane & Trude Schermer. 1984. Natural phonetic processes underlie historical change and register variation in American Sign Language. *Sign Language Studies* 13, 97–119. doi:10.1353/sls.1984.0014

Rosen, Russell S. 2004. Beginning L2 production errors in ASL lexical phonology: A cognitive phonology model. *Sign Language & Linguistics* 7(1), 31–61. doi:10.1075/sll.7.1.04beg

Rudner, William A. & Rochelle Butowsky. 1981. Signs used in the deaf gay community. *Sign Language Studies* 30, 36–48. doi:10.1353/sls.1981.0009

Sacks, Oliver. 1989. *Seeing voices: A journey into the world of the deaf.* Oakland, CA: University of California Press.

Sandler, Wendy. 1989. *Phonological representation of the sign. Linearity and nonlinearity in American Sign Language.* Dordrecht: Foris.

Sandler, Wendy. 1993. Hand in hand: The roles of the nondominant hand in sign language phonology. *The Linguistic Review* 10, 337–390. doi:10.1515/tlir.1993.10.4.337

Sandler, Wendy. 1996a. Representing handshapes. In: W. H. Edmondson & R. B. Wilbur (eds.), *International review of sign linguistics*, 115–158. Mahwah, NJ: Lawrence Erlbaum.

Sandler, Wendy. 1996b. Phonological features and feature classes: The case of movements in sign language. *Lingua* 98, 197–220. doi:10.1016/0024-3841(95)00038-0

Sandler, Wendy. 1999. The medium and the message: Prosodic interpretation of linguistic content in Israeli Sign Language. *Sign Language & Linguistics* 2(2), 187–215. doi:10.1075/sll.2.2.04san

Sandler, Wendy. 2012. Visual prosody. In: R. Pfau, M. Steinbach & B. Woll (eds.), *Sign language. An international handbook*, 55–76. Berlin: De Gruyter Mouton.

Sandler, Wendy, Mark Aronoff, Irit Meir & Carol Padden. 2011. The gradual emergence of phonological form in a new language. *Natural Language and Linguistic Theory* 29(2), 503–543. doi:10.1007/s11049-011-9128-2

Sandler, Wendy & Diane Lillo-Martin. 2006. *Sign language and linguistic universals.* Cambridge: Cambridge University Press. doi:10.1017/CBO9781139163910

Sandler, Wendy, Irit Meir, Carol Padden & Mark Aronoff. 2005. The emergence of grammar: systematic structure in a new language. *Proceedings of the National Academy of Sciences* 102(7), 2661–2665. doi:10.1073/pnas.0405448102

Sapountzaki, Galini. 2012. Agreement auxiliaries. In: R. Pfau, M. Steinbach & B. Woll (eds.), *Sign language. An international handbook*, 204–227. Berlin: De Gruyter Mouton.

Sasaki, Daisuke. 2007. Comparing the lexicons of Japanese Sign Language and Taiwan Sign Language: A preliminary study focusing on the difference in the handshape parameter. In: D. Quinto-Pozos (ed.), *Sign languages in contact*, 123–150. Washington, DC: Gallaudet University Press.

Schauwers, Karen, Paul Govaerts & Steven Gillis. 2005. Language acquisition in deaf children with a cochlear implant. In: P. Fletcher & J. F. Miller (ed.), *Developmental theory and language disorders*, 95–119. Amsterdam: John Benjamins. doi:10.1075/tilar.4.07sch

Schembri, Adam. 2003. Rethinking 'classifiers' in signed languages. In: K. Emmorey (ed.), *Perspectives on classifier constructions in sign languages*, 3–34. Mahwah, NJ: Lawrence Erlbaum.

Schembri, Adam, Kearsy Cormier, Trevor Johnston, David McKee, Rachel McKee & Bencie Woll. 2010. Sociolinguistic variation in British, Australian and New Zealand Sign Languages. In: D. Brentari (ed.), *Sign languages (Cambridge Language Surveys)*, 476–498. Cambridge: Cambridge University Press. doi:10.1017/CBO9780511712203.022

Schembri, Adam & Trevor Johnston. 2012. Sociolinguistic aspects of variation and change. In: R. Pfau, M. Steinbach & B. Woll (eds.), *Sign language. An international handbook*, 788–816. Berlin: De Gruyter Mouton.

Schermer, Trude. 1990. *In search of a language. Influences from spoken Dutch on Sign Language of the Netherlands*. PhD dissertation, University of Amsterdam.

Schermer, Trude 2003. From variant to standard: An overview of the standardization process of the lexicon of Sign Language of the Netherlands (SLN) over two decades. *Sign Language Studies* 3, 469–486. doi:10.1353/sls.2003.0017

Schermer, Trude. 2004. Lexical variation in Sign Language of the Netherlands. In: M. Van Herreweghe & M. Vermeerbergen (eds.), *To the lexicon and beyond. Sociolinguistics in European deaf communities*, 91–110. Washington, DC: Gallaudet University Press.

Schermer, Trude. 2006. Sign language lexicography. In: K. Brown (ed.), *Encyclopedia of Language and Linguistics* (2nd ed.), 321–324. Amsterdam: Elsevier. doi:10.1016/B0-08-044854-2/00231-5

Schermer, Trude. 2012. Language planning. In: R. Pfau, M. Steinbach & B. Woll (eds.), *Sign language. An international handbook*, 889–908. Berlin: De Gruyter Mouton.

Schermer, Trude, David Brien & Mary Brennan. 2001. Developing linguistic specifications for a sign language database: The development of SignBase. *Sign Language & Linguistics* 4, 253–274. doi:10.1075/sll.4.1-2.18sch

Schermer, Trude, Jacobien Geuze, Corline Koolhof, Elly Meijer & Sarah Muller. 2006. *Standaard lexicon Nederlandse Gebarentaal, deel 1 en 2 (DVD-ROM)*. Bunnik: Nederlands Gebarencentrum.

Schermer, Trude, Rita Harder & Heleen Bos. 1988. *Handen uit de mouwen: Gebaren uit de Nederlandse Gebarentaal in kaart gebracht*. Amsterdam: NSDSK/Dovenraad.

Schermer, Trude & Corline Koolhof. 1990. The reality of time-lines: Aspects of tense in Sign Language of the Netherlands (SLN). In: S. Prillwitz & T. Vollhaber (eds.), *Proceedings of the Forth International Symposium on Sign Language Research*, 295–305. Hamburg: Signum.

Schermer, Trude & Corline Koolhof (eds.). 2009. *Van Dale basiswoordenboek Nederlandse Gebarentaal* [Basic dictionary NGT]. Utrecht: Van Dale.

Schermer, Trude, Corline Koolhof, Sarah Muller & Richard Cokart. 2014. *Online gebarenwoordenboek* [Online dictionary NGT]. Bunnik: Nederlands Gebarencentrum.

Schermer, Trude & Myriam Vermeerbergen. 2004. Nederlandse Gebarentaal en Vlaamse Gebarentaal: zussen of verre nichtjes? *Ons Erfdeel, Vlaams-Nederlands Cultureel Tijdschrift* 47, 569–575.

Schick, Brenda S. 1990. The effects of morphosyntactic structure on the acquisition of classifier predicates in ASL. In: C. Lucas (ed.), *Sign language research: theoretical issues*, 358–374. Washington, DC: Gallaudet University Press.

Schick, Brenda, Marc Marschark & Patricia E. Spencer (eds.). 2006. *Advances in the sign language development of deaf children*. Oxford: Oxford University Press.

Schmaling, Constanze. 2000. *Maganar hannu: Language of the hands. A descriptive analysis of Hausa Sign Language*. Hamburg: Signum.

Schuit, Joke. 2013. *Typological aspects of Inuit Sign Language*. PhD dissertation, University of Amsterdam [http://dare.uva.nl/record/463559].

Schwager, Waldemar & Ulrike Zeshan. 2008. Word classes in sign languages: criteria and classifications. *Studies in Language* 32, 509–545. doi:10.1075/sl.32.3.03sch

Senghas, Ann. 1995. *Children's contribution to the birth of Nicaraguan Sign Language*. PhD dissertation, MIT, Cambridge, MA.

Senghas, Ann. 2005. Language emergence: clues from a new Bedouin Sign Language. *Current Biology* 15(12), R463–R465. doi:10.1016/j.cub.2005.06.018

Sexton, Amy L. 1999. Grammaticalization in American Sign Language. *Language Sciences* 21, 105–141. doi:10.1016/S0388-0001(98)00017-5

Shaffer, Barbara. 2002. CAN'T: The negation of modal notions in ASL. *Sign Language Studies* 3, 34–53. doi:10.1353/sls.2002.0026

Siple, Patricia. 1978. Visual constraints for sign language communication. *Sign Language Studies* 19, 95–110. doi:10.1353/sls.1978.0010

Skliar, Carlos & Ronice M. de Quadros. 2005. Bilingual deaf education in the south of Brazil. In: A. M. de Méjia (ed.), *Bilingual education in South America*, 35–47. Clevedon: Multilingual Matters.

Smith, Wayne H. 1990. Evidence for auxiliaries in Taiwan Sign Language. In: S. D. Fischer & P. Siple (eds.), *Theoretical issues in sign language research. Vol. 1: Linguistics*, 211–228. Chicago: University of Chicago Press.

Smith, Wayne H. 2005. Taiwan Sign Language research: an historical overview. *Language and Linguistics* 6(2), 187–215.

Spencer, Patricia E. & Marc Marschark (eds.). 2006. *Advances in the spoken language development of deaf and hard-of-hearing children*. Oxford: Oxford University Press.

Stamp, Rose, Adam Schembri, Jordan Fenlon, Ramas Rentelis, Bencie Woll & Kearsy Cormier. 2014. Lexical variation and change in British Sign Language. *PLoS ONE* 9(4), e94053. doi:10.1371/journal.pone.0094053.

Steinbach, Markus & Roland Pfau. 2007. Grammaticalization of auxiliaries in sign languages. In: P. Perniss, R. Pfau & M. Steinbach (eds.), *Visible variation: Cross-linguistic studies on sign language structure*, 303–339. Berlin: Mouton de Gruyter. doi:10.1515/9783110198850

Stokoe, William C. 1960. Sign language structure. An outline of the visual communication system of the American deaf. *Studies in Linguistics Occasional Papers 8*. Buffalo: University of Buffalo Press [Re-issued 2005, *Journal of Deaf Studies and Deaf Education* 10, 3–37].

Stokoe William C. 1970. Sign language diglossia. *Studies in Linguistics* 21, 27–41.

Stokoe, William C., Dorothy C. Casterline & Carl G. Cronenberg. 1965. *A dictionary of American Sign Language*. Silver Spring, MD: Linstok Press.

Stone, Christopher. 2012. Interpreting. In: R. Pfau, M. Steinbach & B. Woll (eds.), *Sign language. An international handbook*, 980–998. Berlin: De Gruyter Mouton.

Stroombergen, Marianne & Trude Schermer. 1988. *KOMVA Notatiesysteem voor Nederlandse gebaren*. Amsterdam: NSDSK.

Supalla, Ted. 1986. The classifier system in American Sign Language. In: Craig, C. (ed.), *Noun classes and categorization*, 181–214. Amsterdam: John Benjamins. doi:10.1075/tsl.7.13sup

Supalla, Ted & Elissa L. Newport. 1978. How many seats in a chair? The derivation of nouns and verbs in American Sign Language. In: P. Siple (ed.), *Understanding language through sign language research*, 91–132. New York: Academic Press.

Sutton-Spence, Rachel & Bencie Woll. 1999. *The linguistics of British Sign Language. An introduction*. Cambridge: Cambridge University Press. doi:10.1017/CBO9781139167048

Takkinen, Ritva. 1994. Sign articulation of a deaf boy at the age of 2–3 years, 6 years and 8 years. In: I. Ahlgren, B. Bergman & M. Brennan (eds.), *Perspectives on sign language usage. Papers from the Fifth International Symposium on Sign Language Research*, 357–368. Durham: ISLA.

Tang, Gladys. 2006. Questions and negation in Hong Kong Sign Language. In: U. Zeshan (ed.), *Interrogative and negative constructions in sign languages*, 198–224. Nijmegen: Ishara Press.

Tang, Gladys (ed.). 2007. *Hong Kong Sign Language. A trilingual dictionary with linguistic descriptions.* Hong Kong: Chinese University Press.

Tang, Gladys & Prudence Lau. 2012. Coordination and subordination. In: R. Pfau, M. Steinbach & B. Woll (eds.), *Sign language. An international handbook*, 340–365. Berlin: De Gruyter Mouton.

Taşçı, Süleyman S. 2013. Hand reversal and assimilation in TİD lexicalized fingerspelling. In: E. Arık (ed.), *Current directions in Turkish Sign Language research*, 71–100. Newcastle upon Tyne: Cambridge Scholars Publishing.

Taub, Sarah F. 2001. *Language from the body. Iconicity and metaphor in American Sign Language.* Cambridge: Cambridge University Press. doi:10.1017/CBO9780511509629

Taub, Sarah F. 2012. Iconicity and metaphor. In: R. Pfau, M. Steinbach & B. Woll (eds.), *Sign language. An international handbook*, 388–412. Berlin: De Gruyter Mouton.

Tellings, Agnes. 1995. *The two hundred years' war in deaf education. A reconstruction of the methods controversy.* PhD dissertation, Radboud University Nijmegen.

Thompson, Henry. 1977. The lack of subordination in American Sign Language. In: L. A. Friedman (ed.), *On the other hand: New perspectives on American Sign Language*, 181–195. New York: Academic Press.

Thompson, Robin, Karen Emmorey & Tamar H. Gollan. 2005. "Tip of the fingers" experiences by deaf signers. *Psychological Science* 16(11), 856–860. doi:10.1111/j.1467-9280.2005.01626.x

Thompson, Sandra A. & Robert E. Longacre. 1985. Adverbial clauses. In: T. Shopen (ed.), *Language typology and syntactic description. Vol. II: Complex constructions*, 171–234. Cambridge: Cambridge University Press.

Thoutenhoofd, Ernst. 2006. Cochlear implanted pupils in Scottish schools: 4-year school attainment data (2000–2004). *The Journal of Deaf Studies and Deaf Education* 11, 171–188. doi:10.1093/deafed/enj029

Tyrone, Martha E. & Claude Mauk. 2010. Sign lowering and phonetic reduction in American Sign Language. *Journal of Phonetics* 38, 317–328. doi:10.1016/j.wocn.2010.02.003

Valli, Clayton (ed.). 2005. *The Gallaudet dictionary of American Sign Language.* Washington, DC: Gallaudet University Press.

Valli, Clayton & Ceil Lucas. 1992/1995. *Linguistics of American Sign Language: An introduction.* Washington, DC: Gallaudet University Press.

Vallverdú, Rosa. 2001. The sign language communities. In: M. T. Turell (ed.), *Multilingualism in Spain: Sociolinguistic and psycholinguistic aspects of linguistic minority groups*, 183–214. Clevedon: Multilingual Matters.

Van Herreweghe, Mieke. 2002. Turn-taking mechanisms and active participation in meetings with deaf and hearing participants in Flanders. In: C. Lucas (ed.), *Turntaking, fingerspelling and contact in signed languages*, 73–106. Washington, DC: Gallaudet University Press.

Vanhecke, Eline & Kristof De Weerdt. 2004. Regional variation in Flemish Sign Language. In: M. Van Herreweghe & M. Vermeerbergen (eds.), *To the lexicon and beyond. Sociolinguistics in European Deaf communities*, 27–38. Washington, DC: Gallaudet University Press.

Vercellotti, Mary Lou & David R. Mortensen. 2012. A classification of compounds in American Sign Language: an evaluation of the Bisetto and Scalise framework. *Morphology* 22, 545–579. doi:10.1007/s11525-012-9205-1

Vermeerbergen, Myriam, Mieke Van Herreweghe, Philemon Akach & Emily Matabane. 2007. Constituent order in Flemish Sign Language (VGT) and South African Sign Language (SASL). A cross-linguistic study. *Sign Language & Linguistics* 10, 25–54. doi:10.1075/sll.10.1.04ver

Vinson, David P., Kearsy Cormier, Tanya Denmark, Adam Schembri & Gabriella Vigliocco. 2008. The British Sign Language (BSL) norms for age of acquisition, familiarity, and iconicity. *Behavior Research Methods* 40(4), 1079–1087. doi:10.3758/BRM.40.4.1079

Vivolin-Karén, Riitta & Kaisa Alanne. 2003. *Draft curriculum and the structure of Finnish Sign Language*. The Finnish Association of the Deaf.

Vos, Connie de & Roland Pfau. 2015. Sign language typology: The contribution of rural sign languages. *Annual Review of Linguistics* 1, 265–288. doi:10.1146/annurev-linguist-030514-124958

Walker, Elizabeth A. & J. Bruce Tomblin. 2014. The influence of communication mode on language development in children with cochlear implants. In: M. Marschark, G. Tang & H. Knoors (eds.), *Bilingualism and bilingual deaf education*, 134–151. New York: Oxford University Press. doi:10.1093/acprof:oso/9780199371815.003.0006

Wallin, Lars. 1983. Compounds in Swedish Sign Language. In: J. Kyle & B. Woll (eds.), *Language in sign*, 56–68. London: Croom Helm.

Waters, Dafydd & Rachel Sutton-Spence. 2005. Connectives in British Sign Language. *Deaf Worlds* 21, 1–29.

Wauters, Loes & Annet de Klerk. 2014. Improving reading instruction to deaf and hard-of-hearing students. In: M. Marschark, G. Tang & H. Knoors (eds.), *Bilingualism and bilingual deaf education*, 242–271. Oxford: Oxford University Press. doi:10.1093/acprof:oso/9780199371815.003.0010

Whitebread, Geoff. 2014. A review of stuttering in signed languages. In: D. Quinto-Pozos (ed.), *Multilingual aspects of sign language communication and disorder*, 143–161. Bristol: Multilingual Matters.

Wilbur, Ronnie B. 1990. Metaphors in American Sign Language and English. In: W. H. Edmondson & F. Karlsson (eds.), *SLR '87: Papers from the Fourth International Symposium on Sign Language Research*, 163–170. Hamburg: Signum.

Wilbur, Ronnie B. 1996. Evidence for the function and structure of wh-clefts in American Sign Language. In: W. H. Edmondson & R. B. Wilbur (eds.), *International review of sign linguistics*, 209–256. Mahwah, NJ: Lawrence Erlbaum.

Wilbur, Ronnie B. 2012. Information structure. In: R. Pfau, M. Steinbach & B. Woll (eds.), *Sign language. An international handbook*, 462–489. Berlin: De Gruyter Mouton.

Wilbur, Ronnie B. 2013. The point of agreement: Changing how we think about sign language, gesture, and agreement. *Sign Language & Linguistics* 16(2), 221–258. doi:10.1075/sll.16.2.05wil

Wilbur, Ronnie B. 2016. Preference for clause order in complex sentences with adverbial clauses in American Sign Language. In: R. Pfau, M. Steinbach & A. Herrmann (eds.), *A matter of complexity: Subordination in sign languages*, 36–64. Berlin: De Gruyter Mouton.

Wilbur, Ronnie B. & Cynthia G. Patschke. 1998. Body leans and the marking of contrast in American Sign Language. *Journal of Pragmatics* 30, 275–303. doi:10.1016/S0378-2166(98)00003-4

Wilbur, Ronnie B. & Brenda S. Schick. 1987. The effects of linguistic stress on ASL signs. *Language and Speech* 30(4), 301–323.

Wilcox, Phyllis P. 2000. *Metaphor in American Sign Language*. Washington, DC: Gallaudet University Press.

Wilcox, Phyllis P. (ed.). 2005. *Metaphor in signed languages*. Special issue of *Sign Language Studies* 5(3).

Wilcox, Sherman. 2004. Gesture and language. Cross-linguistic and historical data from signed languages. *Gesture* 4(1), 43–73. doi:10.1075/gest.4.1.04wil

Wilcox, Sherman & Phyllis Wilcox. 1995. The gestural expression of modality in ASL. In: J. Bybee & S. Fleischman (eds.), *Modality in grammar and discourse*, 135–162. Amsterdam: John Benjamins. doi:10.1075/tsl.32.07wil

Wilson, Margaret & Karen Emmorey. 1997. Working memory for sign language: A window into the architecture of the working memory system. *Journal of Deaf Studies and Deaf Education* 2(3), 121–130. doi:10.1093/oxfordjournals.deafed.a014318

Woll, Bencie. 1987. Historical and comparative aspects of British Sign Language. In: J. Kyle (ed.), *Sign and school: Using signs in deaf children's development*, 12–34. Clevedon: Multilingual Matters Ltd.

Woll, Bencie. 2012a. Atypical signing. In: R. Pfau, M. Steinbach & B. Woll (eds.), *Sign language. An international handbook*, 762–787. Berlin: De Gruyter Mouton. doi:10.1515/9783110261325

Woll, Bencie. 2012b. Second language acquisition of sign language. In: C. A. Chapelle (ed.), *The encyclopedia of applied linguistics*. Oxford: Wiley-Blackwell.

Woll, Bencie. 2013. The history of sign language linguistics. In: K. Allan (ed.), *The Oxford handbook of the history of linguistics*, 91–104. Oxford: Oxford University Press.

Woll, Bencie & Paddy Ladd. 2003. Deaf communities. In: M. Marschark & P. E. Spencer (eds.), *Oxford handbook of deaf studies, language, and education*, 151–163. Oxford: Oxford University Press.

Woodward, James. 1973a. Language continuum: A different point of view. *Sign Language Studies* 2, 81–83. doi:10.1353/sls.1973.0007

Woodward, James. 1973b. Some characteristics of Pidgin Sign English. *Sign Language Studies* 3, 39–46. doi:10.1353/sls.1973.0006

Woodward, James. 2000. Sign languages and sign language families in Thailand and Viet Nam. In: K. Emmorey & H. Lane (eds.), *The signs of language revisited: An anthology to honor Ursula Bellugi and Edward Klima*, 23–47. Mahwah, NJ: Lawrence Erlbaum.

Wrigley, Owen, et al. (eds.). 1990. *The Thai Sign Language dictionary (Revised and expanded edition)*. Bangkok: NAD in Thailand (NADT).

Yau, Shun-Chiu. 1977. *The Chinese signs: Lexicon of the standard sign language for the deaf in China*. Paris: Ed. Lang. Croisés.

Zeshan, Ulrike. 2000. *Sign language in Indo-Pakistan. A description of a signed language*. Amsterdam: John Benjamins. doi:10.1075/z.101

Zeshan, Ulrike. 2003a. 'Classificatory' constructions in Indo-Pakistani Sign Language: Grammaticalization and lexicalization processes. In: K. Emmorey (ed.), *Perspectives on classifier constructions in sign languages*, 113–141. Mahwah, NJ: Lawrence Erlbaum.

Zeshan, Ulrike. 2003b. Indo-Pakistani Sign Language grammar: A typological outline. *Sign Language Studies* 3(2), 157–212. doi:10.1353/sls.2003.0005

Zeshan, Ulrike. 2004a. Hand, head, and face: Negative constructions in sign languages. *Linguistic Typology* 8, 1–58. doi:10.1515/lity.2004.003

Zeshan, Ulrike. 2004b. Interrogative constructions in signed languages: cross-linguistic perspectives. *Language* 80, 7–39. doi:10.1353/lan.2004.0050

Zeshan, Ulrike (ed.). 2006a. *Interrogative and negative constructions in sign languages*. Nijmegen: Ishara Press.

Zeshan, Ulrike. 2006b. Negative and interrogative structures in Turkish Sign Language (TİD). In: U. Zeshan (ed.), *Interrogative and negative constructions in sign languages*, 128–164. Nijmegen: Ishara Press.

Zeshan, Ulrike. 2008. Roots, leaves and branches – The typology of sign languages. In: R. M. de Quadros (ed.), *Sign languages: spinning and unraveling the past, present and future*, 671–695. Petrópolis (Brazil): Editora Arara Azul.

Zimmer, June & Cynthia Patschke. 1990. A class of determiners in ASL. In: C. Lucas (ed.), *Sign language research: theoretical issues*, 201–210. Washington, DC: Gallaudet University Press.

Zucchi, Sandro. 2009. Along the time line: Tense and time adverbs in Italian Sign Language. *Natural Language Semantics* 17, 99–139. doi:10.1007/s11050-008-9032-4

Zwitserlood, Inge. 2003. *Classifying hand configurations in Nederlandse Gebarentaal*. PhD dissertation, University of Utrecht. Utrecht: LOT [www.lotpublications.nl/Documents/78_fulltext.pdf].

Zwitserlood, Inge. 2012. Classifiers. In: R. Pfau, M. Steinbach & B. Woll (eds.), *Sign language. An international handbook*, 158–186. Berlin: De Gruyter Mouton.

Zwitserlood, Inge & Ingeborg van Gijn. 2006. Agreement phenomena in Sign Language of the Netherlands. In: P. Ackema, et al. (eds.), *Arguments and agreement*, 195–229. Oxford: Oxford University Press.

Zwitserlood, Inge & Sibylla Nijhof. 1999. Pluralization in Sign Language of the Netherlands. In: J. Don & T. Sanders (eds.), *OTS Yearbook 1998–1999*, 58–78. Utrecht: UiL OTS.

Zwitserlood, Inge, Pamela Perniss & Aslı Özyürek. 2012. An empirical investigation of expression of multiple entities in Turkish Sign Language (TİD): Considering the effects of modality. *Lingua* 122, 1636–1667. doi:10.1016/j.lingua.2012.08.010

Websites

Of general interest

ENDANGERED LANGUAGES DOCUMENTATION PROGRAM (including some sign languages):
http://www.eldp.net/

ETHNOLOGUE www.ethnologue.com/

DEAF CULTURE www.deafculture.com/

DEAF RESOURCE LIBRARY (by Karen Nakamura) with many links:
www.deaflibrary.org/

SIGN LANGUAGE LINGUISTICS SOCIETY (SLLS): http://slls.eu/

WORLD ATLAS OF LANGUAGE STRUCTURES (WALS): http://wals.info/

Sign language dictionaries

GENERAL	www.yourdictionary.com/languages/sign.html
AMERICAN SL	www.lifeprint.com
ASL–WITH AVATAR:	http://signsci.terc.edu/SSD/about/animation.htm
AUSTRALIAN SL	www.auslan.org.au
BRITISH SL	www.signbsl.com/
FINNISH SL	http://suvi.viittomat.net
FLEMISH SL	http://gebaren.ugent.be/
FRENCH SL	www.lsfdico-injsmetz.fr/
GERMAN SL	www.sign-lang.uni-hamburg.de/ALex/Start.htm
NGT	www.gebarencentrum.nl/gebaren/mini-gebarenwoordenboek/ (sample dictionary)
	www.gebarencentrum.nl/gebaren/van-dale-ngt-uitgebreid/ (15.000 signs accessible via subscription)
SOUTH AFRICAN SL	www.youtube.com/watch?v=ufRlTMcYxbA
TURKISH SL	http://turkisaretdili.ku.edu.tr/

Sign language transcription and spoken language glossing conventions

BERKELEY TRANSCRIPTION SYSTEM: http://ihd.berkeley.edu/Slobin-Sign%20Language/(2001)%20
Berkeley%20Transcription%20System%20(BTS)%20-%20Manual.pdf
ELAN SOFTWARE   https://tla.mpi.nl/tools/tla-tools/elan/
HAMNOSYS   www.sign-lang.uni-hamburg.de/dgs-korpus/index.php/hamnosys-97.html
LEIPZIG GLOSSING RULES (MPI): www.eva.mpg.de/lingua/resources/glossing-rules.php
SIGNWRITING   www.signwriting.org

Sign language research, journals, language technology, and corpora

ASIAN SIGNBANK   http://cslds.org/asiansignbank/
ASL LINGUISTIC RESEARCH PROJECT (ASLLRP): www.bu.edu/asllrp/
AUSLAN CORPUS   http://elar.soas.ac.uk/deposit/0001
AUTOMATIC TRANSLATION: www.babelfish.org
BSL CORPUS   www.bslcorpusproject.org/
CATALAN SL LAB   http://parles.upf.edu/en/content/catalan-signs-language-laboratory
DEAFNESS, COGNITION, AND LANGUAGE RESEARCH CENTRE (London):
                        www.ucl.ac.uk/dcal
DGS CORPUS   www.sign-lang.uni-hamburg.de/dgs-korpus/
ECHO-PROJECT   sign-lang.ruhosting.nl/echo/
NGT CORPUS   www.ru.nl/corpusngten/
JOURNAL OF DEAF STUDIES AND DEAF EDUCATION:
                        http://jdsde.oxfordjournals.org/
SIGN LANGUAGE & LINGUISTICS (journal):
                        https://benjamins.com/#catalog/journals/sll/main
SIGN LANGUAGE STUDIES (journal): http://gupress.gallaudet.edu/SLS.html
SPREAD THE SIGN   www.spreadthesign.com/
VISICAST-PROJECT   www.visicast.co.uk

Manual alphabets from various sign languages

ASL   www.lifeprint.com/asl101/fingerspelling/
BSL   www.british-sign.co.uk/fingerspelling-alphabet-charts
CHINESE SL   www.sinosplice.com/life/archives/2007/04/02/
                chinese-sign-language-fingerspelling
SASL   https://commons.wikimedia.org/wiki/File:SASL-Fingerspelled-Alphabet.png
VARIOUS SLs   http://www.deafblind.com/worldsig.html
                (includes Lorm alphabet for the deafblind)

Index

verb phrase (*see* phrase)
VGT (*see* Flemish Sign Language)
Vietnamese   206, 228
Vietnamese Sign Language   206, 228
village sign language   6, 22, 24, 214, 223, 227
visual field   56, 59, 77, 236–237, 247
visual perception   34, 236–237, 247
visual-spatial   2, 11–12, 22, 27, 36, 39, 301, 310

visual-spatial modality   11–12, 22, 48, 178, 218, 301
visuo-spatial loop   36, 47

W
war of methods   328, 335–336
Warlpiri   216, 228
weak drop   233, 239, 247, 249, 271, 276, 278, 287
working memory   35f, 47, 49
Wernicke, area of   26, 29
wh-cleft   84, 89, 157, 169
wh-doubling   133, 135, 144

wh-questions   60, 83, 132, 134, 144–146, 157
writing system   9, 15, 23, 242, 244, 247, 320

Y
yes/no questions   42, 60, 80–81, 130–131, 134, 144, 147, 159, 244, 273
Yimas   127, 147

Z
zero marking   215